Cutting the Fuse

Cutting the Fuse

The Explosion of Global Suicide Terrorism and How to Stop It

ROBERT A. PAPE
JAMES K. FELDMAN

Chicago Project on Security and Terrorism

THE UNIVERSITY OF CHICAGO PRESS   CHICAGO AND LONDON

The University of Chicago Press, Chicago 60637
The University of Chicago Press, Ltd., London
© 2010 by The University of Chicago
All rights reserved. Published 2010.
Paperback edition 2012.
Printed in the United States of America
21 20 19 18 17 16 15 14 13 12   4 5 6 7 8

ISBN-13: 978-0-226-64560-5 (cloth)
ISBN-13: 978-0-226-64565-0 (paper)
ISBN-10: 0-226-64560-6 (cloth)
ISBN-10: 0-226-64565-7 (paper)

LIBRARY OF CONGRESS CATALOGING-IN-PUBLICATION DATA

Pape, Robert Anthony, 1960–
Cutting the fuse : the explosion of global suicide terrorism and how to stop it / Robert A. Pape,
James K. Feldman.
        p. cm.
    "Chicago Project on Security and Terrorism."
    Includes index.
    ISBN-13: 978-0-226-64560-5 (cloth: alk. paper)
    ISBN-10: 0-226-64560-6 (cloth: alk. paper)
    1. Suicide bombings. 2. Terrorists—Suicidal behavior—Middle East. 3. War on Terrorism,
2001–2009. 4. United States—History, Military—21st century. 5. United States—Military policy. 6.
Terrorism—Prevention. I. Feldman, James K. (James Kendrick) II. Chicago Project on Security and
Terrorism. III. Title.
HV6431.P355 2010
363.325—dc22

                                                                                    2010019947

♾ This paper meets the requirements of ANSI/NISO Z39.48-1992 (Permanence of Paper).

TO OUR WIVES AND CHILDREN,
LISA, JONATHAN, ELIZABETH, AND ANNE PAPE
AND
SHARON, JAMES, AND DAVID FELDMAN

Contents

Acknowledgments

This book represents a true team effort at every level, from the collection of the underlying information, to the creation of a state-of-the-art interactive database, to the discovery and analysis of causal patterns, and to the generous support from academic, governmental, and philanthropic institutions for the Chicago Project on Security and Terrorism (CPOST).

The Chicago Project supports broad-based, original research on terrorism and international security. CPOST maintains a complete worldwide knowledge base of suicide attacks and attackers, martyr videos, terrorist group profiles, and multidisciplinary analyses confronting core international security challenges (http://cpost.uchicago.edu). Over several years, funding for these efforts was provided by the University of Chicago Division of the Social Sciences, the U.S. Department of Defense (the Defense Threat Reduction Agency and the Office of Naval Research), Argonne National Laboratory, and the Carnegie Corporation of New York. The Chicago Project on Security and Terrorism is currently made possible through the generous support of the Carnegie Corporation of New York.

Funding support for CPOST is vital, but without the dedication of its outstanding researchers, this book would never have been possible. Time after time they have gone the extra mile to ensure the high standards required for the CPOST database development, campaign research, and analysis. We have been honored to work with these exceptional young professionals: Jacob Homan (CPOST executive assistant); Maryam Almirah, Josie Bechara, Ahsan Butt, Zenab Chowdry, Sylvia Hammad, Rajika Jayatilake, Kaan Kadioglu, Jenna McDermit, Rana Mikati, Dana Rovang, Keven Ruby, Ezra Schricker, Martin Wolberg-Stok, and Susan Young (research associates); Mohammand Abdeljalil, Almad Baasiri, Vanessa Bernick, Julia Clemons, Osama Eledam, Alicia May, Dina Rashed, Dahlia Rizk, Dana

Rovang, Nicolaj Zemesaraja, and Brenda Kay Zylstra (research assistants); Nicole Argo, David Benson, Keren Fraiman, Jenna Jordon, Rose Kelanic, Chad Levinson, Michelle Murray, Lindsey O'Rourke, Neegen Pegahi (research fellows); Amir Wielinski, Emily Hauser, Rani Fedson, Omar Cheta, Rochdi Younsi, Sevag Kechichian, Edward Cohn, Sophia Akbar, and Dina Rashed (native language consultants).

Deserving special recognition are those members of the Chicago Project who were major contributors to the key suicide campaign chapters: Chad Levinson and Maryam Almirah (Iraq and Al Qaeda); Ezra Schricker and Susan Young (Afghanistan and Pakistan); Sylvia Hammad and Martin Wolberg-Stok (Lebanon and Israel/Palestine); Sophia Akbar (Israel/Palestine and Sri Lanka); Jenna McDermit (Chechnya); and Jenna Jordon and Keven Ruby (Sri Lanka).

And finally, Jacob Homan, the CPOST executive assistant, has been extraordinary, keeping the entire effort coordinated and on schedule and contributing numerous ideas to every chapter, while motivating everyone to do their best. He has a natural ability to lead and work with others.

The University of Chicago is a remarkable intellectual community that encourages a vigorous competition of ideas and where the quality of thought—rather than academic rank—is paramount. The University of Chicago Press exemplifies these high intellectual values, and we are honored to have this respected institution publish our book. We would like to thank our editors, David Pervin and John Tryneski, for recruiting superb reviewers for our manuscript, providing excellent comments of their own, and ensuring the timely publication of our book. We greatly appreciate the valuable insights and thoughtful guidance on our manuscript from Robert Art, Risa Brooks, Darcy Burner, Michael O'Conner, Paul Staniland, and the anonymous reviewers.

We continue to be driven by the professionalism and achievements of two remarkable scholars and individuals. John Mearsheimer inspired Bob Pape to pursue a career in social science to better the world, and continues to challenge him to do so. Thomas Schelling changed the way Ken Feldman approaches problems and still does.

Our highest appreciation goes to our wives, Lisa Pape and Sharon Feldman, who are both registered nurses. Their love for us and our families, and their duty and sacrifice for others, reminds us every day of what is really important in life. In a small way, dedicating this book to them recognizes their contribution to its completion, and also their unselfish service to others and their love for our country.

Why Focus on *Suicide* Terrorism

The right kind of public debate on terrorism is finally beginning.
For years after 9/11, the national discussion about how to deal with terrorism seemed to be frozen with little true debate about the root causes of the threat we face. First, we lived through the fear and anger in the immediate aftermath of that terrible day. Next, we lived through a period of hastily constructed responses, which led not only to the necessary war in Afghanistan to eliminate Al Qaeda's sanctuary there, but also the poorly based threat assessments that led up to the invasion of Iraq. After that came years of dealing with the repercussions of these decisions made in anger, fear, and haste, including the rise of the largest anti-American suicide terrorist campaigns in history in Iraq, Afghanistan, and Pakistan; the losses of over 100,000 Iraqi civilians who died in the civil war resulting from the U.S. invasion; and the emergence of a new Al Qaeda sanctuary in the tribal regions of Pakistan from which numerous plots have been hatched to kill Americans and their allies.[1]

Throughout these years, many have presumed that the root cause of the terrorist threat confronting us is Islamic fundamentalism—a religiously motivated hatred of American and Western values among a tiny fringe of Muslims scattered across the globe, and not related to any foreign or military policies by the United States or its allies. The idea that terrorists were willing to kill themselves to achieve religious martyrdom independently of any political goal seemed to explain why Islamic fundamentalists would

---

1. Major contributors to this book were Jacob Homan and the contributors listed individually by chapter. Research assistants for this book were Mohammand Abdeljalil, Almad Baasiri, Vanessa Bernick, Julia Clemons, Osama Eledam, Alicia May, Dina Rashed, Dahlia Rizk, Dana Rovang, Nicolaj Zemesaraja, and Brenda Kay Zylstra and the assistants listed individually by chapter.

commit suicide attacks, a tactic that appeared to reinforce just how much "they hate us."

This presumption fueled the belief that future 9/11s can be avoided only by wholesale transformation of Muslim societies, which was a core reason for the invasion of Iraq.[2] Indeed, for those advocating transformation, Iraq appeared to be the perfect place to start, since its leader Saddam Hussein had already spent decades to diminish Islamic fundamentalism in the country, and so the United States could conquer Iraq without fear of much terrorism in response, establish a base of operations, and then move on to transform other Middle Eastern countries.[3] If the presumption was right—if religion independent of American and Western foreign policy was driving the threat—then the use of heavy military power to bring democratic institutions to Muslim countries should have reduced the frequency of anti-American inspired terrorist attacks, especially suicide terrorism, by eliminating the authoritarian regimes that were thought to be the breeding grounds for Islamic radicalism

Events, however, have not turned out as the presumption would have expected. Far from declining, anti-American–inspired terrorism—particularly suicide terrorism—is more frequent today than before 9/11 and even before the invasion of Iraq. In the 24-year period from 1980 to 2003, there were just under 350 suicide terrorist attacks around the world—of which fewer than 15% could reasonably be considered directed against Americans. By contrast, in the six years from 2004 to 2009, the world has witnessed 1,833 suicide attacks—of which 92% are anti-American in origin. America has made progress in bringing Western institutions to Iraq, but democracy has not proved to be a panacea for reducing terrorism directed toward Americans and American allies. As this book shows, the Madrid and London terrorist bombings of 2004 and 2005, respectively, and numerous plots against Americans were specifically inspired by the invasion of Iraq.

2. Not just among the public, but within the Bush administration as well. Long before President George W. Bush received high-level classified briefings on Iraq's weapons of mass destruction in December 2002, he was briefed in the days after the September 11 attacks about Bernard Lewis's famous explanation for why Islamic fundamentalism is the root of Muslim rage leading to anti-Western terrorism, and in the subsequent weeks Lewis himself advocated for "a military take-over of Iraq to avert still-worse terrorism" by "seeding democracy in the Mideast" to White House officials, including Condoleezza Rice and Vice President Richard Cheney. Peter Waldman, "A Historian's Take on Islam Steers U.S. in Terrorism Fight," *Wall Street Journal*, February 3, 2004.

3. David Frum and Richard Perle, *An End to Evil: How to Win the War on Terror* (New York: Random House, 2003).

The more we've gone over there, the more they've wanted to come over here—and the absence of another 9/11 is due more to extensive American domestic security measures, immigration controls, intelligence, and pure luck than to lack of intent or planning by our enemies.

As the facts have not fit our presumptions, public discussion on the root causes of terrorism has grown in recent years. During the 2008 presidential campaign, candidates, columnists, and commentators in the United States, Europe, and around the world critically examined the U.S. strategy in the "war on terror," and even whether the U.S. actions have inadvertently contributed to more terrorism. In recent years, news media have stopped running the endless stories about "why do only Muslims do it?" and more wide-ranging and informative debate on "who becomes a suicide terrorist" is occurring.

Why Suicide Terrorism Is Important

In the 1990s, any American watching the evening news or CNN, and even those closely following daily events in print and online, could be excused for not seeing an evolving terrorist threat to the United States.

To be sure, many violent problems consumed our attention. Crime in New York, Chicago, Los Angeles, and other major cities; ethnic cleaning in Bosnia, Rwanda, Kosovo, and other civil wars; and conventional military conflicts involving Iraq versus Kuwait and China versus Taiwan all attracted remarkable coverage in the national and international media and called for dedicated plans of action by leading policy makers in the United States, Europe, Asia, and other countries around the world.

What did not seem to matter much was terrorism. The main concern—some would say obsession—of publics and leaders in many major countries for years now was hardly a blip on our radar in the 1990s.

What changed? Today, many people might instinctively answer "9/11," meaning a terrorist attack in the heart of the United States against a leading symbol of America's freedom and prosperity—the World Trade Center. This instinctive answer is obviously true, as far as it goes. But it also masks an important, deeper reality about the new threat facing the United States after September 11, 2001.

The new threat was not "terrorism"—at least not the old-fashioned kind that has been with the world for centuries. Ordinary terrorism occurred in the United States for years before 9/11. Indeed, the first terrorist attack on the World Trade Center occurred on February 26, 1993, when Islamic terrorists detonated a car bomb in the parking garage of Tower One, seeking to knock it down. Although the tower did not fall that day, six people were killed—something few people now remember and something that did not turn the American government, our military, and much of the country upside down to prevent from happening again. No, the new threat was not simply "terrorism."

What made 9/11 different was the willingness of 19 individuals to give their lives to kill a large number of Americans. No doubt, the attack was evil—the 3,000 innocent people who died that day did nothing to deserve their horrible fate. No doubt, the attackers were terrorists, but what made 9/11 very different from the terrorism Americans had experienced in the 1990s was the element of *suicide* by the attackers. The element of suicide is what made it possible for 19 hijackers to kill thousands of people. Even though these 19 were surely dead, the thought of more *suicide terrorist attacks* propelled anxiety and fear to levels few Americans had experienced in their lifetimes.

More consequences followed. The element of suicide is what instantly persuaded millions of Americans that future attacks could not be deterred by the threat of retaliation against the attackers. Indeed, the element of suicide called into question all our standard ways of responding to violence and so opened the door to all manner of "out of the box" strategic thinking—from the idea of preventive war against countries not immediately attacking us to the concept of almost unlimited surveillance of virtually any person in the United States by agencies in the executive branch of the U.S. government without observing the normal (and constitutionally mandated) rules of congressional and judicial oversight.[4] Since suicide terrorists must be stopped before they strike, it seemed necessary to look for them almost everywhere, even if no evidence existed that "they" were "there" at all.

In the years since 9/11, these "out of the box" responses have come under increasing scrutiny. Even defenders of staying the course would hardly deny that many of the domestic and foreign policies associated with the "war on terrorism" have produced their own costs and risks—in lives, national debt, and America's standing in the world. As painful as side effects are, however, they do not really call into question the basic logic of the

---

4. For a riveting account, see Jack L. Goldsmith, *The Terror Presidency: Law and Judgment inside the Bush Administration* (New York: W. W. Norton, 2007).

threat we face and how we should respond to it. They are a bit like a doctor telling a patient to stop smoking to avoid the risk of lung cancer and the patient asking, "won't I gain weight?" The side effect is real, but far from clearly more worrisome than the main threat.

Suicide terrorism is like lung cancer in other ways too. Just as there are numerous forms of cancer, and some quite benign, there are a various forms of terrorism, not all of which are worth the dedicated attention of our national leaders for sustained periods of time. Lung cancer justifies inordinate resources and attention because it is the leading cause of death among all cancers (and many other diseases). So too suicide terrorism. It merits special attention, because this type of terrorism is responsible for more deaths than any other form of the phenomenon—from 1980 to 2001, over 70% of all deaths due to terrorism were the result of suicide terrorism even though this tactic amounted to only 3% of all terrorist attacks.

Lung cancer can also exist for years, hardly creating symptoms until its most virulent stage. So too suicide terrorism. Although it may sound surprising, the United States did not begin to keep statistics on suicide terrorism until the fall of 2000,[5] even though it had been tracking ordinary terrorism around the world for decades. This omission goes a long way toward explaining why 9/11 was so hard to see coming.

If one looks at the U.S. government data on the global patterns of ordinary terrorism from 1980 to 2001, there is an unmistakable decline in the threat. Indeed, the peak is 1988 when some 666 terrorist attacks occurred globally, and this number declined more or less steadily over the next 10 plus years to 348 in 2001. At the same time, what started out as a tiny number of suicide terrorist attacks around the world was climbing at an alarming rate, from an average of only 3 suicide attacks per year in the 1980s to 10 per year in the 1990s to 50 per year from 2000 to 2003 and to 300 per year from 2004 to 2009.

These facts help explain why there was such a broad failure of imagination before 9/11—not only among the public, not only among national policy makers, but even by "terrorism experts" at the time. Since all terrorism was dropping like a rock and we were not tracking suicide terrorism in anything like a comprehensive way, it was hard to see that the threat was growing.

5. This was confirmed by correspondence between Argonne National Laboratories and the data manager for the U.S. government's database on terrorism located at the Naval Post-Graduate School in Monterey California, in fall 2003.

To prevent future 9/11s, it is crucial to focus our attention on preventing anti-American suicide terrorism. True, other forms of terrorism also matter. Conventional truck bomb attacks against bridges, antiaircraft missile shots at civilian airliners, the proliferation of chemical, biological, or nuclear weapons that leads to their use by terrorists—every one of these other terrorist threats is nontrivial. Every one was with us in the 1990s. But, the crucial point is that every one is greatly magnified by the willingness of the terrorists to kill themselves in order to carry the attacks out. Although suicide terrorism is not the only kind of terrorism, it is the most virulent form of the phenomenon and makes every other form of terrorism far more deadly than before.

Consider the following thought experiment. Imagine for the moment that you are Osama bin Laden and you have finally achieved your heart's desire—possession of a working nuclear warhead. Its explosive power is about the size of the atomic bomb that destroyed most of Nagasaki in World War II, the likes of which could devastate Manhattan, Boston, or Los Angeles, surely killing tens of thousands, perhaps over a hundred thousand, of Americans if the bomb actually goes off in one of these cities. You, bin Laden, have hated America for years. You cannot wait to fulfill your dream of inflicting a sucking chest wound on the "far enemy." You want the world to know your power.

But you have a problem. What if you send this one nuclear warhead in a container on a merchant ship, unescorted by anyone, and something goes wrong? What if the port authorities—now so widely criticized in the media—come across the bomb either by accident or through unreported heightened security measures? What if the bomb gets through to the port, but then fails to explode either because the atomic triggers were faulty in the first place or became so during the 1,000-mile-plus voyage? What if tens of other problems occur that you cannot even now foresee? Will former Secretary of Defense Donald Rumsfeld's famous "unknown unknowns" make you look like a fool in front of the world and waste this precious asset?

Getting nuclear weapons for terrorists is hard, much harder than fearmongers in the Western media like to suggest.[6] You know this and know that you cannot count on getting more for years or may be ever. What do you, bin Laden, do?

6. John E. Mueller, *Atomic Obsession: Nuclear Alarmism from Hiroshima to Al Qaeda* (New York: Oxford University Press, 2009).

The answer should now be rushing to your mind. You look for individuals willing to escort the nuclear bomb all the way to its target, to protect the weapon from discovery and seizure along the way, to execute a suicide attack if the bomb works as advertised, and to bring the bomb back for repair if it does not. Just as finding 19 people willing to kill themselves was the key to killing thousands of Americans on 9/11, so too would relying on suicide attackers make all the difference in the likely success of killing 10 or more times as many Americans in a nuclear 9/11. Suicide attack is not the only way to strike the United States or any other country with a nuclear weapon. It is, however, the most reliable way to employ the one, or at most handful, of nuclear weapons likely to come your way.

This thought experiment could be multiplied many times over for truck bombs, chemical and biological attacks, and virtually any kind of terrorist strike plan that truly sought to kill large numbers of people. In all of these, adding the element of suicide to the attack drastically increases the odds of success. And this is the point of a suicide terrorist attack. From the perspective of the terrorist organization, the purpose of a suicide terrorist attack is not for the attacker to die—this is the easy part, once an attacker is willing to participate in such a mission at all. Rather, the purpose is to kill large numbers of people, which is true whether the suicide terrorist attack involves conventional explosives or weapons of mass destruction. Suicide terrorists are the ultimate smart bomb.

What We Know about Suicide Terrorism

Suicide terrorists are superpredators. They murder vast numbers of innocent people in each attack. They are the subject of seemingly endless "three-minute" discussions on Fox, CNN, and MSNBC. Yet, many people still wonder about the motives and dynamics that lead man after man, and increasingly woman after woman, to strap on bombs, load up their cars with explosives, or ram planes into buildings and kill themselves on missions to kill others.

To answer the question, we need to look at more than pictures of mangled bodies, blown out busses, and collapsed buildings. To know why suicide terrorist campaigns occur in some places and not others, why they start at some times and not others, and why they end, we need to look at more than the evil of suicide terrorism. It is all well and good to condemn suicide terrorists as murderers or "homicide terrorists." But when moral

posturing comes to replace reasoned assessment of data and dispassionate consideration of the causes of a phenomenon, we may end up with a
visceral response rather than an effective plan of action to protect those
we care about. In the 1940s and 1950s, lung cancer was spreading, killing
more and more people and causing more and more heartbreak, seeming
more and more out of control each year. What helped was not simply more
aggressive treatments after the fact, but new studies that explained the root
causes of the phenomenon so that that lung cancer could be stopped before
it started. In the decades since, this research probably did more than any
treatment to save lives.[7]

We should learn from our experience with lung cancer. If collection of
comprehensive data, reasoned assessment of the facts, and debate about
how information we have fits or does not fit alternative explanations can
help reduce suicide terrorism even modestly, this is all worth the effort.

Recently, academic research on the causes of terrorism has made significant progress, particularly on suicide terrorism. Although our understanding of the phenomenon is still growing, knowledge about the causes,
conduct, and consequences of suicide terrorism has substantially improved
since 9/11, much of which is embodied in the chapters in this volume. Important methodological advances and new data have helped to make this
progress possible, as has the influx of new scholars.[8] In particular, we now
have the first complete data set of all suicide terrorist attacks around the
world from 1980 to 2009, which greatly improves our ability to assess possible causes of the phenomenon. As with lung cancer, we now know more
clearly who is struck and who is not, and this significantly helps us understand why.

A central result has been the advent of a new theory to explain the phenomenon of suicide terrorism. Prior to 9/11, the expert debate on the causes
of suicide terrorism was divided largely between two explanations, religious fanaticism and mental illness.[9] In the years after 9/11, new research
on who becomes a suicide terrorist showed that virtually none could be di-
agnosed as mentally ill, while many were religious and, most striking, nearly
all emerged from communities resisting foreign military occupation. *Dying*

7. Evelyn N. Powers and Jasmina B. Cabbot, *Smoking and Lung Cancer* (Hauppauge, NY:
Nova Science Publishers, 2008).

8. For example, see the new research on terrorism in the special issue of *Security Studies*,
December 2009.

9. For a good assortment of the 1990s literature, see Walter Reich, ed., *Origins of Terrorism*
(Washington, DC: Woodrow Wilson Center Press, 1998).

to Win, published in 2005, was prominent in advancing this new explanation for the origins of suicide terrorism. From 1980 to 2003, there were 345 completed suicide terrorist attacks by 524 suicide terrorists who actually killed themselves on a mission to kill others, half of whom are secular. The world leader was the Tamil Tigers (a secular, Hindu group) who carried out more attacks than Hamas or Palestinian Islamic Jihad (PIJ) during this period. Further, at least a third of the suicide attacks in predominantly Muslim countries were carried out by secular terrorist groups, such as the Kurdistan Workers Party (PKK) in Turkey. Instead of religion, what over 95% of all suicide terrorist attacks before 2004 had in common was a strategic goal: to compel a democratic state to withdraw combat forces that are threatening territory that the terrorists' prize. From Lebanon to Sri Lanka to the West Bank to Chechnya, the central goal of every suicide terrorist campaign has been to resist military occupation by a democracy.[10]

What Is New in *Cutting the Fuse*

The years since 2004 have witnessed a substantial growth in the number of suicide terrorist attacks, nearly 500% more than all the years from 1980 to 2003 combined. This leads to three questions:

1. Do the global patterns of suicide terrorism since 2004 validate or invalidate the hypothesis that foreign military occupation, or the imminent threat of it, is the root cause of suicide terrorism?
1. Do the global patterns of suicide terrorism since 2004 indicate new factors that add to the causal logic of existing theories, telling us more about when and where suicide terrorism will occur?
2. Do the global patterns of suicide terrorism since 2004 suggest new solutions or major improvements to existing solutions to the threat we face?

The purpose of this book is to answer these questions, analyzing all suicide terrorist attacks around the world from 1980 to 2009, nearly 2,200 attacks in all. Each suicide terrorist attack is defined in the classic sense of an individual killing himself or herself on a mission to kill others and has been verified by two or more independent sources by a research team flu-

10. Robert A. Pape, *Dying to Win: The Strategic Logic of Suicide Terrorism* (New York: Random House, 2005).

ent in the key native languages associated with suicide terrorism (Arabic, Hebrew, Tamil, Russian, Urdu, etc.), and members of the team have also contributed to the analysis of individual suicide terrorist campaigns in this book.

In brief, the new research finds the following.

1) Strong confirmation for the hypothesis that military occupation is the main factor driving suicide terrorism. The stationing of foreign combat forces (ground and tactical air force units) on territory that terrorists prize accounts for 87% of the over 1,800 suicide terrorist attacks around the world since 2004. The occupation of Pakistan's western tribal regions by local combat forces allied to American military forces stationed across the border in Afghanistan accounts for another 12%. Further, the timing of the deployment of combat forces threatening territory the terrorists prize accounts for the onset of all eight major suicide terrorist campaigns[11] between 1980 and 2009, which together comprise 96% of the 2,188 attacks during that period. Simply put, military occupation accounts for nearly all suicide terrorism around the world since 1980. For this finding to be wrong, our research team would have had to miss hundreds of suicide attacks during this period, which is unlikely as readers can judge for themselves by reviewing the database of suicide attacks available online.[12]

Although each of the major suicide terrorist campaigns is important, perhaps the most urgent finding within specific campaigns concerns the recent abrupt spike of suicide terrorism in Afghanistan, where starting in early 2006 the number of suicide attacks suddenly rose from a handful to over 100 per year. The key reason was United States and NATO military deployments, which began to extend to the Pashtun southern and eastern regions of the country beginning in late 2005. In 2006, the United States pressured Pakistan to deploy large military forces in the Pashtun areas of western Pakistan, which also led to a large increase of suicide attacks in the country. In effect, the more the United States and its military allies have militarily occupied the Pashtun homeland, the more this has inspired suicide terrorism to end the occupation.

11. To be clear, a suicide terrorist campaign occurs when one or more suicide attacks are intended as part of a cluster organized by one or more groups to achieve a specific political goal. Suicide attacks that do not occur as part of campaigns are called "isolated" attacks.

12. For the specific sources for each attack, see the searchable database on suicide attacks by the Chicago Project on Security and Terrorism at http://cpost.uchicago.edu.

2) Strong evidence for new hypotheses about the causes of transnational suicide terrorism. *Dying to Win* explained that nationalism—the desire to perpetuate the local political, religious, and social institutions of a community independent of foreign interference—is the taproot explanation for why individuals from a community facing foreign military occupation would undertake costly measures to defend it, including, in extremis, suicide terrorism. This causal logic is important since the overwhelming number of suicide attackers do live in the occupied country or in immediately adjacent border regions that are also under spillover threat from the occupation. However, *Dying to Win* left unanswered the causal logic of transnational suicide attackers—individuals living in countries far removed from the occupied countries—who comprise about 10% of the over 2,600 suicide attackers from 1980 to 2009 and as much as a fifth to a third of some prominent suicide terrorist campaigns (Iraq and Al Qaeda).

Cutting the Fuse provides a new causal logic for the phenomenon of transnational suicide terrorism. Although existing theories contend that it is a product of religious fanaticism or economic alienation, this volume shows that the logic of military occupation should be extended to account for transnational suicide terrorism.

Transnational suicide terrorism is a classic instance of individuals with multiple national loyalties to different stable communities of people associated with a territory, distinctive culture, and common language, one loyalty for their kindred community and another for their current country of residence, in which the loyalty for their kindred community wins out. However, these dueling loyalties do not exist in a vacuum, but are powerfully influenced by external circumstances. Specifically, the hierarchy of competing national loyalties can be strongly influenced by which community, the kindred or local, is most under threat. The hierarchy of multiple loyalties is not an a priori weighting among demographic factors such as place of birth, current residence, ethnicity, or religion, but is often constructed by circumstances in the international environment that shape individuals' perceptions of the relative importance of their loyalties, most particularly the level of threat to the different communities valued by the individuals. Hence, the foreign military occupation of kindred communities can compel individuals with multiple loyalties to adopt a hierarchy that privileges the kindred community over the local one. Perhaps most important, for transnational suicide attackers, this hierarchy of loyalties is normally established among preexisting groups of individuals who become progressively more radical as a group over time. As *Cutting the Fuse* explains, only exceptionally rare social dynamics are likely to lead to this progressive radicalization of groups, which accounts for why transnational suicide terrorism is such a rare, Black Swan phenomenon.

3) Important evidence for the value of a new approach to more effectively combat suicide terrorism, likely to improve the effectiveness of already well-known solutions.   As *Dying to Win* explained, the key to stopping suicide terrorism campaigns, which by their nature necessarily involve a series of attacks by different individuals over time, is to prevent the rise of a new generation of suicide terrorists. Given the close association between foreign occupation and suicide terrorism, the goal of thwarting the rise of the next wave of suicide terrorism will likely require a major shift in military strategy by those target states with a military presence in foreign areas. This strategy is "offshore" balancing, which seeks to achieve foreign policy interests in key regions of the world by relying on military alliances and offshore air, naval, and rapidly deployable ground forces rather than heavy onshore combat power. In essence, this strategy would resemble America's military commitment to the Persian Gulf from the end of World War II in 1945 to the period before the first Iraq War up to 1990, when the United States successfully pursued its interests and obligations in the region despite local instabilities and wars without stationing tank, armor, or fighter aircraft units there—and without provoking terrorism against us or our allies. After the 1991 Iraq War, America left tens of thousands of heavy combat forces on the Arabian Peninsula as a residual force, which became the chief rallying cry for Osama bin Laden's terrorism against the United States and its allies. Conversely, as Israel withdrew combat forces from Gaza and large parts of the West Bank and relied on defensive measures such as the "wall" in 2004 and as the United States and its allies drew down the total number of combat forces from Iraq after January 2008, suicide terrorism in both conflicts substantially declined.

However, something else happened in Iraq. Starting in late 2006, the United States began to offer local political control and economic resources directly to large Sunni tribes in Anbar Province, which gave them significant wherewithal to provide for their own security. At the same time, the United States deployed ground forces to the most vulnerable Sunni neighborhoods in Baghdad, protecting them and allowing more vulnerable Sunnis to move to safe havens within the city and bordering Anbar Province, enabling the Sunni community as a whole to better secure itself in the future. This strategy of empowering a key local community to better provide

balancing

for its security independently of the United States, the central government in the country, and the terrorists led to a decline of Iraqi suicide terrorism by over a third in the next year.

Most important, the strategy of "local empowerment" works by recognizing that suicide terrorism is driven by a strategic logic that seeks to remove foreign threats to local culture. A foreign state can remove a local population's primary reason for supporting suicide terrorist campaigns— safeguarding the local way of life—by providing the political, economic, and military wherewithal for the local community to detect and destroy terrorists, tasks that often require deep local knowledge to achieve success. Of course, the foreign occupier is often so powerful than it could still overwhelm newly empowered local groups, and so suicide terrorism may continue at a robust level so long as foreign ground forces remain in or near their community's area. However, the strategy of local empowerment is likely to moderate suicide terrorism over several years and serve as a useful transition strategy to offshore balancing, the grand strategy likely to work best over decades.

The Perspective of This Book

In the chapters that follow, *Cutting the Fuse* seeks to contribute to the growing public debate about the root causes of the threat we face by explaining the key findings about the new patterns of suicide terrorism since Iraq and by providing readers with the conceptual and empirical tools to assess these findings on their own. Chapters 1 and 2 explain what is driving the precipitous rise of suicide terrorism over the past five years and the special logic of transnational suicide terrorism. The body of this volume systematically assesses the causes, conduct, and consequences of the largest contemporary suicide terrorist campaigns: Iraq, Afghanistan, Pakistan, Al Qaeda, Palestine, Lebanon, Chechnya, and Sri Lanka. The conclusion offers policy recommendations, particularly why a strategy of local empowerment and offshore balancing is our best approach for safeguarding America and its allies from the threat of suicide terrorism.

This book is not written from a specific worldview, ideological orientation, or Democratic or Republican program. It is not authored by individuals who have voted consistently for one party (even in the past 10 years) or are committed to any political agenda. It is based fundamentally on a consideration of the facts of the matter and on the assumption that dispassionate consideration of the facts can create consensus and hope for a new future in American foreign policy.

To take a fresh look at the facts, it is helpful to keep a few basic ideas in mind:

First impressions can be faulty.   After 9/11, it seemed easy to think that Islam, poverty, social alienation, or the more sinister-sounding "Islamo-fascism" were the root cause of our problems. Yet, these did not just suddenly emerge in recent decades and so are poor explanations for the rise of suicide terrorism during our lifetimes. The key to improving our security is to find out what has changed and how it is propelling suicide terrorism against us.

Spectacular problems can have hard to see causes.   The ultimate cause of a deadly attack is not always the most obvious. Smokers often have no symptoms of the cancer growing in their bodies for decades until just before it becomes terminal. The root causes of suicide terrorism can also fester for years before producing spectacular harm.

"Patriots"—even the most well meaning—can let their emotions get the best of them.   As Ronald Reagan used to say, "Going over a cliff, carrying flags, is still going over a cliff." Americans should take pride in our country. This should be our reason for wanting to improve our security even if this means developing new courses of action, not for staying the course with policies that actually reduce it.

Understanding what to track helps clarify a complex situation.   In recent years, Americans have been inundated with an array of complicated concerns associated with the "war on terrorism"—the ebb and flow of potential proliferation of weapons of mass destruction in numerous countries, the rise and leveling off of the civil war in Iraq, and the capture of old and emergence of new Al Qaeda leaders and operatives—and these various and cross-cutting issues obscure the core question of whether the United States is winning or losing ground. Focusing on the trajectory of anti-American suicide terrorism helps to cut through the fog and provides a baseline for American security.

This book, then, seeks to demystify the terrorism threat we face. It recognizes that this threat has multiple causes and that solutions are not merely about "strong" versus "weak" policies. Being tough did not stop

Gary Cooper and Paul Newman from dying from lung cancer. Aggressive policy is sometimes the right and indispensable course of action, but aggression for aggression's sake, "getting two of them for one of us," and all other manner of blind fury can make matters worse.

Great victories often depend on a clear-eyed view of the merits of the case. Whether these facts help Democrats or Republicans in their domestic contests is far less important than whether they help improve the general welfare of the United States and our allies. The key is a willingness to consider information that may run against some of our first impressions, to see if the new data changes the overall picture in fundamental ways. Since there is no more common conventional wisdom than that the "war on terrorism" is making us safer, let us first ask: Why is anti-American suicide terrorism skyrocketing?

PART I

Analytic Overview

CHAPTER ONE

Why Occupation Ignites Suicide Terrorism

Almost every week, suicide bombers attack—either a military convoy or market, either in Afghanistan, Pakistan, Iraq, or other targets in other countries around the world. We know the horror. We know not to be surprised, even though attacks in certain countries can come after long periods of relative calm. But, do we understand what would drive seemingly ordinary people to strap explosives to their bodies and deliberately kill themselves on a mission to kill others?

Recently, we have made strides in understanding suicide terrorism. Years ago, one could listen to seemingly endless journalistic reports asking, why do only Muslims carry out suicide attacks? Such news stories dovetailed with the popular notion that suicide terrorism is a product of religious extremism where a poor, desperate (Islamic fundamentalist) soul seeks to escape the troubles of this world for a quick trip to paradise.

To make progress on understanding the root cause, it is important to clarify what we wish to explain. What matters most is not why one person carries out one suicide attack, but why many people would carry out a campaign of suicide attacks, since it is the possibility of more attacks to come that presents the greatest threat to our future. Until recently we have not had the benefit of comprehensive data on the global patterns of suicide attacks and so have had little clarity about the real world circumstances under which a suicide terrorist campaign is, or is not, carried out—the critical information necessary to confirm the general causes of the phenomenon.

Today, we know much more. Much challenges the conventional wisdom. Some is a bit disconcerting. Most important, our new knowledge rests on more thorough information, particularly the availability of the first complete data set on suicide terrorist attacks around the world from 1980 to 2009. When this is combined with the increasingly available martyr videos—the last video will testimonials of suicide attackers[1]—the wealth of new information about both the general circumstances and individual motives of suicide attackers paints a powerful picture of the root cause of the threat we face.

To bring this new picture into focus, it is helpful to analyze the global patterns of suicide attacks around the world in two stages. The first is the pattern of attacks from 1980 to 2003, involving nearly 350 suicide attacks and over 500 individuals who actually killed themselves. The second is the pattern from 2004 to 2009, when the number of suicide attacks around the world escalated sharply and became more focused against America, with over 1,800 attacks, more than five times the number in the previous 24 years combined. This division allows us to account for whether the tremendous rise of anti-American suicide terrorism in recent years in Iraq, Afghanistan, and elsewhere is due to general causes or special circumstances.

The Root Cause of Suicide Terrorism

Examination of the universe of suicide terrorist around the world from 1980 to 2003 shows that the principal cause of suicide terrorism is resistance to foreign occupation, not Islamic fundamentalism. Even when religion matters, moreover, it functions mainly as a recruiting tool in the context of national resistance.

For the purpose of understanding suicide terrorism, it is imperative to view occupation from the perspective of the resistance movement (e.g., terrorists) because it is the behavior of the local actors, not the foreign power, that determines whether suicide terrorism occurs. Whether the foreign power regards itself as a "stabilizing" ally rather than an "occupier" is not relevant.

"Occupation" means the exertion of political control over territory by

1. The statements in martyr videos are important for two reasons. First, as last testimonials, they are the best window available into the individual motives of suicide attackers who, once they complete their mission, cannot be questioned or psychoanalyzed. Second, and as important, martyr videos are publicized by terrorist organizations in part for recruitment purposes, and so reveal what the organizations believe motivates individuals to become suicide attackers.

an outside group. The critical requirement is that the occupying power's political control must depend on employing coercive assets—whether troops, police, or other security forces—that are controlled from outside the occupied territory, an issue often salient when foreign military forces cause collateral damage to local civilians but are not held accountable in local courts for their actions. The number of troops actually stationed in the occupied territory may or may not be large, so long as enough are available, if necessary, to suppress any effort at independence. The best test is the political decisiveness of political control: if the local government requires the power of foreign "stabilizing" troops or police in order to maintain order—or if large segments of the local community believes this is the case—then, from the perspective of the resistance, these foreign troops are occupying forces that are preventing a change of government that would otherwise occur. From the perspective of a resistance movement, a "threat of occupation" is imminent when a foreign military power stations troops in territory immediately adjacent to another country and has the strength to invade the neighboring territory, either to impose political control on a significant region for its own interests or to suppress local opposition to the current government.

Among members of the local community, foreign occupation can create fear that they would lose the ability to perpetuate their political, social, economic, and religious institutions, leading some members to make extreme sacrifices to prevent the loss of their community's way of life. Accordingly, factors that influence the intensity of the local community's fear of the occupation—such as number of foreign troops, degree of foreign influence over local institutions, and harm to the local population caused by the presence of foreign troops—are likely to impact the ebb and flow of self-sacrifice to protect the community.

In some cases, an outside power may exert military or economic pressure on a local government that is sufficient to compel the local government to alter key foreign policies, but not to control the domestic institutions of the country. This case is best termed an "indirect occupation," meaning large segments of a local community believe their government's foreign policy goals are under the control of an outside group. In a traditional alliance, member countries pursue mutual goals of interest independently of coercion by other members. For instance, Great Britain and the United States both viewed Germany as a military threat in World War II and neither coerced the other to make this calculation. By contrast, in indirect occupation, the indirectly occupied country gives a higher priority to the goals of the indirect occupier than its national interest alone would warrant, typically as a result of military or economic pressure. For example, India contributed large numbers of troops to the fight against Italy in World War II, an army third in size to the British and American armies, and did so because India was under indirect occupation by Great Britain.[2]

From 1980 to 2003, the connection between suicide terrorism and Islamic fundamentalism is weaker than many might have thought. Although there are prominent Islamic suicide terrorists—most particularly from Hezbollah in Lebanon and Hamas in the West Bank and Gaza—the world leader during this period was not an Islamic group. It was the Hindu, avowedly antireligious Liberation Tigers of Tamil Eelam (LTTE) in Sri Lanka, whose 157 suicide terrorists totaled more than Hamas and all other Palestinian suicide groups combined. Of the Palestinian suicide terrorists, more than a third were from secular groups, such as the Al-Aqsa Martyr's Brigade and the Popular Front for the Liberation of Palestine (PFLP). Of the suicide terrorists associated with Hezbollah in Lebanon during the 1980s, only 21% were Islamic fundamentalists while 71% were communists and socialists; 8% were Christians. In Turkey, 100% of the PKK's suicide attackers were secular. Overall, Islamic fundamentalism cannot account for over half of the known affiliations of the 524 total suicide terrorists from 1980 to 2003—184 were from Islamic fundamentalist groups (35% comprising 73 Al Qaeda, 5 Lebanese, 5 Kashmiri Rebels, 69 Hamas, 34 Palestinian Islamic Jihad) and 236 from secular groups (45% comprising 157 Tamil Tigers, 42 Al-Aqsa, 22 Lebanese, 15 PKK), while 12 (21%) had unknown ideological affiliations. Even if we assume every unknown was an Islamic fundamentalist, at most 56% of all suicide terrorists worldwide would count as Islamic fundamentalists.

By contrast, foreign occupation accounted for nearly all suicide terrorism. The vast majority of suicide terrorist attacks (95%) from 1980 to 2003 occurred as part of coherent and organized campaigns designed to compel democratic societies to abandon the occupation or political control of territory the terrorists view as their national homeland. From Lebanon to Israel to Sri Lanka to Kashmir to Chechnya, every suicide terrorist campaign has been waged as part of a national liberation strategy against a democracy with military forces stationed on territory the terrorists value.

Al Qaeda fits the pattern. Osama bin Laden's principal objective has

2. On the nature of alliances, see Hans J. Morthenthau, *Politics among Nations* (New York: Alfred A. Knopf, 1978), pp. 190–92. on the Indian Army in World War II, see Peter W. Fay, *The Forgotten Army: India's Armed Struggle for Independence, 1942–1945* (Ann Arbor: University of Michigan Press, 1993).

long been the expulsion of American troops from the Persian Gulf. From 1995 to 2003, there were 71 suicide terrorists who actually killed themselves on a mission for Al Qaeda. Of these, 44, or 62%, came from Saudi Arabia or other Muslim countries with thousands of American combat troops stationed on their soil, and 13, or 18%, came from the Muslim countries whose regimes are the most supported by the United States. It is important to recall that 1990 was a benchmark year in America's military deployment to the Persian Gulf. Before this point, the United States had only tiny numbers of troops stationed in Muslim countries (mostly guards protecting embassies), but no tank, armor, or tactical aircraft combat units since World War II. The United States deployed large numbers of combat forces to the region starting in August 1990 to deal with Iraq's invasion of Kuwait and has kept tens of thousands of combat forces there every year since; Al Qaeda's attacks began in 1995.Foreign occupation also accounts for the motives of individual suicide terrorists from 1980 to 2003. Many suicide terrorists are acting on the basis of altruistic motives for their communities, not on the purely personal motives that are typical of almost all other suicides. Many individual suicide attackers see themselves as powerfully related to the presence of foreign combat forces on territory the terrorists prize. For instance, the martyr videos made by the 9/11 hijackers strongly emphasize the motive of ending foreign occupation of the Arabian Peninsula. Here are three of the Saudi hijackers:

ABU AL-JARAAH AL-GHAMIDI: What is happening in Muslim countries today? Blatant occupation about which there is no doubt. . . . There is no duty more obligatory after faith than to repel him.

ABU MUS'AB WALID AL-SHEHRI: The occupation and deterioration in the land of the Two Sanctuaries is a plot by the Jew and Nazarenes, foremost among them America, may Allah destroy it, which has been among the chief causes of every misfortune suffered by Islam and the Muslims. Thus, repelling the Americans occupying the land of the Two Sanctuaries . . . is the most obligatory of obligations

HAMZA AL-GHAMDI: And I say to America: if it wants its armies and people to be safe, then it must withdraw all of its forces from the Muslim lands and depart from all our countries. If not, then let it await the men, prepare its coffins and dig graves for its citizens.

To be sure, some foreign occupations are more likely to result in suicide terrorism than others. Especially when the predominate religion in the occupier's society is different from the prevailing religion in the occupied society, this religious *difference* enables terrorist leaders to more easily portray the conflict in zero-sum terms, demonize the enemy, and legitimate martyrdom. Although the religions vary, the suicide terrorist campaigns by the Lebanese against the United States, France, and Israel, Palestinians against Israel, Sikhs against India, and Tamils against Sri Lanka, and Al Qaeda against the United States all contain a religious difference, and this contributed to community support for martyrdom in these cases. When a foreign occupation with a religious difference leads to rebellion, suicide terrorism often results as a weapon of last resort once more conventional strategies of resistance fail, a pattern observed in nearly all disputes that escalated to suicide terrorism. However, when foreign occupation does not engender local rebellion—as in the case of the U.S. occupation of Japan and South Korea during the Cold War, where local resistance to American military presence was offset by greater concern with the Soviet threat— suicide terrorism rarely occurs.

Further, suicide terrorism started rising around the world during the period 1980 to 2001 in part because terrorists have learned that it can work. From America and France's complete military exit from Lebanon in the 1980s to Israeli partial military withdrawals from the West Bank and Gaza in 1994 and 1995 to Sri Lanka's initial willingness to negotiate autonomy conditions with the Tamil Tigers in 1994 and 2001, suicide terrorism achieved important political concessions, especially for groups with so few other options.

In general, suicide terrorism has important, but limited coercive power— it might bring concessions on issues that are only modestly important for target states, but has little effectiveness in changing their core goals. Of course, issues that are only moderately important for target states may be of central importance to suicide terrorist groups or communities that support them.

Suicide terrorism makes punishment more effective than in traditional military campaigns. Targets of suicide terrorism remain willing to countenance high costs for important goals, but administrative, economic, or military adjustments that will prevent suicide attack are harder to make, while suicide attackers themselves are unlikely to be deterred by the threat of retaliation. Accordingly, suicide attack is likely to present a threat of continuing limited civilian punishment that the target government cannot completely eliminate, and the upper bound on what punishment via suicide attacks can gain for coercers is recognizably higher in suicidal terrorist campaigns than in conventional military coercion in international disputes.[3]

This is because suicide terrorism makes the target state's adjustment to reduce damage more difficult than for states faced with military coercion or economic sanctions because the when and where are unpredictable. However, it does not affect the target state's interests in the issues at stake. As a result, suicide terrorism can coerce states to abandon limited or modest goals, for example, by withdrawing from territory of low strategic importance, as in America's withdrawal from Lebanon in 1984, or, as in Israel's case in 1994 and 1995, by a temporary and partial withdrawal from a more important area. However, suicide terrorism is unlikely to cause targets to abandon goals central to their wealth or security, for example, by allowing a loss of territory that would weaken the economic prospects of the target state or strengthen its rivals.

Data on suicide terrorism since 2004 reinforces this conclusion. While suicide terrorism has achieved modest or very limited goals, it has so far failed to compel target democracies to abandon goals central to wealth, security, or integrity of core territory. When Israel withdrew from Gaza and parts of the West Bank in 2005, it abandoned territory of marginal value to the security of some Israelis, while actually increasing the security of the vast majority of the Jewish settlers by retaining the major settlements in East Jerusalem, Ariel, and elsewhere and by building a triple fence "wall" to protect them. Although Israel's concessions are modest, they almost surely would not have occurred without the large-scale suicide terrorism from 2000 to 2004, as many Israelis recognize. For example, on July 18, 2005, Haaretz's Danny Rubinstein wrote "Sharon, who never once mentioned or alluded to the need to withdraw from Gaza before, needed suicide bombers, rockets, and mortars to persuade him."[4] Further, in the period 2004 to 2009, suicide terrorism has not succeeded in evicting the United States from Iraq, in preventing the United States from escalating its commitment in Afghanistan, or in stopping Russia from crushing Chechen rebels, while the Sri Lankan government went for broke and wiped out the Tamil Tigers as an organized force.

The bottom line, then, is that suicide terrorism is mainly a strategic response to foreign occupation with important, but limited, coercive power.

3. On the limits of conventional punishment strategies, see Robert A. Pape, *Bombing to Win: Air Power and Coercion in War* (Ithaca, NY: Cornell University Press, 1996).

4. Danny Rubinstein, "Palestinian Pride, Israeli Capitulation," *Haaretz,* March 21, 2005.

Isolated incidents in other circumstances do occur. Religion plays a role. However, modern suicide terrorism is best understood as an extreme strategy for national liberation against democracies with troops that pose an imminent threat to control the territory the terrorists view as their homeland or prize greatly. Lasting victory over suicide terrorism requires that we consider this fact.[5]

Trajectory of Suicide Terrorism, 2004–2009

By almost any measure, recent years have witnessed a remarkable rise in the number of suicide terrorist attacks around the world. In aggregate, for the six-year period 2004 to 2009, there were a total of 1,833 completed suicide terrorist attacks by 2,136 individuals who actually killed themselves on such missions, nearly five times more than the 345 suicide attacks from the preceding 24-year period from 1980 to 2003. Further, the number per year has also risen remarkably, from a handful of attacks annually in the 1980s and 1990s to 303 attacks in 2006, 531 in 2007, 402 in 2008, and 281 in 2009.

The geographic distribution of the suicide attacks in figure 1.2 also reveals important patterns. Although isolated suicide attacks do occur in many countries, the overwhelming share are concentrated in campaigns of suicide terrorism that are located in only a handful of places. As figure 1.2 shows, the large suicide terrorist campaigns over the past six years include Iraq, Afghanistan, Pakistan, Sri Lanka, Palestine, Chechnya, and Al Qaeda, while small campaigns (15 attacks or fewer) have occurred in Kashmir, Uzbekistan, and Somalia, with only a tiny number of other attacks occurring in the rest of the world.

These patterns are important. First, the timing and geographic concentration of the suicide attacks cast sharp doubt on the explanation that Islamic fundamentalism is driving the threat, even though the overwhelming number of attacks have been committed by Muslims. Islamic fundamentalism cannot account for the steep upward trajectory of the annual rates of suicide terrorism—from an average of three attacks per year in the 1980s to over 500 in 2007—since it is implausible (and no authorities on the subject claim) that the number of Islamic fundamentalists around the globe

---

5. For a full analysis of the strategic, social, and individual logic of suicide terrorism around the world from 1980 to 2003, see Robert A. Pape, *Dying to Win: The Strategic Logic of Suicide Terrorism* (New York: Random House, 2005).

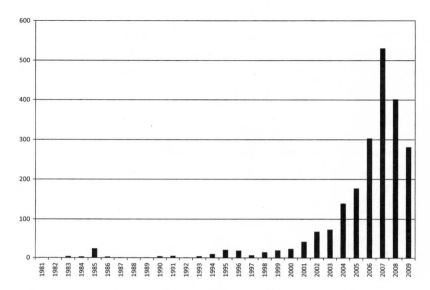

FIGURE 1.1 Global patterns of suicide terrorism

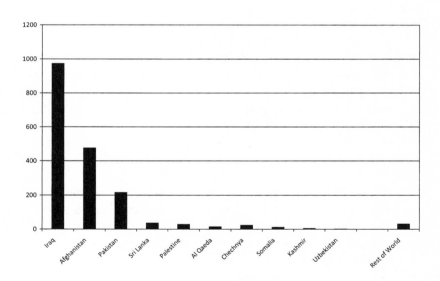

FIGURE 1.2 Suicide terrorism, 2004–9. U.S. combat operations: 92%. Foreign occupation: 98%.

rose by a similar astronomical rate (over 16,000%). Further, the geographic concentration also casts doubt on the causal force of Islamic fundamentalism. If religious fanaticism or any ideology was driving the threat, we would expect a spread of more or less proportionately scattered attacks around the globe or, in the case of Islamic fundamentalism, at least spread randomly across the 1.4 billion Muslims who live in nearly every country in the world. However, we are observing nearly the opposite of random, scattered attacks that would fit the pattern of a "global jihad," but instead tightly focused campaigns of suicide terrorism that are limited in space and time and so would appear related to specific circumstances. Finally, Islamic fundamentalism cannot explain the termination of important suicide terrorist campaigns in recent years. Since Israeli combat forces left Lebanon in 2000, there has not been a single Lebanese suicide terrorist attack—not even during Hezbollah's war with Israel in the summer of 2006—an end of suicide terrorism that cannot be explained by religion since Hezbollah has remained an Islamic fundamentalist group.

At the same time, the geographic concentration and timing of the upward trajectory of the attacks provide strong confirmation of the strategic logic of suicide terrorism. What every campaign of suicide terrorism has in common is that they are occurring as a central feature in violent resistance to foreign military occupation of territory that the terrorists view as their homeland or prize greatly. Many of the previous suicide terrorist campaigns in opposition to foreign military occupation (Palestine, Sri Lanka, Chechnya, Kashmir, and Al Qaeda) have continued, while all the new suicide campaigns have been in response to foreign military occupation (Iraq, Afghanistan, Uzbekistan, and Somalia) or to occupation by a local army working under the de facto direction of a foreign military force in immediately adjacent territory (Pakistan). Further, the target society of every suicide terrorist campaign from 2004 to 2009 has been a democracy where there has been a religious difference between the occupier and occupied communities.

Most important, the strategic logic of suicide terrorism accounts for the timing of the new suicide terrorist campaigns. As we shall explain below, the campaigns in Iraq, Afghanistan, Pakistan, Uzbekistan, and Somalia emerged only after the onset of military occupation, not after the fact, and declined as the occupation declined.

Overall, foreign military occupation accounts for 98.5%—and the deployment of American combat forces for 92%—of all the 1,833 suicide terrorist attacks around the world in the past six years. For this pattern to be wrong or simply due to random chance, there would have to be hundreds of additional suicide terrorists attacks since 2004 not counted in our census that are occurring in countries other than those listed in figure 1.2. Although no research can claim perfection, such a great degree of missing data is unlikely, particularly since suicide terrorist attacks are highly salient events that are prominently covered by national and international news media and elicit high profile responses by societies under attack.

These findings have important implications for assessing how the United States and other democracies under fire have responded to the threat of suicide terrorism. Since 2001, the United States and many Western governments have devoted enormous resources to a "war on terrorism," while many government officials and commentators have stressed the need to better measure and evaluate progress in that war. The most useful way to measure progress in dealing with the threat to the American homeland is the number of anti-American suicide terrorist attacks around the world. Although some might think the best measure of the future threat to the homeland is the historical occurrence of actual attacks on the homeland, this is a mistake if the event is rare and the underlying causal mechanism is influenced by factors that could change significantly over time. Worse, measuring the degree of threat to the homeland only by the existence of an attack could easily create false optimism or hysteria—by this measure, the threat to the U.S. homeland on September 10, 2001, was zero and on September 12 it was 100%, both wildly wrong. However, focusing on the trend of anti-American suicide terrorism around the world helps to reveal the relative likelihood of an attack to the homeland before such an attack occurs. By this measure, the threat is higher today than before 2001, and the United States and its allies are not winning the "war on terrorism."

To "win" against terrorism in the sense of making America and its allies safer against 9/11s in the future, it is crucial to prevent the rise of a new, larger generation of anti-American terrorists, particularly suicide terrorists—since without the willingness of the 9/11 hijackers to kill themselves they could never have killed 3,000 innocents on that terrible day. The most important metric for measuring this threat is not the amount of territory controlled by Al Qaeda or any terrorist group, but a more direct benchmark: the number of people willing to be recruited as suicide attackers to carry out missions to kill Americans and their allies. Further, what mainly motivates individuals to become suicide terrorists is not the existence of a terrorist sanctuary for indoctrination and training, but deep anger at the presence of foreign combat forces on territory they prize. This is the main reason why as American and allied forces have increasingly occupied

Muslim countries from 2001 onward, the number of suicide attacks—over-whelmingly occurring in Iraq, Afghanistan, and Pakistan in opposition to control by the United States and its allies—has skyrocketed and why there are more anti-American suicide attacks today than before 9/11.

New Suicide Terrorist Campaigns versus the United States and Allies

To understand the sudden rise of suicide terrorism around the world since 2004, it is helpful to briefly explain the emergence of these attacks in the three largest cases, Iraq, Afghanistan, and Pakistan, and two small ones, Uzbekistan and Somalia. Subsequent chapters will analyze all of the eight major suicide terrorist campaigns since 1980 in depth to answer the many issues related to the causal dynamics and ebbs and flows of suicide ter-rorism in the cases. Here our purpose is simply to allow readers to easily track the main casual relationship between the threat of foreign military occupation and suicide terrorism by showing the basic trajectory of these two factors in the prominent current cases.

Iraq

Iraq is a prime example of the strategic logic of suicide terrorism. As figure 1.3 shows, prior to our invasion in March 2003, Iraq never experi-enced a suicide attack in its history. The first suicide attacks occurred at the end of March and during the first week of April 2003 against Ameri-can military forces entering the country, and rose against an expanding target set over the course of the next five years until they began to decline in early 2008 and particularly after summer 2008. Thereafter, Iraqi suicide attacks continued on a particularly steep decline, with about 24% less in 2009 compared to 2007.

What motivates the Iraqi suicide attackers? Although we can confi-dently identify with reliable sources only a small number (72) of the iden-tities of the suicide attackers in Iraq, this information still paints a helpful picture that clarifies their main motive. As figure 1.4 shows, the largest pools come from Iraq or Saudi Arabia, the next from Kuwait. That is, the overwhelming majority are from Iraq or the immediately adjacent border areas, most of which have been mentioned prominently as possible targets of American military control after Iraq, and only a smaller portion from

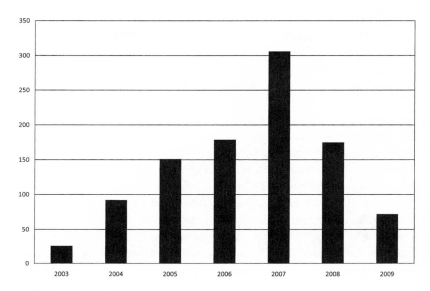

FIGURE 1.3 Suicide attacks in Iraq

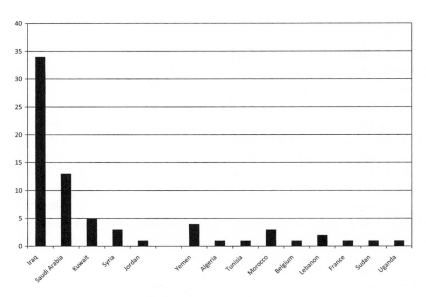

FIGURE 1.4 Nationality of suicide attackers in Iraq

outside the immediate conflict region. This is a pattern of regional resistance to American military occupation, not a global jihad.[6]

Further, notice that there are no suicide attackers from Iran—one of the largest Islamic fundamentalist populations in the world, with a population greater than Iraq, Saudi Arabia, Kuwait, Jordan, and Syria combined. Moreover, all the Iraqi suicide attackers are Sunnis, and none are Shia, who comprise 60% of the population and have large Islamic fundamentalist militias in the country. If Islamic fundamentalism were driving suicide terrorism in Iraq, we should be seeing at least as much suicide terrorism from the approximately 100 million Shia as from the approximately 50 million Sunnis in the region, but that is not the pattern that we observe. Instead, suicide terrorism is associated with the group most threatened by American occupation—Iraqi Sunnis, who widely believe that it is the American military that toppled the previous Sunni-dominated regime in Iraq and is key to installing the current Shia-dominated government there, and populations from countries in the region with little or no significant state-organized military capability to oppose American military power. If the United States were to use military force to weaken or destroy Iran's large security capabilities or to prevent the Shia majority from proportionally ruling the central government in Iraq, then Shia in the region may also come to fear they would soon lose their autonomy and become motivated to adopt suicide attacks to preserve it.

Why the decline of suicide terrorism in Iraq from 2007 to 2009? As the Chicago Project on Security and Terrorism data show, the trajectory of suicide terrorism in Iraq rises from 2003 to 2007 and then declines in two major "steps," a 40% decline from 2007 to 2008 (when suicide attacks fell from 307 to 175) and then a further 60% decline from 2008 to 2009 (175 to 72). Each of these declines reflects a different set of causal factors.

To unpack the causal dynamics of the first period, 2007 to 2008, it is important to discuss separately the two most critical geographic regions—Baghdad and Anbar Province—where violence has been most prominent and problematic, because each has different underlying causes for the decline in suicide attacks. Baghdad experienced a dramatic decline in suicide

---

6. Among numerous stories about the Bush administration's wider plans, see Nicholas Blanford, "Syria Worries US Won't Stop at Iraq," *Christian Science Monitor,* September 9, 2002; Robert Fisk, "US Sets Out to Redraw Map of Middle East," *New Zealand Herald,* September 10, 2002; and Michael Ledeen, "America's Revenge: To Turn Tyrannies into Democracies: After Iraq Will Come Iran, Syria, and Saudi Arabia," *Daily Telegraph* (London), September 11, 2002.

violence beginning in 2007 after four years of steady year-after-year increases. The primary causes of this reversal are (1) the geographic separation of the population along sectarian lines when from 500,000 to 1 million residents moved from mixed Sunni-Shia neighborhoods to homogenous ones and (2) the deployment of Coalition troops in the city, and a change in military strategy to population protection of a modest number of remaining mixed neighborhoods.

Anbar Province also saw a decline in suicide violence, but not for the same reasons operating in Baghdad. First, Anbar is overwhelmingly Sunni, so ethnic separation is not relevant. Second, Anbar experienced virtually no "surge" of the Coalition troops, whose deployment in the province remained almost constant (34,000–38,000) from September 2006 to September 2008. Rather, suicide terrorism declined mainly because local Sunnis in Anbar turned against the insurgency, a fundamental shift in popular support caused by the willingness of the Coalition to enlist local tribal cooperation, commonly known as the Anbar Awakening. From September 2006 to September 2008, the size of local tribal groups cooperating with the Coalition grew from a meager 5,000 to 100,000 strong. The result was an actual reduction in the relative power of Western combat forces in the province that empowered large numbers of Sunnis to provide for their own security and autonomy, not merely a change in the perception of foreign occupation by making American forces less apparent. *Hence, the success attributed to the surge in 2007 to 2008 was actually less the result of an increase of Coalition forces and more to a change of strategy in Baghdad and the empowerment of the Sunnis in Anbar.*

The reduction in suicide terrorism from 2008 to 2009 is due more to the reduction of the size and geographic deployment of U.S. and Coalition forces and official agreements for a schedule of further force reductions than to additional ethnic separation or enlistment of Sunni tribes. Indeed, the total number of American and Coalition combat forces in Iraq began to decline steadily from its peak in January 2008 of 174,000 to 115,000 in November 2009.[7] Further, in fall 2008 the United States signed official agreements with the Iraqi government for the schedule of further withdrawals of American combat forces, first, from all major Iraqi cities by June 2009 (which occurred) and, then, the vast majority of forces throughout Iraq by the end of 2010.

Overall, the decline of suicide terrorism in Iraq from 2007 to 2009 shows

7. According to the Department of Defense's official records.

the value of doing more than simply reverse engineering the causes of the phenomenon. Although America's invasion of Iraq triggered the rise of suicide terrorism in the first place, its reduction was driven by 1) the moderation of underlying sources of ethnic tension; 2) the empowerment of local groups, encouraging them to abandon support for terrorism; and, of course, 3) withdrawal of foreign combat troops on an orderly schedule, signaling the imminent independence of the central government. As the evidence shows, Iraq is an exemplar of the decline of suicide bombing when foreign occupation starts to go down, either when the power of local communities rises or the power of foreign militaries declines.

Afghanistan

Afghanistan also shows a close fit with the strategic logic of suicide terrorism. Prior to America's toppling of the Taliban in fall 2001, Afghanistan never had a suicide terrorist attack in its history, even with Osama bin Laden living there since the mid-1990s—with the sole exception of the suicide assassination by Al Qaeda of the leader of the Northern Alliance on September 9, 2001, in anticipation of America's military response to 9/11.

In the immediate aftermath of America's conquest, Afghanistan experienced only a small number of suicide attacks—fewer than 15 total attacks from 2002 through 2005. Suddenly, suicide attacks began to increase by an order of magnitude—with 93 in 2006, 137 in 2007, 136 in 2008, and 98 in 2009. Moreover, the overwhelming percentage of the suicide attacks (80%) has been against security targets related to American and allied forces and nearly all (90%) carried out by Afghan nationals.

So, what happened in late 2005 or early 2006 to suddenly motivate a large number of Afghans to willingly kill themselves to attack American and NATO military targets?

Although there are multiple causes, one stands out: the growth and redeployment outside of Kabul of Western forces in Afghanistan. For the first two years after toppling the Taliban, American and NATO forces were effectively limited to occupying Kabul, not the country as a whole. Partly this was due to the small number of troops available (given Iraq) and partly because of the intense security threat against America's chosen political leader, Hamid Karzai, whom the United States helped install in 2001.

Figure 1.6 represents the coalition strength at the beginning of each year.

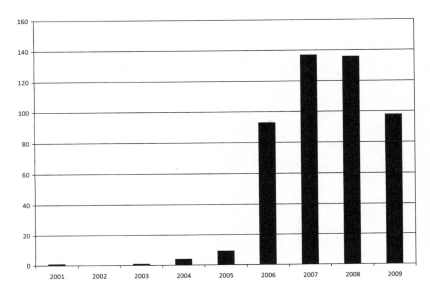

FIGURE I.5 Suicide attacks in Afghanistan

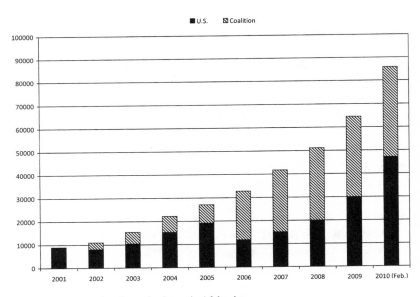

FIGURE I.6 International security forces in Afghanistan

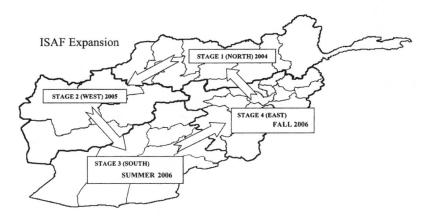

FIGURE 1.7 ISAF expansion

In October 2003, the United Nations granted permission to extend NA-TO's mission, and Western military leaders developed a plan to increase troops and expand their military deployment around the country in stages. Expanding NATO's military mission was part of a larger strategy to democratize Afghanistan by broadening central government control and combating the low level of insurgency that then existed.

As you can see in figure 1.7, NATO began by first moving to the northern region in 2004, effectively moving in with our friends, the Tajiks and Ezbeks in the Northern Alliance who helped us topple the Taliban. Next, NATO moved into the western region, again with more of our Tajik and Uzbek friends. It was not until later in 2005 that NATO began to move into the truly dangerous areas in the south and east inhabited by the Pashtuns who had supported the Taliban before 2001. This is what triggered the enormous spike in suicide terrorism in Afghanistan.

The more U.S. and NATO troops have occupied the Pashtun homeland, the more Pashtuns have renewed their support for the Taliban and the more they have engaged in suicide (and other) terrorist attacks to resist Western military occupation.

To win in Afghanistan, the United States and its allies must prevent the rise of a new generation of anti-American terrorists, particularly suicide terrorists. The metric for measuring this threat is not the amount of territory controlled by the Taliban or Al Qaeda, but the number of people willing to be recruited as suicide terrorists. These individuals are motivated not by indoctrination in a terrorist sanctuary, but by deep anger at the presence of foreign forces on land they prize. To decrease the number of suicide attacks given the ethnic divisions of the country, our best tactic is to use political and economic means to empower local Pashtuns to feel that they have greater autonomy from both Taliban and Western domination and less need to respond violently. A similar strategy toward Sunni groups in Anbar Province reduced anti-American suicide terrorism in Iraq and is our best way forward in the Pashtun provinces of Afghanistan.

Pakistan

These findings on Afghanistan also help to explain the similar explosive rise in suicide terrorism in Pakistan in 2007. Prior to 2001, Pakistan experienced only a single instance of suicide terrorism (in 1995). From 2002 to 2006, after American combat forces deployed to Afghanistan and adjacent countries, apparently including covert use of bases inside Pakistan, Pakistan began to experience a small number of suicide attacks each year.[8] However, in early 2007, the number of suicide attacks abruptly rose about 5 times (figure 1.8). These suicide attacks were mainly against military targets (figure 1.9), and were mainly in the western regions of Pakistan (figure 1.10).

So, what accounts for the escalation in suicide attacks against military targets in the western regions of Pakistan from late 2006 onward?

The key factor is the deployment of Pakistan's army against the Taliban. From April 2004 to September 2006, Pakistan concluded a series of peace agreements with various Taliban leaders with the result that there was little fighting between Pakistan and Taliban forces during this period. Following American pressure to change course, the Pakistan Army conducted a major air attack in October 2006 against a madrassa suspected of training Taliban militants, and the Taliban retaliated with a suicide attack against the Pakistan Army camp in November. This began a spiral of conflict between Pakistan's army and the militants, including the deployment of 100,000 Pakistani Army troops to the western region of the country where the Taliban are located and retaliatory Taliban suicide attacks against the Pakistani Army there and elsewhere in the country. Osama bin Laden and leaders of the

---

8. According to U.S. Senator Dianne Feinstein, the United States operates unmanned aerial vehicles that attack Al Qaeda and other targets from bases in Pakistan to the present day, while American special forces operated from Pakistani bases at least from fall 2001 to 2006. "Pakistan Lets CIA Use Airbase to Strike Militants," *Times* (London), February 17, 2009; and "Feinstein Comment on U.S. Drones Likely to Embarass Pakistan," *Los Angeles Times*, February 13, 2009.

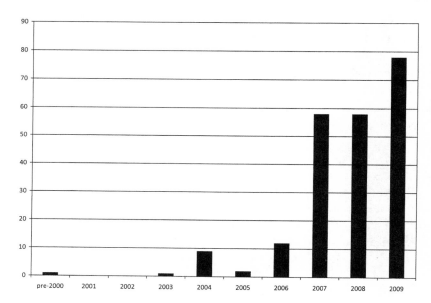

FIGURE 1.8 Suicide attacks in Pakistan

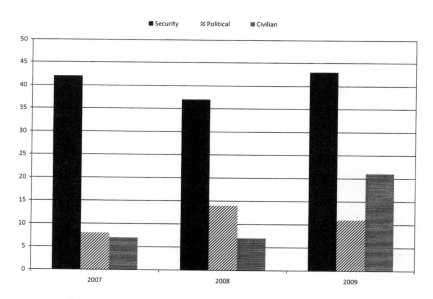

FIGURE 1.9 Pakistan attacks by target type

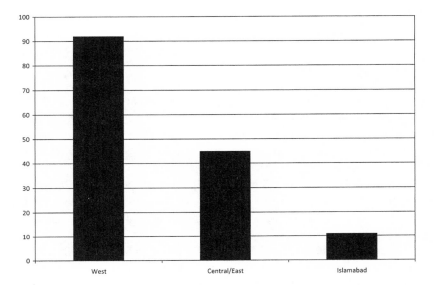

FIGURE I.10 Geography of suicide attacks in Pakistan

Taliban encouraged suicide attacks against the Pakistani government and army by stressing that they were simply an extension of American military domination of the region. In September 23, 2007, Osama bin Laden said:

> So to sum up: It is obligatory on the Muslims in Pakistan to carry out Jihad and fighting to remove Pervez, his government, his army and those who help him. . . . Rather than moving to break the siege placed on the Muslims of Afghanistan, they moved to break the siege placed on the bases and airports which Pervez gave to America and from which the planes were taking off to pound us in Tora Bora, Kabul, Kandahar, Paktia, Nangarhar and other places. . . . The tribes of Waziristan have made a great stand in the face of international Kufr— America, its allies and its agents—and the major states have been unable to make the stands they have made.[9]

Unlike the empowerment of 100,000 local Sunnis in Anbar that dampened suicide terrorism in Iraq, the imposition of 100,000 Pakistani Army troops to suppress insurgents in western Pakistan, according to the wishes

9. Osama Bin Laden, "Come to Jihad: A Speech to the People of Pakistan," September 20, 2007, transcript online at http://www.informationclearinghouse.info/article18449.htm.

of a foreign power with strong military forces in a neighboring country, increased suicide terrorism.

Uzbekistan

Uzbekistan experienced a tiny suicide terrorist campaign in 2004. Although one should not overread the implications from only a handful of attacks, a brief consideration of this case provides evidence for the relationship between suicide terrorism and even modest foreign military presence, at least by the world's most powerful state.

In late 2001, the United States established an airbase with 1,500 troops in Uzbekistan as part of its regional military operations to topple the Taliban and dislodge Al Qaeda from Afghanistan. Prior to this point, Uzbekistan had no history of suicide attack.

The first suicide attack in Uzbekistan occurred on March 29, 2004, when two female suicide attackers exploded bombs under their garments at a civilian market adjacent to the U.S. airbase, killing three policemen and a child, presumably seeking to threaten shopping opportunities for U.S. servicemen. The second attack occurred on July 30, 2004, when three male suicide attackers struck the U.S. and Israeli embassies and an Uzbek government office in Tashkent, killing four people, and apparently signaling continued opposition to American and Western presence in the country even if sanctioned by the central government.

In 2005, the United States withdrew its airbase, and there has not been a suicide attack in Uzbekistan since.[10]

Somalia

The rise of suicide terrorism in Somalia is the direct result of a foreign occupation by a democracy with a different religion. On July 20, 2006, the army of (Christian and semi-democratic) Ethiopia[11] invaded (Muslim) Somalia with the support of the United States, ultimately deploying as many as 30,000 troops in order to weaken the growing influence of Is-

10. On the establishment and removal of the U.S. airbase, see Robin Wright and Ann Scott Tyson, "US Evicted from Air Base in Uzbekistan," *Washington Post,* July 30, 2005.

11. Since 2000, Ethiopia has held multiparty elections that are commonly viewed as mostly fair and are scored as "partly free" by Freedom House, i.e., on the same level of democracy as Turkey and Pakistan.

lamic radicals in the country. In January 2009, the Ethiopian forces helped to install the new "transitional" government in the country that incorporated some insurgent splinter groups but not the main rebel faction and withdrew from the country. Thus far, at least 16,000 Somali civilians, 500 Ethiopian troops, and 2,000 insurgents have been killed.[12]

From September 2006 to 2009, a campaign of 14 suicide attacks occurred as part of a general insurgency against the Ethiopian Army and Somali government officials backed by the United States and Ethiopia. The targets of the suicide attacks were Ethiopian troops and military bases, international peacekeeping agencies supporting the Somali government, and Somali government officials.

The purpose of the suicide attacks is to compel the Ethiopian Army to withdraw and to overthrow the Somali government backed by its army. As the Somali rebel leader Sheikh Sharif Ahmed said in October 2006, "Heavily-armed Ethiopian troops have invaded Somalia. They have captured Buur Hakaba, History shows that Somalis always win when they are attacked from outside. We will counter them soon. I urge all the Somali people to wage holy war against the Ethiopians."[13]

Although nearly all the suicide attackers have been Somali, this suicide campaign has also become notable for support among American Somalis, including the first American suicide bomber, a Somali immigrant who struck Ethiopian troops in Somalia in October 2007. This transnational support for terrorism in Somalia is also motivated by the presence of foreign combat forces in the country, according to the most detailed investigation of the Americans fighting in Somalia:

> It took a major geopolitical event—the Ethiopian invasion of their homeland in 2006—to spur them to join what they saw as legitimate resistance movement, said friends of the men. . . . While the United States had defended the Ethiopian invasion as a front in the global war on terrorism, many Somalis saw it as a Christian crusade into a Muslim land. They were outraged at reports of Ethiopian troops raping Somali women, looting mosques, and killing civilians.[14]

12. "US Support Key to Ethiopia's Invasion," *USA Today,* January 7, 2007; "Evaluating Ethiopia's Presence" (January 31, 2009), http://allafrica.com/stories/200902020072.html.

13. "Call for Jihad as Ethiopian Troops Go into Somalia," *Daily Telegraph,* October 10, 2006.

14. Andrea Elliott, "A Call to Jihad, Answered in America," *New York Times Magazine,* July 12, 2009.

Conclusion

Since 2004, the world has witnessed a spectacular rise in suicide terrorism. Although there are multiple reasons, the central cause is that the United States and its allies have waged the "war on terrorism" according to the faulty premise that the threat to the American homeland and U.S. overseas interests is mainly due to Islamic fundamentalism. If this were right, then transforming Muslim societies to wring out the religious extremists, if necessary using heavy military force, would make sense. However, the premise does not fit the facts, and the conquest of Muslim countries since 2001 has vastly increased anti-American suicide terrorism around the world. If judged by its central purpose—reducing the number of individuals willing to die to kill Americans and their allies—the "war on terrorism" from 2001 to 2009 has failed to make Americans safer.

CHAPTER TWO

What Really Motivates Transnational Suicide Terrorists

Many people around the world ask how Muslims, many of whom are middle class and well educated, can kill themselves to kill Americans and others in the West. The answer is both simple and disturbing: deep anger at the presence of Western combat forces in the Persian Gulf region and other predominately Muslim lands.

As explained in *Dying to Win,* nationalism—the desire to protect and perpetuate their community's political, religious, and social institutions—is the central explanation for why some individuals, whose community is facing foreign military occupation, willingly chose to defend their community's way of life by sacrificing their own in carrying out suicide attacks. However, left unanswered was the causal logic of transnational suicide attackers—individuals living in distant countries from those occupied—who comprise about 10% of all suicide attackers from 1980 to 2009 and as much as a fifth to a third of some prominent suicide terrorist campaigns (Iraq and Al Qaeda).

This book explains the phenomenon of transnational suicide terrorism. While existing theories contend that it is a product of religious fanaticism or economic alienation, this volume shows the causal logic for transnational suicide terrorism is best explained as an extension of the logic of military occupation.

Transnational suicide terrorists are individuals with colliding communal loyalties, one for a kindred community and another for their home country of citizenship. Which is most demanding of an individual's loyalty is significantly influenced by the foreign threats to each. Specifically, an individual's hierarchy of communal loyalties can be strongly influenced by which community, the kindred or home, is most under threat. Hence, the foreign military occupation of the kindred community can result in an individual's hierarchy of loyalties elevating the kindred community over the home one. Once this ranking of loyalty is established, then effects similar to nationalism follow. The individual is more willing to make sacrifices to defend the kindred community, since it is the more threatened community. This theory cannot tell us how many individuals with divided loyalties will become suicide terrorists, but it does conclude that transnational suicide terrorism is more likely in response to a kindred community's foreign occupation than the result of an individual's religious fanaticism or economic alienation.

However, what is striking about transnational suicide terrorism is not only that it is rare, but that it is also commonly a group phenomenon, with individuals who were first friends collectively becoming more radical together. Accordingly, a theory of transnational suicide terrorism should seek to explain the rare circumstances under which the group forms, becomes focused on political action for a kindred community, and moves to intentional action to execute a specific plan of suicide attack. This chapter develops such a theory and shows that it better accounts for cases of transnational suicide terrorism than the leading alternatives.

The "Black Swan" Issue

Suicide terrorists are often referred to as "extremists" who are "radicalized" by some "scattered global networks." These references do fit with the reality that suicide terrorists are most often shadowy, hard-to-find attackers whose existence is rarely known until they strike. They also reflect the fact that many suicide terrorists are individuals with little connection with terrorism until just a few months or even a few weeks prior to their attack and would commonly appear, even to those who know them moderately well, as fairly ordinary people.

The multitude of references to suicide terrorists as extremists radicalized by global networks also suggests—incorrectly, as we shall see—that most such attackers are transnational individuals scattered from fringe populations across the world and who carry out strikes in countries outside their own homelands and for reasons that have little to do with helping their local communities. Whether viewed as the product of economic alienation, social isolation, or cultlike brainwashing, suicide terrorists are often portrayed as mainly transnational. Assaf Moghadam writes, "the new globalized phenomenon of suicide attacks is transnational in nature."[1] Similarly, Scott Atran claims, "most suicide terrorists today are inspired by a global jihadism . . . the problem is transnational."[2]

The existing literature on transnational suicide terrorism is valuable, calling attention to a complex phenomenon that eludes easy explanation. The literature also has a clear conception of the meaning of transnational terrorism, although it is not always well articulated. To be clear, what defines a transnational terrorist is not the distance traveled to do an attack, although traveling a long distance is a suggestive indicator. Nor is the defining characteristic that the terrorist is attacking a target in a foreign country, because a terrorist with multiple loyalties could attack his own country of citizenship. Rather, the defining feature is the motive—to carry out an attack beyond supporting the particular interests of the terrorist's home nation, normally the terrorist's community of birth or adopted community through naturalization. By this definition, the 15 Saudi 9/11 hijackers who attacked America in response to U.S. military presence on the Arabian Peninsula were not transnational, while Mohammad Atta, an Egyptian national who led the attack, was a transnational suicide terrorist.

However, the idea that suicide terrorism is mainly transnational is factually inaccurate. As discussed earlier, over 96% of all suicide attacks from 1980 to 2009 have occurred in campaigns of suicide terrorism that are tightly focused in specific areas of the world. This pattern is also reflected in the identities of the suicide attackers themselves, the overwhelming number of whom come directly from the local population resisting a foreign occupation. Overall, the vast majority of suicide attackers carry out attacks in their home countries, often just miles from their homes, as part of campaigns to resist foreign occupation of land they prize. Hence Lebanese carried out the suicide attacks against Israeli occupation of Lebanon, Sri Lankan Tamils the suicide attacks against the Sri Lankan military occupation of their home areas, Palestinians the suicide attacks against Israel's occupation of the Palestinian West Bank and Gaza, Chechens the suicide attacks against Russia's occupation of Chechnya, and Turkish Kurds the suicide attacks by the PKK against the Turkish military presence on their home areas, and Iraqis, Saudis, Syrians, Kuwaitis, and Jordanians the suicide attacks against America's military occupation of Iraq and America's threat to countries adjacent to Iraq.

1. Assaf Moghadam, "Suicide Terrorism, Occupation, and the Globalization of Martyrdom," *Studies in Conflict and Terrorism* 29 (2006): 707–29, quote at p. 707
2. Scott Atran, "The Moral Logic and Growth of Suicide Terrorism," *Washington Quarterly* 29, no. 2 (2006): 127–47, quote at p. 139.

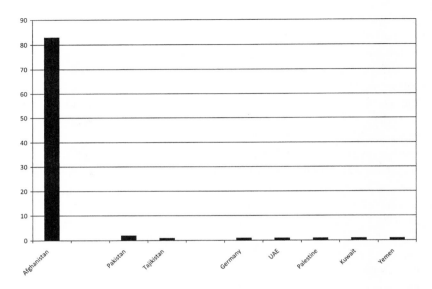

FIGURE 2.1 Nationality of suicide attackers in Afghanistan

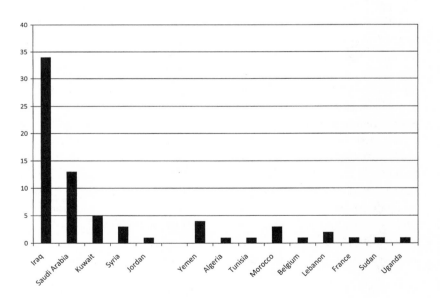

FIGURE 2.2 Nationality of suicide attackers in Iraq

Moreover, transnational suicide terrorists are in the minority even in the campaigns where they do occur, and have only occurred after or in conjunction with national suicide terrorists from the country resisting occupation. As figure 2.1 shows, we can confidently identify 91 suicide attackers in Afghanistan, of which 90% are Afghan nationals and another 4% are from the zone of conflict.

In Iraq, we can confidently identify the nationalities of 72 suicide attackers who actually killed themselves on missions to kill others. Of these, the largest group is Iraqi Sunnis (34), the next largest Saudis (13), and the overwhelming majority (60) from Iraq or the immediate adjacent border areas to Iraq both to the west and south on the Arabian Peninsula, areas that have frequently been mentioned as possible targets of expanded U.S. military control after Iraq. Compared to the 83% coming from Iraq and the Persian Gulf region, only 17% (12) come from areas beyond the conflict zone, and only 6% (4) from non-Muslim countries. Notably, there has not been a single Iraqi suicide attacker from Iran and none from Iraq's Shia and Kurdish populations (which, respectively, comprise 60% and 20% of the inhabitants of the country). Although we have far more missing than complete data, the verifiable evidence suggests that the lion's share of the suicide terrorists attacking in Iraq have been from the populations in Iraq and surrounding communities most vulnerable to American military occupation and not from a global jihad more or less randomly drawn from the Muslim world. Put differently, there are nearly five times the number of attackers from Iraq and the region, which comprises roughly 55 million Muslims, than from the remaining 1.4 billion Muslims around the globe, a population 25 times larger. This is mainly a pattern of regional opposition to foreign military presence, not a global jihad.

Al Qaeda also fits the pattern of opposition to American military presence. From 1995 to 2009, a total of 97 individuals have killed themselves on missions supported by Osama bin Laden. Of these, we know the names and nationalities of 81. Of these, the largest number, 37, come from Saudi Arabia and the great majority, 54 (67%), from the Arabian Peninsula where the United States first began to station combat forces in 1990 or other Sunni countries with American combat presence.[3] About one-third are transnational, using the conservative definition adopted in this study,

3. As noted in chapter 1, American special forces and unmanned aerial vehicles have been based in Pakistan since the fall of 2001, and so the two Pakistani Al Qaeda attackers qualify as from a Sunni country with American combat presence.

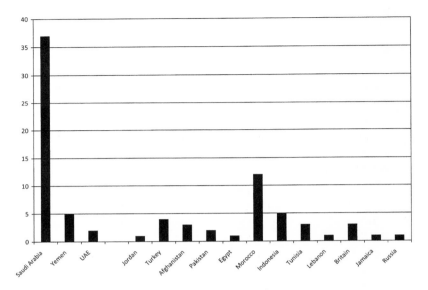

FIGURE 2.3 Nationality of Al Qaeda attackers

i.e., these 27 are from countries not immediately threatened by American combat presence, and of these, only five are from non-Muslim countries.

However, even these 27 do not fit the idea that transnational suicide attackers represent a global jihad, coming more or less at random from Islamic fundamentalist populations. Most of the transnational attackers (18 of 27) come from Morocco, Indonesia, and Egypt, which have been among the highest recipients of American foreign aid (and labeled by Al Qaeda as U.S.-backed regimes that "repress" Muslims). At most nine are from countries not directly under American military influence or whose regimes are not strongly underpinned by American resources, while none are coming from some of the largest Islamic fundamentalist populations in the world, such as Iran, Bangladesh, or Sudan (all with the same or larger population than Saudi Arabia).

Transnational suicide attackers do exist. They are important. But, they are the "Black Swans" of suicide terrorism. From 1980 to 2009, there have been a total of 2,668 suicide attackers around the world. Although we cannot be sure given missing data, most likely there have been 255, or 10%, transnational suicide terrorists, counting all those we know are transnational in all campaigns other than Iraq and Afghanistan and applying the fraction of known transnational attackers in Iraq and Afghanistan to those campaigns.

Understanding that transnational suicide attackers are Black Swans has important implications for explaining their existence. Although in many ways they are especially fascinating, it is important to recognize that they are anomalies rather than the norm. Sometimes anomalies require wholly new explanations that are radically different from the phenomenon as a whole. Sometimes anomalies require only a modest extension of a main explanation. However, to know just how radically our explanations of anomalies and the norm differ, it is helpful to begin with the baseline explanation of the norm and then compare the anomalies to it.

Occupation and Nationalism

One of the most important patterns about suicide terrorism is its geographic concentration. As discussed earlier, over 96% of all suicide attacks since 1980 have occurred in campaigns of suicide terrorism that are tightly focused in specific areas of the world. This pattern is also reflected in the identities of the suicide attackers themselves, the overwhelming number of whom come directly from the local population resisting a foreign occupation.

The close association between suicide terrorism and foreign military occupation is explained by the phenomenon of nationalism, the idea of valuing the distinct political, cultural, religious, and other characteristics that define a group of people as a distinct community. National identities rest on the idea of a primary division of the world between "us" and "them," a boundary that tends to harden under the circumstances of a foreign military occupation. Indeed, the wider the difference between the identities of the foreign occupier and the local community, the more likely is the local community to view the occupier as "alien," and since the "alien" is also the stronger power, the more the local community is likely to fear that occupation will lead to radical and permanent transformation of its way of life and so is more willing to make sacrifices to resist the occupation. Religious differences are among the most extreme, which is why nearly all suicide terrorist campaigns occur when a foreign occupying community has a predominately different religion than the occupied community, even those suicide terrorist campaigns that are carried out by secular groups—since secular (as well as religious) individuals may fear even indirect influence by the occupier's religion. This is why Osama bin Laden and the leaders of other suicide terrorist campaigns often demonize the foreign occupier as driven by a religious agenda that necessarily damages local ways of life.

Nationalism also accounts for the existence of regional suicide attackers, those from the zone of conflict who join campaigns of opposition to foreign military presence on territory immediately adjacent or otherwise vulnerable to domination by the same foreign force. Especially when the foreign military power is extremely strong, its military presence in one country is likely to produce fears of a more expansive military design for the region as a whole, on grounds similar to the "domino theory"—the foreign military control of one country is likely to encourage more ambitious adventures in immediately adjacent areas. Hence, foreign military presence in one community can mobilize national resistance from other communities in the region, even those that have not yet come under the same degree of foreign occupation. This is why the defining feature of transnational suicide terrorism is not the crossing of a political boundary, but a motive beyond supporting the particular interests of the terrorists' home country.

The key point is that the association between suicide terrorism and national resistance to foreign occupation, for the overwhelming proportion of events, hinges on the existence of a community of individuals with a single national loyalty, which accounts for extreme self-sacrifice. However, what explains the rare events, those in which individuals carry out suicide attacks in circumstances far removed from the occupation of the community in which they reside?

To answer this question, let us begin by examining the evidence on the actual motives of transnational suicide terrorists.

The Motive of Transnational Suicide Terrorists

There is strong evidence that transnational suicide terrorists are powerfully motivated by the strategic goal of compelling a democracy to withdraw combat forces from the foreign occupation of territory, and not economic alienation or religious fundamentalism independent of this circumstance.

Aggregate Patterns

Consider the patterns in the aggregate data. First, the largest pool of transnational suicide attackers occurs in the Iraq campaign, likely about 200 total attackers. These Iraqi transnational suicide attacks tightly correlate to the timing of the onset of military occupation by the United States and its allies. They began only after the United States invaded Iraq in March 2003 and have dramatically declined along with all the suicide terrorism in Iraq from 2008 onward as the occupation has declined.

Second, transnational suicide attacks have not spread to other areas around the world as they have declined in Iraq. The fact that transnational suicide terrorism is not "moving" from one region to another, but is largely disappearing as the external circumstances that inspired it in one region are removed, casts doubt on the idea that this pool of attackers are being produced from global religious or economic causes, since these global phenomenon—to the extent they exist—existed prior to the Iraqi transnational suicide attacks and after their decline.

Third, the next largest pool of transnational attackers is associated with Osama bin Laden's campaign against the United States and its military allies in response to their military occupation of the Arabian Peninsula, at most 48 attackers overall. These attackers are also closely linked to the foreign military presence, striking only after U.S. forces were stationed in significant numbers in the Persian Gulf region after 1990. Further, although these attacks have occurred in many countries, they focus on killing the citizens of countries with combat forces stationed side by side with the United States in Muslim lands. Indeed, bin Laden's public statements routinely highlight Western occupation as the central rallying point for encouraging extremists to attack the countries participating in occupation and as the focal point explaining the targeting logic in Al Qaeda's campaign of attacks. Mocking President George Bush's claim that Al Qaeda "hates freedom," bin Laden said, "No, we fight because we are free men who don't sleep under oppression. We want to restore freedom to our nation. Just as you lay waste to our nation, so shall we lay waste to yours.... [This is] contrary to Bush's claim that we hate freedom. If so, let him explain why we don't strike for example—Sweden?"[4]

If economic alienation were driving transnational suicide terrorism, different global patterns should occur. In particular, we would expect those engaged in transnational suicide terrorism to be predominantly from economically disadvantaged immigrant communities within prosperous Western countries and the timing of their attacks to occur independently of the trajectory of foreign military presence in any country. Indeed, those who

---

4. Osama bin Laden videotape (November 1, 2004), translated and published on Aljazeera.net.

advocate this theory expected such a pattern in recent suicide terrorist events.

Following the London suicide attacks by British citizens with Pakistani and Jamaican heritage in July 2005, many terrorist experts ascribed the cause to economic disadvantages of Muslims in Britain, a social phenomenon quite common across Europe. Accordingly, these experts warned that Europe was heading for a major wave of "homegrown" suicide attacks, particularly in France where the population is 10% Muslim, many of whom were unemployed and engaged in violent protests about their economic circumstances.[5] However, although the prediction of widespread European transnational suicide terrorism would make sense if this type of terrorism were the product of economic alienation, the predicted wave did not occur—a major failure for the theory.

Further, the timing and geographic distribution of transnational suicide terrorists do not fit well with the economic alienation theory. Transnational suicide terrorists are mainly coming from Muslim countries, not Europe or other Western nations, and the few from Western countries do not correspond to periods of immigrant violence related to economic alienation. In Britain, there has been a history of immigrant violence, including riots by Pakistani immigrants, but these violent events have typically occurred in clusters that coincide with serious economic downturns, such as the multiple immigrant riots that occurred during the spring and summer of 1980, which are closely associated with Britain's severe recession of 1979–81. Most important, although Britain has experienced repeated patterns of economic alienation and immigrant violence, the last riots among immigrants occurred in 2001, and since then there has been no rioting among Pakistani or any other immigrant group in the country.[6] Accordingly, there is little reason to think that the July 2005 London bombers are an extension of a general pattern of economic alienation affecting Muslims or other immigrants in Britain at the time.

Similarly, if Islamic fundamentalism were the principal factor driving transnational suicide terrorism, such attacks should not be related to the ebb and flow of foreign occupation of particular countries. Islamic fun-

---

5. For instance, see Oliver Roy, quoted in "Paradigm of Terror Changing," *Toronto Star,* July 16, 2005; Francis Fukuyama, quoted in "Don't Ignore Western Europe, Terrorism Expert Warns," *Washington Post,* September 8, 2005; and Marc Sageman, quoted in "Hearts and Minds," *Boston Globe,* August 20, 2006.

6. For an excellent study of immigrant violence in Britain from 1950 to 2006, see Rafaela M. Dancygier, "Immigration and Conflict" (Ph.D. dissertation, Yale University, December 2007).

damentalism is a global phenomenon, one that has been in existence in a variety of forms, not just for many decades, but almost since the inception of Islam itself. Hence, Islamic fundamentalism cannot account for the rise of transnational suicide terrorism over the past 30 years, why it occurs intensely at some times and not others at specific places and times within this 30-year time span, and—most especially—why transnational suicide terrorism declines. For instance, some argue that the rise of global communication networks that allow for "leaderless" association among ideological extremists scattered across the world is a central cause of transnational terrorism—except that, in the past few years, global use of the Internet is increasing while transnational suicide terrorism has been declining.

Specific Cases

Examination of specific transnational suicide terrorists shows that the presence of foreign combat forces occupying land they prize is powerfully motivating their behavior. Consider the individuals who carried out the London suicide attacks in July 2005, surely a part of Al Qaeda's transnational support. The attackers, mostly British citizens of Pakistani extraction, were not ethnically related to those suffering under foreign occupation. They were, however, individuals with multiple loyalties, and sympathy with the plight of kindred Muslims suffering under foreign military occupation. This empathy with fellow Muslims played a powerful role in the suicide bombers' motivations. And in this case, as well as others, suicide terrorism was seen as an effective weapon with which to coerce the democratic nations occupying the prized territory.

First, the Al Qaeda group that claimed responsibility for the London attacks said that they were intended to punish Great Britain for its military operations in Iraq and Afghanistan. The Al Qaeda statement was released just hours after the July 7 attack and went on to threaten Italy and Denmark with terrorist attacks if those states "did not withdraw their troops from Iraq and Afghanistan."[7]

Second, Hussein Osman, one of the four would-be July 21 bombers, who attempted a follow-on attack of London two weeks after the July 7 bombings and was later captured in Rome, said in his interrogation by Italian

---

7. Elaine Sciolino, "The Ghosts of Madrid Stalk the Bloodied Streets of London," *International Herald Tribune,* July 8, 2005.

authorities: "Religion had nothing to do with this. . . . We were shown videos with images of the war in Iraq."[8]

Third, two of the four July 7 bombers made "martyr videos"—last will video testimonials released by Al Qaeda several months after their attack—which leave little doubt as to their motives.

MOHAMMAD SIDIQUE KHAN: I'm going to keep this short and to the point. . . . Our words are dead until we give them life with our blood. This is how our ethical stances are dictated. Your democratically-elected governments continuously perpetuate atrocities against my people all over the world. And your support of them makes you directly responsible—just as I am directly responsible for protecting and avenging my Muslim brothers and sisters. Until we feel security, you will be our targets, and until you stop the bombing, gassing, imprisonment, and torture of my people, we will not stop this fight. We are at war and I am a soldier.

SHEHZAD TANWEER: To the non-Muslims of Britain, you may wonder what you have done to deserve this. You are those who have voted in your government, who, in turn, have and still continue to this day to oppress our Muslim mothers, children, brothers, and sisters, from the East to the West. . . . Your government has openly support the genocide of over 150,000 innocent Muslims in Fallujah [Iraq]. . . . What you have witnessed now is only the beginning of a series of attacks, which will intensify and continue until you pull all your troops out of Afghanistan and Iraq, until you stop all financial and military support to the U.S. and Israel, and until you release all Muslim prisoners from Belmarsh and your other concentration camps. And know that if you fail to comply with this, then know that this war will never stop and that we are ready to give our lives 100 times over for the cause of Islam. You will never experience peace until our children in Palestine, our mothers and sisters in Kashmir, our brothers in Afghanistan and Iraq feel peace.[9]

Finally, the British government also found that, to the extent that British Muslims sympathized with Al Qaeda's call for suicide attacks on the West, they did so for reasons related to Western occupation of Muslim countries. In April 2004, the British Home Office conducted a survey of the attitudes of the 1.6 million Muslims living in Britain at the time. It found that be-

8. David Leppard and John Follain, "Third Terror Cell on the Loose?" *The Times* (London), July 31, 2008.

9. The transcripts of both videos will be available on the CPOST Web site.

tween 8% and 13% believed more suicide attacks against the United States and the West were justified. These numbers are troubling enough, but they also reveal the limits of multiple loyalties: according to the report, "the great majority of British Muslims (up to 85%) regarded the attacks on Western targets, including the 9/11 attacks, as unjustified." Further, among those who endorsed suicide terrorism, the survey identified the number one reason—Iraq.

While it is clear that the July 2005 London bombers were motivated by the goal of ending the foreign occupation of kindred communities, there is little evidence that they were acting out against social or economic alienation or to achieve Islamic fundamentalist religious objectives. What would count as evidence for these alternative explanations is nicely presented by the most important official American report claiming that alienation and religious indoctrination are the key factors driving "homegrown" terrorism, the 2007 study by the New York Police Department, "Radicalization in the West." This report identifies the key standards for each factor, stating with regard to alienation: "failure to integrate the 2nd and 3rd generation of immigrants into society, both economically and socially, has left many young Muslims torn between the secular West and their religious heritage"; and stating with regard to religious motives: "to attack institutions and societies in order to overthrow non-Islamic governments and to bring about a 'pure' Islamic society . . [based on] sharia law."[10] As the report points out, these two broad motives apply so broadly that virtually any ordinary second- or third-generation Muslim male under the age of 35 living in Western liberal democracies is potentially vulnerable to radicalization, causing many to think that the NYPD report characterizes Muslims as intrinsically dangerous or intrinsically linked to terrorism and so serving as a license for blanket surveillance of the majority of the adult male Muslim population.[11]

If Islamic fundamentalism were driving the motives of Khan and Tanweer, then we should find their martyr videos teeming with calls for the overthrow of non-Islamic governments in order to create new governments in the West based on sharia law and so spread a "pure" Islamic society to

10. Mitchell D. Silber and Arvin Bhatt, "Radicalization in the West: The Homegrown Threat" (New York: City of New York Police Department, 2007), pp. 8, 19.

11. For the association of alienation and religious motives to under 35-year-old Muslim immigrants in the West, see ibid., p. 25. For complaints about the NYPD report, see "Concerns with Mitchell D. Silber and Arvin Bhatt, NYPD, *Radicalization in the West*" (New York: Brennan Center for Justice, New York University School of Law, August 30, 2007).

Great Britain or other Western societies. However, there is no evidence that Khan or Tanweer sought to attack Britain in order to create a change of government that would lead to the establishment of sharia law. Only Khan even mentions "sharia" and then as a condition for Muslims to feel safe, but not as a factor justifying the attack of non-Muslims in Britain or anywhere else.

If social or economic alienation were driving the motives of the London bombers, we would expect to find evidence from their last testimonials or interviews of family, friends, and acquaintances of rejection by their surrounding community. However, even the NYPD report rules this out, saying "to many who knew [the London bombers], all four were described as being well-integrated into British society."[12]

In short, the principal factor among radicalized British Muslims was not "Islamo-fascism" or economic alienation, but deep anger over British military policies in the Persian Gulf region, policies that were seen to impose great harm on a kindred people.

Occupation and Multiple Loyalties

Knowing more about the patterns and motives of transnational suicide terrorists helps us to specify what we are seeking to explain. The main issue is not why virtually all suicide terrorists are transnational, but nearly the opposite: why do a tiny fraction of individuals carry out extreme acts of self-sacrifice to coerce a target country to change its policies toward a community that is not their home nation?

Limits on the "Radicalization of Individuals" Approach

In the years since the July 2005 London suicide bombings, government analysts, scholars, and policy experts have sought to explain how an individual becomes a transnational terrorist by seeking to track points along a spectrum of radicalization. Their basic idea is that there is a large pool of potential extremists who become progressively radicalized either through elite manipulation (say, indoctrination by Islamic fundamentalist leaders in mosques) or through economic alienation (say, unemployment or other economic or social disadvantages in their daily lives), which then leads to

---

12. Silber and Bhatt, "Radicalization in the West," p. 28.

anger that can grow and fester, through either (more) elite manipulation or membership in small circles of similarly disadvantaged individuals.[13]

However, the fundamental problem with the "spectrum of radicalization" approach is that it is grossly overpredictive. Consider the London suicide attacks. Even if we restrict the pool of potential extremists to the 1.6 million Muslims living in Britain in 2004, both the religious indoctrination and economic alienation versions of the spectrum of radicalization approach would expect orders of magnitude more "homegrown" suicide attackers than actually occurred, since tens of thousands, if not hundreds of thousands, would, at some point in their lives, have been exposed to Islamic fundamentalist leaders in mosques or faced difficulty in jobs or school that they might think was related to their ethnicity. Further, these same alleged factors existed for many decades before the 2005 attacks and have not disappeared since, and so poorly account for the timing of the strikes.

Beyond extreme overprediction, however, the spectrum of radicalization approach rests on a problematic assumption. The spectrum of radicalization approach focuses on the transition of an individual, when there is substantial evidence that transnational suicide attackers strike in groups of individuals with preexisting social ties. This observation was first made by Marc Sageman about Al Qaeda terrorists,[14] but seems to fit a broader pattern. From 9/11, to the July 2005 London bombings, to Moroccans carrying out suicide attacks in Iraq in recent years, one of the most important characteristics of transnational suicide attacks is that they often involve a group of attackers who knew each other well—often living together—in the years prior to their attack, effectively progressing from a group of friends to a group of suicide attackers. This observed pattern is quite different from what is commonly found among national suicide attackers. Although there are exceptions (such as the members of the Hebron soccer team who carried out suicide attacks for Hamas during the Second Intifada), national suicide terrorists are often walk-in volunteers who join suicide terrorist groups individually, most frequently carry out their attacks individually,

13. For a spectrum of individual radicalization that emphasizes religious indoctrination, see Silber and Bhatt, "Radicalization in the West," and Thomas Precht, "Homegrown Terrorism and Islamist Radicalization in Europe: From Conversion to Terrorism" (Danish Ministry of Justice Report, December 2007) . For a similar approach that emphasizes personal economic and social alienation, see Marc Sageman, *Leaderless Jihad: Terror Networks in the Twenty-First Century* (Philadelphia: University of Pennsylvania Press, 2008).

14. Marc Sageman, *Understanding Terror Networks* (Philadelphia: University of Pennsylvania Press, 2004).

and when they do strike as a team, often appear to be organized for team attacks by the organization (meeting, for instance, in training camps as appears to be the case with Sri Lankan and national Al Qaeda suicide attackers who strike in teams) rather than on the basis of friendship or other social ties prior to joining the group.

There are limits to even the most well formulated of the spectrum of radicalization theories. Marc Sageman develops "four prongs of radicalization" of Muslims: a) moral outrage; b) war against Islam; c) resonance with personal experiences ("perceived discrimination" by host country); d) membership in like-minded group or Internet chat room.[15] Sageman's theory does recognize the importance of anger over Western military polices and the role of groups in turning that anger into violent action. However, his theory still greatly overpredicts the expected amount of transnational terrorist attacks by Muslims living in Western countries. As noted, there were 1.6 million Muslims in Britain in 2004. If the British government's polls are valid and 8%–13% believed that Western occupation of Iraq justified suicide attacks on Western countries and if Sageman is right that they are unemployed at two or three times the rate of natives (4.8% in 2004), we would expect at a minimum of between 12,000 to 31,000 individuals in Britain alone to fit his model—nearly all of whom would have easy access to Internet chat rooms or Muslim group activities. Of course, there would be many times more Muslims in France, Germany, and elsewhere in Europe who would fit as well. What Sageman's theory predicts are numerous White Swans that we do not observe, not the rare Black Swans we do.

Accordingly, an explanation of transnational suicide terrorism should seek to explain not why one individual evolves along a spectrum of radicalization from ordinary person to suicide attacker, but why dynamics occur among a group of people that can account for their group decision to carry out a team suicide attack. This theory should take into account the fact that the individuals involved may have multiple loyalties and also explain why the phenomenon is so rare.

Transnational versus National Loyalties

Whereas a national identity is an attachment to a single nation of people with a common understanding of their ancestry and all their shared political,

---

15. Sageman, *Leaderless Jihad.*

cultural, linguistic, religious, and other characteristics, a transnational identity is an attachment to a "kindred" community, defined either by a single
characteristic common across multiple nations or by a loyalty to a particular
nation different from one's country of citizenship. Kindred communities can
be based on ideology, religion, or latent commitments to specific nations, but
in all cases the depth of a transnational attachment is reflected in the willingness of individuals to sacrifice for a kindred community.

Throughout history, various transnational loyalties have motivated
individuals to sacrifice their lives. For instance, 40,000 loyal communists
from 52 countries (including 2,800 Americans) fought for a kindred community of communists in the Spanish Civil war from 1936 to 1939, and
one-third lost their lives in this struggle. In 1948, 3,500 overseas Jews
from 40 countries fought for the nascent Israeli state in its War for Independence, making great sacrifices for both their religion and the Israeli
homeland. In 2007, dozens of first- and second-generation Somali immigrants in America fought to defend Somalia in response to Ethiopia's
2006 invasion.[16]

What these episodes of transnational violence have in common is not
a particular type of kindred community, but the willingness of individuals
to risk their lives for a community other than their country of citizenship
and, more specifically, in defense of that kindred community in the face of
a military threat to it. Indeed, the existence of a foreign military threat to
the kindred community appears to be a crucial condition for large numbers
of individuals to choose transnational loyalties over national ones. Additionally, local members of the kindred community are actively engaged in
resistance against the military threat, and this local resistance provides a
magnet encouraging transnational actors to emulate the action. Further,
the existence of transnational violent action is rare in all the above cases,
comprising only a tiny fraction of the possible pool of individuals loyal to
a kindred community.

As a result, there is no one single hierarchy between national and transnational loyalties that is constant in the sense that the country of current

16. Peter N. Carroll, *Odyssey of the Abraham Lincoln Brigade: Americans in the Span-
ish Civil War* (Stanford, CA: Stanford University Press, 1994); Craig and Jeffrey Weiss, *I Am
My Brother's Keeper: American Volunteers in Israel's War of Independence 1947–1949* (Atglen,
PA: Schiffer Military History 1998). The American Somalis are discussed below. For a broad
discussion of transnational fighters in civil conflicts, see David S. Malet, "Foreign Fighters:
Transnational Identity in Civil Conflicts" (Ph.D. dissertation, George Washington University,
August 31, 2009).

citizenship always dominates kindred community loyalties. Instead, the hierarchy of loyalties is a function of the degree of relative threat to the multiple values an individual may hold. If there is a military threat to one's home nation, this will likely take precedence over transnational values. Alternatively, if there is a military threat to a kindred community, this may take priority, particularly under circumstances that encourage emotional spirals of fear and anger and a collective commitment for self-sacrifice among groups of individuals.[17] The next section explains when this rare Black Swan event may happen, particularly with respect to contemporary transnational suicide terrorism.

Explaining the Black Swans

Sociologists and professional militaries in many countries have long known that primary group cohesion plays a significant role in why armies fight. While individuals may volunteer for military service or accept conscription for motives based on national loyalties, a key reason why they fight hard under circumstances of extreme personal risk on the battlefield is the degree of primary group cohesion at the squad or platoon level—that is, when the chips are down, soldiers fight and die for their friends. Indeed, a core purpose of boot camp and other professional military training is to foster primary group cohesion through long days over many weeks of intense face-to-face contact that builds deep bonds of intrasquad loyalty based on devotion to the mission of the small group even at the expense of the physical survival of individual members.[18]

17. For discussion of the flexibility of communal identities and how emotions can trigger priorities among competing identities, see Lisa Wedeen, "Conceptualizing Culture," *American Political Science Review* 96, no. 4 (2002); Roger Petersen, *Understanding Ethnic Violence* (New York: Cambridge University Press, 2002); and Kanchan Chandra, *Why Ethnic Parties Succeed* (New York: Cambridge University Press, 2004). For alternatives to military threat creating priorities among identities (in circumstances not leading to transnational violence), see Benedict Anderson, *Imagine Communities: Reflections on the Origins and Spread of Nationalism* (London: Verso, 1983); and Daniel Posner, *Institutions and Ethnic Politics in Africa* (New York: Cambridge University Press, 2005).

18. The seminal work explaining the relationship between primary group cohesion and why soldiers fight is Edward A. Shils and Morris Janowitz, "Cohesion and Disintegration in the Wehrmacht in World War II," *Public Opinion Quarterly* 12, no. 12 (Summer 1948): 280–315. For further research extending the original analysis, see Guy L. Siebold, "The Essence of Military Group Cohesion," *Armed Forces and Society* 33, no. 2 (January 2007): 286–95; and W. D. Henderson, *Cohesion: The Human Element in Combat* (Washington, DC: National Defense University Press, 1985). For evidence that ideological homogeneity mattered more than primary group cohesion in the German Army on the Eastern front in World War II, see Omer

Transnational suicide terrorism likely stems from a version of primary group cohesion often found in professional militaries. Like military squads willing to fight to the last man to achieve their unit's mission, transnational suicide attackers frequently operate in small groups who coordinate their individual suicide attacks closely in time and for a concerted purpose. The main difference is that, while professional militaries construct elaborate environments in which to infuse raw recruits with value for their small unit and other elements of the military, the phenomenon of primary group cohesion leading to suicide terrorism occurs largely spontaneously, without a well-defined institutional structure and without preexisting values that groups are expected to internalize.

In the case of transnational suicide terrorism, the process of primary group cohesion follows a sequential logic: a) individuals come together and form continuing interactions around religious discussions, athletic interests, and social programs, during which they b) discover that they share deep anger over particular political issues—typically anger over the presence of foreign military forces occupying kindred lands—and c) this anger becomes the basis for still more intense small group interactions over periods of months, with the individuals choosing to meet frequently in face-to-face meetings and reducing their interactions with those outside the primary group, either living together or in close proximity to one another. Once the primary group is formed on this basis, then d) some event—possibly occurring exogenously to the group, such as a spectacular suicide attack by others—directs their shared anger toward executing their own suicide attack.

More generally, the progressive radicalization of the group can be viewed as a four-stage causal process: a) "filtering"—the subprocess of individuals socially interacting in ways that allow each to compare their interests with others; b) "discovering"—the subprocess of individuals finding others with like political concerns; c) "cutting"—the subprocess of group members moving toward intentional action by voluntarily cutting preexisting social ties and meeting each other with greater frequency; and d) "determining"—the subprocess by which the group agrees on a particular course of action, which may be triggered by a common salient experience.[19]

Bartov, *Hitler's Army: Soldiers, Nazis, and War in the Third Reich* (New York: Oxford University Press, 1991). Ideological homogeneity as an explanation for transnational suicide terrorism is discussed later in this chapter.

19. Although there have been few attempts to theorize the radicalization of terrorist groups, the large literature on the social structure and frequency of interaction among social networks and groups helped to formulate the theory developed in this chapter. Most helpful

Understanding that transnational suicide terrorism rests on primary group cohesion that occurs spontaneously helps to explain why it is such a rare phenomenon. The above process of primary group radicalization is sequential, with each step depending on the previous one, and so open-ended that group interactions could easily break down at any step or simply never move from one to the next. The fragility of the process of primary group cohesion and action in unstructured environments accounts for why transnational suicide terrorist attacks are Black Swans.

For instance, even with frequent social interaction, a primary group may not form at all or, if it does, not focus near exclusively on a single policy problem. If the individuals who initially come together are quite homogeneous in backgrounds and interests, with many touch points in common in their socioeconomic status, previous experiences, and level of education, then a primary group may form, but along so many possible dimensions that any shared political anger is either not salient or heavily diluted. In this case, homogeneity among individuals makes the primary group more likely to form, but far less likely to become focused on any one political, social, or economic program—they are just a group of friends.

Conversely, while heterogeneous individuals may be less likely to form primary groups spontaneously, such groups when formed may be more focused on a single political, social, or economic issue. If the individuals are quite heterogeneous in background and interests, with relatively few touch points in common, then shared political anger may well become magnified as the defining characteristic of the small group. However, the small group may never progress beyond this stage, if only because each member likely has preexisting ties to many other people who do not share this common political anger and because each member may have such strong attachments to these other people (e.g., to family, friends, and colleagues) that their shared political anger is diluted or limited by multiple interactions outside the group. The members are just a discussion group.

Without either a high degree of homogeneity or a constraining institutional structure, primary groups composed of heterogeneous members

───────────────

are Peter Blau, *Inequality and Heterogeneity: A Primitive Theory of Social Structure* (New York: Free Press, 1977); Peter Blau and Joseph Schwartz, *Cross-Cutting Social Circles* (Orlando, FL: Academic Press, 1984); J. Miller McPherson, Pamela A. Popielarz, and Sonja Drobnic, "Social Networks and Organizational Dynamics," *American Sociological Review*, 57 (1992): 153–70; Doug McAdam, "Recruitment to High-Risk Activism," *American Journal of Sociology* 92, no. 1 (July 1986): 64–90; and Harrison C. White, *Identity and Control: How Social Formations Emerge* (Princeton, NJ: Princeton University Press, 2008). Thanks to John Padgett.

may simply remain a discussion group—endlessly discussing alternative courses of action without reaching agreement and without taking any action at all.[20] Movement toward action requires the still further unlikely step that members of the group voluntarily cut their ties to individuals outside the group—effectively creating a separate environment in which they can agree on the need for action and a willingness to commit themselves to executing the mission even at the expense of personal sacrifice and costs to their (previously) significant others. This step of cutting previous attachments in favor of politically motivated action is likely to be especially rare, if only because it requires individuals with varying degrees of previous attachments to withdraw from them at nearly the same point in time. However, if cutting does occur, this is likely to greatly increase the likelihood of action, since members would then gain confidence from the group as a whole that some collective action would be valuable.

Finally, even if the primary group exists, focuses on political anger, and cuts ties to those beyond the group, the members may never reach agreement on pursuing a course of action—if only because they are clearly a small group with little obvious power to influence events. Absent some salient event that triggers agreement on a course of action, the group may never settle on a policy—in the case of a suicide attack, their last.

Accordingly transnational suicide terrorism should be a rare event, commonly occurring by teams of attackers, who spontaneously formed a primary group long before their attack, composed of individual members with heterogeneous socioeconomic and educational backgrounds, who share deep anger over the presence of foreign military forces on a kindred land, and who experience some external event that directs their shared anger toward a suicide attack. Although transnational suicide terrorism is so rare that it may be impossible to fully test any theory of its occurrence with the available data, as we see below, a number of prominent instances do accord with the theory of transnational suicide terrorism offered in this chapter.

Evidence

STANDARDS OF EVIDENCE FOR RARE EVENTS.   Testing any social theory for the radicalization of a group calls for extremely detailed information about a

---

20. For how group homogeneity and institutional structure encourages members of a primary group to concur on a course of action for the problem they are confronting, see Irving L. Janis, *Group Think: Psychological Sudies of Policy Decisions and Fiascoes* (Boston: Houghton, Mifflin, 1982), p. 250.

myriad of interactions of individual members of a group. Even in the best of environments in which group members may wish to share this information, such detailed data on social ties and individual characteristics are not likely to be widely available. Among terrorist groups, who are often actively seeking to obstruct surveillance of their activities, such information is still less available. When social information on terrorists is available, it is collected through extensive investigations by government officials and journalists who typically do not conduct comparable investigations of nonviolent groups or, at least, do not make them publicly available. Accordingly, the current evidence on the radicalization of transnational suicide terrorist groups is limited in quantity and subject to potential bias, which means that extensive testing of theories across large numbers of cases is not now possible.

When dealing with large populations, one might be able to explain behavior at the macrolevel by testing for significant correlations between the main independent and dependent variables even without a thorough understanding of the underlying individual and group causal mechanisms. However, when dealing with rare events, it is essential to examine the underlying casual mechanisms in each case for which information is available, since the key question is whether the rare events are occurring randomly or in a consistent fashion that can be accounted for with the same theory. Of course, the more cases whose causal mechanisms can be explained by the same theory, the better for the theory. But, the central methodological standard for systematically accounting for rare events must be demonstrating consistency across any two or more of the rare events, and this is the standard established in this book for evaluating the theory of group radicalization leading to transnational suicide terrorism. If these multiple events are consistent with one theory and not others, this further increases our confidence in the strength of the validated theory, and so our assessment also compares our theory to the most prominent alternatives.

Transnational suicide terrorism has been and may well remain rare. Accordingly, our methods of assessment should not be held hostage to awaiting a large number of cases and more data on them. Instead, we should seek to examine multiple cases of this rare event to evaluate whether the causal mechanism in each case is consistent with the theory offered here or with the leading alternative explanations.

Significant information about the social environment and individual characteristics of groups of transnational suicide terrorists is available in a number of important instances of the phenomenon. These three cases—1) the Hamburg cell of the 9/11 attack; 2) the July 2005 London suicide attackers; and 3) a Moroccan group who went on to carry out suicide attacks in Iraq in May 2006—vary across time, target countries, and resident countries. Further, there is a consistent pattern across these cases that closely fits the theory developed in this chapter and does not fit the leading alternative explanations. Although more information would help to determine if the theory of the progressive radicalization of groups truly accounts for nearly all instances of transnational suicide terrorism, the information we do have suggests that it is the most plausible existing explanation now available. For analytic clarity, these cases are discussed not in chronological order, but rather in descending order of the information available.

LONDON BOMBERS.   The four July 7, 2005, London suicide bombers are a prime example of the progressive radicalization of a group of transnational suicide attackers according to the theory offered in this chapter. Although little was known about these individuals at the time of their attack, the British government and numerous journalists conducted detailed investigations, including multiple interviews with the immediate social circles of the bombers including family, friends, colleagues, and other associates. The British government also found important (and previously overlooked) information about their activities from recorded conversations among the many Muslims they had under surveillance in the years before the 2005 attacks.[21]

The results strongly challenge the most common explanations of transnational suicide terrorism. First, there is little evidence that any of the four attackers were economically or socially alienated. Mohammad Khan, age 30, was a "learning mentor" at a primary school with an exemplary employment record, spoke passionately about his work in a *Times Educational Supplement* interview in 2002, and took part in a school trip to the Houses of Parliament in 2004. He did begin to miss work in the fall of 2004, but only as he began traveling to Pakistan when planning for his attack began in earnest. Shehzad Tanweer, age 22, drove his own red Mercedes, worked in one of his father's several businesses, and was a trophy-winning cricket player who rarely missed his Wednesday night matches. Hasib Hussain,

21. MI5, "Report of the Official Account of the Bombings in London on 7th July 2005" (London: Stationary Office of the House of Commons, May 2006); Intelligence and Security Committee, "Could 7/7 Have Been Prevented? Review of the Intelligence on the London Terrorist Attacks on 7 July 2005" (London: Report to Parliament by the Prime Minister, May 2009). Also helpful are the online profiles for Khan, Tanweer, Hussein, and Lindsay at julyseveth.co.uk, which compile numerous journalistic investigations.

age 18, was known for his clubbing, occasional run-ins with authority and frequent discussions about girls and cars, and was little different from any other teenager according to his friends. Germaine Lindsay, age 19, was unemployed, lived on government benefits, and married to a British woman. None had a history of outbursts or violence, or other signs of significant opposition to British life.

Second, religious indoctrination is also a poor explanation for the behavior of these individuals. All four were Muslims, but all had secular upbringings. None were educated in Islamic schools (e.g., madrassas) and instead attended state schools and pursued modern studies. Further, their personal experience with Islam varied considerably. According to MI5's investigation, Khan and Tanweer showed no signs of religious extremism, while Lindsay was a recent convert to Islam (2000) who was frequently unfaithful to his wife. Hussain was particularly religious, undertaking a hajj visit to Saudi Arabia in 2002, but there is no evidence that he—or the other bombers—were motivated to pursue their attack by their local religious leaders; for instance, none even consistently attended the same mosque, and all stopped attending mosque specifically because local religious leaders refused to allow political discussions about Western military policies toward Iraq, Kashmir, Chechnya, and elsewhere at the mosque.[22]

So, how did these four British citizens become transnational suicide attackers? The evidence suggests that it was socialization into a primary group that became progressively radicalized over time over the issue of Western military policies toward Muslim countries, the kindred communal attachment that they all shared.

Stage 1: Filtering.   "Filtering" is the subprocess of individuals socially interacting and forming initial points of contact among individuals to form a group. The London bombers appear to have initially met and interacted frequently face-to-face at varying social events: gyms, youth centers, bookshops, and mosques near Leeds, in the metropolitan county of West Yorkshire, particularly in the neighborhoods of Beeston and Dewsbury. (It is unlikely that any significant filtering occurred over the Internet, as investigation of their homes found.) All four shared a common interest in martial arts, sports, and athletic fitness, and so gyms may have been most important, but most of

22. Amy Waldman, "Seething Unease Shaped British Bombers' Newfound Zeal," *New York Times,* July 31, 2005.

TABLE 2.1 **Characteristics of July 2005 London suicide bombers**

	Khan	Tanweer	Hussain	Lindsay
Age	30	22	18	19
Ethnicity	Pakistani	Pakistani	Pakistani	Jamaican
Marital status	Married, child	Single	Single	Married, child
Economic class	Low middle	Upper middle	Low middle	Low, on welfare
Employment status	School staff	Father's business	Unemployed	Unemployed
Education	College degree	College degree	1 yr college	Secondary
Aptitude	Studious	Bright	C student	Smart
Personality	Passionate	Outgoing	Quiet	Erratic
Religion	Islam	Islam	Islam	Islam

the social settings were within a few hundred of yards of each other, and so members of the group likely attended them all at different times.

Stage 2: Discovering.   "Discovering" is the subprocess of identifying common interests. Perhaps most important, the members of the group were heterogeneous across most demographic or social categories. As MI5 reports, some were reasonably "well-educated, some less so. Some genuinely poor, some less so. [Some] single, but some family men with children.... In a few cases there is evidence of abuse or trauma, but in others their upbringing has been stable and loving."[23]

Table 2.1 summarizes the most salient characteristics for each terrorist found by MI5. With the exception of a shared Islamic identity, the group as a whole varied considerably. Even when three of the four share common features, the outliers vary, with no homogenous subcliques. Hence, as the theory expects, for this heterogeneous group, interacting in various settings would likely enable them to discover their shared political anger over the Western military policies toward Muslim countries.

Stage 3: Cutting.   "Cutting" is the subprocess of group members voluntarily cutting their other preexisting social ties to individuals outside of the group, which enables a deepening of shared anger and commitment to the need for a course of action in response to it. From early 2003 to fall 2004, all four future bombers increasingly spent time together, including "days and

23. MI5, "Official Account of the Bombings in London," p. 31.

nights away from home"—which would be unusual especially when two of the four members of the group were married with young children. From 2003 onward, Khan and Tanweer took trips together outside of the Leeds area, including camping and rafting trips and a several month trip to Pakistan. From May 2005 onward, all four rented an apartment in which they continued meeting and began assembling materials for their operation.[24]

Stage 4: Determining. "Determining" is the subprocess by which the clique focuses on a specific course of action—beyond discussions. The commitment to action and the selection of a particular course of action may be triggered by a highly publicized terrorist event in which the perpetrators are viewed as martyrs. After the London attack, MI5 combed voluminous records it has acquired of face-to-face and other conversations documented from surveillance of many British Muslims. They found that the 7/7 bombers were involved in conversations just a few weeks after the Madrid bombings, which brought a new government to power in Spain that ordered Spanish troops out of Iraq. During these conversations, they agreed: "amazing isn't it, everything turns around . . . look on the success of the Madrid bombing, change of power."[25]

9/11 HIJACKERS.   Of the 19 hijackers in the September 11 attacks, three qualify as transnational suicide terrorists. Two—Mohammad Atta, an Egyptian, and Ziad Jarrah, a Lebanese—are transnational suicide attackers, strictly defined as motivated by reasons other than foreign combat forces on or threatening their home nation. One—Marwan al-Shehhi from the United Arab Emirates—is best qualified as a transnational attacker by virtue of his years-long association with Atta and Jarrah in Hamburg, Germany, which at least partly motivated his behavior, and the lack of any evidence to suggest that he was motivated by American forces threatening the UAE. The other 16 are national suicide attackers, native-born citizens of countries from the Arabian Peninsula (15 from Saudi Arabia and 1 from the United Arab Emirates), where American combat forces have been stationed since 1990.

In the years since 9/11, a reasonably robust picture of the personal backgrounds and social interactions of the Hamburg group—Atta, Jarrah, and

24. Ibid., pp. 16, 24, 36.
25. "Could 7/7 Have Been Prevented? Review of the Intelligence on the London Terrorist Attacks on 7 July 2005," (London: Intelligence and Security Committee of Parliament, May 2009), p. 28.

al-Shehhi—has come to light. Prior to the attack, the group was under regular surveillance by German authorities, including eavesdropping on their communications, important parts of which have become public. Further, numerous journalists and government investigations have also been conducted into the Hamburg group's personal history and social life, including interrogations of Ramzi Bin al Shibh, who was part of the Hamburg group until he was unable to obtain a visa to America in 2000.[26]

This detailed picture of the Hamburg group is strongly at odds with the conventional wisdom on the motives of transnational suicide terrorists. First, members of the Hamburg group were not economically or socially alienated from their surrounding society in Germany. Atta, age 33, did have problems finding a job in Egypt, but not after he moved to Germany where he held numerous positions with respected firms that treated him as a valued employee, all while progressing through professional education programs at his own pace. Although both Shehhi, age 23, and Jarrah, age 25, occasionally held odd jobs, they each had independent means of support. Shehhi was being paid by the UAE military as a scholarship student while in Germany. Jarrah relied on his parents for support, and, according to a long-time roommate, always had plenty of money.[27] Strikingly, in all the detailed investigations of this group, there is not a single reference to any one of them reacting to personal discrimination in their surroundings in Hamburg, either real or perceived.

Second, religious indoctrination, at least as normally understood to mean religious instruction guided by a religious leader, did not play a significant role. Although it is true that Atta, Shehhi, and Jarrah were especially devout Muslims and even attended the same Al Quds mosque in Hamburg, there is no evidence that a religious leader significantly influenced their radicalization. Indeed, the group began to separate themselves from others at the mosque and held their own religious and political meetings in their apartment in part because the local mosque was not meeting the group's needs.

So, how did Atta, Shehhi, and Jarrah become transnational suicide attackers? The evidence suggests that it was socialization into a primary

---

26. Especially helpful are Terry McDermott, *Perfect Soldiers: The Hijackers: Who They Were, Why They Did It* (New York: HarperCollins, 2005); Lawrence Wright, *The Looming Tower: Al-Qaeda and the Road to 9/11* (New York: Alfred A. Knopf, 2006); Canadian Broadcasting Corporation News, "The Story of Zaid Jarrah" (January 19, 2005); and the Final Report of the 9/11 Commission.

27. 9/11 Commission Report, p. 132

group that became progressively radicalized over time by anger about Western military policies toward Muslim countries, the kindred communal attachment that they all shared.

Stage 1: Filtering. "Filtering" is the subprocess of individuals socially interacting and forming initial points of contact among individuals to form a group. Atta, Shehhi, and Jarrah all immigrated to Hamburg, Germany, at various points in the 1990s on student visas and appear to have met each other initially as part of a study group associated with the Al Quds mosque, with Atta first meeting Jarrah in 1997 and then both meeting Shehhi in early 1998. During these first months, the three men interacted in a variety of local settings, frequenting the same mosque and restaurant and working in the same odd jobs, with numerous opportunities for discussion.[28]

Stage 2: Discovering. "Discovering" is the subprocess of identifying common interests. Perhaps most important, the members of the group were quite heterogeneous across most demographic or social categories. Aside from a shared interest in technical education, what the group mainly had in common was deep anger over the political condition of Muslims, and particularly Western military policies toward Muslim countries. According to one of Atta's roommates, Atta "was very emotional about political issues . . . [he] saw a worldwide conspiracy at work, bolstered by the Americans, but run always by Jews." Jarrah's wife said Jarrah first spoke about jihad in Hamburg in 1997, when he "enlightened me about the problems Muslims have in the Middle East. He spoke about the intifada . . . the freedom struggle of the Palestinians." She also told a friend, "I don't want to be left behind with children, because my husband moved into a fanatical war." When a friend visiting from the UAE asked why he no longer laughed, Shehhi responded "How can you laugh when people are dying in Palestine?"[29]

Stage 3: Cutting. "Cutting" is the subprocess of group members voluntarily cutting their other preexisting social ties to individuals outside of the group, which enables a deepening of shared anger and commitment to the need for a course of action in response to it. Starting in spring 2008, "the group for the first time began to act as a group, not as a collection of individuals" as the most thorough account puts it. They rented a new apart-

---

28. McDermott, *Perfect Soldiers*, p. 58.
29. Ibid., pp. 67, 80; 9/11 Commission Report, p. 162.

TABLE 2.2 **Characteristics of 9/11 transnational suicide attackers**

	Atta	Shehhi	Jarrah
Age	33	23	25
Ethnicity	Egypt	UAE	Lebanon
Marital status	Single	Single	Married
Economic class	Middle	Working (mil)	Wealthy
Employment status	Often full-time	Part-time	Part-time
Education	2 college degrees	Enrolled in college	Enrolled in college
Aptitude	Intelligent	Struggled	Above average
Personality	Leader, intolerant	Convivial, regular guy	Fun loving, party goer
Religion	Muslim	Muslim	Muslim

ment, spent considerable time there in near-isolation from others, being rarely seen with people outside the group, with no telephone or computers, effectively "moving in a pack." Neighbors report that their collective routines included long discussions most nights and collective physical fitness training. In the fall 2008, they moved to still another, somewhat larger apartment, and began severing ties in their personal affairs, assigning powers of attorney over bank accounts to acquaintances and quickly completing education programs or abandoning them. Jarrah grew distant from his wife, hardly seeing her for weeks at a time.[30]

Stage 4: Determining. "Determining" is the subprocess by which the clique focuses on a specific course of action—beyond discussions. The commitment to action and the selection of a particular course of action may be triggered by a highly salient event or experience for the group as a whole. Starting in 1997, German secret services began to track and record conversations among members of the Hamburg group, and particularly their interactions with Mohammad Haydar Zammar, already known as a follower of Osama bin Laden and for routing would-be jihadists to terrorist camps in Afghanistan. Zammar had frequent conversations in various settings with members of the group, always encouraging them to do more than offer money or public support for Muslims suffering under Western military policies and to actively fight on their behalf. In these meetings with Zammar, the members of the group appear to have moved beyond merely considering intentional action and to agreeing on the idea of carrying out a suicide attack. At this time, acquaintances report Atta and Shehhi would

30. McDermott, *Perfect Soldiers*, pp. 62–63, 79–80.

often become agitated about Americans and Jews, sometimes out of no-where reacting with "Our way! Jihad!" In early October, Jarrah wrote: "The victors will come. We swear to beat you. The earth will shake beneath your feet.... I came to you with men who love death just as you love life. The mujahideen give their money for weapons, food and journeys to win and to die for Allah's cause ... Oh, the smell of paradise is rising." In December all would go to Afghanistan, meet Osama bin Laden, and commit to carry out the 9/11 attacks as a group in his presence.[31]

MOROCCAN SUICIDE ATTACKERS IN IRAQ.   In the fall of 2006, five men left their homes in a crowded neighborhood of the Moroccan city of Tetouan called Jamaa Mezuak for Iraq. According to Moroccan security officials, Muncif and Bilal Ben Aboud, Hamza Akhlifa, Younes Achbak, and Abdelmunim Amakchar Elamrani all had a common purpose: "to become martyrs by fighting the American occupation." As best we can tell, three achieved their goal, since documents for them were later found among a trove of documents related to foreign suicide attackers during an American military operation in Iraq in September 2007, making the group an example of the many transnational suicide attackers known to have come to Iraq from Morocco.[32]

Although details of most transnational suicide attackers are cloudy, this instance is more transparent than most. Thanks to superb investigative reporting by a *New York Times* reporter we have remarkable insight into the backgrounds and social experiences of the group. The reporter spent several weeks in the attackers' neighborhood, interviewing their relatives and friends to provide the only thoroughly researched account of the Moroccan attackers currently available.

The Moroccan attackers don't appear to have been economically or socially alienated from their small community. Their neighborhood is desperately poor, and at least three of the five attackers came from families who owned one or more businesses. The Ben Aboud brothers—Muncif and Bilal—were perhaps the best off. Their parents own an ornately decorated

31. Ibid., pp. 72–74, 82, 86, 88.

32. Andrea Elliott, "Where Boys Grow Up to Be Jihadis," *New York Times,* November 25, 2007. A number of Moroccans have carried suicide attacks both for Osama bin Laden, such as the May 2003 Casablanca attacks, and in Iraq. A key motive appears to be anger at the close relationship between the United States and the authoritarian government of Morocco. See Pape, *Dying to Win*, chap. 7. Elliott quotes a Moroccan terrorism expert who says the Casablanca attack was "the price that Morocco paid for collaborating with the United States."

three-story home, a Mercedes, a Peugeot, and three shops in the heart of Tetouan's market area. Muncif Ben Aboud was the star of the family, first in his class at school, achieving especially high marks in math and languages. He was politically engaged, reading newspapers and watching documentaries on Al Jazeera. He was selected for the prestigious Moroccan air force academy, and his father was positioning him to run one of his shops later in life. Bilal Ben Aboud was nearly the opposite, dropping out of school in the ninth grade, filling his time with music, and he was especially fond of a song deriding President Bush by the American rapper Eminem, even translating it into Arabic. He frequently crossed his parents, and his father disapproved of his efforts to become an artist. Akhlifa was a high school dropout who worked selling car parts in his father's auto shop, which he planned to run in the future. He was a gifted athlete who admired Europe, was enamored with Western style, and spent what little money he had on a John Travolta haircut. Elamrani was the son of a poor sheep trader, and he flunked out of school and became a smuggler. He married and had a child, but often kept to "boyish pursuits," watching *Conan the Barbarian* and playing video games with his little brother. Little is known of the fifth member of the group, Younes Achbak.

Religious indoctrination does not appear to have played a significant role in the group's radicalization. According to Aklifa's close friend, the mosque was not how they found their way to Iraq. He said, "they weren't recruited." They became interested in jihad on their own and then sought out those who could help them get to Iraq.

Stage 1: Filtering.   The group lived in the same small neighborhood of about 6,000 people, often played soccer together on Fridays, and attended the same mosque as most in the neighborhood. At first they would chat before and after soccer games, drifting from topic to topic.

Stage 2: Discovering.   Members of the group were quite heterogeneous across most demographic and social categories, although they shared a strong anger at Western military policies. After the Madrid bombings, they became consumed by one subject: the Iraq War. Muncif Ben Aboud saw the occupation of Iraq as part of a broader threat, saying to a relative, "Maybe if Iraq doesn't have sovereignty, Morocco will be the next country invaded." His brother, Bilal, began talking the same way, saying to a relative that the "the war was not simply aimed at conquering Iraqis but also at defeating Islam."

TABLE 2.3 **Characteristics of Moroccan transnational suicide attackers**

	Muncif Ben Aboud	Bilal Ben Aboud	Hamza Akhlifa	Abdelmunim Amakchar Elamrani	Younes Achbak
Age	21	26		21	25
Ethnicity	Moroccan	Moroccan	Moroccan	Moroccan	Moroccan
Marital status	Single	Single	Single	Married	
Economic class	Middle	Middle	Working	Poor	
Employment status	Student	Musician	Auto shop	Smuggler	
Education	College	HS dropout	HS dropout	HS dropout	
Aptitude	Top of class	Struggled	Struggled		
Personality	Politically engaged	Artistic	Athletic	Immature	Athletic
Religion	Islam	Islam	Islam	Islam	Islam

Stage 3: Cutting. They began meeting after evening prayers, at an area near a middle school. Friends later said the group "became obsessed with the war . . . traded details of the day's news, stirring the anger in one another. They were outraged by the graphic deaths they saw on television and by the American contractors they heard were profiting from the occupation."

Stage 4: Determining. The Madrid bombings were especially salient to the group, perhaps because the leader of the Madrid attacks was from the same small neighborhood and had become something of a legend for his transformation from a heroin dealer and murderer to a person obsessed with the war in Iraq, who "couldn't sleep at night knowing that women and children were dying at the hands of Americans, all in the greedy pursuit of oil," according to his brothers. According to Aklifa's friend, the Madrid bombers were the key salient event, he said, "They wanted to be like them. What they wanted was to die, to become martyrs."

American Transnational Suicide Terrorism

How well does our theory of transnational group radicalization apply to America? Thus far, there has been little "homegrown" Islamic terrorism in the United States and no cases at all of Americans carrying out a suicide attack on their shores. Further, there are important questions about the seriousness of the cases of homegrown terrorism that do exist. As a result, with one possible exception, U.S. cases do not fall squarely in the domain of the theory and so cannot strongly confirm or falsify it.

However, there are important questions about U.S. cases that bear on alternative explanations to our theory and on the degree of fit between our theory and close call events. For instance, many argue that European Islamic terrorists greatly outnumber those in the United States and that the difference is driven by social and economic alienation, a factor outside our theory of foreign occupation and transnational group radicalization. So, if our theory is valid, why would there be more Islamic transnational terrorists in Europe than America?

Further, what about the motives in the close calls, the homegrown Islamic terrorist plots that have occurred? Are the motives, at least of the most serious plots, consistent or not with our analysis of the role of foreign occupation of kindred communities driving the Hamburg cell, 7/7 London bombers, and the Moroccan suicide attackers in Iraq?

Let us take these questions in order, beginning with the apparent differences between the number of Islamic terrorists in Europe and the United States. Although this argument has many advocates,[33] its most detailed rendition is by Sageman. He argues that from 2001 to 2005, there were 2,300 individuals arrested for Islamic terrorism in Europe compared to only 60 in the United States, and even when accounting for differences in size of the Muslim community (2.3 million in United States versus 12–20 million in Europe), "the rate of arrests on terrorism charges per capita among Muslims is six times higher in Europe than in the United States."[34]

Alas, Sageman's own sources reveal a mistake in his analysis. The number 60 used by Sageman as a count of U.S. Islamic terrorists refers to convictions while the number 2,300 in Europe refers to arrests. Moreover, the source used by Sageman for U.S. Islamic terrorists counts 400 U.S. arrests from 2001 to 2005, with the result that the proportion of Muslims arrested for terrorism in the United States and Europe is virtually identical.[35]

Moreover, closer examination of the pattern of arrests casts serious doubt on this measure—since arrests occurred disproportionately following major terrorist events (after 9/11 in the United States and after

33. For instance, see Robert S. Leiken, "Europe's Angry Muslims," *Foreign Affairs,* July/August 2005.

34. Sageman, *Leaderless Jihad*, p. 90.

35. Dan Eggen and Julie Tate, "US Campaign Produces Few Convictions on Terrorism Charges," *Washington Post,* June 12, 2005.

the Madrid and London bombings in Europe), suggesting that fear of the next attack was an important factor in making the arrests in the first place. A better measure would be convictions for offenses related to acts of terrorist violence (not merely charges associated with support for terrorist groups or immigration violations and controlling for the possibility of convictions on multiple charges for the same person). Although a comprehensive study using this measure does not exist, we do know that, from 2001 to 2009, 139 Americans were convicted on charges related to acts of terrorism compared to 193 in Great Britain, France, and Italy (with the most aggressive prosecutions in Europe), suggesting that any meaningful differences across the Atlantic on this score are likely to be small, if they exist at all.[36]

As numerous journalists are now reporting, over the past few years there has been a notable number of transnational terrorists from the United States,[37] and, especially when viewed in light of still earlier U.S. cases, these paint a different picture than the conventional wisdom—the reality is that there are American as well as European cases of transnational terrorism and roughly in the same tiny magnitude, once we account for the different Muslim populations across the Atlantic and appropriately use the same measure—either arrests or convictions for comparable charges associated with acts of terrorism.

Overall, the phenomenon of "angry European Muslims" as compared to American Muslims has been exaggerated and hence the evidence most commonly asserted for the main alternative explanation to our theory of transnational terrorism does not exist. But, do we have evidence in American cases for our theory? Most especially, what can we learn about the motives of the homegrown Islamic terrorist plots that have originated in the United States?

Thus far, few U.S. cases would qualify as relevant to our theory about transnational suicide terrorism. As of early 2010, there has been only one successful suicide attack by a resident of the United States—a Somali immigrant who blew himself up in Somalia in October 2007. Also, only one

36. David Schanzer, Charles Kurzman, and Ebrahim Moosa, "Anti-Terror Lessons of Muslim Americans" (Washington, DC: National Institute of Justice, U.S. Department of Justice, January 6, 2010), pp. 54–61; and "Ethnic Profiling in the European Union," (New York: Open Society Institute, 2009), pp. 82–90.

37. Scott Shane, "New Incidents Test Immunity to Terrorism on U.S. Soil," *New York Times,* December 12, 2005; Peter Bergen, "Reassessing the Evolving al Qaeda Threat to the Homeland" (Washington, DC: Testimony before House of Representatives Committee on Homeland Security, November 19, 2009).

(alleged) plot has involved a martyr video—a common last testimonial of suicide attackers—which was found with the five Virginia Muslims arrested in Pakistan in December 2009. Examination of these two U.S. cases in which we have reason to take the element of suicide attack seriously reveals firm evidence that the motive behind the plots was rooted in responding to a foreign occupation of a kindred community.

The first involves a group of young Somali immigrants in Minnesota who left the United States as a group for Somalia in late 2007 and at least one of whom carried out a confirmed suicide attack. According to the most detailed investigation, this group was radicalized by the foreign military occupation of Somalia: "In December 2006, Ethiopian troops crossed the border and routed the Islamist forces with intelligence support from the United States, beginning a two-year occupation. These events triggered a political awakening among young Somalis in Minneapolis. They had long viewed their homeland's problems as hopelessly clan-based, but the Ethiopian campaign simplified things. Here was an external enemy against which young Somalis could unite. Spurred by a newfound sense of nationalism, college students distributed T-shirts emblazoned with the Somali flag and held demonstrations during a frigid Minnesota winter."[38]

The second case involves the five U.S. Muslims arrested in Pakistan in December 2009 for planning to carry out terrorist attacks in support of the Taliban against American forces and their allies in Afghanistan and Pakistan. At least one of these individuals made a "farewell" video, an 11-minute last video will testimonial comparable to the martyr videos of many suicide attackers. According to reliable reports of those who watched the video, it calls "for the defense of Muslims in conflicts with the West," while officials say the men, from suburbs of Washington, were en route to North Waziristan for training with the Taliban and Al Qaeda to fight American troops in Afghanistan.[39]

What if we broaden our examination to consider U.S. terror plots that are not closely associated with suicide attack? Some involve evidence of an intention to commit violence, some evidence of planning and preparation for specific acts of violence, and one major act of actual violence short of a suicide attack. Nearly all involve important questions about the serious-

38. Andrea Elliot, "A Call to Jihad, Answered in America," *New York Times* July 12, 2009; Craig Witlock, "Terrorist Networks Lure Young Moroccans to War in Far-Off Iraq," February 20, 2007 (available at Washington Post.com).

39. Scott Shane, "Pakistan Detains Five Americans in Raid Tied to Militants," *New York Times,* December 10, 2009.

ness of the plots, both because many court convictions for terrorism were based on charges of "support" for terrorist groups rather than the intention to commit specific acts of violence,[40] and because most serious plots were stopped prior to their completion, leaving doubt that even planning and preparations would have resulted in actual violence.

Although an assessment of all U.S. plots is beyond our study, examination of three highly salient cases involving at least planning and preparation for terrorist violence finds important evidence for the foreign occupation motive. The Fort Dix Group, the six Muslims living in the United States convicted in 2008 for terrorism, conducted onsite surveillance of a New Jersey U.S. military base for months, planned a coordinated shooting designed to kill 100 soldiers, purchased fully automatic machine guns, and carried out live fire exercises, in order to "defend Islam" from American military operations.[41] The Virginia Paintball Jihad were 11 U.S. Muslim citizens and legal residents convicted for terrorism in 2004, five of whom traveled to Pakistan in 2001 with the intention of fighting against India's military occupation of Kashmir and trained in terrorist camps for this purpose, but returned to the United States and were arrested before carrying out their mission.[42] Finally, Major Nidal Malik Hasan killed 13 people and wounded over 30 others at Fort Hood on November 5, 2009, in protest against America's occupation of Afghanistan and soon after receiving orders to deploy there.[43] While the Hasan case departs from our group radicalization theory in an important respect, together these three events demonstrate that ordinary

40. For instance, the Lackawanna Six, who were convicted in 2002, provide little evidence on the motives for violence articulated in our theory, since they were charged merely with "support" for a terrorist group based on participation in Al Qaeda camps in the 1990s and their trial revealed no evidence of any intention to commit violence. Other convictions have involved even less substantial connection to terrorism, such as the Portland Seven (initially six), convicted for attempting to travel to Afghanistan after 9/11 to fight the "American invaders" did not ultimately associate with Al Qaeda. To the extent they tried, their motive was rooted in a response to a foreign occupation. "No Choice but Guilty," *Washington Post,* July 29, 2003; "The Portland Six," *Newsweek,* October 14, 2001; "Portland Seven Figure Gets Seven Years for Taliban Aid," *Oregonian,* February 10, 2004.

41. U.S. District Court, District of New Jersey, United States versus Mohammad Ibrahim Shnewer, Criminal Complaint, May 7, 2007; "Al Qaeda Inspired Fort Dix Plot," *Associated Press,* October 20, 2008.

42. U.S. District Court for the Eastern District of Virginia, Alexandria Division, United States versus Randall Todd Royer, et al., Indictment, June 2003 term.

43. "Radical Yemeni Cleric Blesses Fort Hood Rampage," *Agence France Presse,* November 16, 2009.

transnational Islamic terrorist plots in the United States are significantly associated with foreign occupation of kindred people.

Is Transnational Suicide Terrorism Particularly Islamic?

One might think that there is an Islamic-specific dynamic at play in transnational suicide terrorism that is not operative for other religions or transnational ideologies, for two reasons. The first is the absence of contemporary cases of transnational suicide attack by non-Muslims. Second, the rare instance of transnational suicide attack among Muslims could be better explained by adherence to a specific Islamic ideology, Salafism, than by our theory of the progressive radicalization of transnational groups.

Only Muslims?

At first glance, the absence of transnational suicide attacks among non-Muslims appears to be strong evidence that only Muslims would do it. For instance, Orthodox Christians did not launch suicide attacks in the United States in protest of the 1995 or 1999 U.S. armed interventions against Serbs in the Balkans, while non–Sri Lankan Buddhists did not execute suicide attacks against Indian interests when Indian troops were on Sri Lankan soil from 1987 to 1990, nor were there suicide attacks against China by non-Tibetan Buddhists for its occupation of Buddhist Tibet, against India by non-Naga Christians when Indian security forces were engaged in a brutal counterinsurgency in Christian-majority Nagaland, against Burma by people with kindred identities to the Christian and Muslim peripheral minorities under assault by the Burmese state, or in other conflicts involving local communities with international diasporas or other people who could reasonably be thought to have transnational kindred attachments to them.[44]

However, what is also absent in these conflicts is national suicide terrorism carried out by local resistance fighters, a key precondition for transnational suicide terrorism. As *Dying to Win* explains, the above cases generally lack crucial enabling factors beyond foreign occupation for national

44. Thanks to Paul Staniland for calling attention to these potentially disconfirming cases.

suicide terrorism, most commonly the belief that suicide attack is necessary because nonsuicide operations had failed to achieve desired concessions.[45] Simply put, without a local suicide campaign, there is no self-martyrdom in the local community for transnational actors to emulate.

Salafism—an Alternative Explanation?

One might wonder whether ideological homogeneity is a more powerful explanation than our theory based on primary group cohesion, especially since all the terrorists discussed are Muslims and are often devout. Perhaps it is ideological homogeneity that is pivotal, and the specific ideology is extremely rare and that is why transnational suicide attacks are rare.

There are, however, several reasons to doubt that one ideology is driving the rare event of transnational suicide terrorism. First, since 1980 suicide terrorism has been associated with a variety of secular and religious ideologies—including the avowedly Marxist PPK in Turkey and PFLP on West Bank, the vocally nationalist SSNP in Lebanon and LTTE in Sri Lanka, the non-Islamic religious groups of the Vanguard of Arab Christians in Lebanon and Hindu BKI in India, the Shia Islamic groups of Hezbollah in Lebanon and PIJ in Palestine, and many varieties of Sunni Islamic groups, from the Taliban (Deobandi) to Al Qaeda (Salafi) and Hamas (Salafi). Marxism, Shiism, Deobandism, Salafism, and most ideologies associated with suicide terrorism are transnational phenomenon. Based on the fact that multiple ideologies have been linked to national suicide terrorist campaigns, there is no reason to think that transnational suicide terrorism must be limited to one—and only one—transnational ideology.

Second, the specific type of religious fundamentalism most commonly alleged to produce the rare event of transnational suicide terrorism—Salafism—is in fact not rare and would poorly account for the timing of transnational suicide terrorism. Salafism is widely practiced and one of the oldest forms of Islamic fundamentalism. In the year 2000 alone, there were over 200 million Muslims significantly exposed to Salafi religious and political movements, but only an infinitesimal number of individuals became transnational suicide terrorists and then only in response to Western military occupation of Muslim countries.[46] If the Salafist ideology were the primary cause, we would have reasonably expected many more transnational sui-

---

45. For discussion of Nagaland and other cases, see Pape, *Dying to Win*, p. 100.
46. For a survey of Salafism in many countries in 2000, see ibid., pp. 287–95.

cide terrorists attacking Western democracies for many decades prior to America's establishment of active combat bases in the Persian Gulf and in other Muslim countries, starting in the 1990s.

Third, Salafism is not a unified movement. There is no single authority. As with many transnational religions—such as Protestantism—there are broad varieties and numerous microdifferences across specific geographic areas. As a result, there is no single authoritative understanding of Salafism that could produce ideological homogeneity independent of other circumstances.[47] Although it is common to refer to "jihadi Salafism," which supports the use of violence for Islamic goals,[48] it would be virtually circular to claim that this belief "causes" Islamic terrorism—because then support for violence would cause violence, begging the question of what is driving the support for violence in the first place.

Fourth, there are no reliable ideological profiles for any transnational suicide terrorists, none of whom can be interviewed and all of whom went to great lengths to mask their true beliefs from their families and close acquaintances. Hence, we lack the critical information necessary to show that individuals did embrace the tenets of Salafism, or any specific ideology, prior to carrying out their attacks.

Finally, what evidence we do have suggests that transnational suicide attackers sought to marry their religious beliefs to their prior political views, not the other way around. Transnational suicide terrorists are not the product of long-standing inculcation in particular religious institutions. For instance, all of the terrorists studied in this chapter attended secular public schools, and many abandoned their parents' religious institutions as young adults, seeking religious ideologies more in line with their political beliefs. Further, far from consistently accepting Salafi religious teachings, several of the London bombers only occasionally attended the local Salafi mosque, and rejected and had contempt for its religious teachings when the mosque leaders would not embrace their political opposition to West-

---

47. "The divisions within the Salafi community, in part, represent a generational struggle over sacred authority—the right to interpret Islam on behalf of the Muslim community." Quintan Wiktorowicz, "Anatomy of the Salafi Movement," *Studies in Conflict and Terrorism* 29, no. 3 (May 2006): 207–39, at p. 221. On different varieties of Salafism and other forms of Islamic fundamentalism, see Roxanne L. Euben, *Enemy in the Mirror: Islamic Fundamentalism and the Limits of Modern Rationalism* (Princeton, NJ: Princeton University Press, 1999), pp. 3–19; and Mansoor Moadel and Kamran Talattof, *Modern and Fundamentalist Debates in Islam* (New York: Palgrave, 2002); and Daniel Brown, *Rethinking Traditional in Modern Islamic Thought* (New York: Cambridge University Press, 1996).

48. See Moghadam, "Al-Qaida, Salafi Jihad, and Spread of Suicide Attacks," p. 62.

ern military policies. In effect, Salafi religious leaders tried to dampen, not increase, extremism.

Conclusion

Understanding that transnational suicide terrorism is a rare phenomenon largely associated with the progressive radicalization of specific types of groups of individuals with multiple national loyalties under extremely unusual circumstances has important implications.

First, both national and transnational suicide terrorism stem from the same root cause, which is foreign military occupation of particular countries. Hence, so long as such occupation continues, one must expect both.

Second, domestic policies designed to reduce economic and social alienation of specific immigrant populations, to encourage immigrant religious leaders to condemn terrorist activities, or to monitor Internet chat rooms are unlikely to have significant impact on the progressive radicalization of future transnational suicide terrorist groups. Such policies may have other social benefits, such as improving relations between native and immigrant communities in general, and so may be quite valuable on their own terms. However, in the context of counterterrorism, such policies provide little obvious benefit and may in fact be detrimental if they create the impression that an entire community is a potential threat and so discourage citizens from such communities from closely cooperating with authorities who view them with suspicion.[49]

Third, the group logic of transnational suicide terrorism is not a one-way process in which everyone who enters one stage necessarily goes forward to the next, but instead is an open-ended process with many off-ramps and two-way avenues. Accordingly, the idea that Muslim communities in Western societies present an accelerating, irreducible threat is at odds with the facts and logic of transnational suicide terrorism.

Fourth, counterterrorism operations should focus on what makes these rare events dangerous—that is, the point at which politically active groups seek detailed information and actual materials for lethal action, commonly

---

49. On how profiling may increase the threat, see Bernard E. Harcourt, *Against Prediction: Profiling, Policing, and Punishing in an Actuarial Age* (Chicago: University of Chicago Press, 2007).

from international terrorist organizations or their local representatives. For law enforcement to attempt to track the large numbers of young Muslim men who are religious or have personal difficulties would incorrectly profile and target an entire community and takes resources away from the most productive counterterrorism measure: the search for specific preparations for violent acts.

PART II

The Largest Suicide Terrorist Campaigns

In Part II, the eight largest suicide terrorist campaigns from 1980 to 2009 are examined: Iraq, Afghanistan, Pakistan, Al Qaeda, Lebanon, Israel and Palestine, Chechnya, and Sri Lanka.

Thus far, analysis of the global patterns of modern suicide terrorism provides strong evidence for the following:

- Foreign occupation is the principal trigger for suicide terrorist campaigns.
- Religious difference between the foreign occupier and the occupied is a key enabling factor that explains why some occupations and not others lead to suicide campaigns.
- Foreign occupation of kindred communities is the principal factor driving transnational suicide terrorism.

There remain, however, important unanswered questions, most especially what accounts for the ebb and flow of the trajectory of suicide attacks over time once a campaign begins. Is the trajectory a function of the key dimensions of the foreign occupation—such as, the extent of foreign military presence, the degree of foreign political control over political, economic, and social institutions, or the amount of harm foreign military forces impose on local civilians—or something else? This question is important both because understanding the operational dynamics within suicide campaigns deepens our understanding of the principal mechanisms influencing the phenomenon and may widen the range of the policy recommendations for ameliorating the frequency of suicide attacks in campaigns.

Within each campaign, our main purpose is to understand the variation in the trajectory of suicide attacks, once a campaign begins. Accordingly, each campaign analysis is structured using a framework that disentangles the origins and goals of the terrorist groups from the internal dynamics of the campaign—the trajectory of the suicide attacks, popular support for the campaign, recruitment of individuals to carry out suicide attacks, and operational patterns in targets and weapons. For each campaign, we consider the targets and trajectory of the suicide campaign in terms of the terrorist group's goals and the occupier's operational strategy, as described by the dimensions of the occupation.

Overall, there is powerful evidence that the campaign trajectory within each major suicide campaign is a function of factors related to the foreign occupation. As we shall see, changes in the extent of foreign military presence, degree of foreign control over local political, economic, and social institutions, and the amount of harm foreign military forces impose on civilians are all important factors in influencing the variation in the frequency of suicide attacks within major campaigns. Consequently, there are multiple dimensions of a foreign occupation that contribute to the intensity of suicide campaigns.

CHAPTER THREE

Iraq

B efore the invasion by Western Coalition forces in 2003, there had never been a suicide terrorist attack in Iraq.[1] Since then, the country has experienced the world's most prolific and deadliest suicide attack campaign.[2] In two short years, Iraq's tally of suicide attacks went from 26 in 2003 to a then record-setting 125 in 2005. The data we have collected reveals that this trend continued to rise into 2007, after which time the number of attacks began declining substantially. Over the past seven years, suicide attacks have killed between 7,800 and 13,000 people.

This chapter explains the composition, goals, objectives, cohesion, popular support, trajectory, and state sponsorship status of the five key groups that have engaged in suicide terrorist tactics in Iraq. Each of the groups is comprised predominantly of Sunni Muslims, although one would be mistaken to conclude that religion acts as the prime motivator of suicide terrorism. An evaluation of the goals of the several campaigns reveals the common strategic objectives of removing the coalition presence in Iraq and undermining the new Iraqi government in its current form. However, the groups disagree substantially with respect to the role that religion should play in the future of Iraqi governance. Analysis also reveals critical differ-

---

1. Major contributors to this chapter were Chad Levinson and Maryam Alimirah.

2. Recent literature on Iraq includes Thomas E. Ricks, *The Gamble: General David Petraeus and the American Military Adventure in Iraq, 2006–2008* (New York: Penguin Press, 2009); Nora Bensahel, *After Saddam: Prewar Planning and the Occupation of Iraq* (Santa Monica, CA: RAND, 2008); Thomas R. Mockaitis, *Iraq and the Challenge of Counterinsurgency* (Westport, CT: Praeger Security International, 2008); Mohammed M. Hafez, *Suicide Bombers in Iraq: The Strategy and Ideology of Martyrdom* (Washington, DC: U.S. Institute of Peace Press, 2007); Ahmed S. Hashim, *Insurgency and Counter-Insurgency in Iraq* (Ithaca, NY: Cornell University Press: 2006); George Packer, *The Assassin's Gate: America in Iraq* (New York: Farrar, Straus and Giroux, 2005).

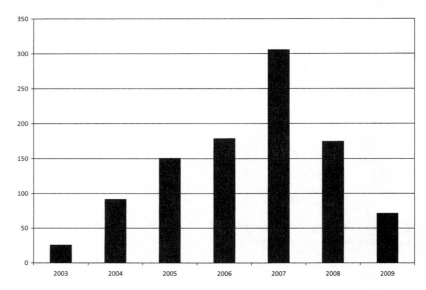

FIGURE 3.1 Suicide attacks in Iraq, 2003–9

ences among the groups that create the potential for serious conflict among the groups themselves. A review of Iraqi public opinion suggests a waning of support for some of the groups' goals and tactics. Finally, the information currently available is consistent with the idea that state sponsorship does not play a significant role in the suicide terrorist campaign in Iraq.

Groups and Goals

As with the campaigns in Lebanon and Palestine, suicide terrorism in Iraq is not a self-contained, independent phenomenon, but rather a component of a broader insurgency employing a variety of tactics, including kidnappings, beheadings, improvised explosive device (IED) attacks, and more typical guerilla tactics. Also similar to Lebanon and Palestine, there are several well-defined and largely independent groups carrying out these attacks, although many observers seem eager to attribute most of the suicide campaign to Al Qaeda in Mesopotamia; this serves the interests of simplicity by identifying a single prominent group to which blame can be assigned as well as setting the Iraq suicide campaign more firmly in the framework of the U.S. "global war on terror" and the fight against Osama bin Laden and Al Qaeda proper. However, this treatment of suicide terrorism in Iraq is not only inaccurate, but also fails to recognize the opportunities for disrupting the campaign presented by ideological and organizational cleavages among the different groups. At the peak of its lethality, the campaign's various players coordinated, often tacitly, around a common strategic objective—ending the U.S. occupation. As with all coalition politics, the maintenance of unity is difficult and only masks temporarily fundamental disputes over more specific cultural, religious, and political objectives.

Insurgent Groups

Of the dozens of insurgent groups operating in Iraq since the Coalition invasion, only five have engaged in martyrdom operations. The difference in impact between minor and major actors in the suicide campaign depends mainly on the regularity, continuity, and stability of the groups' communications and military operations in terms of both suicide attacks and more conventional combat. We do not have a particularly strong basis for determining the relative impact of each group, mainly because over half of all suicide attacks in Iraq have gone unclaimed by one organization or another. Nevertheless, we use the volume of their communications and known operations as a rough proxy for relative size and impact.

The groups differ along two broad dimensions, first in terms of the geographic origin of their membership, some of them consisting of Iraqi nationals, others drawing from locations outside Iraq. The vast majority of foreign-born fighters hail from the Arabian Peninsula and Mediterranean North Africa; there is no evidence of foreign fighters arriving from major Sunni population centers located to the east of Iraq, such as Bangladesh, Pakistan, India, and Indonesia. Thus, despite the nearly exclusively Sunni[3] composition of these groups, geography seems to have stronger influence than religion in attracting fighters to the cause of the suicide terrorism campaigns in Iraq.

3. Some reports indicate that there may a scattering of non-Sunni members in these groups.

The second dimension of distinction among the suicide campaign groups reflects a difference of ideology. On one side of the divide is Islamic fundamentalism. Much, but not all, of this religious extremism is accounted for by a particular brand of fundamentalist religious nationalism referred to as Salafism. Adherents reject secular authority entirely, adhering instead to divine doctrine, and explicitly favoring the Sunna, the body of writings by the companions of Mohammad. Salafists not only privilege these early writings by those who knew the prophet during his lifetime and wrote recollections of his words and deeds, they explicitly reject much of the interpretations of the faith that originate from after the seventh century. On the other side of the divide, some groups are substantively more secular in their nationalism, retaining a partisan loyalty to the deposed Baathist power structure. These groups follow a leadership that draws from former members of the ruling Baath party. This lineage gives them a certain claim to popular Sunni support and a highly trained cadre of interrogators, tacticians, and communications specialists.

ISLAMIC ARMY IN IRAQ (AL-JAYSH AL-ISLAM FIL-'IRAQ).   Iraqi in origin, the Islamic Army in Iraq (IAI) blends Salafic and secular rhetoric and consists overwhelmingly of Sunnis, both former Baathists and other Iraqis disillusioned with the prospect of political inclusion in the new regime. Their goal of expelling Western forces is clearly stated, "[w]e have prepared an efficient plan to target these [U.S. and Coalition] bases with the available ordinance . . . it is imperative to state that the [IAI] army's emir has ordered a heightened military offensive against the occupation forces during this period so that to incur heavy loses upon them and to force them to withdraw."[4] Among the oldest insurgent groups in Iraq, IAI was established prior to and in anticipation of the Coalition invasion, having secured weapons caches looted from former Iraqi arms depots.[5] The military leader of IAI is Abu al-Abbas al-Baghdadi, and their official spokesman is Dr. Ibrahim al-Shammari. Comprised largely of former Iraqi military personnel, they have a relatively high degree of competent professional training.

4. Islamic Army in Iraq, *Al-Fursan Magazine,* 18 (July 2009). Translated by Chicago Project on Security and Terrorism. Available at http://www.iaisite.org/index.php?option=com_content&id=780_Itemid=71.

5. Abdul Hameed Bakier, "Military Commander of the Islamic Army of Iraq Describes Rift with al-Qaeda," *Terrorism Focus* (2008): 3–4.

The IAI consists of 13 brigades,[6] and operates primarily in Baghdad, al-Anbar, Diyala, and Salah Al-Din.[7]

FIRST FOUR CALIPHS ARMY (JAYSH AL-RASHIDIN).   The name of this group indicates its Sunni sectarian affiliation, since Shiites as a matter of doctrine reject the first three Caliphs of Islam. Like the Islamic Army in Iraq, the First Four Caliphs Army (FFCA) is comprised of Iraqi nationals, and their rhetoric blends Islamic and nationalist tendencies. They began their suicide attack campaign in 2006. One of the more minor groups engaging in suicide attacks, its consists of roughly six brigades.[8] They state their purpose as follows, "[i]t is indeed true that since its establishment, the armed resistance has sworn to pursue Jihad in order to expel and remove the occupying forces from the borders of proud Iraq."[9]

VICTORIOUS GROUP'S ARMY (JAYSH AL-TA'IFA AL-MANSOURA).   Another minor group in the wider scope of the overall suicide terror campaign, VGA consists of about three brigades. They are believed to be primarily Salafist in ideology and Iraqi in origin, although they have operated in coordination with foreign-sourced terrorist groups such as Al Qaeda in Mesopotamia (AQM). Like IAI, they are believed to be comprised largely of former Baath party members. Unlike AQM, they restrict themselves to targeting military personnel (Coalition and Iraqi), attempting to avoid civilians.

JAYSH ANSAR AL-SUNNA (ARMY OF THE PROTECTORS OF FAITH).   Formed out of the remnants of Ansar al-Islam, which itself began in the Kurdish

---

6. Detailed information on the size of each group remains elusive. This report uses the term "brigade" to describe the groups, but should not be taken to indicate the precise size of a group's membership. The term itself does not imply a uniformly sized combat unit. Instead, the number of brigades more aptly describes the complexity of a group's organizational structure. In other words, brigades may refer to geographically distributed cells, functional or tactical divisions, or even the personal characteristics of brigade members. For example, Al Qaeda in Mesopotamia has two suicide attack brigades, one of which is exclusively Iraqi in the origin of its martyrs while the other is comprised of foreigners.

7. Anthony Cordesman, "Iraq's Sunni Insurgents: Looking beyond Al Qa'ida" (Washington, DC: Center for Strategic and International Studies, 2007).

8. "In Their Own Words: Reading the Iraqi Insurgency" (Washington, DC: International Crisis Group, 2006).

9. First Four Caliphs Army (2010). "Jaish Al-Rashdeen's Stance on the Ongoing Iraqi Election" (February 26, 2010). Available at http://www.malafy.com/2010/02/20100226.pdf.

territories of Iraq in September 2003, Jaysh Ansar al-Sunna (JAS) is the most Salafic of the indigenous Iraqi insurgent groups using suicide tactics.[10] Claiming to have some 16 brigades, they are led by Abu Abdullah al-Hassan Bin Mahmoud. They believe that the occupation force's strategy is to divide the Iraqi nation and thereby conquer it politically as well as militarily. Their chief aim is to expel occupation forces and collapse the government that JAS views as a Western puppet regime. They write, "[t]here is no credibility to any political action that does not address Iraq's tribulations, primarily by dispelling the occupiers."[11] They operate primarily in Mosul, Baghdad, al-Anbar, Diyala, Kirkuk, and Salah Al-Din.[12]

AL QAEDA IN MESOPOTAMIA (TANDHIM AL-QA'IDA FI BILAD AL-RAFI-DAYN). The most well known of all suicide terrorist organizations operating in Iraq, the group goes by several names depending on the time frame and context. It began as a renegade guerilla organization under the old Saddam Hussein regime, founded by the late Abu Mus'ab al-Zarqawi. After the onset of the Coalition invasion, Zarqawi formed an alliance with the larger Al Qaeda organization and its leader, Osama bin Laden, in 2004. It is decidedly Salafist in its constitution, and highly organized. The group has attempted to bring together the Sunni insurgent groups under several auspices. Initially, they created the Mujahideen Shura Council (MSC) as a general umbrella organization, and later they created the Islamic State of Iraq (ISI), a shadow government of sorts. Despite efforts to "Iraqify" its image, it is the only group that has a significant contingent of foreign fighters, most of whom have crossed the border from Syria to enter the country.[13] Since Zarqawi's demise, the leadership has been assumed by Abu Abdullah al-Rashid al-Baghdadi, who claims the title of emir. In significance, they resemble both the IAI and JAS, with roughly 15 brigades.

In October, 2007, Coalition forces recovered a cache of documents containing AQM personnel files known as the Sinjar Records. These documents provide stunning insight into the composition of AQM's forces. Among other things, they show the national origins of the group's foreign

---

10. It should be noted that, despite its predominantly Sunni character, the name of the organization does not imply a strictly Sunni sectarian meaning.

11. Ansar al-Sunna (2007). Available at http://www.ansar11.org/show.php?state=cat&idn ews=49&idsec1=8&idsec2=10.

12. Cordesman, "Iraq's Sunni Insurgents."

13. Best estimates consistently put the number of foreign fighters (suicide attackers and conventional forces) at about 2,000, roughly 10% of the total insurgency.

fighter contingent.[14] The raw numbers indicate that Saudi Arabia provides a strong plurality of fighters, followed rather distantly by Libya, Syria, Yemen, Algeria, and Tunisia. Scaled to reflect the population differences in the countries of origin, the numbers are somewhat different: Libya and Saudi Arabia switch places when measuring the per-capita contribution of fighters to AQM's forces. Furthermore, the content of the records and the location of the recovery indicate that even though the foreign sources are spread rather widely throughout the Arabian Peninsula and North Africa, the porous Syrian border is the main point of entry and a rallying point for jihadists traveling to Iraq to join in the conflict.[15] They operate in al-Anbar, Diyala, Kirkuk, Salah Al-Din, Ninewah, and parts of Babil and Wasit.[16]

Goals and Objectives

All the insurgent groups employing martyrdom tactics share the common strategic goals of expelling Western occupation forces and collapsing the current Iraqi government. These groups hold little hope of participating in the politics of Iraq, which are built upon a Shiite-dominated coalitional alignment. The timing and targeting of suicide attacks serve to demonstrate durability and persistence while discouraging collaboration with and participation in the new regime. Suicide attacks often follow counterinsurgency operations and target Iraqi security forces as well as nongovernmental organizations seeking to provide support to the Iraqi population. Together, these aspects of suicide tactics aim to show that the groups will not be deterred in their mission to create chaos, thus undermining the promise of security by the ruling political order.[17]

The differing goals and objectives of the various suicide campaign groups follow closely the pattern established by their origins and ideology. While all groups seek to expel the occupying Coalition forces and collapse the existing Iraqi government as currently configured, they differ

14. The Sinjar cache is a valuable source of information on foreign recruitment for the insurgency. Although there is significant overlap between the Sinjar records and the Chicago Project on Security and Terrorism database, there are discrepancies, likely for two main reasons. First, the Sinjar records track all foreign fighters, not just suicide bombers. Second, these records only account for a span of several months in 2007, while CPOST data covers attacks between March 2003 and December 2009.

15. Joseph Felter and Brian Fishman, "Al-Qa'ida's Foreign Fighters in Iraq: A First Look at the Sinjar Records" (West Point, NY: Combating Terrorism Center, 2007).

16. Cordesman, "Iraq's Sunni Insurgents."

17. Hafez, *Suicide Bombers in Iraq.*

in terms of the character and scope of the regime they aim to establish in its place. Along one dimension, secular nationalists seek to restore a Sunni-dominated regime similar to that which existed prior to the Coalition invasion, while Salafi nationalists aim to establish a theocratic state founded on a particular interpretation of sharia law. Along a second dimension, indigenous all-Iraqi groups seek to establish a state with sovereignty over the current territory of Iraq, while multinational groups envision a transnational pan-Arabic state with Iraq merely acting as its territorial foundation.

Iraqi secular nationalism, best represented by IAI, motivates the goal of expelling the occupation forces and collapsing the Shia-dominated Iraqi regime, followed by a restoration of the deposed Baathist minority-Sunni–led government. Several historical trends underpin this motivation and belief in its possibility. First, the Baath party came to power in a coup very much like the one they imagine would be possible to repeat. Second, sectarian prejudice and decades of dominance over the majority Shiite population instilled a belief among the Baathist holdouts in their exclusive claim on the authority to govern Iraq. They see themselves as having superior organization and experience to manage the affairs of state. In contrast, they see the Shia population as utterly unfit. Furthermore, they view the Shiite government as an affiliate of the ruling powers in Iran. Thus, they reject any power-sharing arrangement, especially one which reflects the Shiite popular majority. Their animosity toward the current regime is thus based on decades of domination and animosity toward Iranian Shiites. Their animosity toward occupation forces is twofold: they would turn the tables on their invaders, those who deprived them of their status, employment, and power; they also expect the current regime to crumble in the absence of their Western benefactors. Finally, the oppressive manner in which they dominated their countrymen has convinced them that they would be subjects to a vengeful Shiite. The haste with which they themselves were summarily dismissed at the beginning of the occupation only cemented the impression that they would be shut out of future political participation.

Iraqi Salafism has a similar initial goal of expelling Western forces and collapsing the government. However, the flavor of the government they hope to establish in its place differs greatly from that of the local nationalists. Whereas the Baathist ideology is more secular in nature (despite the Islamic rhetoric they have adopted), the Salafi ideology is one of religious fundamentalism. They aspire to create an explicitly Islamic state based on sharia, rejecting all "man-made" laws and secular governing institutions (democracy or political parties, for example). Like the Iraqi secular nationalists, they reject the elevation of non-Sunni sectarians to political power, but for reasons of religious doctrine, not 20th-century political history. Thus, they view the current regime as both heretical and an illegitimate creation of invading Western powers.

Transnational Salafism takes this thinking one step further by adding to it the notion that Iraq is merely one component (albeit a critical one) of a pan-Arabic state, a restoration of the Caliphate. Like the Iraqi Salafis, the transnationals seek to expel Western forces and establish an Islamic state. Toward this latter end, they have adopted the name "Islamic State of Iraq" and established their own quasi-official bureaucracy, a provisional government with 10 official administrators including a minister of education. However, for the transnational Salafis, the boundaries of this state extend well beyond Iraq. They justify their presence in Iraq and the motivation behind their goals by claiming the right to combat non-Muslim forces throughout what they consider exclusively Muslim territory. Thus the invasion and occupation of Iraq is seen by them as an invasion and occupation of their rightful state territory.

In summary, the goals and objectives of the major insurgent groups engaging in suicide attacks against Western and Iraqi government forces vary along two dimensions reflecting the distinctions among the groups' origins and ideologies. The first dimension represents a difference in kind, with secular nationalists aspiring to restore a Baathist-style regime and Salafists aiming at building an Islamic religious state. The second dimension represents a difference in scope, with Iraqi Salafists aspiring to create a religious state within the boundaries of Iraq and transnational Salafists aiming to create a similarly constituted state over a much wider geographic area. Despite these differences, both Iraqi and transnational, secular and Salafi groups seek to expel Western forces and collapse the current governing regime.

Cohesion

There appears, in certain cases, to be strong cohesion among some of the groups. For instance, VGA has joined AQM as part of the ISI. However, this might also be interpreted simply as a more robust group subsuming a lesser one with some similar characteristics. Additionally, the IAI has joined with JAS to form the Jihad and Reform Front, which in its mission statement rejects the current Iraqi regime and the elections upon which its legitimacy is founded.[18] Thus, we observe between-group cohesion along both dimensions of our frameworks for interpreting ideology and objectives. Theocratic, Salafi nationalist groups have joined together, as have locally originating groups with the goal of governing Iraq within its current boundaries.

The hard test of cohesion among the groups would address the relations between major groups whose origins and ideology, as well as goals and objectives, overlap as little as possible. This entails examining the dynamics between the Iraqi nationalists (IAI) and the transnational Salafis (AQM). Both groups have existed in one form or another since before the Coalition invasion, so they have had ample opportunity to form a partnership or, alternatively, engage in overt competition with one another. Neither has occurred completely. On the one hand, each group has recognized the rhetorical value of the other's self-branding. So, despite its essentially secular nationalism, IAI has adopted some of the religious rhetoric of its rival (even in its very name). Likewise, AQM has recognized that they had previously done damage to their own image by relying too heavily on foreign fighters, causing the local population to see them as an invading force, especially given AQM's acceptance of civilian targets. IAI's reluctance to target civilians has succeeded in pressuring AQM to develop a domestically grown suicide bomber brigade.

On the other hand, despite sharing short-term goals, they have ultimately conflicting long-term goals given the differences in the religious aspect of the new government they seek to establish and the fact that they have overlapping territorial claims. The 2006 National Intelligence Estimate noted these intergroup differences, and its insights along these lines helped lay the foundation for supporting the Anbar Awakening, discussed elsewhere in this chapter. Thus, we expect to see some evidence of conflict, which we do. AQM has accused IAI of collaborating with the established government and participating in the so-called Awakening (a movement of Sunni groups that have begun collaborating with the government and occupation forces), which their spokesman has denied. Furthermore, IAI and AQM have engaged in open violent conflict with one another.[19] This could be, in part,

18. Jihad and Reform Front (2008), "JR Front Establishing Statement," http://rjfront.info/english/index.php?option=com_content&task=view&id=12&itemid=28.

19. Islamic Army in Iraq (2007), "A Press Statement on the Events on al-Latifiyah and Samarra areas," http://iaisite.org/index.php?option=com_contents&task=view&id=839&itemid=37.

caused by their differences with respect to Salafism. While AQM is clearly dedicated to these principles and these alone, IAI's willingness to accommodate Baathists reveals some potential to compromise in order to achieve influence. Either Salafism is merely an empty rhetorical gambit, or the group has managed to craft a division of labor between rhetorical and organizational strategies. If the former were the case, this would further explain their conflict with AQM along the lines discussed above. If it were the latter, then there would emerge a vulnerability to potential loss of within-group cohesion for IAI. Nevertheless, the cohesion patterns seem to indicate a consolidation of similarly constituted groups alongside an increase in the tensions among groups that represent different constituencies and diverge in terms of the long-term objectives.

State Sponsorship

There is no direct evidence of state sponsorship of suicide terrorist groups operating in Iraq. Two adjacent states warrant some attention on this particular issue. First, while there is evidence of Iran's involvement in aspects of the insurgency, such behavior is restricted to support for Shiite groups, none of which have committed martyrdom operations. Second, as mentioned above, Syria has become a common point of entry for foreign fighters joining transnational Salafi groups that do engage in suicide tactics. Although these foreign fighters find material support in Syria, the evidence appears to indicate that these smuggling operations are likely criminal in nature and thus are not sanctioned by the Syrian government.[20] Furthermore, we note the absence of any multinational secular groups seeking to establish a transnational secular state. Syria is governed by a primarily secular Baathist regime, and might be expected, were it sponsoring suicide terrorism, to choose to align itself with a group fitting these characteristics, not one seeking to establish a transnational theocracy. It is therefore consistent with the idea that Syria is not materially supporting suicide terrorist groups in Iraq. However, given the prolific supply of foreign fighters crossing the porous border between the two countries and the failure of the Syrian government to shut down these smuggling networks, its behavior could best be characterized as neglect or incompetence.

20. Felter and Fishman, "Al-Qa'ida's Foreign Fighters in Iraq."

Trajectory of the Suicide Campaign

The U.S. invasion of Iraq began on March 20, 2003. Two days later, Abdul Aziz ibn Saud Al-Gharbi detonated a car bomb in the northern Iraqi city of Halabja. Ansar al-Islam (later Ansar al-Sunna) at the time operated a base near the location of the attack, which killed at least five people.[21] On March 25, a suicide bomber in the southern al-Basrah Province destroyed a Coalition tank.[22] Four U.S. Marines were killed by a suicide car bomb in Najaf on March 29.[23] And on April 4, two female Iraqi suicide bombers killed three U.S. soldiers and two Iraqi civilians, one of them pregnant, near Haditha in Anbar Province. Thus, the suicide bombing campaign begins immediately upon the arrival of Coalition forces, and is aimed at disrupting military operations.

A clear majority (over 65%) of the attacks have been aimed at security targets—at first primarily U.S. forces, but as the Iraqi security and police forces grew so did the number of attacks on their personnel. This figure is actually a reduction in the proportion of attacks aimed exclusively at security targets from the first three years of the campaign, during which time such events comprised over 80% of the data. This reduction is due primarily to the emergence of a greater number of mixed target-type attacks, with combined civilian/security target bombings making up most of the difference. This indicates a strategy on the part of suicide attacker groups directed at sowing chaos among the security apparatus and simultaneously sending a message to the civilian public that their safety cannot be assured by either Coalition or Iraqi forces.

Chaos among security forces is indeed the goal of the suicide campaign factions of the insurgency. The logic of this targeting strategy is revealed in a 2004 letter sent by the now-deceased leader of Al Qaeda in Mesopotamia, Abu Mus'ab al-Zarqawi, to Osama bin Laden, where he describes the official Iraqi security forces as "the eyes, ears, and hands of the occupier, through which he sees, hears, and delivers violent blows. God willing, we are

21. "Explosion Kills Five at Northern Iraq Checkpoint," *Associated Press,* March 22, 2003.

22. "Iraqi Commits Suicide Attack, Destroys Tank: Army," *Agence France Presse,* March 25, 2003.

23. "U.S. Troops Surround Najaf as Basra Fighting Heats Up and Suicide Attackers Volunteer for Iraq," *Associated Press Worldstream,* March 29, 2003.

determined to target them strongly."[24] Specifically, Zarqawi aims to disrupt the organizational capacity of the state and prevent the formation of a capable security infrastructure. The goal, then, is to prevent (or at least delay) the establishment of order, and thereby weaken the governing regime.

This disruption is also the primary objective of the broader insurgency, which is distinct from the civil war between Sunnis, Shiites, and Kurds. The insurgency, including but not limited to the suicide bombing campaign, begins with the onset of the invasion and subsequent occupation, starting small and growing substantially through 2007. The sectarian civil war, on the other hand, does not begin in earnest until 2006, after the bombing of the Golden Mosque in Samarra in February.[25] The civil war is a three-sided[26] struggle for power and territory within Iraq, leading to widespread population displacement, the homogenization of previously multiethnic neighborhoods, and the virtual emptying out of certain areas. The insurgency, on the other hand, is primarily a Sunni movement, motivated by their removal from power in the toppling of the Baath regime.[27]

Suicide terrorism in Iraq has declined substantially over the past three years. At the same time, the prevalence of Islamic religious fundamentalism in general and Salafism in particular have remained steady. It remains an essential law of causality that you cannot explain variation with a constant. On the other hand, several important causal factors have varied. Iraqis have become more confident in their capacity for maintaining their own security and perpetuating their own way of life, especially among the Sunni population in Anbar Province. This growing confidence is largely attributable to two factors. First, Sunnis have been invited to become more active partners in securing their own territories. Second, the Coalition presence and influence in Iraqi governance have declined substantially.

The trajectory of suicide attacks in Iraq follows a fairly straightforward pattern, illustrated in figure 3.1. Beginning in 2003, suicide attacks increase steadily through 2006, then jump dramatically in 2007, and finally begin to

---

24. Abu Mus'ab al-Zarqawi, "Letter to Osama bin Laden" (2004). Available at http://www.globalsecurity.org/wmd/library/news/iraq/2004/02/040212/zarqawi.htm.

25. "Blast Destroys Shrine in Iraq, Setting Off Sectarian Fury," *New York Times*, February 22, 2006.

26. Although the majority of civil war violence has occurred between Shiites and Sunnis.

27. A notable exception is Muqtada al-Sadr's Mahdi Army, which clashed violently with Coalition forces starting in 2004, and vacillated between open opposition and peaceful political participation with the new regime through 2008. Since then, Sadr's militia has been, for the most part, placated.

fall off in 2007 and continue to drop through 2009. In this section, we discuss the most likely causes of this pattern. Summarized briefly, the onset of suicide violence coincides with the arrival of Coalition forces, jumps between 2006 and 2007 following the bombing of the Golden Mosque in Samarra and the escalation of the sectarian civil war, and then begins to subside due to three main factors: the so-called surge of Coalition troops in the summer of 2007, the mutual separation of Sunni and Shiite populations in Baghdad, and the creation of the Awakening Councils in Anbar Province. The first two of these factors explain the majority of the reduction in suicide violence in Baghdad, while the last factor helps explain the reduction in violence in Anbar.

In order to unpack the causal dynamics of the post-2006 reduction in suicide violence in Iraq, it is necessary to make an important distinction: namely, that the two most critical geographic regions, where violence has been most prominent and problematic, have different underlying causes for the decline in suicide attacks. In the first case, Baghdad has experienced a dramatic decline in suicide violence beginning in 2007 after four years of steady year-over-year increases. The primary causes of this reversal are the deployment of additional Coalition troops in the city along with a change in military strategy to one of population protection and the geographic separation of the population along sectarian lines. We call for a balanced causal assessment, crediting both factors with helping reduce suicide terrorism. The first of these causes has achieved a great deal of attention in the press, as many in the United States have accepted the surge as the main contributing factor behind the reduction in both suicide and ordinary violence. To credit the surge itself as the single main solution to the problem of increasing violence, however, obscures the fact that the transition to a population protection strategy had already begun before the announcement by President Bush of his intention to increase the U.S. troop presence in Iraq. Furthermore, we argue that this also overstates the contribution of the surge by ignoring the second factor, population separation. Although both Sunni and Shiite residents have been forced by sectarian violence to abandon their home neighborhoods, the majority of this burden has fallen upon the Sunnis. An analysis of nighttime artificial light emanations undertaken by geographers at the University of California, Los Angeles, reveals that many predominantly Sunni neighborhoods have literally gone dark.[28]

28. John Agnew, Thomas W. Gillespie, and Jorge Gonzalez, "Baghdad Nights: Evaluating the US Military 'Surge' Using Nighttime Light Signatures," *Environment and Planning* 40 (2008): 2285–95.

The logic behind this argument is straightforward: violence motivated by sectarian conflict necessarily diminishes as adversarial populations become separated. There are simply fewer provocations and opportunities for violence as proximity to one's enemy declines.

The second geographic region where violence has decreased substantially is Anbar Province. Neither of the two factors underlying the pacification of Baghdad are at work in this region, namely, because neither really occurs in Anbar between 2006 and 2008. First, the population of the province traditionally has been predominantly Sunni, so there simply has been little opportunity for separation. Second, an increase in Coalition personnel cannot represent an important reason for the reduction in suicide violence because the overall size of the deployment remained constant over the time period in question. In particular, the Coalition counterinsurgency force (COIN) in Anbar Province remained fairly flat at roughly 34,000–38,000 from 2006 to 2008. However, at the same time, the Coalition strategy expanded to include an enlistment of local tribal cooperation known commonly as the Anbar Awakening. The local tribal groups with whom the Coalition has formed partnerships, known variously as the Anbar Salvation Council, the Awakening Councils, and the Sons of Iraq, grew from a meager 5,000 to 100,000 strong between 2006 and 2008, and represent the critical factor leading to the abatement of violence. For the most part, the partnership focuses on providing the material means and incentives for the local Anbar Sunni population to combat insurgent and terrorist forces, namely, Al Qaeda in Mesopotamia.[29] This had two salutary effects: it transformed a former source of insurgent violence into a strategic partner and it added to antiterrorist elements in the province.[30]

The second phase of the reduction in suicide violence began in November 2008 following the signing of key agreements between the United States and the Iraqi government over the scheduled withdrawal of Coalition forces. These agreements were widely publicized and likely shifted expectations almost immediately regarding the duration of the occupation, while the actual drawdown of Western troops from Iraqi cities beginning in the summer of 2009 lent credibility to these expectations. Moving beyond the progress gained through the promotion of the Awakening movement, the withdrawal agreement has itself worked to reduce the level of violence.

29. Austin Long, "The Anbar Awakening," *Survival* 50, no. 2 (2008): 67–94.

30. For a more thorough analysis of the strategy in the province, see ibid. Long not only narrates many of the important aspects of the program, but also argues that the late Iraqi president Saddam Hussein followed a similar tribal cooptation strategy in the area.

Both factors helped to pacify elements of Iraqi society that previously supported the suicide terrorism campaign. These two separate phases, the first from 2007–2008 and the second from 2008 to the present, reflect distinct but overlapping causes for the improvement in Iraqi security.

Although these downward trends, beginning after 2007 and continuing to the present day, represent a great improvement in the security environment in the country, the situation clearly remains dangerous. Furthermore, the primary causes of the reduction in violence are themselves somewhat problematic. The promise of full inclusion of the Sons of Iraq in the governance of Iraq remains uncertain, as the Shiite-majority authorities frequently waver on their commitments to the partnership. The separation along sectarian lines in Baghdad has created widespread population displacement. If refugees seek to return to their former neighborhoods in the city, violence might return as well. Abandoned neighborhoods might be difficult to repopulate, and reintegration of mutually hostile populations might result in increased provocations and opportunities for violence. Nevertheless, these trends represent significant improvement over the past several years. Still, this analysis is not a declaration of victory, but rather an examination of the most likely causes of the campaign-level changes in suicide violence in Iraq.

Weapons and Targeting

The overall suicide attack campaign in Iraq is dominated by the use of car and truck bombs. It was not until 2007, three years into the campaign, that groups began using belt bombs in significant numbers. Insofar as we have been able to identify the type of weapons used in attacks, it was not until the current year that belt bombs have been utilized in numbers comparable to car and truck bombs.

Despite smaller numbers, belt bombers have generally proven either equally or more lethal than their counterparts using automobile-loaded explosives. Although the 2004 lethality figure is exaggerated by the low number of attacks that year (two), and the fact that one of those attacks killed 109 people, the overall average lethality for belt bombers exceeds the average for car and truck bombers by 40% (slightly over 10 killed per attack for the latter, compared to over 14 for the former). Nevertheless, the sheer number of car and truck bomb attacks has meant that over twice as many people, over 3,600, have been killed by these weapons, compared to just over 1,500 people killed in belt-bomb suicide attacks.

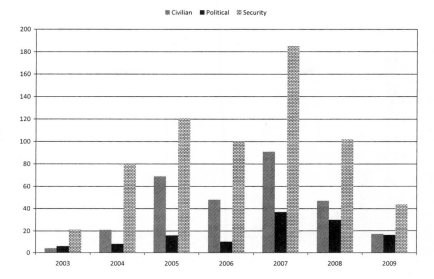

FIGURE 3.2 Attacks by target type, 2003–9

Measured by the number of attacks, the campaign has primarily been an offensive against security targets, followed by civilian targets. Predictably, given that they are generally better defended, the lethality for security targets is, with the exception of 2005, lower than that for civilian and political targets. For political targets, the lethality is trending mostly downward, possibly indicating a heightened caution among political protection services, while the lethality for security targets has remained mostly constant with the exception of 2005, when lethality was over double the next highest year. Furthermore, attacking these targets destabilizes the security situation, leaving room for militias to increase their presence, thus escalating the civil war and weakening the government. A desire to promote the civil war also accounts for a large number of the civilian-targeted attacks.

Recruitment

At this point, it is possible to identify confidently the demographics of suicide attackers in Iraq for only a small portion. During ongoing suicide

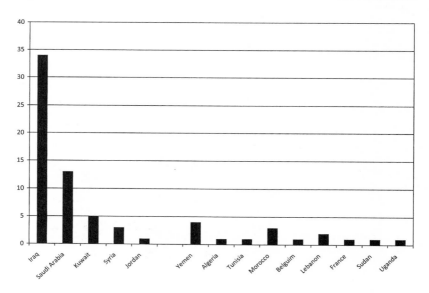

FIGURE 3.3   Nationality of suicide attackers in Iraq

terrorism campaigns, it is not unusual for terrorist organization to conceal information regarding their recruits. However, our data collection methodology insures that the information is of the highest quality—requiring double-verification from reputable news organizations, government agencies, or the suicide terrorist groups themselves, and not relying on unverifiable or anonymous speculation, such as Internet chat rooms. In short, while to date we have detailed information on just 72 of the 1,000-plus suicide attackers in Iraq, our confidence in the accuracy of the data is extremely high.

The data reveal that the Iraqi suicide terrorism campaign remains a mostly localized phenomenon, with the vast majority of known recruits (83%) originating from Iraq and elsewhere in the Arabian Peninsula. Far from indicating a global jihad, the geographic distribution of suicide attackers appears to be a function of their home countries' proximity to Iraq. Only 7% of the known attackers originated from outside the Persian Gulf region. Furthermore, when adjusted to account for population size in the countries of origin, Iraq, Saudi Arabia, and Kuwait far outpace all others, with Jordan, Yemen, and Syria following at some distance. Notice that each of these countries except Yemen shares a land border with Iraq. In addition to challenging the idea that Iraqi suicide attacks represent an arm of a global jihad, these data also refute the claim that "we're fighting them over there so we don't have to fight them over here." Instead, we are fighting them over there because that is where they live.

Given the geographic distribution of country of origin for attackers in Iraq, geopolitical factors are a stronger causal factor than Islam in the Iraqi suicide campaign. A true, worldwide religiously motivated campaign would look very different, likely including recruits from Indonesia, India, Bangladesh, and other populous countries with large Muslim populations. Thus, while our demographic data set is far from complete, the pattern that has emerged is consistent with the proposition that geopolitical influences, like U.S. policy in the region, are at the root of the recruiting strategy for the Iraq suicide terrorism campaign.

Popular Support

Large-scale suicide terrorism campaigns cannot function for long without substantial local support for the goals of terrorist groups, if not for the tactics they employ. Otherwise, these groups would threaten the security of a population without any potential upside for the public at large. In particular, the goal of removing foreign occupation forces must resonate with the people. A key factor in estimating local support for the objectives of the suicide terrorism groups is whether the public both desires the removal of the current regime and believes that absent the foreign occupation, such an outcome would become likely. With respect to the campaign in Iraq, the critical facet of public opinion resides among the Sunni population, which has both a reason to desire the toppling of the new regime and to believe in such a possibility. After all, they held power for decades under Saddam Hussein, and were subsequently marginalized when the Coalition forces took over and sponsored the creation of a Shiite-dominated government.

In the early years of the new government, Sunni populations were clearly disillusioned with the situation. In 2004, they almost completely refused to vote in the national elections, signaling profound doubt about the expectations for enjoying political influence within the new system. Subsequent to this mass protest, suicide terrorism increased dramatically, demonstrating empirical plausibility for the causal mechanism we propose as underpinning the bombing campaign: political alienation under the circumstance of foreign occupation motivates extreme measures by the disempowered.

However, as the Anbar Awakening progressed, and gained first the im-plicit then later the open support of the Coalition and the central govern-ment, Sunnis began to believe that they would gain a meaningful voice in their own self-determination. Especially in Anbar Province, this entailed a return to local, often tribal control, as had often been a successful strategy of governance in Iraq.[31] This period, as is shown in table 3.1, corresponds with a rise in public confidence in the central government, moving from 6% to 39% over the course of two years. By the time the 2008 national elections were held, Sunnis voted in significant numbers, signaling an acceptance of the new political process and a withdrawal from violent extremism.

A review of public opinion polling in Iraq shows an improving situation, but still reveals substantial differences along sectarian lines with respect to important questions of support for postinvasion political arrangements. Support for governing institutions and occupation forces have always been highest among Shiites and lowest among Sunni populations. This helps to explain why the suicide bombing campaign has remained a Sunni phe-nomenon despite the country having a Shiite majority overall. Although Shiites have been active in the insurgency, they have not resorted to suicide tactics. This is consistent with the notion that while certain Shiite factions may object to specific aspects of the governing arrangement, they have by and large accepted the broader institutional layout of the government. In other words, the insurgent Shiite factions have not sought regime collapse, but merely a greater share of power within the current configuration, using violence to strengthen their negotiating position. Overall, as Sunni support for the status quo institutional arrangements have improved, their use of suicide tactics has diminished.[32]

Polling in Iraq has not provided direct evidence of support for or op-position to the particular suicide-practicing insurgent groups. However, a review of polling done at various times by ABC News (and a rotation of affiliates including the BBC and others)[33] sheds some light on support for some of the goals of the various types of groups. Helpfully, the ABC data are aggregated by ethnic group, so we can tease out the differences in

31. Ibid.

32. The major exception to this has been consistently high Sunni support for keeping some form of strong centralized governance, but this has more to do with the fact that a more regionally divided solution would leave Sunni areas without a significant share of Iraq's oil revenues.

33. "Iraq: Where Things Stand," ABC/BBC/NHK Poll (March 16, 2009). Data were col-lected at various times between November 2003 and February 2009.

TABLE 3.1 **Public opinion (percentages)**

	3/5/2007			2/20/2008			2/25/2009		
	Sunni	Shia	Kurd	Sunni	Shia	Kurd	Sunni	Shia	Kurd
Confidence—Iraqi Army	25	80	80	43	75	78	55	85	71
Confidence—Iraqi police	24	87	82	40	81	79	67	79	77
Confidence—Occupation	3	12	67	3	18	55	7	25	66
Confidence—Iraqi government	6	68	71	10	55	71	39	73	63
Support—Occupation	3	17	75	5	23	77			
Support—Attacks against coalition	94	35	7	62	43	2			
Support—Attacks against Iraqi government	34	1	1	6	4	0			
Support—Centralized government	97	41	20	95	67	10	91	74	18
Support—Regional government	2	40	49	3	31	35	5	23	39
Support—Separate states	1	19	30	2	1	52	1	1	39
Support—Baathist inclusion in government	96	35	31	94	63	45			
U.S. withdrawal—Now	55	28	11	61	33	10			
U.S. withdrawal—Security restored	41	39	28	33	37	33			
U.S. withdrawal—Stronger government	3	18	28	4	17	23			
U.S. withdrawal—Before 2011							61	47	23
U.S. withdrawal—2011							31	38	31
U.S. withdrawal—After 2011							4	15	41

Source: ABC/BBC/NHK Poll. Iraq: Where Things Stand (March 17. 2008. and March 16. 2009).

opinion along sectarian lines. Since all of the suicide-practicing groups are Sunni, this gives some extra purchase on determining local popular support for the groups' goals and motivations.

The data in table 3.1 show that while the Sunni population is substantially less confident than Shiites and Kurds in the ability of Iraqi government institutions to provide security, the percentage of those Sunnis expressing confidence increased steadily and significantly between early 2007 and 2009. This indicates that the suicide campaigns have largely failed to undermine confidence in public security institutions through the creation of chaos. However, it does not necessarily follow that the Sunni opinion has grown more favorable toward the ruling regime.

Despite the steady increase in confidence in official security forces, confidence in the underlying government institutions has fluctuated over time. The Sunni population's confidence in the Iraqi government had not surpassed 10% until 2009. Furthermore, the last time the population was polled on their confidence in the U.S. occupation, the Sunni response remained in the single digits. This inconsistency between confidence in the security apparatus and the government leads to two possible conclusions: either the Sunnis do not closely associate official security forces with the governing regime or, more likely, their survey responses reflect confusion with respect to whether the question referred to official government forces or to the Sunni-controlled Awakening Council forces.

Public opinion data from Anbar Province shed important light on the basis for the Sunnis growing confidence in public institutions to provide security. In Anbar, the proportion of respondents reporting a positive assessment of the security situation jumps from zero in 2007 to 71% in 2008.[34] Although it is impossible to determine with absolute certainty just how much the improvement in public opinion is due to the central government versus the Awakening Councils, it is clear that virtually none is attributable to a more favorable assessment of the Coalition. From 2007 to 2008, respondents in Anbar report no greater confidence in Coalition forces or in approval of their performance—which both remain essentially at zero[35]—and so this factor cannot account for the Sunnis growing confidence in security institutions. Given that the Awakening movement represents the predominant development in security policy in the region during this time period, it is likely that the growth of the Awakening Councils accounts for the change in public opinion in Anbar. Accordingly, the reduction in suicide violence among Sunnis from 2007 to 2008 is largely a consequence of the increasing confidence among the residents of Anbar in home-grown security forces, not any improvement in their attitudes toward a continuing U.S. military presence in the region.

As of 2008, virtually no support exists among Sunnis for making the strength of the Iraqi government a condition for withdrawal, while majorities of Sunnis consistently support an immediate departure. By contrast, the Iraqi population as a whole shows some nontrivial support for waiting to establish a stronger government. A significant portion of both the total population and the Sunnis supports making withdrawal contingent

---

34. "Iraq Five Years Later: Where Things Stand," ABC/BBC/ARD/NHK Poll (March 17, 2008).

35. Ibid.

upon improved security conditions. However, a similar proportion of the total population supports an immediate withdrawal. These data show that the Sunni population is substantially similar to the rest of Iraq's people with respect to their belief that their security depends at least in part on the presence of Coalition forces. On the other hand, the Sunni population remains unconvinced of the idea that the Coalition should remain in Iraq to protect the Iraqi government. The most plausible interpretation is that the Sunni population's desire to see the occupation forces leave swamps their belief in the government. Subsequent to the Status of Forces Agreement (SOFA) signed by the U.S. and Iraqi governments in late 2008, these patterns remain largely in place, with a clear majority of Sunnis in favor of speeding up the U.S. departure, and a very small minority in support of extending the occupation beyond the agreed-upon date of 2011. In other words, substantial Sunni support exists for one of the primary goals of suicide campaign groups, the removal of Coalition forces from Iraq.

Support for such attacks against occupation forces is consistently higher among Sunnis than other groups, but that it dropped off substantially between August 2007 and February 2008, while support for attacks against the government drops steadily over the same time period to a low 6%. This corresponds with the movement known as the Anbar Awakening, discussed previously. While the questions do not specify the type of attacks in question, we can infer broadly that the support for suicide attacks takes roughly the same shape. As a matter of simple logic, support for suicide attacks is a subset of support for all attacks, so we can conclude that support for suicide attacks against government institutions is minimal among Sunnis. This clearly shows a lack of support for martyrdom tactics against the Iraqi government. We might be witnessing the beginning of an abandonment of popular support for suicide tactics against the occupation forces as well.

Support for a central government is highest among Sunnis, followed by Shiites, with the latter group increasing over time and reaching a three-quarters majority in the latest poll. Furthermore, Shiite support for including former Baathists in the government has increased to roughly two-thirds by 2008; there is no data on this question in the 2009 poll.[36] At first, these

36. This particular finding should not be overemphasized, as it is based on only two surveys. Furthermore, the wording of the question changed from "Thinking about ex-Baathists in the country, do you think they should or should not be allowed to take government jobs?" in March 2007 to "Thinking about former mid-level or low-level Baathists in the country, do you think they should or should not be allowed to take government jobs?" in February 2008. Thus

data might seem to imply that a centralized Sunni-Shiite Coalition government is supported by both groups, undermining one of the motivations of Sunni secular nationalist martyrdom groups, the refusal to share power with Shiites. However, two factors bear mentioning that call into question this optimistic conclusion. First, the survey did not ask Sunnis whether they would accept Shiites into a government under their control. Second, in a regionally divided government, Sunnis would likely lose out on resource extraction revenues, since major oil supplies reside outside of Sunni-controlled areas of the country. Thus, these data do not necessarily indicate an enthusiasm on the part of Sunnis to share power with Shiites. Still, the fact that Shiites have come to accept the prospect of sharing power with Sunnis, one of the primary concerns motivating the Sunni insurgency (fear of political marginalization) has waned.

Conclusion

The sectarian character of suicide terrorism in Iraq remains overwhelmingly Sunni. However, to posit this religious affiliation as the main causal factor for the campaign is to make a fundamental attribution error, falsely favoring the influence of personal over situational characteristics of the actor, making the mistake of seeing religion instead of rebellion against foreign occupation as the primary culprit. First of all, while nearly all suicide bombers and the groups supporting them are indeed Sunni, the degree of religious orthodoxy varies from group to group within Iraq. Furthermore, attributing cause to Islamic fundamentalism more generally ignores the fact that this proposed causal factor does not vary during the time frame examined in this analysis, but the level of suicide violence varies considerably. Since 2007, all of the active terrorist groups have remained in existence, and their religious doctrine has not changed, but the violent activity has dropped precipitously. By contrast, key factors associated with foreign occupation have changed, and these factors explain both the initial rise and subsequent fall in the severity of the campaign. With the onset of the occupation and the formation of a Shiite-dominated central government, Sunni insurgents turned to suicide bombing as a method of promoting chaos and undermining the regime. As local self-

---

the increase could be due in part to a stronger specification of the type of former Baathist that would be eligible for inclusion.

governance has returned to Sunni populations and as the Coalition presence has diminished, the level of violence has dropped correspondingly. For these reasons, Islamic fundamentalism remains a poor explanation for the phenomenon of suicide terrorism.

Overall, suicide violence in Iraq has fallen by about 85% from its peak in January 2007, as local Sunnis have been empowered and Western occupation has declined. Whether suicide violence in Iraq remains at these low levels and falls even further depends not only on maintaining the key policies that have led to these reductions, but also on not adding new pressures on the Sunnis—the most obvious being oppressive policies by the Shia-dominated central government after Western military forces have completely left Iraq. Given Western interests in stability in Iraq, it is important for the United States and other major powers to remain closely engaged with the government of Iraq to encourage equitable internal policies in the country.

CHAPTER FOUR

Afghanistan

Since the 1970s, Afghanistan has been in a state of nearly constant warfare.[1] Infamously called the "graveyard of empires," Afghanistan is renowned for its harsh mountainous terrain, stalwart guerilla fighters, and complex tribal organizations.[2] Catapulted into Western consciousness after September 11, 2001, Afghanistan is the site of a deadly suicide terrorist campaign waged by Afghan rebels against U.S. forces and their allies. Figure 4.1 details the ebb and flow of suicide attacks that have taken place in Afghanistan since 2001.

Despite Afghanistan's violent past, suicide terrorism is a relatively new phenomenon in the country; the first attack occurred on September 9, 2001. Scholars and knowledgeable observers have struggled to explain the initiation of suicide terrorism in Afghanistan as well as the subsequent trajectory of suicide attacks. Some have pointed to Islamic fundamentalism as the root cause of suicide terrorism while others have blamed Afghanistan's illegal opium trade for financing the upswing of suicide attacks that began in 2006. In our analysis, we find severe deficiencies with the existing explana-

---

1. Major contributors to this chapter were Ezra Schricker and Susan Young. The research assistant for this chapter was Zenab Chowdry.

2. For further reading on Afghanistan, the Taliban, and Al Qaeda, recent literature includes David Kilcullen, *The Accidental Guerrilla: Fighting Small Wars in the Midst of a Big One* (New York: Oxford University Press, 2009); Ahmed Rashid, *Descent into Chaos: The United States and the Failure of Nation Building in Pakistan, Afghanistan, and Central Asia* (New York: Viking Press, 2008); Seth Jones, *In the Graveyard of Empires: America's War in Afghanistan* (New York: W. W. Norton and Company, 2009); Steve Coll, *Ghost Wars: The Secret History of the CIA, Afghanistan, and Bin Laden, from the Soviet Invasion to September 10, 2001* (New York: Penguin Books, 2005); David Loyn, *In Afghanistan: Two Hundred Years of British, Russian, and American Occupation* (New York: Palgrave Macmillan, 2009).

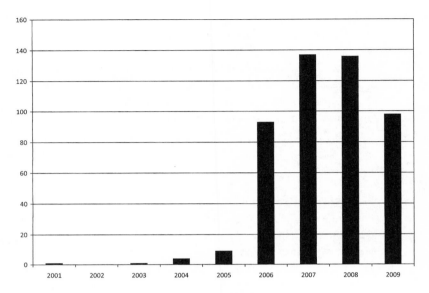

FIGURE 4.1 Suicide attacks in Afghanistan, 2001–9

tions for suicide terrorism in Afghanistan, despite their recent popularity among politicians, government officials, and journalists.

In this chapter, we show that the initiation and trajectory of suicide terrorism in Afghanistan is the direct result of foreign occupation. Western military operations and a crisis of confidence in the Afghan central government have caused many Afghans to see their country as under foreign military occupation and to support suicide attacks as a strategy to end it. Given the link between foreign occupation and suicide terrorism, General McChrystal's new counterinsurgency strategy—increasing the number of American forces and expanding military operations into Pashtun provinces—has the potential to aggravate rather than ameliorate the complex security environment in Afghanistan, with potentially negative consequences for the stability of the Karzai government in Kabul and American national security.

This study explores the origins and goals of the two principle groups responsible for suicide terrorism in Afghanistan—the Taliban and Al Qaeda—in order to better understand the trajectory of their suicide attacks, local community support, and recruitment methods. In particular, we examine the Taliban's hard targeting[3] tactics, which reveal important insight into how the Taliban has used suicide terrorism and what these targeting patterns reveal about the organization's strategic goals. In addition, we analyze Pakistan's close ties to the Taliban and Al Qaeda, which continue to frustrate U.S. counterterrorism efforts in the region. Lastly, we assess the recent introduction of nearly 40,000 additional U.S. and allied troops on the overall trajectory of suicide attacks.

Groups and Goals

In the current discourse on Afghanistan, the word "Taliban" is often used to broadly categorize three subgroups—all of which oppose the Afghan government, but for disparate reasons. The first is the Religious Taliban, led by Mullah Muhammed Omar, which is sometimes described as the hard-core Taliban and is the primary focus of this section. The second subgroup consists of the drug lords—based in southern provinces such as Helmand and Kandahar—who are motivated by profit, not ideology. Third, there are numerous local Pashtun groups, such as the Haqqani network, whose allegiances shift depending on what is best for their particular group. To understand the relative size of the Religious Taliban compared to the other two factions, David Kilcullen, a counterinsurgency scholar and advisor to U.S. General David Petraeus, estimated that the broad "Taliban" movement numbered around 40,000 in 2008, but only 10,000 were hard-core Religious Taliban. This suggests that the majority of fighters who support the Taliban do not share their ideological motivations. While it may be impossible for the United States to negotiate with the hard-core Religious Taliban, separating out these three subgroups is essential because it may be possible for the United States to encourage many of the local Pashtun groups to break away from the broader Taliban movement.[4]

The roots of the current conflict in Afghanistan can be traced back to the end of the Soviet-Afghan War. After the Soviet Union withdrew from Afghanistan in February 1989, Afghanistan entered a three-year period of

3. In the discussion of terrorism, "hard" commonly refers to security forces, such as military, police, and intelligence targets. Hard targeting is also part of the lexicon of nuclear warfare. However, in that lexicon, not all military targets are labeled "hard."

4. Kilcullen, *The Accidental Guerrilla*, p. 48. Translated from Pashto to English, "Taliban" means "Students" or "Knowledge Seekers."

civil war between the Soviet-backed Democratic Republic of Afghanistan and mujahideen fighters. The final collapse of the Soviet Union in August 1991 ended all financial support to the Republic, which further destabilized the tenuous coalition that held the government together. In April 1992, Kabul was finally captured by mujahideen guerillas, and Afghanistan entered a second phase of civil war. During this tumultuous period, competing guerilla factions fought for control of the capital and government.

The Taliban's birth and subsequent success was largely a byproduct of the anarchic conditions in war-torn Afghanistan. The Taliban sought to implement a strict legal code called sharia law and end the rampant corruption among the mujahideen warlords. Journalist Ahmed Rashid argues that it was neither ideology nor religious fervor that attracted local Afghans to the Taliban's cause. Instead, indigenous support for the Taliban arose from "the war weariness of the populace which stood ready to welcome any force that promised the disarming of the local brigands, the restoration of peace, the semblance of an honest administration, no matter how rough and ready the system of justice [sharia law]."[5] Afghans, tired of lawless civil war, welcomed the Taliban as a stabilizing force. In a matter of months, Mullah Omar succeeded in uniting many warring factions under the Taliban banner.

As the Taliban continued to gain momentum in the summer of 1996, Osama bin Laden decided to leave his base in Sudan after numerous assassination attempts on his life.[6] Bin Laden returned to Afghanistan where he had previously fought in the Afghan jihad against the Soviets, a personal legacy that endeared him to many of the local mujahideen. Soon after bin Laden's arrival, Mullah Omar gave bin Laden and his followers formal sanctuary in Afghanistan. In return for protection, bin Laden offered his reputation, politicking skills, and large coffer to help consolidate the Taliban's power within Afghanistan. Only months after he arrived, bin Laden convinced the Hezb-i-Islami commander, Jalalluddin Haqqani, to integrate his veteran fighters with Taliban forces.[7] Financially, bin Laden provided money to buy defections from many commanders of the Northern Alliance, the main opposition group to the Taliban. Bin Laden also

5. Ahmed Rashid, "Pakistan and the Taliban," in *Fundamentalism Reborn? Afghanistan and the Taliban,* ed. William Maley (New York: New York University Press, 1998), p. 72.

6. Anonymous, *Through Our Enemies' Eyes* (Washington, DC: Brassey's Inc., 2003), p. 156.

7. Hezb-i-Islami is an Islamist political and militant organization that was founded by Gulbuddin Hekmatyar in the 1970s and which gained prominence by fighting against the Soviets during the Soviet-Afghan War; ibid.

contributed his personal band of veteran guerrilla fighters who trained and fought alongside Taliban forces, often turning the tide of key battles. By September 1996, the Taliban had captured Kabul and gained effective control over the country.

While Mullah Omar's political objective for the Taliban was localized—the establishment of Afghanistan as an Islamic state ruled by sharia law—bin Laden's interests were more global and specifically anti-American. In the 1990s, bin Laden was concerned with expelling U.S. forces from the Arabian Peninsula. During his stay in Afghanistan, bin Laden endeared himself to the local ulema (Islamic legal scholars), resulting in a 1998 fatwa (religious edict) sanctioning the "use of all means to expel American forces from the [Arabian] Peninsula."[8] However, as time went on, bin Laden broadened his strategic goals to include the removal of U.S. forces from all Muslim lands.[9] However, while the Taliban have borrowed many ideological narratives from Al Qaeda over the years, the two groups have retained their clearly disparate political objectives.

Northwest Pakistan, including the Federally Administrated Tribal Areas (FATA) and the North West Frontier Province (NWFP), has become a major recruiting and training ground for suicide terrorists destined for Afghanistan or Pakistan. Over the last several decades, thousands of Afghan refugees have settled in the tribal regions of Pakistan to escape Soviet occupation and years of civil war. Interestingly, as Al Qaeda was driven into these border sanctuaries following the 2001 invasion, many foreign fighters began to marry into the local Pashtun tribes—most notably Al Qaeda's second in command, Ayman al-Zawahiri.[10] These marriages demonstrate how deeply intermeshed Al Qaeda and the Taliban have become with local Pashtuns along the Afghan-Pakistan border.

It is impossible to discuss the creation of the Taliban without addressing Pakistan's long history of involvement in Central Asia, which is related as much to geopolitics as it is to terrorism. During the Soviet-Afghan War, the CIA used Pakistan's Inter-Services Intelligence (ISI) to smuggle guns and money to mujahideen fighters. When CIA support dried up after Soviet troops left Afghanistan in 1989, the ISI began to provide financial and military support to local Pashtun groups. To fill the power vacuum created by the Afghan civil war, the ISI decided to support Mullah Omar in an at-

8. Ibid., p. 158.
9. Ibid., p. 160.
10. "Peter Bergen, Assessing the Threat in Afghanistan," *Fresh Air,* December 3, 2009, available at http://www.npr.org/templates/transcript/transcript.php?storyId=121020669.

tempt to consolidate authority under a Pakistani-influenced Taliban. Mullah Omar's close ties to the Pakistani religious establishment made him an ideal candidate for ISI sponsorship.

Through the ISI, the Pakistani government provided the Taliban with money, weapons, food, and even connected the Taliban to Pakistan's phone grid.[11] Pakistan's rationale for supporting the Taliban was twofold. First, they believed that a Pakistan-friendly regime in Afghanistan would be strategically beneficial in case of a war with India. Second, the ISI reasoned that the militant groups developed in Afghanistan could be used for Pakistan's ongoing guerrilla war in Kashmir against India. This second reason was an important factor in Pakistan turning a blind eye to Al Qaeda's involvement in the region. As Ahmed Rashid noted, "the ISI had never bothered to rein in Al Qaeda's extensive logistics networks in Pakistan because the terrorist group helped train Kashmiri militants willing to fight India."[12] As time went on, the links between the Taliban, Al Qaeda, and the ISI began to grow. In early 2001, an anonymous U.S. diplomat stated that "the Taliban and al Qaeda are one enterprise and we see Pakistan as backing that enterprise." To underscore these connections, the diplomat went on to list nine senior ISI officers stationed inside Afghanistan who were advising the Taliban on military policy.[13]

After September 11, 2001, Pakistan President Pervez Musharraf publically accepted a list of U.S. demands that included publicly renouncing support for the Taliban and detaining all Al Qaeda operatives along the Afghan-Pakistan border.[14] This agreement created a unique dilemma for the Pakistani government. In effect, Musharraf had pledged to fight against the same groups that the ISI had helped create. However, in a meeting of top Pakistani generals and cabinet ministers, Musharraf was clear that he never intended to follow all of the U.S. directives.[15] Musharraf's strategy for handling U.S. demands was simple: "first say yes and later say but ..."[16] This policy enabled Pakistan to play a double game with the Americans where they would agree to U.S. demands while continuing to support the Taliban. True to his strategy, Musharraf agreed to let the ISI continue to

11. Robert Kaplan, "The Lawless Frontier," *The Atlantic,* September 2000, available at http://www.theatlantic.com/doc/200009/kaplan-border/2.

12. Rashid, *Descent into Chaos,* p. 48.

13. Ibid., p. 60.

14. Anonymous, *Through Our Enemies' Eyes,* p. 166; Rashid, *Descent into Chaos,* p. 28.

15. Rashid, *Descent into Chaos,* p. 28.

16. Ibid.

supply the Taliban in the spring of 2002—in clear defiance of his earlier acceptance of U.S. demands.

Over the course of the next eight years, the double game being played by the ISI and the Pakistani government led to halfhearted efforts to eliminate elements of the Taliban from the tribal regions of Pakistan. Perhaps the most striking example of this lukewarm commitment was the Pakistani military's repeated failures to control or pacify the Afghan border regions that were crawling with Taliban and Al Qaeda militants. A 2006 peace deal between Pakistan and the Taliban left the majority of the FATA effectively ungoverned—creating a safe haven for Taliban fighters.

Outwardly, the Pakistani government maintains that it has officially severed ties with the Taliban and cooperated with U.S. efforts in Afghanistan. However, most authorities within the U.S. intelligence community believe that the ISI continues to support the Taliban and other local militant groups. After the July 7, 2008, bombing of the Indian embassy in Kabul, American intelligence agencies claimed to have intercepted communications linking the ISI to Lashkar-e-Taiba, the militant group reportedly behind the attack.[17] In November of 2009, U.S. officials accused the ISI of helping Taliban leader Mullah Omar evade CIA drone strikes.[18] General McChrystal's latest report[19] on Afghanistan directly linked Pakistan to the Taliban: "Afghanistan's insurgency is clearly supported from Pakistan. Senior leaders from the major Afghan insurgent groups are based in Pakistan, are linked with al Qaeda and other violence extremist groups, and are reportedly aided by some elements of Pakistan's ISI."[20]

After the U.S. invasion in 2001, India established consulates in Afghanistan and developed an extensive aid program there. These moves infuriated the Pakistani military, which fears India's presence in Central Asia.[21] In the coming years, it seems likely that Pakistan will continue their covert support for Afghan militant groups in an effort to counter India's growing

17. "Pakistan Aided Attack in Kabul, Officials Say," *New York Times,* August 1, 2008, available at http://www.nytimes.com/2008/08/01/world/asia/01iht-01pstan.14929392.html.

18. "Taliban Chief Hides in Pakistan," *Washington Times,* November 20, 2009, available at http://www.washingtontimes.com/news/2009/nov/20/taliban-chief-takes-cover-in-pakistan-populace/.

19. Stanley A. McChrystal, "Commander of International Security Assistance Force's Initial Assessment," August, 30 2009.

20. Ibid., p. 18.

21. "Right at the Edge," *New York Times,* September 15, 2008, available at http://www.nytimes.com/2008/09/07/magazine/07pakistan-t.html.

influence in Afghanistan. As one former Pakistani official stated, "We are saving the Taliban for a rainy day."[22]

For the American government, the ISI's continued support for the Taliban is a double-edged sword. On the one hand, the United States may be able to weaken the Taliban by coercing the Pakistani government to sever the links between the ISI and the Taliban. However, any American pressure on the Pakistani government for this purpose comes at the risk of breaking the Pakistani government apart by putting the ISI at odds with the army—with uncertain consequences for the security of Pakistan's nuclear weapons.

Trajectory of the Suicide Campaign

In the 1980s, the Soviet military occupied Afghanistan for over nine years. One of the most puzzling aspects of the Soviet-Afghan War is that the mujahideen fighters never resorted to suicide terrorism to fight the Soviet occupying forces. Interestingly, Osama bin Laden and other groups now associated with suicide terrorism were in the country during that time, yet suicide terrorism was nonexistent. On the one hand, the lack of suicide terrorism during this period could be due to the success of the mujahideen's guerilla strategy. Because of this success, the mujahideen were never forced to use suicide terrorism as a last resort. However, we believe the more compelling explanation for the lack of suicide attacks is that suicide terrorism is a coercive strategy used against democracies. Within the universe of modern suicide campaigns, the target state has always been a democracy. Suicide terrorism is more likely to be used against democracies primarily because democracies are commonly perceived as vulnerable to coercive punishment. The reasoning behind this logic is that democratic populations are often thought to have a very low cost tolerance and a high ability to affect state policy.

Recent empirical studies[23] indicate that democracies are not uniquely vulnerable to coercion compared to other regime types. However, the perception of democracies as vulnerable is what matters. Terrorist leaders such as Osama bin Laden and his second-in-command, Al-Zawahiri, have repeat-

22. Ibid.
23. For the view that democracies are not vulnerable to terrorism, see Max Abrahms, "Why Democracies Make Superior Counterterrorists," *Security Studies* 16, no. 2 (April–June 2007): 223–53. For the opposite view, see Andrew Kydd and Barbara Walter, "The Strategies of Terrorism," *International Security* 31, no. 1 (Summer 2006): 59–62.

edly stated that they believe the United States is vulnerable to suicide attacks. Bin Laden noted, "America is a great power possessed of tremendous military might and a wide-ranging economy, but all this is built upon an unstable foundation which can be targeted, with special attention to its obvious weak spots."[24] In other statements, bin Laden declared rather bluntly, "We believe that America is weaker than [Soviet] Russia," while Al-Zawahiri has repeatedly underscored "the need to inflict the maximum casualties against the opponent, for this is the language understood by the West."[25] Therefore, the lack of suicide attacks during the Soviet-Afghan War is most likely the result of the USSR not being a democracy, and therefore it was viewed as more resistant to suicide terrorism as a form of coercive punishment.

The Afghanistan suicide campaign began on September 9, 2001, in anticipation of American military occupation. The subsequent ebb and flow of the campaign has been a function of the strategies used by Western forces and their effect on the local population's perception of foreign occupation. Critically, the Western military presence augmented an evolving crisis of confidence in the central government, which convinced many Afghans that the government would not survive without continued foreign military support. Once the perception of foreign occupation was in place, many local Pashtuns allied with the Taliban to drive out the occupiers using any means necessary.

On September 9, 2001, Al Qaeda operatives, posing as Belgian journalists, gained access to Ahmad Shah Masood, a war hero from the Soviet-Afghan War and the leader of the anti-Taliban Northern Alliance. Eyewitness reports state that the attackers asked Masood several pointed questions that implicitly defended Osama bin Laden before they detonated explosives concealed within their camera equipment.[26] Masood became the first casualty of suicide terrorism in Afghanistan, although his death was overshadowed by the enormity of the September 11 attacks that occurred two days later. Al Qaeda calculated that the United States would retaliate against the Taliban regime following the September 11 attacks. As leader of the Northern Alliance, Masood was the most

24. "Bin Laden's Sermon," *Middle East Media Research Institute,* March 5, 2003.

25. Ibid.; and Ayman al-Zawahiri, "Knights under the Prophet's Banner," *Middle East Media Research Institute,* December 2, 2001, part 11.

26. "Threats and Responses: Assassination; Afghans, Too, Mark a Day of Disaster; A Hero Was Lost," *New York Times,* September 9, 2002, available at http://www.nytimes.com/2002/09/09/world/threats-responses-assassination-afghans-too-mark-day-disaster-hero-was-lost.html.

prominent potential ally for the United States. Despite Masood's death, the United States galvanized the Northern Alliance and, with the aid of precision airpower and U.S. Special Forces, captured most of Afghanistan in a few months.

In the aftermath of the invasion, Afghanistan experienced only 14 suicide attacks between 2001 and 2005. Then suddenly, the number of suicide bombings skyrocketed, with 93 in 2006 alone.[27] By 2007, that number had increased to 137, and in 2008, 136. In 2009, there were 98 suicide attacks in Afghanistan. It is worth examining some of the more prominent explanations for this sharp rise in suicide attacks that started in 2006 and continues into the present day.

Many scholars have argued that Islamic fundamentalism is the driving force behind suicide terrorism. At first glance, this argument appears compelling because Osama bin Laden subscribed to radical Islamic principles and his terrorist organization, Al Qaeda, used suicide terrorism against the United States. The problem with this logic is that many different variations of Islamic fundamentalism existed in Afghanistan well before bin Laden arrived.[28] As we mentioned earlier, many Islamic extremists—including bin Laden—fought against the Soviets during the 1980s without the use of suicide terrorism. Perhaps most importantly, from 1996 onward, bin Laden's brand of Islamic fundamentalism was a constant feature of the Afghan consciousness, and, therefore, it fails to account for the specific timing of suicide terrorism—including the initiation of the suicide terrorism campaign, the low level of suicide attacks from 2001 to 2005, and the subsequent spike in 2006.

Another popular explanation for this surge in suicide terrorism is that profits from poppy production allowed the Taliban to finance and train more suicide terrorists. Afghanistan produces around 90% of the world's opium, and 80% of the poppies used for this opium trade are grown in the southern provinces of Afghanistan, an area where the Taliban has strong local support. In 1997, the United Nations estimated that the illegal poppy harvest made $4 billion, nearly half of Afghanistan's annual income from legal products. Within the last decade, the Taliban has encouraged local farmers to plant poppies, taxed their crops, and used the money to finance

27. IED attacks also increased dramatically over this same period according to Joint IED Defeat Organization estimates quoted in "Soaring IED Attacks in Afghanistan stymie U.S. Counteroffensive," *Washington Post*, March 18, 2010.

28. For a discussion of the different variants of fundamentalist Islamic thought, including Deobandism, Wahhabism, and Salafism, see Jones, *In the Graveyard of Empires*, pp. 54–63.

their insurgency—a component of which certainly includes suicide terrorism.[29] However, the poppy production explanation for suicide attacks has fallen out of favor in recent years as extensive NATO efforts to curb poppy growth has had little effect on the rate of suicide bombings.

We argue that foreign occupation is the best explanation for the initiation and the subsequent ebb and flow of suicide attacks in Afghanistan. Occupation matters because it suggests a loss of control over the future of a country's political and social institutions. Faced with this loss of control, citizens may embrace coercive tactics such as suicide terrorism to remove the foreign occupier.

Foreign troops are one conspicuous factor that contributes to the perception of occupation. However, foreign troops are not always so conspicuous. From 2001 to 2005, the United States and NATO had fewer than 30,000 troops in Afghanistan, with most stationed in and around the Afghan capital of Kabul. The reason for this limited presence was due to NATO strategy. NATO strategy in Afghanistan evolved in distinct phases that were implemented over time.[30] In Phase 1: Assessment and Preparation, the International Security Assistance Force (ISAF) was predominately concentrated in Kabul and a few key bases scattered throughout Afghanistan. These troops had little direct contact with the local population and because of this limited footprint, the perception of foreign occupation was minimal as was the number of suicide attacks—only 15 during the first period of the campaign. However, in October of 2003, NATO began Phase 2: Geographic Expansion, which called for the systematic introduction of troops into the north, west, south, and east, consecutively. The goal of this expansion was twofold. First, the ISAF sought to suppress the small Taliban insurgency that existed at the time by clearing out the Taliban and providing security for the local population. Protection of the population was not a new goal for the ISAF, but its commitment to providing security throughout Afghanistan was a noticeable change in ISAF policy. Second, the ISAF expansion was designed to help the central government extend its new powers—provided in the January 2004 constitution—throughout the country.[31]

29. "UN Report Hails Progress in War against Opium Trade in Afghanistan," *The Times* (London), August 27, 2008.

30. For an overview of the NATO mission in Afghanistan along with timeline and discussion of the evolving NATO deployment strategy, see http://www.nato.int/cps/en/natolive/topics_8189.htm.

31. UN Security Council, *Resolution 1510,* October 13, 2003, available at http://www.nato.int/isaf/topics/mandate/unscr/resolution_1510.pdf.

The new Afghan constitution, which the United States drafted and ensured passage of in 2004, gave near absolute authority to the central government, without any checks and balances to executive power. This top-down power structure was a radical shift from the weak central government and dominant tribal organization that had constituted Afghanistan's past political systems. Afghan President Hamid Karzai used this newfound power to help install members of his own tribe, the Popalzai, in key provincial government positions, including his own brother, Ahmed Wali Karzai, as provincial council leader of Kandahar Province.[32]

In the early stages of the expansion (October 2003 to December 2005), the ISAF moved into the north of Afghanistan and met little resistance. The Taliban presence in the north was very light because of strong indigenous support for the anti-Taliban Northern Alliance. However, in early 2006, the ISAF transitioned to the west and south, which placed large numbers of foreign soldiers into regions previously controlled by the Taliban, including the southern provinces of Kandahar and Helmand. Coinciding with this force redeployment, suicide attacks and security incidents rose dramatically, especially in the southern provinces, as many local tribes joined up with Taliban militants to fight the ISAF forces. This upward trend in suicide attacks continued as the ISAF moved into the eastern region, along the Afghan-Pakistan border.[33]

Alongside the ISAF redeployment, U.S. forces were also expanding into previously unoccupied regions with Operation Mountain Thrust. Beginning in June 2006, Mountain Thrust moved nearly 11,000 troops into Helmand Province in southern Afghanistan.[34] From June to July, U.S., Canadian, and Afghan forces engaged in some of the bloodiest fighting since the war began. The Americans transferred command of the region to ISAF forces after the worst of the fighting had subsided.

One result of this large expansion of Western troops into the south, west, and east was that the local population began to increasingly view Western

32. "Tribal Leaders Say Karzai's Team Forged 23,900 Votes," *New York Times,* September 1, 2009.

33. For a discussion of the rise in security incidents from 2005 to 2006, see NATO, *Afghanistan Joint Collaboration and Monitoring Board Report,* November 12, 2006; "NATO Readies Combat Brigade for Afghanistan," *New York Times,* January 25, 2007, available at http://www.nytimes.com/2007/01/25/world/asia/25iht-afghan.4348698.html. For NATO security incident statistics from 2007 to 2008, see "NATO Figures Show Surge in Afghanistan Violence," *Guardian* (London), January 31, 2009, available at http://www.guardian.co.uk/world/2009/jan/31/afghanistan-nato-violence.

34. Rashid, *Descent into Chaos,* p. 359.

forces as foreign occupiers. Part of this perception stemmed from the ISAF's use of airstrikes that frequently resulted in collateral damage among the local population. As Ahmed Rashid noted, "NATO's unwillingness to take casualties forced it to depend more heavily on air power than the Americans had ever done, but in doing so it lost any hope of winning over the population."[35] British Captain Leo Docherty referred to the heavy use of airstrikes as "a textbook case of how to screw up a counterinsurgency."[36] NATO's increased use of airstrikes was stunning; there were an estimated 2,100 airstrikes in the last six months of 2006, which was more than the total number used in the first four years of the war.[37] In comparison, there were only 88 airstrikes in Iraq during the same period.[38] After the United States reevaluated its Afghanistan strategy in 2009, it soon became clear that collateral damage was a major impediment to gaining the confidence of the Afghan population that the United States and NATO were trying to protect. General McChrystal's report on Afghanistan finds that, "over-reliance on firepower and force protection have severely damaged the International Security Assistance Force's legitimacy in the eyes of the Afghan people."[39] This heavy use of airpower contributed to the perception that Western troops cared little about the well-being of the local population.

The perceived illegitimacy of Western troops was further exacerbated by the rampant corruption and nepotism in the Afghan central government. In a 2009 worldwide corruption survey, Afghanistan ranked 179 out of 180 countries—beaten only by Somalia as the most corrupt country in the world.[40] To make matters worse, President Karzai alienated many Pashtuns by failing to appoint members of majority tribes as provincial governors. For instance, in the large Pashtun province of Kandahar, Karzai installed childhood friend and member of the Mohammadzai tribe Tooryalai Wesa as governor, rather than someone from the majority Ghilzai tribe.[41] This blatant nepotism contributed to widespread feelings of disempowerment

35. Ibid., p. 365.

36. Ibid.

37. Ibid.; "US Air Strikes Climb Sharply in Afghanistan" *New York Times,* November 17, 2006, available at http://www.nytimes.com/2006/11/17/world/asia/17bomber.html.

38. "US Air Strikes Climb Sharply in Afghanistan."

39. McChrystal, *Commander of International Security Assistance Force's Initial Assessment,* p. 18.

40. Transparency International, *Corruption Perceptions Index 2009,* available at http://www.transparency.org/policy_research/surveys_indices/cpi/2009/cpi_2009_table.

41. "City of Kandahar Is Key That Unlocks Afghanistan," *Star* (Toronto), June 18, 2008; "Kandahar Gets New Governor," *Pajhwok Afghan News,* December 19, 2008.

among the local population—as local Pashtuns failed to believe that they had a voice in their central government. Furthermore, the United States and President Karzai gave former warlords such as Muhammad Fahim, Abdul Rashid Dostum, and Abdul Rasul Sayyaf prominent positions within the Afghan government.[42] As we mentioned earlier, the Taliban gained popularity during the 1990s by overthrowing these warlords who were hated by the public for their widespread injustice and corruption.[43] The Taliban have capitalized on the fact that these same warlords are back in power by branding the government as a return to the lawlessness and corruption of the pre-Taliban era. Kathy Gannon, a journalist and fellow at the Council on Foreign Relations, argues that the United States' biggest mistake was to believe that the warlords "who caused Afghanistan so much misery in the past will somehow lead it to democracy and stability in the future."[44] Given the close association between Western forces and the Afghan government, the public perceives that the United States and NATO are complicit in this corruption.

Combined with the expansion of military forces in 2006, these political factors created an ideal recruiting environment for the Taliban. The perception of a corrupt, puppet authoritarian government controlled by a foreign occupying force led to a rise in suicide bombings and other forms of terrorist attacks. This synthesis of NATO's expansion strategy, high collateral damage from ISAF operations, and a crisis of confidence in government has made the Afghan people doubt whether they will control their political and social institutions in the future. These factors coalesced in 2006 and caused a spike in Afghan suicide attacks. In the years that followed, the number of suicide attacks fluctuated slightly in response to a buildup of Western forces from 2007 to 2009. To understand these small changes in the number of suicide bombings, it is important to examine in detail the Taliban's targeting tactics.

Targeting and Weapons

After the surge in suicide attacks in 2006, the U.S. military and many political analysts throughout the world began to talk about the "Iraqification" of the Afghan War. However, the Afghan suicide terrorism campaign has

---

42. Seth Jones, "Averting Failure in Afghanistan," *Survival* 48, no. 1 (Spring 2006): 111–27.

43. Kathy Gannon, "Afghanistan Unbound," *Foreign Affairs,* May/June 2004, available at http://www.foreignaffairs.com/articles/59891/kathy-gannon/afghanistan-unbound.

44. Ibid.

unique tactical dynamics that set it apart from Iraq and shape our understanding of the conflict. In Iraq, suicide attackers kill between 7.61 and 13.18 people per attack,[45] but in Afghanistan, suicide bombers rarely achieve a kill count that high. From 2001 to 2009, suicide attacks in Afghanistan killed between 3.17 and 4.61 people per attack. In comparison, global suicide terrorist attacks from 1980 to 2009 killed between 8.65 and 12.55 people per attack—excluding the 9/11 attacks, which are clearly an outlier.

Although some observers[46] have attributed this disparity to Taliban ineptitude, there is little reason to believe the Taliban is any more or less inept than their counterparts in Iraq. The primary reason for this difference appears to be targeting patterns. While jihadi groups in Iraq target soft targets such as markets, checkpoints, and recruitment lines, Taliban bombers prey almost exclusively on hard targets, such as the police and military. In figure 4.2, the Taliban's concentration on security targets becomes apparent.

Unlike civilians, ISAF and U.S. forces commonly operate in small numbers when on patrol, and are well defended when in garrison. Therefore, the Taliban's tactical focus on hard targets explains their relatively low kill ratios.

Rather than copying Iraqi insurgent tactics, the Taliban employs hard targeting to safeguard the hearts and minds of the Afghan people—in particular, local Pashtuns. In a statement to the Associated Press, Mullah Omar stated, "I would again ask *mujahidin* to intensify their attacks, but they should avoid any harm to innocent people and children."[47] After a Taliban attack on ISAF troops killed approximately 15 civilians, the Taliban spokesperson apologized saying, "We are sorry about the loss. We are trying our best to avoid civilian casualty [*sic*]. This is war."[48] In addition, when a suicide attack near Kandahar killed 26 civilians, the Taliban later told Agence France-Presse, "We strongly condemn this attack on innocent people. The Taliban leadership convey their condolences to the relatives of the victims."[49] Whether these statements express genuine concern for innocent civilians is unclear. The Taliban's concept of "innocent" and "guilty" is a complicated distinction. The Taliban often targets civilians who aid

---

45. CPOST codes a "low" kill count and "high" kill count to capture the inconsistencies of casualty reporting.

46. "Afghan Suicide Attacks Seen as Less Effective," *New York Times,* February 15, 2010, available at http://www.nytimes.com/2010/02/16/world/asia/16bomber.html.

47. Human Rights Watch, *The Human Cost: The Consequences of Insurgent Attacks in Afghanistan,* April 15, 2007, available at http://www.hrw.org/en/node/10984/section/1.

48. Ibid.

49. Ibid.

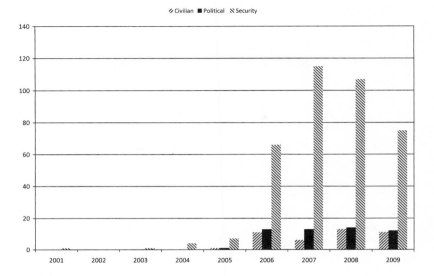

FIGURE 4.2 Afghanistan suicide attacks by target

and abet the Afghan central government. Moreover, despite Taliban reassurances, 272 Afghan civilians were killed just in 2006, although the vast majority were not directly *targeted* by the Taliban.[50]

Regardless of whether the Taliban's concern for civilian casualties is genuine, the fact remains: their overwhelming focus is on hard targets. What accounts for this tactical disparity between Iraqi insurgents and the Taliban? In terms of political objectives, both Iraqi insurgents and the Taliban seek to undermine what they term "infidel proxy" governments. However, where Iraq's insurgency is comprised of numerous sectarian groups, all competing for power, the Taliban is relatively monolithic, with very little infighting between ancillary insurgent groups such as the Haqqani Network and Hezb-i-Islami Gulbuddin. Importantly, the disparate nature of Iraq's population—comprised of Sunni, Shia, and Kurd—provides sectarian groups with civilian targets that range outside of their base of support. In essence, the combination of numerous competing factions and a heterogeneous population make soft targeting viable in Iraq. However, in Afghanistan, the Taliban is focused on cultivating Pashtun support and

50. Ibid.

soft targeting of civilians would undermine that objective.[51] In addition, Pashtuns have largely abstained from collaborating with the Karzai government, giving the Taliban few reasons to target them in the first place. Because of these conditions, the Taliban have centered on a coercive strategy of punishment by attacking military forces. The goal of this strategy is to undermine ISAF resolve and the Karzai government's ability to secure its citizens. As General McChrystal's report explains: "Violent attacks are designed to weaken the government by demonstrating its inability to provide security, to fuel recruiting and financing efforts, to provoke reactions from ISAF that further alienate the population, and also to undermine public and political support for the ISAF mission in coalition capitals."[52]

Car bombs are used in 43% of all suicide attacks and are the most common weapon for suicide terrorism in Afghanistan. Belt bombs are the second most common weapon type with 28%. In general, lethality per attack is fairly consistent between weapon types, with truck bombs having the highest lethality per attack, but being used in only 1% of all bombings. As we noted earlier, security targets are the most prevalent form of suicide attacks (78%), and they also have the lowest lethality per attack.

In 2006, three principal factors—NATO's troop expansion, collateral damage from ISAF operations, and Afghan government corruption—created an environment that fostered the perception of foreign occupation at the local level. Many locals as well as Afghan government officials believed that the Karzai government would collapse without continued U.S. and Western military presence throughout the country—a presumption widely shared in the West, as well.[53] In fact, this was one of the principal

51. In general, a population is heterogeneous when two or more ethnic groups live in physically intermixed settlements in provinces, cities, or neighborhoods. Under these conditions, terrorist groups who utilize suicide terrorism may demonize other ethnic groups living in their midst as "part of the oppressors," and target them with suicide terrorism. Once groups begin targeting opposing ethnic groups, this civilian targeting logic may expand to co-ethnic groups cooperating with what may be perceived as the "other." Palestine and Lebanon are two excellent examples of how heterogeneous versus homogeneous populations can affect targeting patterns. In Palestine, the West Bank population is heterogeneous with hundreds of thousands of Jews settled in the midst of 3 million Palestinians. In this heterogeneous environment, Hamas has frequently targeted Israeli civilians. By contrast in southern Lebanon, the population is homogeneous Shia Muslim, and the suicide terrorist groups associated with Hezbollah have almost exclusively targeted the military rather than civilians.

52. McChrystal, *Commander of International Security Assistance Force's Initial Assessment,* pp. 13–14.

53. "Afghans Fear Talk of Exit Strategy Will Play into Taliban's Hands," Associated Press, December 1, 2009; "Threats by Taliban May Sway Vote in Afghanistan," *New York Times,* August 16, 2009.

reasons for America's decision to add combat forces in the fall of 2009. The perception of foreign occupation angered segments of the Afghan population, which bolstered Taliban recruiting efforts and led to a spike in suicide terrorism. Once the perception of foreign occupation was in place, a steady increase of Western forces continued to provide the Taliban with hard targets—leading to the small changes in the frequency of suicide attacks from 2007 to 2009. Therefore, rather than a simple linear relationship between suicide attacks and Western troop levels, analysis of the data suggests that mitigating factors, such as troop deployment patterns, local disempowerment, and Taliban tactics, also play an important role in explaining the ebb and flow of suicide attacks in Afghanistan.

Local Community Support

Local community support is an important element of any sustained suicide terrorism campaign. A sympathetic local community can provide shelter for terrorist groups as well as a pool of potential recruits.[54] In the 1990s, the Taliban gained community support by ending the lawlessness that was rampant throughout the country following years of civil war. In the current climate, the Taliban derives its support in two important ways: (1) by protecting poppy farmers, and (2) by providing opposition to foreign intervention in the region.

First, U.S. and Afghan efforts to eradicate poppy farms have led many Pashtun poppy farmers to embrace the Taliban. Poppy farms are prevalent in the southern provinces of Afghanistan, including Helmand and Kandahar, where the Taliban enjoy strong local support. A coalition between the Taliban and poppy farmers has resulted in an agreement in which the Taliban protect farms from the government's eradication efforts in return for a share of the opium profits.[55] Because poppy production is such an integral part of Afghanistan's economy, the Taliban's protection of poppy farms has engendered a considerable amount of community support.

Second, the Taliban provide opposition to foreign intervention in the region. The Taliban commands respect within the communities from which

54. For more information on the Taliban's civilian support network, see Jones, "Averting Failure in Afghanistan."

55. John Lee Anderson, "The Taliban's Opium War: The Difficulties and Dangers of the Eradication Program," *New Yorker,* July 9, 2007, available at http://www.newyorker.com/reporting/2007/07/09/070709fa_fact_anderson?currentPage=all.

they recruit because they are seen as pursuing legitimate nationalist goals. Militant leaders such as Haqqani have historically fought against any foreigner who dared to invade Afghanistan. For many militant groups, alliance with the Taliban is considered the best hope for liberation from foreign occupation.

Historically, the vast majority of Taliban support comes from the ethnic Pashtun tribes in the southern and eastern regions of Afghanistan.[56] Pashtuns make up 40% of the population of Afghanistan, and the remaining 60% of the population—composed of Hazaras, Uzbeks, and Tajiks—have no great love for the Taliban and many fought against them during the 1990s. Poll data from Afghanistan is aggregated with no separation between ethnic groups, but the clear ethnic differences in support for the Taliban allow us to roughly disaggregate the poll data.[57] Because 60% of the population is non-Pashtun and historically anti-Taliban, we believe the most crucial segment of the population is the 40% Pashtun contingent. We posit that this 40% Pashtun contingent is the most important barometer for gauging Afghanistan polls because the non-Pashtun 60% of the population has been reliably opposed to Taliban rule.

The results of a 2009 BBC/ABC opinion poll suggest that the number of Afghans who oppose the presence of Taliban fighters in Afghanistan remains high but is in slight decline.[58] From 2006 to 2009, those who "strongly oppose" the presence of Taliban fighters fell from 81% to 70%. This result

56. Hillary Synnott, "What Is Happening in Pakistan?" *Survival* 51, no. 1 (February–March 2009): 72–73.

57. It is important to question the reliability of survey results in Afghanistan for three main reasons. First, the Taliban controls large areas of the country, and the war has made much of Afghanistan unsafe to travel through. The Taliban does not conduct surveys, so Afghans approached by someone collecting survey data know that the person either represents foreign troops, the central government, or a private company associated with one or both. This often translates into a progovernment and procoalition bias because participants may feel pressured in these situations. Afghanistan's history also works against reliable data reporting—the Soviet-backed government and the Taliban were known for punishing government detractors. Second, it is difficult to accurately gauge the opinions of women due to the patriarchal nature of Afghan society, which prohibits freedom of expression. While surveys often attempt to sample men and women equally, it is almost impossible in many tribal areas. Third, polling is primarily conducted in urban areas where Western troops have bases or off major highways where the Afghan government maintains a notable presence. Outside of areas controlled by Western forces, data is limited and often nonexistent. Surveyors are often forced to find participants among people that they personally know, voiding the idea of a random sample and diminishing the value of the results.

58. "Afghan People 'Losing Confidence,'" *BBC News,* February 9, 2009, available at http://news.bbc.co.uk/2/hi/south_asia/7872353.stm.

supports two main conclusions: (1) there is little chance of the Taliban taking over the country in the foreseeable future because of strong opposition from the non-Pashtun population, and (2) if we subtract the 60% of
non-Pashtuns who would never support the Taliban, the data indicate that
around 50% (21/40) of the Pashtun population supported the Taliban in
2006 and 75% (30/40) in 2009. This implies that support for the Taliban is
growing among the Pashtun population. In addition, there has also been a
slight uptick in those "strongly supporting" and "somewhat supporting" the
existence of Taliban fighters in Afghanistan, although the numbers remain
small (between 2% and 6%, respectively).

On the question of the Taliban as a whole—not the presence of Taliban
fighters—respondents reporting a "very unfavorable" view rose slightly
from 74% in 2005 to 79% in 2009.[59] Support for the presence of jihadi
fighters from other countries has seen little change from 2006 to 2009, with
"somewhat supporting" hovering around 9% and "strongly oppose" remaining at 60%. Because only 9% of all Afghans support the presence of
jihadi fighters, this suggests that around 75% of Pashtuns reject foreign
fighters.

From 2005 to 2009, when asked "who would you rather have ruling
Afghanistan today?" support for the Taliban only reached 4%.[60] Again,
by assuming Taliban support comes from the 40% Pashtun population,
the poll indicates that around 90% (36/40) of Pashtuns do not want to be
ruled by the Taliban. Even without our attempts to disaggregate the data,
the fact that 96% of the population would rather have other groups ruling Afghanistan suggests that there is very little support for the Taliban's
ideology in any segment of the population. The poll also found that public
support for the current government remained high from 2006 to 2009, but
has experienced some decline—from 91% to 82%. Public opposition for
NATO/ISAF military forces has remained steady at 60%.

These results suggest that, on the whole, the population is unlikely to
embrace the Taliban on ideological grounds, especially if local groups are
empowered to oppose them. In fact, since 2005, the Taliban has been most
cited as the problem that poses the greatest threat to Afghanistan—increasing from 41% in 2005 to 58% in 2009.[61] Moreover, 49% of respondents blame the Taliban and Al Qaeda/foreign jihadis for the majority of

59. Ibid.
60. Ibid.
61. Ibid.

violence occurring in Afghanistan. When asked about their confidence in the Taliban to provide security and stability to Afghanistan, 79% reported that they were "not at all confident." This result is intriguing because it suggests that around 50% (19/40) of Pashtuns are skeptical of whether the Taliban could actually represent their local interests. We believe that support for the Taliban is likely to erode if local Pashtuns were able to provide for their own security.

These poll numbers reinforce the idea that local Pashtun tribes may split allegiance with the Taliban if they are empowered to do so. Declining support for the central government and Western troops underscore the necessity of curbing corruption, empowering local groups, and ameliorating the perception of Western forces as foreign occupiers. Fortunately, the current instability in Afghanistan is fundamentally different from the instability of the 1990s, and popular support shows that Taliban and foreign jihadi fighters are not the favored remedy.

Recruitment

Although the available data on attacker demographics is sparse, CPOST has identified 177 Afghan suicide attackers by name and 91 by birth country. Of those identified, 91% were Afghan nationals, 3% came from Tajikistan and Pakistan, and 6% were born outside the region of conflict (United Arab Emirates, Yemen, Palestinian Territory, and Germany). All known attackers were male. The lack of data on suicide attackers is fairly common; many terrorist groups delay the release of identities to protect the attacker's family and community from reprisals.

The high concentration of suicide attackers from Afghanistan and the surrounding region suggests that suicide terrorism is primarily a localized reaction to Western occupation. Because of the small number of suicide bombers from outside the region and a noticeable lack of attackers from South Asian countries with large Muslim populations, there seems to be little evidence that supports the idea of a global jihad. Instead, our data suggests that suicide bombing has become a way to exert force as a means of local resistance.

Many scholars have argued that people do not usually support or volunteer for suicide missions based on situations involving *absolute* conditions of political repression, poverty, unemployment, and illiteracy. Rather, support and volunteerism tend to occur where there is a convergence of

political, economic, and social trends that result in diminished opportunities relative to individual expectations. This "relative deprivation" may
generate social and individual frustration, which groups like Al Qaeda can
exploit. It has long been thought that that better educated people experience this deprivation more acutely.

At a glance, these findings do not appear to hold true in Afghanistan
where suicide attackers are generally poor, young, and uneducated. Looking more closely, however, suicide bombers in Afghanistan are poor and
uneducated because the Afghani population is overwhelmingly poor and
uneducated. In large part, this atypical sample of suicide attackers is a
byproduct of the demographics of Afghanistan—over 72% of the population is illiterate, 70% are below the age of 22, and over 50% live below the
poverty line.[62] The United Nations' Human Development Index, which
measures a variety of indicators of well-being including life expectancy,
standard of living, and education, rated Afghanistan second to last in their
most recent survey.[63] Shockingly, these statistics may not sufficiently capture the depth of illiteracy and poverty in Afghanistan because it is difficult
to conduct accurate surveys in the mountainous tribal regions along the
Afghan-Pakistan border. Because the poor and uneducated make up such
a very large segment of the population, they also represent a similar proportion of suicide bombers.

Individual suicide attackers are often motivated by many of the tangible
effects of Western occupation, most notably, collateral damage. On November 9, 2008, 18-year-old Mullah Habibollah carried out a suicide car bomb
attack in the western Herat Province, targeting a joint military convoy of
Western and Afghan forces.[64] Habibollah came from the village of Shindand—a district that was badly damaged by NATO air raids. In Shindand,
bombs intended for Taliban militants had killed over 200 civilians.[65] Before
his suicide attack, Habibollah told his family that he felt compelled to take
revenge against Western troops for the actions they perpetrated against

---

62. UNICEF, *Afghanistan—Statistics,* available at http://www.unicef.org/infobycountry/
afghanistan_statistics.html; World Food Programme, *Where We Work—Afghanistan,* available
at http://one.wfp.org/country_brief/indexcountry.asp?country=004; McChrystal, *Commander
of International Security Assistance Force's Initial Assessment,* p. 44.

63. Human Development Reports, *Human Development Report 2009—Afghanistan,* available at http://hdrstats.undp.org/en/countries/country_fact_sheets/cty_fs_AFG.html.

64. "Afghan Taliban Leaders Urge Spain to Withdraw Troops, Threaten Attacks," *El Pais,*
September 6, 2009.

65. Ibid.

his village.[66] Another suicide attacker, Qari Omar, carried out a suicide car bomb attack against U.S. and Afghan forces on November 20, 2008—days after American soldiers had killed his mother, father, brothers, and sisters in their home.[67] These two stories illustrate the personal revenge motives behind many suicide bombings. Collateral damage by Western forces continues to be a powerful and effective recruiting tool for the Taliban and Al Qaeda.

Conclusion

On December 1, 2009, U.S. President Barack Obama formally outlined his new strategy for Afghanistan before cadets and soldiers at the U.S. Military Academy. Obama's plan calls for an additional 30,000 U.S. troops in Afghanistan coupled with 5,000 to 10,000 from NATO allies. How will the introduction of 40,000 Western soldiers affect the overall trajectory of suicide attacks?

Our prior analysis showed that suicide terrorism in Afghanistan has been a result of foreign occupation, and so there is good reason to believe that the addition of more Western combat forces will increase suicide attacks in Afghanistan. However, although many would like a precise mathematical relationship between the total number of foreign troops in the region and the rate of suicide attacks, such specific point predictions are beyond our current level of understanding.

What we do know is that the Western forces in Afghanistan are already viewed as foreign occupiers and the number of new forces and their envisioned use will do nothing but further reinforce that perception. The perception of occupation rests on two main factors: (1) that Western forces are in Afghanistan to support a corrupt and illegitimate central government in Kabul, and (2) that Western forces are willing to impose harm on Afghan civilians to achieve their aims.

First, at the local level, the addition of 40,000 troops suggests to the Afghans that Western forces support what many believe to be an illegitimate government. Therefore, the increase in troops sends a costly signal to the Afghan people that Western support will continue and this illegiti-

---

66. Ibid.
67. "Taleban Claim Killing Afghan, Foreign Soldiers in Suicide Attack in East," *BBC Worldwide*, November 20, 2008.

mate government will persist, rather than end any time soon. This fosters an already growing sense of disillusionment within the local population that stems from dissatisfaction with government representation and a lack of local empowerment. Rather than working toward local empowerment and a more representative government, the United States and NATO are signaling their support of the Karzai regime and the continuation of its authoritarian rule with a surge of troops. Ending government corruption and empowering the local population must be an integral part of U.S. and NATO strategy if any meaningful changes to the perception of occupation are to be made.

The second factor largely revolves around the issue of collateral damage. Collateral damage is a signal to Afghans that U.S. and ISAF forces are willing to harm civilians to accomplish their objectives. General McChrystal's report outlines a new strategic focus on limiting airstrikes and protecting civilian population centers, "where the population lives and works." This strategy seeks to minimize collateral damage while ceding rural territory to insurgents with the express purpose of providing greater security to areas with high population density. However, minimizing collateral damage is extremely difficult when large numbers of foreign ground troops are present because it is almost impossible to keep troops from defending themselves in a hostile environment.[68] Even with McChrystal's limits on airstrikes, U.S. and ISAF ground troops will remain under orders to engage the enemy, will defend themselves even if engagements are limited to urban areas, and will still use other forms of high powered weaponry in close proximity to many civilians. The continued difficulty of avoiding civilian casualties has been clearly illustrated during the February 2010 NATO offensive in Marja, Afghanistan. On February 20, 2010, a helicopter strike launched by U.S. Special Forces against what they believed to be a group of insurgents resulted in the killing of over 27 civilians.[69] This attack underscores the difficulty of preventing collateral damage, especially when the number and location of engagements are as much a function of the initiative of the Taliban as the decisions of U.S. and Western troops. As a result, significant collateral damage may remain

68. In the U.S. military's lexicon, this self-preservation behavior is generally referred to as force protection. The Department of Defense defines force protection as "actions taken to prevent or mitigate hostile actions against Department of Defense personnel (to include family members), resources, facilities, and critical information."

69. "NATO Airstrike Kills Afghan Civilians," *New York Times*, February 22, 2010, available at http://www.nytimes.com/2010/02/23/world/asia/23afghan.html?emc=eta1.

impossible to avoid, as the United States experienced in other counter-insurgency conflicts, such as Vietnam and Somalia.

Alongside this inability to ameliorate the perception of foreign occupation, the current strategy in Afghanistan falls short on three key points. First, the Afghanistan Social Outreach Program, which attempts to take steps toward empowering local tribes, is severely lacking in resources that are crucial for its success. Of the $65 billion Pentagon budget for Afghanistan, only $8.5 million would be used for the Social Outreach Program. In addition, some of the $8.5 million is slated for use in the Governor's Performance Fund, which may only encourage corruption at the provincial level.[70] Second, there is a severe lack of Pashto speakers in the U.S. military and Foreign Service. By most estimates, the United States needs thousands of Pashto speakers to adequately pursue a hearts and minds campaign that can win over the local population. According to a State Department official, there are only 18 Foreign Service officers who speak Pashto, and only two of them are stationed in Afghanistan.[71] The Defense Language Institute in Monterey, California, produces around 35 Pashto speakers a year, but that is a far cry from the 200–300 a year that many analysts say are needed.[72] In large part, this problem is unsurprising given how long it takes to train fluent speakers of any foreign language. The most glaring error seems to be that, after nine years of the conflict, the United States is only now starting to rectify this problem by increasing efforts to train Pashto speakers. Third, the Afghan National Army (ANA) is increasingly dominated by Tajiks, not Pashtuns. As General Eikenberry acknowledged in 2003, this ethnic disparity within the ANA is a huge problem for the U.S. mission in Afghanistan because it is imperative that the ANA be seen as a representative military force in order to be viewed as legitimate. A United Nations official estimated that no less than 70% of ANA officers are Tajiks.[73] In addition, Tajiks continue to occupy the top positions in the Afghan Ministry of Defense.

Given the likely crosscutting efforts of the current strategy in Afghanistan, the introduction of 40,000 troops appears unlikely to lead to anything

70. U.S. Department of State, *Facts Sheet: United States–Afghanistan Strategic Partnership*, available at http://kabul.usembassy.gov/press_release_25_09.html.

71. "U.S. Lacks the Capacity to Win Over Afghans," *Inter Press Service*, April 21, 2009, available at http://www.ipsnews.net/news.asp?idnews=46578.

72. Ibid.

73. "Tajik Grip on Afghan Army Signals Strife," *Asia Times*, December 1, 2009, available at http://www.atimes.com/atimes/South_Asia/KL01Df02.html.

more than a small fluctuation in suicide attacks. However, it would be misleading to think that the overall consequences for American security are negligible. Since President Obama's commitment of 40,000 troops signals the commitment of his new administration to the long-term occupation of Afghanistan, the main consequence of this troop surge may be a continued threat to the American homeland. As we have already witnessed with the shooting spree at Fort Hood and the 2009 Christmas bomber in Detroit, there is a close relationship between the motives of these attackers and America's continuing occupation of Afghanistan.[74]

74. "Army Doctor Held in Ft. Hood Rampage," *New York Times,* available at http://www.nytimes.com/2009/11/06/us/06forthood.html?pagewanted=all; "Review of Jet Bomb Plot Shows More Missed Clues," *New York Times,* available at http://www.nytimes.com/2010/01/18/us/18intel.html.

CHAPTER FIVE

Pakistan

In 2001, the U.S. invasion of Afghanistan drove large numbers of Taliban and Al Qaeda fighters across the Afghan border into the tribal areas of Northwest Pakistan.[1, 2] The Pakistani government publicly agreed to assist U.S. counterterrorism efforts in the region, but as time went on, it became clear that Pakistan's strategic priorities were often in conflict with the United States. More concerned with India than militant groups, the Pakistani government has vacillated between using tentative military action and appeasement to deal with the terrorist networks and militant groups operating within its borders—many of which the government considers strategic assets in its ongoing conflict with India over the disputed territory of Kashmir. But for the United States, Pakistani support continues to be an essential component of winning the war in Afghanistan. In recent years, the United States has successfully pressured Pakistan to shift its strategic priorities away from India to militant groups

1. Major contributors to this chapter were Ezra Schricker and Susan Young. The research assistant for this chapter was Ahsan Butt.

2. For further reading on Pakistan, the Taliban, and Al Qaeda, relevant literature includes Rizwan Hussain, *Pakistan and the Emergence of Islamic Militancy in Afghanistan* (Burlington, VT: Ashgate, 2005); John Wilson, *The General and Jihad: Pakistan under Musharraf* (New Delhi: Pentagon Press, 2007); Ahmed Rashid, *Descent into Chaos: The United States and the Failure of Nation Building in Pakistan, Afghanistan, and Central Asia* (New York: Viking Press, 2008); Daniel Byman, "Passive Sponsors of Terrorism," *Survival* 47, no. 4 (2009): 117–44; Amin Saikal, "Securing Afghanistan's Border," *Survival* 48, no. 1 (2006): 129–42; John R. Schmidt, "The Unravelling of Pakistan," *Survival* 51, no. 3 (2009): 29–54; Hilary Synnott, "What Is Happening in Pakistan," *Survival* 51, no. 1 (2009): 61–80; Stephen P. Cohen et al., "What's the Problem with Pakistan?" *Foreign Affairs,* March 31, 2009, http://www.foreignaffairs.com/discussions/ roundtables/whats-the-problem-with-pakistan; William Wheeler, "Letter from Mardan: A War of Unintended Consequences," *Foreign Affairs,* May 28, 2009, available at http://www.foreignaffairs.com/features/letters-from/letter-from-mardan-a-war-of-unintended-consequences.

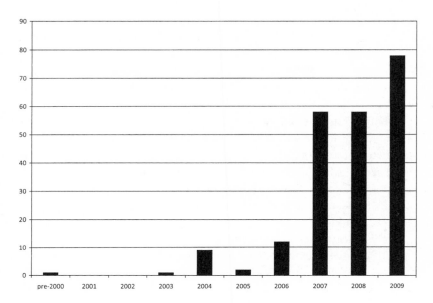

FIGURE 5.1 Suicide attacks in Pakistan

within its borders. In this chapter, we show that initiation and trajectory of the Pakistani suicide campaign is a function of the changing political and military alliance between the United States and Pakistan. Figure 5.1 details the trajectory of suicide attacks.

The suicide campaign and the U.S./Pakistan strategic alliance can be divided into two distinct phases—Phase 1: 2002-2005 and Phase 2: 2006-present.[3] In Phase 1, the low levels of suicide attacks reflect the nascent alliance between Pakistan and the United States, which was primarily political at this stage of the conflict. In Phase 2, the political alliance between the U.S. and Pakistan evolved into—what is better termed—an indirect occupation. In a traditional alliance, member countries pursue mutual goals of interest,[4] but in an indirect occupation, the indirectly occupied country (Pakistan) gives a higher-priority to the goals of the indirect occupier (the

3. A 1995 suicide attack against the U.S. embassy in Karachi appears to be an isolated event.

4. Hans Morgenthau lays out the logic of alliance formation based on mutual interest in his seminal text *Politics Among Nations* (New York: Alfred A. Knopf, Inc, 1978), p. 190: "It is only when the common interests are inchoate in terms of policy and action that a treaty of alliance is required to make them explicit and operative."

United States) than its national interest alone would warrant. For example, in Phase 2, the United States increased pressure on Pakistan President Pervez Musharraf to intervene militarily against Al Qaeda and the Taliban. When Musharraf acquiesced to U.S. demands and shifted around 100,000 troops from the Eastern front against India to engage militant targets in western Pakistan, the alliance transitioned into an indirect occupation.[5] As the relationship between the U.S. and Pakistan began to be increasingly dominated by the United States, large segments of the Pakistani population started to question the legitimacy of the Islamabad government, believing that it served America's interests, rather than Pakistan's. This perceived illegitimacy helped Al Qaeda and the Taliban gain local support and garner recruits for suicide attacks against the Pakistani Army's expansion into Northwest Pakistan.

In this chapter, we examine the groups responsible for suicide terrorism in Pakistan, including their objectives, state sponsorship, targeting patterns, local community support, and recruitment. In addition, we analyze how the evolving strategic partnership between the U.S. and Pakistan has influenced the trajectory of suicide attacks since 2002. Lastly, we assess the consequences of the recent escalation of U.S. drone attacks in the region.

Groups and Goals

Groups

The Pakistani government has a long history of involvement with numerous militant organizations operating in Central and South Asia. During the Afghan civil war in the 1990s, Pakistan's espionage agency, Inter-Services Intelligence (ISI),[6] gave military and economic aid to the Taliban in order to

5. "The [Pakistani] military are convinced Mr. Bush compelled Gen. Musharraf to deploy some 100,000 troops in the tribal agencies on the Afghan border to eradicate Taliban and Al Qaeda infrastructure," according to "Perils of Pakistan," *The Washington Times*, November 6, 2007. "This is going to be a long slog for the Pakistan Army, and they are, or should be, worried about fighting a two front war – with India on the one side, with radical Islamist on the other," said Steven Cohen, senior fellow in Foreign Policy Studies at the Brookings Institution and author of *The Idea of Pakistan*, quoted in "Pakistan Army Counts the Rising Casualties of its War Within," *Indian Express*, July 29, 2007.

6. Pakistan's InterServices Intelligence incorporates aspects of domestic and international surveillance and can best be described as a hybrid of the FBI and CIA.

FIGURE 5.2 District map of Pakistan's NWEP and FATA

consolidate power in Afghanistan under a Pakistan-friendly regime.[7] Within Pakistan, the ISI has created, trained, and abetted a wide variety of militant groups in an ongoing guerilla war against India over the disputed region of Kashmir. Despite the ISI's best efforts, these militant groups have always remained loosely allied with Pakistan and capricious allies at best.

7. For a background on Pakistan's support for the Taliban during the 1990s, see Hussain, *Pakistan and the Emergence of Islamic Militancy in Afghanistan.*

While the Taliban started out as a localized organization based in Afghanistan's Kandahar Province, the movement expanded during the Afghan civil war to control most of the country. Today, the Taliban can best be thought of as a broad umbrella movement, comprised of a variety of distinct militant groups, some more under the guidance of Mullah Muhammed Omar than others. What holds these groups together is the common aim to end Western military presence and political influence in the Pashtun areas of Afghanistan and Pakistan. Each group now operates out of fairly distinct geographic areas with their own senior leadership, although in tacit cooperation with each other.

Within the Taliban umbrella organization there are three primary subgroups operating within Pakistan: the Afghan Taliban, the Pakistani Taliban, and the Punjabi Taliban.[8] Most scholars use the word "Taliban" to describe all three subgroups, but doing so misses an important operational distinction: the Afghan Taliban concentrates the vast majority of its guerrilla and suicide attacks against Western forces in Afghanistan while the Pakistani and Punjabi Taliban focus on Pakistani targets. A fourth organization, Al Qaeda, has ties to all three subgroups, but is primarily linked to the Afghan Taliban.

THE AFGHAN TALIBAN.   Led by Mullah Muhammed Omar, the Afghan Taliban is composed of members of the original Taliban organization that fled Afghanistan after the U.S. invasion, as well as pro-Taliban militant groups such as the Haqqani network.[9] Geographically, the Afghan Taliban operates throughout the Federally Administered Tribal Areas (FATA) with strongholds in North and South Waziristan. Outside of the tribal areas, the Afghan Taliban leadership has an important base in Quetta, a medium-sized city in the Pakistani province of Balochistan.[10] According to Colonel Chris Vernon, a British chief of staff for southern Afghanistan, "The thinking piece of the Taliban is out of Quetta in Pakistan. It's the major headquarters. They use it to run a series of networks in Afghanistan."[11]

8. This chapter uses the word "Taliban" to refer to the broad umbrella movement as a whole, while more qualified names, such as the Afghan Taliban, refer to individual subgroups within the movement.

9. For more information on the origins of the Afghan Taliban, see chapter 4: "Afghanistan."

10. "At Border, Signs of Pakistani Role in Taliban Surge," *New York Times,* January 21, 2007, available at http://www.nytimes.com/2007/01/21/world/asia/21quetta.html.

11. Eben Kaplan and Jayshree Bajoria, "The ISI and Terrorism: Behind the Accusations," *Council on Foreign Relations,* May 28, 2008, available at http://www.cfr.org/publication/11644/.

THE PAKISTANI TALIBAN.   The Pakistani Taliban is responsible for the vast majority of suicide terrorism in Pakistan and is therefore the focus of much of this chapter. The Pakistani Taliban has a headquarters in South Waziristan as well as a strong presence in parts of the North West Frontier Province (NWFP) and throughout the FATA. In general, the tribal areas are the nexus of militant activity in Pakistan. In large part, the FATA have become a breeding ground for Taliban-affiliated groups because the Pakistani government has marginalized the Pashtun population there. The acronym FATA is somewhat misleading because these areas are locally ruled, not "Federally Administered." As a result, FATA tribes are denied constitutional and political rights available to other regions of the country. According to journalist Ahmed Rashid, a lack of political choices and freedoms has kept the Pashtun tribesmen removed from Pakistani mainstream society and disconnected from the government.[12] Al Qaeda and the Taliban have capitalized on this environment by empowering the local tribes and even renaming the region "The Islamic Emirate of Waziristan."[13] Angered by Pakistani military operations into their homeland, these local tribes joined forces with the Taliban movement to oppose government intervention and have since called themselves the Pakistani Taliban.

In December 2007, various Pakistani Taliban groups—more than half a dozen—coalesced into one entity, Tehrik-e-Taliban Pakistan (TTP). The TTP's first elected leader, Baitullah Mehsud, was killed by a U.S. drone strike on August 5, 2009.[14] Baitullah's former bodyguard, Hakimullah Mehsud (no relation), is the current leader of the TTP, and he maintains control over numerous local TTP commanders based throughout FATA and parts of NWFP.[15] Hakimullah is rumored to have several thousand active fighters under his command, but official estimates vary considerably. A local Pakistani senator estimated combined TTP forces at around 25,000, but some analysts believe this number to be inflated.[16]

In the past, the Pakistani Taliban has cosponsored suicide bomb attacks with Al Qaeda, but they are primarily operationally independent from

12. Rashid, *Descent into Chaos,* p. 273.

13. Ibid., p. 273.

14. "Air Strike Kills Taliban Leader Baitullah Mehsud," *Guardian* (London), August 7, 2009, available at http://www.guardian.co.uk/world/2009/aug/07/baitullah-mehsud-dead-taliban-pakistan.

15. Jayshree Bajoria, "Pakistan's New Generation of Terrorists," *Council on Foreign Relations,* October 26, 2009.

16. "Hidden Hand," *Newsline,* February 2008, available at http://www.newsline.com.pk/NewsFeb2008/newsbeatfeb.htm.

their Afghan Taliban counterparts.[17] After an apparent split with certain segments of Al Qaeda, the Pakistani Taliban has emerged as the public face of the terrorism campaign in Pakistan.[18] According to sources within the Pakistani military, the Pakistani Taliban is responsible for over 80% of the terrorist attacks in the country.[19]

THE PUNJABI TALIBAN.   In general, the Taliban movement is comprised of ethnic Pashtuns. However, in recent years, a so-called Punjabi Taliban network has emerged within Pakistan's borders. Operating largely in Punjab Province, and occasionally in FATA, the Punjabi Taliban is a loose collection of individuals from three militant groups: Jaish-e-Mohammed, Sipah-i-Sahaba Pakistan, and Lashkar-i-Jhangvi, all of which were banned by the Pakistani government in 2001 and 2002.[20] According to Teresita Schaffer of the Center for Strategic and International Studies, "Punjab-based groups were initially the creatures of the Inter-Services Intelligence, and had a Kashmir focus."[21] In many cases, the Pakistani government professionally trained the militant groups for guerrilla warfare in Kashmir.[22] These fighters often work as mercenaries and seem to prefer armed confrontation rather than suicide attacks.[23]

Attacks by the Punjabi Taliban add to the growing fears of "Talibanization" within Punjab Province. However, the Punjabi Taliban is quite small—most estimates cite around 5,000 fighters—and their affiliation with the Taliban seems based on profit motives and anger over ISI abandonment rather than shared ideology.[24] While a loose collection of embittered Punjab fighters may be active within the province, most experts believe it

17. Barbara Elias, "Know Thine Enemy," *Foreign Affairs,* November 2, 2009, available at http://www.foreignaffairs.com/articles/65639/barbara-elias/know-thine-enemy; "Old-Line Taliban Commander Is Face of Rising Afghan Threat," *New York Times,* June 17, 2008, available at http://www.nytimes.com/2008/06/17/world/asia/17warlord.html.

18. Sami Yousufzai and Ron Moreau, "Al Qaeda: Internal Power Struggle Looms," *Newsweek,* July 30, 2007.

19. "Pakistani Army Kills 60 Militants in South Waziristan," *Bloomberg,* October 18, 2009, available at http://www.bloomberg.com/apps/news?pid=20601087&sid=aYk10VqJM7Bo.

20. Hassan Abbas, "Defining the Punjabi Taliban Network," *CTC Sentinel,* 2, no. 4 (April 2009): 2.

21. "Rise of Punjabi Taliban," *Hindustan Times,* October 25, 2009.

22. Abbas, "Defining the Punjabi Taliban network," p. 2.

23. Ibid.

24. Ibid., p. 3.

is unlikely that the movement will coalesce into an organized group in the near future.[25]

Despite their small numbers, groups like the Punjabi Taliban, which are outside of the traditional base of Taliban support, have led many security analysts to warn of a possible Taliban takeover of Pakistan. In a March 2009 interview, David Kilcullen, a counterterrorism expert and advisor to U.S. General Petraeus, said, "We're now reaching the point where within one to six months we could see the collapse of the Pakistani state. . . . The collapse of Pakistan, al Qaeda acquiring nuclear weapons, an extremist takeover— that would dwarf everything we've seen in the war on terror today."[26] Fortunately, Kilcullen's grim forecast has not come to pass because groups like the Punjabi Taliban are an anomaly—the vast majority of Taliban support comes from ethnic Pashtuns. In Pakistan, Pashtuns make up only 15% of the population and, as a minority group, they are generally sympathetic to the Taliban movement because the Taliban works hard to empower local Pashtun communities.[27] However, given the relatively small size of the Pashtun population, there is little chance that it could rise up against the Pakistani state. Most importantly, the main obstacle to any extremist takeover—the Pakistani Army—is primarily composed of Punjabis, not Pashtuns, and tensions between the two groups run deep. As Selig Harrison, the director of the Asia Program at the Center for International Policy, noted, "For centuries, Pashtuns living in the mountainous borderlands of Pakistan and Afghanistan have fought to keep out invading Punjabi plainsmen."[28] This tension between the two groups is reflected in opinion polls within Punjab Province that report over three-quarters of the population support tougher

25. Ibid., pp. 3–4; some experts, most notably Daniel Byman, disagree with this assessment, arguing that ideological ties supersede profit motives: "These organizations share an ideological affinity with Al Qaeda, believing in the need for Islamic government, the importance of jihad as an individual duty, the corruption of most Muslim regimes, and the fundamental hostility of India and the United States. In addition, bin Ladin has provided them with both material and operational aid in their struggle in Kashmir, helping direct money to them from the vast network of charities he influences throughout the Muslim world." Quoted in Byman, "Passive Sponsors of Terrorism," pp. 125–26.

26. "A Conversation with David Kilcullen," *Washington Post,* March 22, 2009, available at http://www.washingtonpost.com/wp-dyn/content/article/2009/03/19/AR2009031903038.html.

27. For more information on how the Taliban empowers local Pashtun groups, see Rashid, *Descent into Chaos,* pp. 273–75.

28. "Pakistan's Ethnic Fault Line," *Washington Post,* May 11, 2009, available at http://www.washingtonpost.com/wp-dyn/content/article/2009/05/10/AR2009051001959.html.

measures against the Taliban.[29] Unless the Taliban starts making substantial inroads with Punjabis, a Taliban takeover of Pakistan appears unlikely.

AL QAEDA.   Al Qaeda has ties to all three Taliban subgroups, although its connections with the Afghan Taliban are by far the strongest. Despite a long history between the Afghan Taliban and Al Qaeda, many experts have remained puzzled by what has held the alliance together.[30] The benefits of the alliance are fairly straightforward for Al Qaeda: they use the Afghan Taliban for shelter and support. However, for the Afghan Taliban, the benefits from this arrangement are more ambiguous, considering the severe repercussion the alliance has had on their control of Afghanistan. Georgetown professor and senior fellow at the Brookings Institution Daniel Byman has suggested that Al Qaeda's main benefit to the Taliban in the 1990s was providing essential training and expertise for their fighters: "The majority of Al Qaeda's training camps in Afghanistan focused on training fighters to help defeat the Northern Alliance, not to conduct sophisticated terrorist attacks against the West."[31] Therefore, Al Qaeda provided the Afghan Taliban with practical assistance to consolidate their regional power. Inside Pakistan, Al Qaeda continues to function in this same training and advisory capacity with all three Taliban subgroups by providing logistical and financial assistance for guerrilla and suicide attacks. As we will see in the subsequent sections, Al Qaeda is adept at manipulating regional anger toward the Pakistani government and the United States to serve its own interests.

Goals

The central objective of the Taliban movement is to control territory in the Pashtun areas of Central and South Asia.[32] In a rare interview before his death, former TTP leader Baitullah Mehsud stated that the international border between Pakistan and Afghanistan is largely meaningless

29. Gallop Poll, "Pakistanis Support Tougher Stance on Terrorism," December 17, 2008, available at http://www.gallup.com/poll/113455/pakistanis-support-tougher-stance-terrorism.aspx.

30. For more information on the history between the Taliban and Al Qaeda, see Anonymous, *Through Our Enemies' Eyes* (Washington, DC: Brassey's Inc., 2003), p. 156.

31. Byman, "Passive Sponsors of Terrorism," p. 126.

32. Elias, "Know Thine Enemy"; the smallest and most disorganized of the Taliban subgroups, the Punjabi Taliban, has not released public statements concerning group goals, but given their mercenary background and anti-Shiite bent, profit and sectarian motives seem to be central objectives behind their attacks.

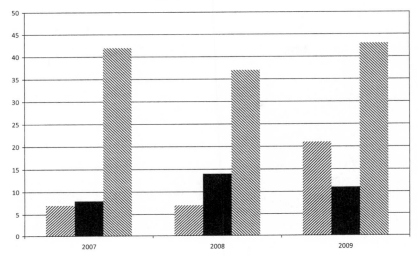

FIGURE 5.3 Pakistan attacks by Target

to the Taliban because "Islam does not recognize any man-made barriers or boundaries."[33] Within Pakistan, the Pakistani Taliban's principal goal is terminating the alliance between Pakistan and the United States. This alliance is damaging to the Pakistani Taliban because it has brought the Pakistani Army into the tribal regions that the Taliban movement wants to control. Baitullah Mehsud noted, "We do not want to fight Pakistan or the [Pakistani] army. But if they continue to be slaves to U.S. demands, then our hands will be forced."[34] As figure 5.3 highlights, starting in 2007, Pakistani military targets have been a top priority for suicide attacks. The Pakistani Taliban targets Pakistan's security forces and the army to punish the Pakistani government for supporting the United States and intervening in Northwest Pakistan.

A second objective shared by both the Pakistani and Afghan Taliban is the withdrawal of U.S. and NATO forces from Afghanistan. Pakistani Taliban spokesman Maulvi Umar called the U.S. government and the NATO alliance "the real enemy" and said that once international forces withdrew

33. "Afghan Jihad Will Continue: Mehsud," *Dawn,* May 24, 2008.
34. "Meeting Pakistan's Most Feared Militant," *BBC News,* May 27, 2008, available at http://news.bbc.co.uk/2/hi/south_asia/7420606.stm.

from Afghanistan, "the mujahideen would return to their homes."[35] However, if Western forces fail to withdraw, Umar stated that the TTP was prepared to employ suicide terrorism: "The suicide bombers are ready to sacrifice themselves. . . . We developed these mujahideen in response to American injustice around the world."[36] Pro-Taliban militant leader Maulvi Jalaluddin Haqqani cited the exit of foreign forces from Afghanistan as "a common mission" for the Taliban and its militant allies.[37] Baitullah Mehsud put it bluntly: "We will continue our struggle until foreign troops are thrown out."[38]

In contrast to the regional goals of the Taliban movement, Al Qaeda's agenda is global and anti-American. Osama bin Laden is principally dedicated to the removal of U.S. forces from all Muslim lands and the global spread of fundamentalist Islam. In a July 2007 statement, Al Qaeda second-in-command Ayman al-Zawahiri outlined a "near-term" and a "long-term" plan for achieving Al Qaeda's objectives: "The near-term plan consists of targeting Crusader-Jewish interests, as everyone who attacks the Muslim Ummah must pay the price, in our country and theirs, in Iraq, Afghanistan, Palestine and Somalia. . . . And the long-term plan is divided into two halves: The first half consists of earnest, diligent work, to change these corrupt and corruptive regimes. . . . As for the second half of the long-term plan, it consists of hurrying to the fields of jihad like Afghanistan, Iraq and Somalia, for jihad preparation and training."[39] Al-Zawahiri's rationale highlights Al Qaeda's more global focus, as well as its dedication to toppling Western-backed governments in Central and South Asia with predominately Muslim populations.

State Sponsorship

During the 1990s, Pakistan was intimately involved with consolidating the Afghan Taliban's power within Afghanistan.[40] After September 11,

35. "Taliban 'Ready for Peace with Islamabad,'" *National* (Abu Dhabi), June 22, 2008, available at http://www.thenational.ae/article/20080622/FOREIGN/250620911/1103/SPORT&Profile=1103.

36. Ibid.

37. "Old-Line Taliban Commander Is Face of Rising Afghan Threat," *New York Times*.

38. "Pakistan Taleban Vow More Violence," *BBC News*, January 29, 2007, available at http://news.bbc.co.uk/2/hi/south_asia/6292061.stm.

39. Christopher Blanchard, "Al Qaeda: Statements and Evolving Ideology" *CRS*, July 9 2007, pp. 13–14.

40. For a detailed discussion of the Pakistan's support for the Taliban during the 1990s, see Ahmed Rashid, "Pakistan and the Taliban," in *Fundamentalism Reborn? Afghanistan and the*

Pakistan President Musharraf claimed that his government severed ties with the Afghan Taliban, but evidence to the contrary is overwhelming. Starting in 2001, a CIA operative in Afghanistan claimed that, "[ISI] advisors were supporting the Afghan Taliban with expertise and material and, no doubt, sending a steady stream of intelligence back to Islamabad."[41] Months after the U.S. invasion of Afghanistan, Pakistan requested clearance from the United States to airlift some of their ISI personnel out of Kanduz in northern Afghanistan. The U.S. government gave the go ahead, and U.S. soldiers estimated that several thousand people, including Afghan Taliban fighters, were airlifted out of Kanduz in what was dubbed by U.S. forces as, "the Great Escape."[42]

In the years that followed, U.S. and NATO officials collected substantial evidence that suggested direct ISI involvement with the Afghan Taliban. The ISI has routinely provided intelligence to the Afghan Taliban and tipped off their forces about U.S. and NATO operations in Afghanistan.[43] While most ISI assistance came from middle- and low-level officers, the United States found connections between senior-level ISI connections and the Afghan Taliban in 2008.[44] More recently, U.S. officials have expressed frustration that Pakistan continues to shelter Afghan Taliban leader Mullah Omar from drone attacks.[45] Most experts agree that Pakistan's continued support for the Afghan Taliban is rooted in fears of growing Indian involvement in Afghanistan. Pakistan and the ISI hope to preserve the Afghan Taliban as a strategic asset to counter India's influence in the region. However, recently, it appears that the relationship between the ISI and the Afghan Taliban is in flux as evidenced by the February 2010 arrest of Mullah Abdul Ghani Baradar, the Afghan Taliban second-in-command. It is unclear whether this arrest suggests a permanent change of attitude within the ISI or a calculated compliance with U.S. demands with possible ulterior motives.

Taliban, ed. William Maley (New York: New York University Press); and Wilson, *The General and Jihad: Pakistan under Musharraf,* pp. 133–35.

41. Seth Jones, *In the Graveyard of Empires: America's War in Afghanistan* (New York: W. W. Norton and Company, 2009), p. 264.

42. Rashid, *Descent into Chaos,* pp. 92–93.

43. Jones, *In the Graveyard of Empires: America's War in Afghanistan,* p. 266.

44. Ibid., pp. 265–66.

45. "Taliban Chief Hides in Pakistan," *Washington Times,* November 20, 2009, available at http://www.washingtontimes.com/news/2009/nov/20/taliban-chief-takes-cover-in-pakistan-populace/.

Trajectory of the Suicide Campaign

The Pakistani suicide campaign can be divided into two distinct phases—
Phase 1: 2002–2005 and Phase 2: 2006–present (see figure 5.1)—which
are based on the changing alliance structure between Pakistan and the
United States and impact of those changes on the frequency of suicide
attacks.

During Phase 1: 2002–2005, the alliance between Pakistan and the
United States was primarily a political one, with each party having great
autonomy over their military actions. The low levels of suicide attacks during Phase 1 (0 in 2001 and 2002, 1 in 2003, 9 in 2004, and 2 in 2005) reflected
the nascent political relationship between the United States and Pakistan.
However, many suicide attacks during this period targeted symbols of the
growing relationship between Pakistan and the United States including:
Pakistan President Musharraf, the U.S. consulate in Karachi, and top government officials who were perceived as pro-American.[46]

During this period, there were more than a half-dozen sectarian suicide
attacks against Shiite mosques throughout Pakistan. Many observers have
struggled to explain the strategic objectives behind this sectarian subcampaign because tensions between Sunnis and Shiites have existed for centuries without the use of suicide terrorism. Our analysis reveals that, while
these attacks are specifically directed against Shiites, the broader goal of
sectarian attacks is to undermine the Pakistani government.

From 2002 to 2005, the militant group Lashkar-e-Jhangvi was responsible for the majority of sectarian suicide bombings. In 2001, Pakistani President Musharraf banned Lashkar-e-Jhangvi along with several other Punjabi
militant groups after they attacked members of the Shiite community.[47]
In the aftermath of Musharraf's decision, Al Qaeda quickly reached out to
these alienated groups and emboldened them to escalate their attacks on
Shiites by using suicide terrorism. Al Qaeda's goal behind these sectarian
suicide attacks was to demonstrate that the government could not protect
its citizens, thereby creating distress among the populace and fostering a
state of anarchy.[48] Talat Masood, a military analyst and retired Pakistani

46. "Continuing Terrorist Attacks Indicate Presence of 'Pakistani Al-Qa'ida,'" *Herald,*
August 30, 2004; and Byman, "Passive Sponsors of Terrorism," p. 127.
    47. Abbas, "Defining the Punjabi Taliban Network," p. 3.
    48. "Unholy Alliance of Al Qaeda and Sectarian Groups Returns to Haunt Pakistan,"
Agence France Presse, May 31, 2005.

Army general, said that sectarian suicide bombing "suits [the] double purpose of destabilizing the state while creating despondency amongst the people, and especially the Shiite."[49] In some cases, these sectarian suicide attacks triggered looting and rioting within the community, furthering the perception of lawlessness.[50] Alliances with anti-Shiite militant groups also provided Al Qaeda with valuable contacts within Pakistani civil society, and, in return, Al Qaeda directly financed the groups' suicide attacks.

Sunnis make up almost 80% of Pakistan's 175 million people with Shiites representing the remaining 20%.[51] The two populations are, for the most part, able to live in peace with one another. Pakistani officials continue to denounce all suicide attacks, branding them as acts of terrorism in an effort to downplay the sectarian elements at work. Pakistan's current president, Asif Ali Zardari, recently cautioned that attacks against Shiites were attempting to "turn the fight against militants into a sectarian clash and make the people fight against one another."[52]

During Phase 2: 2006–present, the alliance between Pakistan and the United States evolved into—what is better termed—an indirect occupation. In a traditional alliance, both countries pursue mutual goals of interest. In an indirect occupation, the indirect occupier (the United States) dictates the strategic priorities to the indirectly occupied country (Pakistan). In essence, U.S. pressure has shifted Pakistan's strategic priorities. For example, between 2002 and 2005, the Pakistani Army made several minor forays against militants in Northwest Pakistan, but, starting in 2006, the American government began to pressure Pakistan to take serious military action against militant targets. This involved shifting around 100,000 troops from Pakistan's Eastern border with India to fight against militant targets in Western Pakistan.[53] The U.S. dominance of the U.S./Pakistan strategic partnership led to growing discontent within Pakistan. The Pakistani populace criticized the government for representing the interests of the United

49. "Militants in Pakistan Strike Shiites Again, Prompting Fears of Sectarian Violence," *New York Times,* December 28, 2009, available at http://www.nytimes.com/2009/12/29/world/asia/29pstan.html.

50. "Two Killed in Clashes during Funeral of Karachi Blast Victims," *Press Trust of India,* June 1, 2004 and "Investigators Suspect Sunni Militants in Suicide Attack on Pakistani Mosque," *Agence France Presse,* June 3, 2004.

51. CIA World Factbook, *Pakistan,* available at https://www.cia.gov/library/publications/the-world-factbook/geos/pk.html.

52. "Militants in Pakistan Strike Shiites Again, Prompting Fears of Sectarian Violence," *New York Times.*

53. "Perils of Pakistan," *Washington Times,* November 6, 2007.; "Pakistan Army Counts the Rising Casualties of its War Within," *Indian Express,* July 29, 2007

States, not Pakistan. This led to a crisis of confidence in the Pakistani central government that reached a boiling point in December 2007 with the assassination of pro-Western politician, Benazir Bhutto and the resignation of President Musharraf in August 2008.[54]

After Pakistan President Musharraf began to accept U.S. military objectives in 2006, his approval rating began to fall precipitously. According to the Pew Research Center, 76% of Pakistanis rated Musharraf favorably in the fall of 2002.[55] By the summer of 2007, Musharraf had a 34% approval rating. Strikingly, a CNN poll from September 2007 found Osama bin Laden had a higher approval rating than Musharraf (46% to 38%, respectively).[56] At the time, former Prime Minister Benazir Bhutto noted: "Increasingly, the West's favorite dictator [Musharraf] is viewed by his own people as nothing more than a foreign puppet. This creates the very environment that works to the advantage of the militants."[57] Public anger toward Musharraf eventually forced him to resign in August 2008. Alongside Musharraf's falling approval ratings, the Pakistani populace also began to identify the United States as the most prominent threat to Pakistan. An August 2009 Al-Jazeera poll found that 60% of Pakistanis identified the United States as Pakistan's greatest threat.[58] This is especially remarkable considering that Pakistan's traditional enemy, India, received 18% of the vote and the Pakistani Taliban only 11%. Growing anger towards the political alliance between the United States and Pakistan helped to oust Musharraf from power and this animosity continues to be a major factor in Pakistani politics.

Within Phase 2, the overall rise in suicide terrorism was largely the byproduct of this indirect occupation of Pakistan by the United States, which pushed the Pakistani Army to engage militant groups in Northwest Pakistan. However, suicide terrorism was also influenced by other salient events, including the politics surrounding the national election in 2008. From 2006 to the present, there have been five reasonably discreet periods

54. Schmidt, "The Unraveling of Pakistan," p. 36.

55. Richard Wike, "Musharraf's Support Shrinks, Even As More Pakistanis Reject Terrorism . . . and the U.S.," *Pew Research Center,* (August 8, 2007), available at http://pewresearch. org/pubs/561/pakistan-terrorism.

56. "Poll: Bin Laden Tops Musharraf in Pakistan," *CNN,* September 11, 2007, available at http://edition.cnn.com/2007/POLITICS/09/11/poll.pakistanis/index.html.

57. Rashid, *Descent into Chaos,* p. 156.

58. "Pakistan: State of the Nation," *Al Jazeera,* August 23, 2009, available at http://english. aljazeera.net/focus/2009/08/2009888238994769.html.

violence sponsored by the Pakistani Taliban, which included, but were not limited to, suicide terrorism.

The first noticeable rise in violence took place in the spring and summer months of 2006 as the Pakistani Army mounted their largest operation yet to maintain order in the tribal areas. Countering the expanded presence of Pakistani military forces, the Pakistani Taliban unleashed a series of suicide bombings and guerrilla attacks. To stem the violence that ensued, President Pervez Musharraf brokered a series of controversial peace deals.[59] On September 5, 2006, the governor of NWFP, General Aurakzai, signed a truce with Pakistani Taliban leaders in North Waziristan, which specified that militants surrender to local tribes and refrain from attacks in Afghanistan.[60] However, the Pakistani government neglected to enforce the terms of the truce, and the peace deal was largely viewed as impotent. In the following months, the U.S. military calculated that "cross-border incursions from the tribal areas into Afghanistan rose by 300 percent."[61]

As the September truce began to weaken in the beginning of 2007, the United States and NATO again pressured the Pakistani government to "do more" in the fight against terrorism. As a result, the Pakistani Army expanded their presence into border regions once again, which led to a second noticeable increase in suicide and guerrilla attacks in the first six months of 2007.

The third uptick in violence took place in July 2007, as the infamous Lal Masjid crisis drew to its violent close. In Pakistan's capital of Islamabad, hundreds of militants, along with male and female religious madrassa students, barricaded themselves inside the Lal Masjid (Red Mosque).[62] After days of the government vacillating between inaction and appeasement with the protesters, the tense standoff ended with the military storming the mosque. In the ensuing clash, several hundred militants and civilians were killed. As the crisis reached its breaking point in July, there was an appreciable increase in suicide terrorism and militant violence as the Pakistani Taliban staged reprisal attacks against the Pakistani military.

The fourth upsurge in Taliban-sponsored violence occurred during a volatile election season (between October 2007 and March 2008) and targeted Pakistani politicians. By the fall of 2007, it was well understood that

59. "Amid U.S. Policy Disputes, Qaeda Grows in Pakistan," *New York Times,* June 30, 2008, available at http://www.nytimes.com/2008/06/30/washington/30tribal.html.

60. Ibid.

61. Ibid.

62. Schmidt, "The Unraveling of Pakistan," pp. 45–46.

the United States was attempting to engineer a power-sharing agreement between Pakistani president Pervez Musharraf and two-time former prime minister Benazir Bhutto. Bhutto issued a number of statements indicating her desire to confront militancy and tackle it aggressively and her strong pro-American foreign policy stance was already well known. Consequently, Bhutto and her Pakistan People's Party (PPP) were targeted on a number of occasions, including a suicide attack against a PPP rally on October 18, 2007, that killed over 134 people in Karachi. Although she never directly blamed President Musharraf, Bhutto accused several government officials of being sympathetic to the militants behind the bombing.[63]

The escalating series of attacks against Bhutto culminated in her assassination on December 27, 2007, as she was leaving a political rally in Rawalpindi, Pakistan. According to conflicting accounts, Bhutto was shot either in the neck or head and, seconds later, a suicide attacker detonated a bomb, killing more than 20 people and wounding over 50. Bhutto's death threw the country into a frenzy less than two weeks before the scheduled parliamentary elections. Until her assassination, Bhutto had navigated the turbulent world of Pakistani politics for 30 years, becoming the first female prime minister of Pakistan in 1988.[64]

American and Pakistani investigators stated that Baitullah Mehsud, the newly elected leader of the TTP, was behind the assassination, perhaps with assistance from Al Qaeda. Weeks before Bhutto's assassination, Al Qaeda operative Ayman al-Zawahiri issued a message warning that Bhutto and anyone else who participated in elections would be killed. In their statements to the press, Al Qaeda explicitly made clear that they viewed Bhutto as "a tool of U.S. influence."[65] Following Bhutto's death, the Pakistani elections were postponed until February. In the short term, it seemed that the TTP had succeeded in signaling their strength and resolve, as the new power brokers in Islamabad—Nawaz Sharif and Asif Ali Zardari—announced their intention to counter militancy with negotiation and compromise, not military crackdowns.

The TTP success was short lived, however, as U.S. pressure led newly elected President Asif Ali Zardari, Benazir Bhutto's widower, to call for

63. "After Bombing, Bhutto Assails Officials' Ties," *New York Times,* October 20, 2007, available at http://www.nytimes.com/2007/10/20/world/asia/20Pakistan.html.

64. "Bhutto Assassination Ignites Disarray," *New York Times,* December 28, 2007, available at http://www.nytimes.com/2007/12/28/world/asia/28pakistan.html.

65. "Bhutto's Death Helps Further Al Qaeda's Pakistan Agenda," *Christian Science Monitor,* December 31, 2007, available at http://www.csmonitor.com/2007/1231/p10s01-wosc.html.

new Pakistani Army operations against militants throughout Northwest Pakistan. As the Pakistani military moved against TTP strongholds in the Swat Valley, a fifth uptick in violence began in the summer of 2009. In the fall, the Pakistani Army invaded South Waziristan, and the TTP responded by staging attacks on security installations throughout the country. This wave of attacks continued into late 2009, with few signs of abatement.

Before 2009, the three previous Pakistani military operations into South Waziristan (2004, 2005, and 2008) had all ended poorly for the Pakistani Army and resulted in controversial peace deals with militant leaders. A distinct pattern of military failure[66] (ending in truce agreements) has continued for the last nine years. In large part, Pakistan's inability to ameliorate the security situation in the FATA and NWFP stems from two central deficiencies: a lack of government resolve and army sympathy for many militant groups.

The Pakistani government's lack of resolve is partly pragmatic—they are worried about opening up a front against every militant group in the region.[67] The Pakistani military insists that it lacks the resources necessary to fight the entire range of insurgent groups, including the Taliban, the TTP, and other minor militant organizations in the tribal areas. In addition, the Pakistani Army remains fixated on guarding the border with India because India has long been viewed as the most important security challenge facing Pakistan. These strategic calculations have led Pakistan to fight mainly against Pakistani Taliban groups, which they regard as the most proximate threat to their security. The army is more reluctant to intervene against the Afghan Taliban, who orchestrate the majority of their attacks across the border in Afghanistan.[68]

Within the Pakistani Army, many commanders are sympathetic to the Taliban controlling large sections of FATA and NWFP. Officers from the ISI and the army's Frontier Corps have supported insurgent groups that eventually ended up fighting against NATO and U.S. forces in Afghanistan.[69] "The army and the Taliban are friends," said an anonymous local tribal elder in South Waziristan, "Whenever a Taliban fighter is killed, army

---

66. For an additional information on the Pakistani Army's recurrent military failures in Northwest Pakistan, see Rashid, *Descent into Chaos*, "Chapter 13: Al Qaeda's Bolt-Hole," pp. 265–92.

67. "Why Pakistan Won't Fight the Afghan Taliban," *Time,* November 20, 2009, available at http://www.time.com/time/world/article/0,8599,1940777,00.html.

68. Ibid.

69. Jones, *In the Graveyard of Empires: America's War in Afghanistan*, p. 265.

officers go to his funeral. They bring money to the family."[70] The ineffec-
tual nature of Pakistani Army operations in the FATA and NWFP is the
result of the close relationship between segments of the Pakistani military
establishment and Taliban-affiliated militants.

In many ways, the Swat Valley of NWFP epitomizes this pattern of Pakistani military failure. During 2009, the Pakistani Army engaged in a recurrent battle with the Taliban for control of Swat. The army moved into the
region and, after sporadic fighting, quickly declared victory. The principal
result of the operation was that over 2.3 million locals were displaced.[71]
The Taliban's response was quite simple; they withdrew with the refugees
and returned to Swat less than a month after Pakistani troops were redeployed elsewhere.[72] The army responded with another operation and,
when fighting escalated, the Pakistani government signed a peace deal with
the militants that formally implemented sharia law in Swat.[73] U.S. Secretary
of State Hillary Rodham Clinton called the truce a sign that "the Pakistani
government is basically abdicating to the Taliban and to the extremists."[74]

In the summer of 2009, the Pakistani Army began their largest ground
offensive into South Waziristan. Although the campaign was prompted by
U.S. pressure, the Pakistani military seemed to conduct the operation with
a newfound resolve that was uncharacteristic of the previous offensives
in the region. "The military's movement is faster than in their previous
campaigns," said a former government official from North Waziristan.[75]
In October, the Pakistani Army launched a three-pronged attack in South
Waziristan that included over 28,000 troops backed with artillery and air
support.[76] Despite this unprecedented show of force, there has been little
evidence of heavy fighting during the entire operation. In fact, there are
indications that the vast majority of militants escaped the Pakistani Army's

70. "Right at the Edge," *New York Times,* September 5, 2008, available at http://www.
nytimes.com/2008/09/07/magazine/07pakistan-t.html.

71. "1.6 million Pakistani Refugees Return Home: UN," *Times of India,* August 22, 2009,
available at http://timesofindia.indiatimes.com/articleshow/4921578.cms.

72. "Taliban Resume Attacks in Swat Valley," *Wall Street Journal,* July 27, 2009, available
at http://online.wsj.com/article/SB124860097152481663.html.

73. "Pakistan Passes Swat Sharia Deal," *BBC News,* April 13, 2009, available at http://
news.bbc.co.uk/2/hi/south_asia/7996560.stm.

74. "Clinton Says Pakistan Is Abdicating to the Taliban," *Reuters UK,* April 23, 2009,
available at http://uk.reuters.com/article/idUKTRE53L69J20090423.

75. "Pakistani Army Captures Taliban Stronghold," *New York Times,* October 24, 2009,
available at http://www.nytimes.com/2009/10/25/world/asia/25pstan.html.

76. "As Pakistan Makes Gains, Resistance from Taliban," *New York Times,* October 19,
2009, available at http://www.nytimes.com/2009/10/20/world/asia/20pstan.html.

advance.[77] "They are fleeing in all directions," stated a Pakistani security official, who requested anonymity.[78] A TTP spokesman, Azam Tariq, told reporters, "We have not been defeated. We have voluntarily withdrawn into the mountains under a strategy that will trap the Pakistan army in the area."[79]

It appears that Pakistan's most recent military offensive has marginally succeeded in disrupting the TTP and destroying its headquarters in South Waziristan.[80] However, the operation has failed to noticeably degrade the TTP's operational capabilities. In the months following the invasion of South Waziristan, the TTP unleashed a deadly campaign of suicide and conventional bombing throughout Pakistan. An American embassy official, speaking on the condition of anonymity, said, "This is a battle of perceptions and beliefs. It's not really a battle about ground you seize or territory you control."[81]

In February 2010, the ISI captured Abu Waqas, a minor Afghan Taliban leader, and Mullah Abdul Ghani Baradar, the Afghan Taliban second-in-command, behind Mullah Omar.[82] Most observers acknowledge that the capture of Waqas and Baradar was less a matter of finding the militants than it was convincing the ISI to go after them. "If Pakistani officials had wanted to arrest him, they could have done it at any time," said Sher Mohammad Akhud Zada, a member of the Afghan Parliament.[83] To explain this apparent shift in ISI behavior, some American officials have suggested that senior Pakistani leaders, including the chief of the army, Ashfaq Parvez Kayani, have begun to question the value of Pakistan's ties to the Afghan Taliban.[84] While it remains too early to judge whether the ISI's decision

77. Rahimullah Yusufzai, "Assessing the Progress of Pakistan's South Waziristan Offensive," *CTC Sentinel*, 2, no. 12 (December 2009): 9; "Pakistani Military Encounters Little Fight as Militants Flee," *New York Times*, November 17, 2009, available at http://www.nytimes.com/2009/11/18/world/asia/18pstan.html.

78. "Pakistani Military Encounters Little Fight as Militants Flee," *New York Times*.

79. "Why Pakistan Won't Fight the Afghan Taliban," *Time*.

80. Yusufzai, "Assessing the Progress of Pakistan's South Waziristan Offensive," pp. 11–12.

81. "Pakistani Army's Victories Fail to Halt Taliban's Blows," *New York Times*, December 15, 2009, available at http://www.nytimes.com/2009/12/16/world/asia/16pstan.html.

82. "Blindfolded and in Chains: The Latest Taliban Commander to Be Captured in Pakistan after Deputy Is Seized," *Daily Mail*, February 18, 2010, available at http://www.dailymail.co.uk/news/worldnews/article-1251379/Top-Taliban-commander-Mullah-Abdul-Ghani-Baradar-captured-Pakistan.html.

83. Ibid.

84. "Secret Joint Raid Captures Taliban's Top Commander," *New York Times*, February 15, 2010, available at http://www.nytimes.com/2010/02/16/world/asia/16intel.html.

represents a more permanent change of heart, the capture of Waqas and Baradar showcases the critical role of ISI loyalty to the success of operations that hurt the Afghan Taliban.

Targeting and Weapons

During Phase 1, there were only 12 suicide attacks—nine of which targeted Shiite civilians. Geographically, these attacks took place outside the tribal areas, in Punjab, Sindh, and Balochistan Province. Lethality per attack was highest in Phase 1 because of the concentration on civilian targets in highly crowded areas such as Shiite mosques and funeral processions.

In Phase 2, there were 206 suicide attacks in Pakistan, and 62% were directed against military targets based in the tribal areas. Suicide attacks outside the tribal areas (17% of all attacks) primarily targeted politicians, especially during the violent election season from fall 2007 to spring 2008. In particular, pro-Western politicians, such as Benazir Bhutto, Nawaz Sharif, and former president Pervez Musharraf, were targeted on a number of occasions with suicide bombs. Lethality per attack was lower during this period because military targets tend to be harder to assail than unsuspecting civilians and political targets often travel with hundreds of vigilant bodyguards and special police, further reducing the likelihood of a successful attack. Throughout the entire campaign, car bombs have been the most prevalent weapon and are used in 42% of all suicide attacks. Belt bombs are the second most common weapon—used 21% of the time.

Local Community Support

Operating from bases along the Afghan-Pakistan border, Al Qaeda and the Taliban movement rely on local community support for shelter and recruitment. The local Pashtun community throughout Northwest Pakistan has historically been the most sympathetic to the Taliban cause. Pashtuns make up only 15% of the Pakistani population, but because of the nebulous border between Afghanistan and Pakistan, the Taliban's support base extends to Pashtun tribes across the porous border. This section examines the Taliban's broader support within Pakistan as well as support for Al Qaeda, the United States, and the Pakistani government.

It is important to note that the available polling data on Pakistan have severe limitations. The most salient problem is that poll data are not collected from the FATA due to continuing violence in the region. The FATA are where the vast majority of Al Qaeda and Taliban-affiliated fighters reside, so its exclusion means that poll data will not reflect their pro-Taliban attitudes. However, it is unclear how much this omission would affect the data as the FATA have around 6 million people,[85] compared to the total population of 175 million.[86]

Overall, the polling data suggest little support for the Taliban as an ideological movement, and opposition to the United States is the primary reason for what little support the Taliban does enjoy. Specifically, polls consistently show (1) continually high opposition to the United States, (2) opposition to the Taliban and Al Qaeda as they pursue their ideology, and (3) the more the Pakistani government has followed American policy, the more it has lost support among the local population.

Throughout the past decade, the Pakistani population has had an overwhelmingly negative opinion of the United States. From 1999 to the present, the United States' favorable rating in Pakistan never rose above 27%.[87] Following the U.S. invasion of Afghanistan in 2001, opinion polls conducted by the Pew Global Attitudes Project indicated that only 10% of Pakistani respondents had a favorable view of the United States.[88] Today, 64% of respondents identified the United States as an enemy, while only 10% considered the United States a partner.[89] In addition, distrust of American foreign policy runs deep; only 22% of respondents believed that the United States considers Pakistan's interest when making decisions.[90] Despite these negative views, 53% of respondents expressed the desire for improved relations between the United States and Pakistan.

Over the last several years, opinion surveys have shown that support for the Taliban and Al Qaeda is in decline. However, Pakistanis did not

85. "Analysis: Pakistan's Tribal Frontiers," *BBC News,* December 14, 2001, available at http://news.bbc.co.uk/2/hi/south_asia/1711316.stm.

86. CIA World Factbook, *Pakistan,* available at https://www.cia.gov/library/publications/the-world-factbook/geos/pk.html.

87. Pew Global Attitudes Project, "Islam and West: Searching for Common Ground," July 18, 2006, available at http://pewglobal.org/commentary/display.php?AnalysisID=1009.

88. Ibid.

89. Pew Global Attitudes Project, "Pakistani Public Opinion: Growing Concerns about Extremism, Continuing Discontent with U.S.," August 13, 2009, p. 17, available at http://pewglobal.org/reports/display.php?ReportID=265.

90. Ibid., p. 1.

always have such unfavorable views of these groups. A month after the September 11 attacks, a Gallop poll found that 83% of Pakistanis said they would support the Taliban in a conflict between the Taliban and the United States.[91] In addition, 82% of respondents identified Osama bin Laden as a "Mujahid" (Muslim holy warrior), not a terrorist, and only 12% believed he was responsible for the September 11 attacks.

Past support for Al Qaeda and the Taliban has given way to strong condemnation of both groups. The most marked shift in opinion occurred from 2008 to 2009, where, in 2008, 33% held a negative view of the Taliban and, nearly a year later, 70% rated it unfavorably. Similarly, the percentage of Pakistanis with an unfavorable opinion of Al Qaeda increased from 34% to 61% during the same period. Among the three most populous provinces in Pakistan, 67% in Punjab Province have a negative view of the Taliban, compared to 75% in NWFP and 82% in Sindh.[92]

Over the past two years, opinions about Osama bin Laden have also grown more negative. In 2009, nearly half (47%) of Pakistanis said they had little or no confidence in bin Laden to do the right things regarding world affairs compared to 18% who indicated they had at least some confidence in him.[93] Compared to a 2004 poll that found Osama bin Laden was viewed favorably by 65% of Pakistanis, the 2009 poll marks a clear shift in public support away from the Al Qaeda leader.[94]

There is also rising concern among Pakistanis about Muslim extremism. In 2009, 69% of Pakistanis indicated that they were worried extremists could take over the country. In turbulent NWFP, 74% of respondents worried about an extremist takeover, along with 70% in Punjab Province and 69% in Sindh Province.[95]

One of the most encouraging trends in Pakistani opinion polls has been a growing aversion to suicide terrorism among the Muslim community. In 2002, 33% of Muslim respondents viewed suicide terrorism as often/sometimes justified while 43% found suicide terrorism rarely/never justified.

91. "Gallop Poll on Current Pakistan Crisis," *YesPakistan.com,* October 13, 2001, available at http://www.yespakistan.com/afghancrisis/gallup_survey.asp.

92. Pew Global Attitudes Project, "Pakistani Public Opinion: Growing Concerns about Extremism," pp. 4–5.

93. Ibid., p. 10.

94. The Pew Research Center for the People and the Press, "A Year after Iraq War: Mistrust of America in Europe Ever Higher, Muslim Anger Persists," March 16, 2004, p. 21.

95. Pew Global Attitudes Project, "Pakistani Public Opinion: Growing Concerns about Extremism," p. 8.

By 2009, only 5% thought suicide terrorism was often/sometimes justified while those that indicated "rarely/never" rose to 90%.[96]

Views of the national government have become more negative in recent years and, in 2009, Pakistanis gave their national government the lowest approval ratings in a decade. In 2002, 72% of respondents believed the national government was having a positive influence in Pakistan, but by 2009, that number had fallen to 40% with a majority (53%) indicating that the government had a negative influence on the way things are going in the country. In 2009, Pakistan President Zardari received even more negative ratings than the national government as 68% of those polled thought the president was having a negative impact on Pakistan.[97] These poll numbers underscore the point that the more Pakistan has acquiesced to U.S. demands, the more it has lost support among the local population.

After examining the public opinion data, it becomes clear that Pakistanis are (1) consistently disenchanted with U.S. involvement in the region, (2) increasingly disenchanted with Al Qaeda and the Taliban as they pursue their ideological agenda inside Pakistan, and (3) increasingly disenchanted with the central government as it sides with the United States. The Pakistani populace appears to support those agents that would preserve their current way of life, and they take a negative view of those who would challenge it.

Recruitment

Of the 218 documented suicide attacks that took place between 2002 and 2009, CPOST has identified the nationalities of 35 attackers: 28 from Pakistan, 1 from Bangladesh, 1 from Uzbekistan, and 5 from Afghanistan. This lack of demographic data is unsurprising; it is fairly common for terrorist organizations to conceal the identity of their attackers during the "heart" of a current campaign because they want to avoid retribution against the families and communities that support martyrdom.

Because of the small sample of identified attackers, it is difficult to reach definitive conclusions about the demographic makeup of attackers. The available data indicate that the Pakistani suicide attackers are a localized reaction to Western forces in Central Asia and the unpopular political and

96. Ibid., p. 10.
97. Ibid., pp. 13, 29.

military alliance between Pakistan and the United States. There is insufficient evidence to support the idea that the Pakistani suicide campaign is the result of a global jihad comprised of foreign fighters. This is not to dispute the existence of foreign fighters in Pakistan, but simply that, throughout the suicide campaign, most estimates of the number of foreign fighters have been below that of indigenous Taliban fighters.[98] Without evidence of more foreign fighters being used for suicide terrorism, we can only conclude that foreign fighters represent a small portion of suicide bombers. However, there have been recent indications that the number of foreign fighters in Pakistan is in flux. In the past, American intelligence officials have stated that the number of foreign fighters has ranged between a few dozen and several hundred.[99] Recent Pakistani estimates place that number around 8,000, but with over half being from nearby Uzbekistan.[100] Other reports indicate that many foreign fighters are leaving Pakistan for Somalia or Yemen.[101] Regardless of the exact numbers, it is clear that U.S. involvement in the region is the primary impetus behind any influx of fighters to Central Asia. Pakistani senator Ibrahim Khan said, "A lot of young Muslims are coming to Afghanistan to fight the U.S. troops who, they believe, have come to Afghanistan not to fight terrorism but to occupy more Muslim lands, including Pakistan, and to plunder their resources."[102]

Despite the lack of data on suicide attackers, most experts agree on why militancy and suicide bombing has become prevalent in Pakistan. Pakistani investigators believe that the sudden U.S.-inspired crackdown on militant Islamist organizations provided the impetus for local citizens to take up

98. For estimates of foreign fighters in Pakistan: "Militant Gains in Pakistan Said to Draw Fighters," *New York Times,* July 10, 2008, available at http://www.nytimes.com/2008/07/10/world/asia/10terror.html; "Taliban and Allies Tighten Grip in Northern Pakistan," *New York Times,* December 11, 2006, available at http://www.nytimes.com/2006/12/11/world/asia/11pakistan.html; "Pakistan Says 300 Foreign Militants Operating in Two Tribal Regions," *Islamic Republic News Agency/GlobalSecurity.org,* December 7, 2008, available at http://www.globalsecurity.org/wmd/library/news/pakistan/2008/pakistan-081207-irna01.htm; "Some in Qaeda Leave Pakistan for Somalia and Yemen," *New York Times,* June 11, 2009, available at http://www.nytimes.com/2009/06/12/world/12terror.html; "Pakistani Senator Says Uzbek Militants Active in Tribal Area," *BBC Worldwide Monitoring,* September 22, 2009.

99. "Pakistan Imposes Sanctions on Tribesmen for Failure to Give Up Militants," *Agence France Presse,* May 30, 2004.

100. "Pakistani Senator Says Uzbek Militants Active in Tribal Area," *BBC Worldwide Monitoring,* September 22, 2009.

101. "Some in Qaeda Leave Pakistan for Somalia and Yemen," *New York Times,* June 11, 2009.

102. Ibid.

arms against the Pakistani government.[103] Militant groups receive financial assistance from Al Qaeda, who primarily recruit members and potential suicide bombers from the ranks of "the poor and enraged."[104]

Fateh Mohammad Burfat, head of the Criminology Department at the University of Karachi in Pakistan, said that suicide bombers are "a new breed [of militants], as suicide bombings are a post 9/11 phenomenon here." According to Burfat, suicide bombers are "unemployed, illiterate, and belong to poor social strata," and they "perceive the U.S. military actions in Iraq and Afghanistan as hostile acts against the Muslim world."[105] Jayshree Bajoria, journalist and member of the Council on Foreign Relations, posited that pro-Taliban tribes in the FATA morphed into "a mainstream Taliban force of their own as a reaction to the Pakistani army's incursion into the tribal areas."[106] Although most men in Pakistan's tribal areas grew up carrying arms, many experts believe it is only recently that they have begun to organize themselves around Islamic ideology similar to that of the Afghan Taliban.

Drone Attacks and Suicide Terrorism

Since 2004, the United States has increasingly relied on Predator drones to attack targets deep within the tribal regions of Pakistan. The Pakistani government has prohibited U.S. troops from engaging targets into Pakistan, and drone attacks are one appealing solution to this proscription. In the last several years, unmanned drones have had considerable success attacking Taliban, Al Qaeda, and TTP targets. According to some U.S. officials, drone strikes have paved the way for a "complete Al Qaeda defeat" in the tribal areas of Pakistan.[107] Despite these optimistic assessments, the recent escalation in the number of drone strikes could be counterproductive. As some scholars have proposed, the primary concern is that drone attacks will generate public anger and collateral damage, both of which feed off each other and facilitate the recruiting efforts of Al Qaeda and

103. "Who Are the Suicide Bombers? Pakistan's Answer," *Christian Science Monitor,* June 17, 2005, available at http://www.csmonitor.com/2005/0617/p07s01-wome.html.

104. Ibid.

105. Ibid.

106. Jayshree Bajoria, "Pakistan's New Generation of Terrorists," *Council on Foreign Relations,* February 6, 2008, available at http://www.cfr.org/publication/15422/.

107. "U.S. Officials: Al-Qaida Leadership Cadre 'Decimated,'" *Morning Edition,* February 3, 2009, available at http://www.npr.org/templates/story/story.php?storyId=100160836.

the Taliban movement.[108] This is not to say the United States should completely abandon the policy of drone strikes to kill terrorist leaders, but these risks suggest that a more selective use of this tactic could minimize potential costs, while preserving the possibility of an extraordinary outcome by a fortuitous strike.

Within Pakistan, there is widespread public indignation toward drone attacks. The Pakistani government has repeatedly protested these attacks as an infringement on its sovereignty and condemned the civilian deaths that have resulted from drone strikes. In January 2010, there were over a dozen CIA drone attacks in Pakistan.[109] A Pakistani newspaper claimed that these attacks killed 123 civilians and only three Al Qaeda operatives.[110] While these numbers may be far from accurate, it is nearly impossible for the United States to counter these accusations. Anger over collateral damage has been echoed in public opinion polls that show drone attacks to be very unpopular among the Pakistani populace. In a 2009 Al Jazeera poll, 67% of Pakistanis reported strong opposition to drone attacks by the United States.[111] Only 9% supported the use of drone strikes.[112] A May–June 2009 Pew poll found that 95% of Pakistanis felt that drone strikes were bad or very bad for Pakistan.[113] This unpopularity of drone strikes has a clearly negative impact on the perception of the United States.

There is also increasing evidence that the Taliban and Al Qaeda use drone strikes to recruit suicide bombers for their campaigns in Pakistan and Afghanistan. In January 2006, a Predator drone destroyed a building thought to house Ayman al-Zawahiri, Al Qaeda's second-in-command. The strike missed al-Zawahiri by several hours and ended up killing numerous civilians. As Ahmed Rashid noted, "The missile attack [aimed at al-Zawahiri] killed five senior AQ figures but generated enormous public anger as politicians accused Musharraf of allowing Washington to undermine Pakistan's sovereignty."[114] In some cases, this public anger has led to suicide

108. Daniel Byman, "Taliban vs. Predator," *Foreign Affairs*, March 18, 2009, available at http://www.foreignaffairs.com/articles/64901/daniel-byman/taliban-vs-predator.

109. Neither the CIA nor the U.S. military release information regarding the number of drone attacks. This number is based on an unofficial CPOST count using open source documents.

110. "US Drones Killed 123 Civilians, Three Al Qaeda Men in January," *The News*, March 1, 2010, available at http://www.thenews.com.pk/daily_detail.asp?id=221847.

111. "Pakistan: State of the Nation," *Al Jazeera*.

112. Ibid.

113. Katherine Tiedemann, "Parsing the Pakistan Polling," *Foreign Policy*, August 14, 2009, available at http://afpak.foreignpolicy.com/posts/2009/08/14/parsing_the_pakistan_polling.

114. Rashid, *Descent into Chaos*, p. 276.

terrorism. Eighteen-year-old Mudasar from Khyber Province enrolled in a camp for suicide bombers after he watched a Pakistani television report that showed the grim footage of dead corpses lying amid the rubble of the house. Several months later, his family received an anonymous phone call informing them that their son had "carried out a suicide operation inside of Afghanistan."[115]

Journalist David Rohdes was held hostage by the Taliban for 11 months and witnessed the complex effects of CIA drone strikes. Rohdes commented, "The drones killed many senior commanders and hindered their operations. Yet the Taliban were able to garner recruits in their aftermath by exaggerating the number of civilian casualties."[116] This trade-off is one of the inevitable consequences of drone attacks, and it is important to assess whether the net benefit of drone strikes outweigh the potential harm.

The most salient question for the Obama administration is whether mass drone attacks can be used in lieu of heavy ground forces along the Afghan-Pakistan border. From 2004 to 2009, drone strikes killed 21 high value Al Qaeda and Taliban targets.[117] However, there is good reason to doubt whether the operational capacity of the Taliban and Al Qaeda has been reduced by these attacks. The year 2009 featured 34 drone attacks, the highest number on record, and yet suicide and IED attacks intensified in late 2009.

Recent scholarship has suggested that leadership decapitation—one of the chief objectives of CIA drone strikes—is generally ineffective.[118] The first comprehensive data set on leadership decapitation looks at 298 cases of leadership decapitation from 1945 to 2004 and shows that the marginal value of leadership decapitation is often negative. In other words, targeting terrorist leaders can actually slow a group's rate of decline. Interestingly, groups with intact leadership fall apart sooner than groups that undergo leadership decapitation. In addition, targeting the leadership of militant groups may strengthen the group's resolve, result in retaliatory attacks, and increase public support for the organization that benefits recruitment.[119]

The succession of Pakistani Taliban leaders illustrates the dubious ef-

115. "Right at the Edge," *New York Times.*

116. "A Drone Strike and Dwindling Hope," *New York Times,* October 20, 2009, available at http://www.nytimes.com/2009/10/21/world/asia/21hostage.html.

117. Unofficial CPOST count using open source documents. See n. 109 above.

118. Jenna Jordan, "When Heads Roll: Assessing the Effectiveness of Leadership Decapitation," *Security Studies* 18, no. 4 (October 2009): 719–55.

119. Ibid.

fects of drone attacks on operational capacity. Barbara Elias, the Director of the Afghanistan, Pakistan, and Taliban Project at the National Security Archive, noted that although former TTP leader, Baitullah Mehsud, was killed by a CIA drone, Mehsud "rose to prominence after a Predator strike killed South Waziristan's rising Taliban commander, Nek Mohammed, in 2004, and Mehsud has already been replaced by a deputy, Hakimullah Mehsud."[120] As suicide attacks intensified in late 2009, there is little evidence that Hakimullah is any less of a threat than Baitullah or that the TTP has been degraded operationally by the drone attacks.

What is clear is that widespread anger over U.S. drone strikes contributes to the already negative image of the United States in Pakistan. The Obama Administration has made Pakistan a central part of its Afghanistan policy and continued use of CIA drones makes it more difficult for Pakistani leadership to assist the politically unpopular United States. In addition, there are indications that the heavy use of drone attacks may be doing more harm than good—working not only to strengthen the resolve of the groups targeted but also providing opportunities for recruitment by angering the Pakistani populace. We conclude that the Obama administration is not well-served by relying on a policy that depends on increasingly numerous drone attacks in lieu of heavy military forces. The Obama administration needs a balanced strategy among military, political, and economic initiatives, not one that simply trades off military alternatives.

120. Elias, "Know Thine Enemy."

CHAPTER SIX

Al Qaeda

O n September 10, 2001, much of the world had paid little attention to the terrorist organization known as Al Qaeda.[1] The following day, that changed. Al Qaeda and its nominal leader, Osama bin Laden, became household names across the globe. However, their mission did not begin on September 11. They had already begun their campaign several years earlier, and the organization itself has its roots in an ideology that reaches back much earlier into the 20th century.[2] Figure 6.1 shows that the campaign itself began well before 2001, and has continued despite the advent of the Global War on Terror.

The group itself formed in Afghanistan following the jihad against the Soviet occupation, but it did not take up the cause of jihad against the United States and its allies until the aftermath of the first Gulf War. This chapter outlines the group's origins, its visionary goals of restoring the Caliphate,[3] its strategic calculus aimed at removing Western military and

1. Major contributors to this chapter were Chad Levinson and Maryam Alimirah.

2. Recent literature on Al Qaeda includes Peter L. Bergen, *Holy War, Inc.: Inside the Secret World of Osama bin Laden* (New York: Simon & Schuster, 2001); Rohan Gunaratna, *Inside Al Qaeda: Global Network of Terror* (New York: Berkeley Books, 2003); Marc Sageman, *Understanding Terror Networks* (Philadelphia: University of Pennsylvania Press, 2004); Marc Sageman, *Leaderless Jihad: Terror Networks in the Twenty-First Century,* (Philadelphia: University of Pennsylvania Press, 2008); Brynjar Lia, *Architect of Global Jihad: The Life of Al Qaeda Strategist Abu Mus'ab al-Suri* (New York: Columbia University Press, 2009); Michael Scheuer, *Through Our Enemies' Eyes: Osama bin Laden, Radical Islam, and the Future of America, Revised Edition* (Dulles, VA: Potomac Books, 2006); Omar Nasiri, *Inside the Jihad: My Life with Al Qaeda* (New York: Basic Books, 2006); Lawrence Wright, *The Looming Tower: Al-Qaeda and the Road to 9/11* (New York: Vintage Books, 2006); Terry McDermott, *Perfect Soldiers: The 9/11 Hijackers: Who They Were, Why They Did It* (New York: HarperCollins, 2005).

3. The Caliphate is a rough Islamic equivalent to the governing system more generally known as "Empire." The term itself derives from Arabic word for "successor," and the

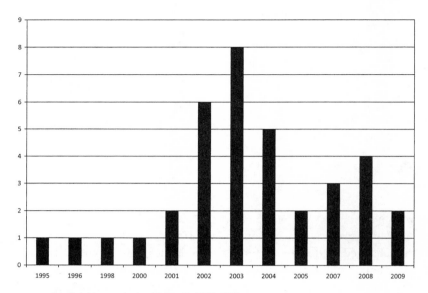

FIGURE 6.1 Suicide attacks by Al Qaeda, 1995–2009

political influence from Muslim lands, and its tactical objectives borne of operational constraints and opportunities. It also examines the group's internal cohesiveness as well as its external alliances with other organizations. Finally, it assesses Arab public support for Al Qaeda's goals and objectives, its targeting strategy, use of weapons, recruitment, and the trajectory of the campaign.

The Al Qaeda suicide terrorism campaign has never produced a high volume of attacks, but they have nearly always been "spectacular" in the sense that they have killed large numbers of people, have been concentrated on high value and high profile targets, and have attracted substantial attention worldwide. The campaign has unfolded in three major phases. First, between 1995 and 2002, Al Qaeda focused on attacking the United States directly,

Caliphate survived in one form or another from the death of Muhammad in the year 632 AD to the abandonment of the Ottoman Empire shortly after World War I. It is an expressly transnational and theocratic mode of governance, rejecting both of the core characteristics of the Westphalian state system (itself premised on the autonomy of nation-states and their independence from centralized religious control). Thus, the idea that Al Qaeda aspires to restore the Caliphate means that they wish to reunite the Muslim world (*ummah*) under a single theocratic governing authority.

targeting U.S. embassies, military forces stationed in Muslim countries, and the U.S. homeland. Second, between 2002 and 2005, they shifted their efforts to attacking the homelands of allies fighting alongside the United States in the Middle East, particularly in Iraq. Third, they returned their attention to attacking the United States directly beginning in 2006 and continuing to the present day. As we discuss later in this chapter, this shifting focus reveals a strategic calculation on the part of Al Qaeda, aimed ultimately at coercing the withdrawal of Western military forces from Muslim territory.

Origins of Al Qaeda

Among the most widely believed notions regarding the origins of Al Qaeda is that its beginnings can be traced to U.S. support of the mujahideen freedom fighters in Afghanistan during their resistance to Soviet occupation forces in the 1980s. The so-called blowback theory of Al Qaeda's ascendance has it that the United States itself helped to create the terrorist organization that visited such death and destruction upon it on September 11, 2001. In an effort to achieve a Cold War victory, the United States failed to observe the well-known rule of unintended consequences, and that by adding fuel to a wildfire, the world's sole surviving superpower cultivated a militant terrorist organization that subsequently turned on its former benefactor. As tidy as this theory appears, this blowback theory is, at best, only marginally true.

Indeed, Al Qaeda's emir-general Osama bin Laden did travel to Afghanistan to join the mujahideen. Bin Laden is known as a talented motivator and skilled organizer. Furthermore, he did indeed distinguish himself in battle as an able mobilizer of men and resources. However, neither bin Laden nor any of the other Afghan Arabs[4] figured prominently in the success of the Afghan resistance to Soviet control. The U.S. involvement in this campaign ran exclusively through the Pakistani Inter-Services Intelligence (ISI). The ISI channeled American resources to their own locally developed Afghan sources. Of the seven parties with which the ISI cooperated, only the Hizb party was significantly tied to bin Laden. Hizb's leader, Gulbuddin Hekmatyar, shared a common ideological fanaticism with bin Laden, and the two men "worked closely together." However,

---

4. Afghan Arabs are those who traveled from Arab countries to join the anti-Soviet jihad.

far from being an integral part of the successful effort to fight the Soviets, "[Hekmatyar] did excel at killing Afghans."[5] So, while bin Laden did benefit from U.S. intervention in Afghanistan, he did so indirectly and in affiliation with a figure who was more subversive than supportive of the freedom fighter movement. There is little evidence that the United States directly trained, armed, or equipped bin Laden himself, separately from the tens of thousands of mujahideen who were indirect beneficiaries of U.S. military support.

Nonetheless, Al Qaeda's origins can be traced, partially, to the Afghan anti-Soviet jihad. Initially, bin Laden worked as a protégé to Sheikh Abdallah Azzam, helping to organize the foreign Muslim fighters. Upon the announcement of the Soviet's withdrawal, the idea of establishing al qaeda ("the base") first gained traction. The premise was to remain in Afghanistan, establishing it as a base of operations upon which to build a worldwide jihad. Azzam took a contradictory position, and some believe his murder in 1989 was prompted by his refusal to support the al qaeda vision.[6] The principal support for this new global vision came from members of the Egyptian Islamic Jihad who had traveled to Afghanistan to join the jihad, most notably Ayman al-Zawahiri, the physician who became (and remains) bin Laden's top lieutenant, whose goals included destabilizing nominally Muslim governments that he considered debased, including the regime in his own native Egypt. With the death of Azzam, bin Laden and al-Zawahiri were left standing as the two pillars upon which Al Qaeda was built and still stands to this day. None of the suicide attackers of the past 15 years were with bin Laden in the early days of Al Qaeda, further evidence against the "blowback" theory.

All three of these leadership figures, Azzam, bin Laden, and al-Zawahiri, are connected to Sayyid Qutb, the mid-century intellectual and ideological leader of the Muslim Brotherhood, founded in 1928. Both Azzam and al-Zawahiri had been members of the Brotherhood (Azzam in Jordan, al-Zawahiri in Egypt), and bin Laden studied with Qutb's brother, Muhammad.[7] Qutb's central guiding principle was a dedication to sharia law and the belief that modern Muslim nations were illegitimate. His mission, thus, was resistance and jihad aimed not only at invading non-Muslim forces, but also against what he considered secular Arab regimes. Al-Zawahiri

    5. Bergen, *Holy War, Inc.*
    6. Sageman, *Understanding Terror Networks.*
    7. Gunaratna, *Inside Al Qaeda.*

carried this idea to Afghanistan, and upon the defeat of the Soviets and the assassination of Azzam, joined bin Laden and helped convert a portion of the Afghan Arabs who had volunteered for a local jihad into the terrorist organization we know as Al Qaeda.

In sum, the notion that the United States created Al Qaeda is revealed as overly simplistic. Osama bin Laden and Ayman al-Zawahiri both did indeed travel to Afghanistan to join the anti-Soviet jihad, where they met and joined forces in creating Al Qaeda. However, this does not support the narrative that emerges from common beliefs in the "blowback" theory, which has it that having defeated the Soviets, a well-supplied and battle-hardened fighting force simply pivoted and aimed its U.S.-provided training and materiel at its former infidel benefactors. Rather, Al Qaeda has its roots an 80-year-old Islamic social movement, and the teachings of one of its chief ideologues. It formed out of the remnants of an Afghan Arab faction (one that contributed little to the actual jihad against the Soviets) in cooperation with imported members of Egyptian Islamic Jihad. In short, the Afghan freedom fighter movement merely provided the opportunity for al-Zawahiri and bin Laden to come together and form Al Qaeda.

However, it took a significant geopolitical event to mobilize the nascent Al Qaeda group to action with a series of terrorist attacks executed by a stream of new recruits. As Marc Sageman notes, "The 1990–1991 Gulf War brought U.S. troops to the Arabian Peninsula. The movement that became the global Salafi jihad might have faded but for the continued presence of these troops. The Salafi mujahedin interpreted this presence as an infidel invasion of the Land of the Two Holy Places. It became the focus of Salafi resentment against the West and breathed new life into the movement."[8] Although U.S. intervention was not necessary for the initial conception of Al Qaeda, it was crucial for the mobilization of the group to violent action.

Goals and Objectives

Among the most popular interpretations of Al Qaeda's objectives among U.S. political commentators and policy makers are the notions that the group wishes to change American cultural values or that they simply view killing Americans as a goal unto itself. When politicians claim that the terrorists "hate us for our freedoms," the clear implication is that their actions

8. Sageman, *Understanding Terror Networks.*

are motivated first by personal hatred and that this hatred, in turn, is motivated by the way we live our lives. It is generally good policy to be skeptical of interpretations that attribute conflict and suffering to one's own virtues. Indeed, the available evidence supports the argument that, rather than our values, culture, or religious status, Al Qaeda's terrorism is aimed at changing the foreign policies of Western nations with respect to military deployments and support of governing regimes in predominantly Muslim countries.

In examining Al Qaeda's goals and objectives, it is helpful to divide them analytically into three parts: tactics, strategy, and vision. In ascending order, these refer to 1) the immediate intended outcomes of their missions, 2) the consequences of those effects, consisting primarily of the anticipated responses of their adversaries, allies, and other audiences, and 3) the shape of the world they hope eventually to create. In any campaign these three levels of goals and objectives ideally work together. However, as will be seen in this case, success at one level does not unerringly and automatically lead to further success one level higher. Tactical success may backfire, leading to strategically adverse outcomes. Furthermore, strategic success might be undermined by the strategy's service to an unrealistic world vision.

First, objectives at the tactical level are the most readily observable. Al Qaeda's specialty, as it were, is mass-casualty suicide terrorism targeting Western populations, either in the victims' home countries or in Muslim lands with a substantial Western presence. Several times, these tactics were successfully carried out, most notably on September 11, 2001, in New York and Washington, DC; on October 12, 2002, in Bali; on March 11, 2004 in Madrid; and on July 7, 2005, in London.[9] Many more times, police and intelligence agencies have thwarted planned attacks. Insofar as one is examining tactical goals, Al Qaeda terrorists do indeed aim to kill large numbers of civilians.

However, to assert that simply killing Westerners represents their ultimate objective would ignore both strategy and their ultimate world vision. At the second level, these acts of mass-casualty suicide terrorism were all intended to bring about a change in the victim nations' foreign policy.[10] The

9. Only the first of these attacks is known with certainty to have been planned by Al Qaeda proper. The others were either carried out by Al Qaeda affiliate groups, inspired by Al Qaeda operations and ideology, or retroactively supported by Al Qaeda communiqués. The issue of Al Qaeda affiliation, inspiration, and public support will be addressed in later sections of this report.

10. Max Abrahms, "Al Qaeda's Scorecard: A Progress Report on Al Qaeda's Objectives," *Studies in Conflict and Terrorism* 29, no. 5 (2006): 509–29.

attacks in the United States were motivated by American military presence on the Arabian Peninsula. The attacks in both London and Madrid were aimed at punishing the British and Spanish people for their government's involvement in the invasion and occupation of Iraq. In short, the strategy was to take the willing out of the coalition.

Finally, the ultimate visionary objective of Al Qaeda goes back to the ideology of Qutb: to revert to a more purely Islamic world. This requires both the expulsion of Western infidel military and even civilian populations from Muslim lands, as well as the overthrow of allegedly corrupt, debased, nominally Muslim domestic governing regimes. In short, it entails the restoration of the Caliphate, and the reemergence of an authentic Muslim empire from Indonesia to North Africa. We can assess the strategic implications of tactical successes, but it is difficult at this point to address how likely Al Qaeda's vision is to follow an as yet hypothetical strategic victory. First, the tactical successes of 9/11, 7/7, and 3/11 reveal a mixed strategic result. In the first case, the strategic result was an abject failure. Rather than decrease military presence in the Middle East and Arabia, the West increased its military deployment to the tune of several hundred thousand additional troops. On the other hand, Spain withdrew its forces from Iraq after 3/11.[11] Finally, Britain did not substantially alter its position in response to 7/7. With respect to assessing the prospects for the success of Al Qaeda's vision, the outcome is far from settled, and the objective so lofty that it seems somewhat absurd to predict the reemergence of the Caliphate—it is no closer today that before Al Qaeda came into being and even the complete withdrawal of Western forces from Muslim lands would hardly ensure it.

Separating the goals and objectives into these three levels affords us some insight into the adaptability of Al Qaeda's thinking, and to observe a prioritization among the various levels. It seems at first self-evident that vision trumps strategy and strategy trumps tactics. However, it gives us some purchase on several of the central questions about the reasons underpinning the terrorism campaign. For instance, the notion that "they hate us for our values" and are motivated primarily by factors intrinsic to their particular religion holds up poorly when one examines the strategic adaptations that have taken place over the course of the campaign. If such

11. For a debate on the strategic success of the Madrid bombings, see William Rose, Rysia Murphy, and Max Abrahms, "Does Terrorism Ever Work? The 2004 Madrid Train Bombings," *International Security* 32, no. 1 (2007): 185–92; and Max Abrahms, "Why Terrorism Does Not Work," *International Security* 31, no. 2 (2006): 42–78.

notions were correct, we might expect to see one or more of the following patterns: 1) Al Qaeda attacks on nations that are either officially or universally non-Muslim, such as Israel (Jewish) or the nations of South America (Christian); 2) nations or institutions that participated in the Crusades such as France, Italy, and the Catholic Church; or 3) nations that are overwhelmingly secular, such as Sweden. We see none of these patterns. Instead, we observe behavior that demonstrates a strategic logic aimed at removing Western political and military influence from Muslim territory.

Subsequent to the attacks of September 11, the United States vastly increased its military presence in the Middle East and Central Asia, just the opposite outcome they were attempting to create. In the face of this strategic backfire, Al Qaeda's response was to execute attacks against Spanish and British populations as well as Australians in Bali, three prominent but second-tier participants in the so-called coalition of the willing. This new strategic wrinkle indicated a shift in thinking by Al Qaeda. Instead of attacking their main enemy, they attacked slightly weaker enemies whose withdrawal from the coalition would be the most costly to the principal occupying nation (the United States). In short, their new strategic calculation was: given the greater presence of the United States in the Middle East, what was the best way to increase its political and military burden?

Those who interpret Al Qaeda's goals as death-seeking and nihilism seem to do so largely from the perspective of broadly observing their tactics: the killing of unsuspecting innocents by suicide terrorists. However, when one looks more closely at the strategic considerations of specific attacks, a different picture emerges. Rather than merely seeking to kill as many infidels as possible, the pattern of attacks by Al Qaeda reveals a strategic adaptation in the service of an unchanging vision. First, they tried to remove U.S. forces from Muslim lands by attacking our embassies in Nairobi and Tanzania, the U.S.S. Cole in the Yemeni port of Aden, and the Pentagon and World Trade Center. When the United States responded by occupying Iraq, this signaled a strategic miscalculation by Al Qaeda, to which they responded by targeting our allies in order to make the continued occupation of Iraq as costly as possible. Both of these strategies ultimately support the objective of recreating a Middle East that is free from the presence of Western military forces.

The question remains as to what role religion plays in the goals and objectives of Al Qaeda. At the tactical level, regarding the use of suicide terrorism, the waters have been muddied by those who highlight fatwas that call for jihad against the West. More accurately, these ad hoc edicts remove the more fundamental religious injunctions against the killing of innocents and against suicide by casting suicide terrorism as martyrdom. The real logic behind the choice of suicide tactics is not religious, but in the service of the strategic objective of removing the Western presence in the Middle East. Al-Zawahiri lays out the logic in four principles:

1. The need to inflict the maximum casualties against the opponent, for this is the language understood by the West, no matter how much time and effort such operations take.
2. The need to concentrate on the method of martyrdom operations as the most successful way of inflicting damage against the opponent and the least costly to the Mujahedin in terms of casualties.
3. The targets as well as the type and method of weapons used must be chosen to have an impact on the structure of the enemy and deter it enough to stop its brutality, arrogance, and disregard for all taboos and customs. It must restore the struggle to its real size.
4. To reemphasize what we have already explained, we reiterate that focusing on the domestic enemy [corrupt Muslim governments] alone will not be feasible at this stage.[12]

Thus, suicide terrorism is chosen not because of some fanatical desire for death, but based on a calculation of the enemy's perceptions, the constraints of asymmetry in military capabilities, and their expectations of the enemy's responses.

At the strategic level, the targeting of the United States and its allies reflects a response to what they interpret as our unjust interference in and control over the affairs of Muslim countries, not (in itself) our presumed Judeo-Christian religious culture: "The call to wage war against America was made because America has spear-headed the crusade against the Islamic nation, sending tens of thousands of its troops to the land of the two Holy Mosques [Saudi Arabia] over and above its meddling in its affairs and its politics, and its support of the oppressive, corrupt and tyrannical regime that is in control. These are the reasons behind the singling out of America as a target."[13] They further interpret U.S. policy in the Middle East as part of a plan to continue and extend what they see as the deliberate fragmen-

12. Ayman al-Zawahiri, "Knights under the Prophet's Banner," *al Sharq al Awsati* (December 2–10, 2001).
13. "Interview with Osama bin Laden," *Frontline*, May 1998.

tation of a unified Islamic nation: "There is a [U.S.] plan to divide Iraq into three—one in the north for the Muslim Kurds, a state in the middle, and a third in the south. The same applies to the land of the two mosques [Saudi Arabia] where there is a plan to divide it into a state for the two mosques, another state for oil in the eastern region, and a state in the middle."[14] In short, they see the United States as the primary actor disrupting the unity of the ummah and sustaining the viability of debased pseudo-Islamic regimes. This leads directly to the strategic objectives of ejecting Western forces, or failing that, making it as costly as possible for the United States to sustain the occupation of Middle Eastern lands.

The most stable, unchanging aspect of the Al Qaeda's goals and objectives is at the level of vision. The operational (i.e., strategic and tactical) goals remain secondary to this vision in the eyes of Al Qaeda: "If the successful operations against Islam's enemies and the severe damage inflicted upon them do not serve the ultimate goal of establishing the Muslim nation in the heart of the Islamic world, they will be nothing more than disturbing acts. . . . The restoration of the caliphate and the dismissal of the invaders from the land of Islam . . . must remain the basic objective of the Islamic jihad movement regardless of the sacrifices and the time involved."[15]

Furthermore, it is at this level that religious faith most directly and consistently motivates its leadership. Central to an examination of Al Qaeda's vision is their adherence to Salafism. Briefly stated, this term refers to a variety of Sunni Muslim movements dedicated to the belief in ancient forms of religious authority.[16] This directly points to the goal of restoring the Caliphate, which served as the governing system of Islam that followed directly upon the death of the Prophet Muhammad himself. However, it would be a mistake to conclude that this religious dogma necessarily leads to strategic targeting of the United States, or the choice of suicide tactics. Granted, the three levels of goals do indeed support one another, but the progression from vision to strategy to tactic requires the interaction with other factors, namely, the deep involvement of Western governments in the affairs of Muslim nations, the material asymmetries between the Salafists and Western forces, and Al Qaeda leaders' perceptions of Western political culture. Bin Laden and the senior Al Qaeda seek to restore the Caliphate, they see the United States as a strategic obstacle to that objective when

14. *ABC News*, December 22, 1998.
15. al-Zawahiri, *Knights under the Prophet's Banner*.
16. The word, *Salaf* is Arabic for "ancient ones."

U.S. forces are stationed on the Arabian Peninsula, and they choose suicide terrorism as the best available tactic for removing that barrier. However, there is little evidence the vision of the Caliphate is motivating Al Qaeda suicide attackers, but rather it is the defense of the Muslim lands occupied by those U.S. and Western forces.

Finally, given Al Qaeda's goal of establishing a state entity, deep collaboration by existing states would indicate substantial progress toward their ultimate objective since building off of an existing governance infrastructure would be significantly easier than founding a new state from scratch. Furthermore, this goal naturally threatens the sovereignty of existing states in the region, so such collaboration would require a high degree of affinity with the Al Qaeda vision. We find that no such deep collaboration exists outside of certain failed states and the Taliban in Pakistan and Afghanistan. Before invading Afghanistan in October 2001, the United States engaged in efforts to persuade the Taliban to hand over bin Laden. These efforts failed, and the Taliban's refusal to comply with the U.S. request stood as a casus belli for the invasion. The common assumption was that the ruling Afghan regime seemed determined to maintain its support of Al Qaeda. However, this belief likely gets the power relations backward. In other words, it was bin Laden supporting failed-state regimes rather than the other way around. In both Sudan and Afghanistan, where bin Laden and Al Qaeda took sanctuary, the ruling government was notoriously weak, financially and with respect to conventional military capabilities. Bin Laden has provided financial acumen and rhetorical support for these dysfunctional regimes. So, when the United States demanded that the Taliban hand over Al Qaeda leadership, it was likely a futile effort from the start. They were in no position to deliver bin Laden and al-Zawahiri.

Cohesion

Al Qaeda is commonly called a "network," and government and policy experts have frequently debated whether the network has changed its character over time from centralized to decentralized, and possibly back to centralized. The cohesion metric commonly used by these experts involves intelligence about the number of specific command orders from Al Qaeda's senior leadership to terrorists carrying out an attack in the name of the group. While this metric does make some sense for intelligence agencies seeking to identify indications of future specific attacks, it weakly captures the nature of the cohesion of the group.[17] Further, the presence or absence of specific intelligence on the communications of Al Qaeda senior leaders gives the impression that organizational structure of the group is changing when, in fact, we are only seeing our ability to monitor specific communication links involving Al Qaeda.

Al Qaeda is best thought of as a "movement" with three key parts all held together by shared ideas, particularly a shared perception of the injustice of Western occupation of Muslim countries and a shared commitment for violent actions to respond to that injustice. One part of the movement is highly centralized, but not always active—these are the senior leaders of Al Qaeda and individuals who have taken loyalty oaths to bin Laden. Another part of the movement is moderately well organized and based on intergroup relationships among a variety of geographically disparate and already-existing terrorist organizations, acting together like partners in a military alliance. The third part is comprised of grassroots volunteers who may join one of the more organized parts of the movement or may act independently, but in any case are motivated by the shared ideas of the movement. This ideologically based aspect of Al Qaeda has been a significant factor in the growth of suicide terrorism overall.[18] In many ways Al Qaeda resembles a typical political movement, part of which is tightly centralized (leadership circle), part of which are alliances of preexisting groups, and part of which are volunteers from local communities and may cooperate only tacitly with the formal parts of the movement.

The most centralized part of Al Qaeda is the central leadership circle and the individuals who have sworn byat to bin Laden—a personal loyalty oath taken in his presence. Estimates as to the size of this contingent vary, but the most plausible among them put the number around 300.[19] Operating in the tribal areas of Pakistan and Afghanistan, this core cohort mainly engages in training, propagandizing, financing, and some high-level elements of the planning of major attacks. However, they typically do not participate in the execution of the attacks themselves (especially not as

17. For a discussion of how the network configuration affects the cohesion of Al Qaeda, see Mette Eilstrup-Sangiovanni, "Assessing the Dangers of Illicit Networks: Why al-Qaida May Be Less Threatening than Many Think," *International Security* 33, no. 2 (2008): 7–44. On the vulnerability of the Al Qaeda network, also see Audrey Kurth Cronin, "How al-Qaida Ends: The Decline and Demise of Terrorist Groups," *International Security* 31, no. 1 (2006): 7–48.

18. Assaf Moghadam, "Motives for Martyrdom: Al-Qaida, Salafi Jihad, and the Spread of Suicide Attacks," *International Security* 33, no. 3 (2009): 46–78.

19. Daniel Byman, "Al Qaeda as Adversary: Do We Understand Our Enemy," *World Politics* 56, no. 1 (2003): 139–63.

martyrs), or in the low-level logistical support. To the extent that they do have contact with operational personnel, it is mostly limited to completing a process of ideological radicalization that usually begins elsewhere and culminates in Al Qaeda's training camps.

The second part of the Al Qaeda movement pertains to its intergroup relationships. As stated above, Al Qaeda proper has ties with various terrorist organizations in different parts of the Muslim world. However, it would be a mistake to overstate the interconnectedness of these organizations. Rather than operate as a tightly coupled operational unit, the various component groups affiliated with Al Qaeda better resemble an international alliance structure. Their mutual sharing of soldiers and materiel is limited. Furthermore, their tactical, and to some extent strategic, behavior differs depending on their immediate situation. The 2002 Bali nightclub bombing offers a good example of these alliance dynamics. Jemaah Islamiyah, a local Indonesian militant group with a grievance against the West, supplied the personnel for the attack, while Al Qaeda proper selected the specific targets and provided $20,000 in financing for the operation. Each group had its own reasons for targeting the largely Australian clientele at the nightclubs (Al Qaeda wanted to deter them from cooperating in the U.S. "coalition of the willing" in the lead-up to the Iraq War; Jemaah Islamiyah wanted to respond to Australian foreign policy over East Timor). The two groups played complementary roles in the planning and execution of the attack.[20]

Within Al Qaeda proper, there have been differences of opinion on whether to target the "far enemy" of the United States or the "near enemy" of domestic regimes in Muslim countries. This distinction between the near and far enemies is important, but not because it creates factions within Al Qaeda.[21] Rather, bin Laden has used the logic of the far enemy as the glue to hold the alliance of local groups together. This is, in fact, bin Laden's main personal innovation and allows cooperation among groups focused on different near enemies. Now we come to the third part of the movement. Marc Sageman argues that Al Qaeda recently has evolved into more of an

20. In January 2002, leaders from Al Qaeda and Jamaah Islamiah met in Bangkok to begin planning the attack. Al Qaeda provided technical expertise as well as substantial financial support for the operation, while JI recruited the bombers. After the attack, both groups claimed a share of the credit.

21. These disagreements have, in the past, led to some degree of factionalization within Al Qaeda, but most of bin Laden's internal rivals have been killed by Western forces. See Vahid Brown, "Cracks in the Foundation: Leadership Schisms in Al Qa'ida" (West Point, NY: Combating Terrorism Center, 2007).

ideological model for self-starting terrorist groups.[22] He is right that there are self-starting militants, but incorrect that this is new in recent years. There has been no change in the organizational form of Al Qaeda—grassroots volunteers have been inspired by bin Laden since the late 1990s, and although the number of grassroots recruits may have grown with America's occupation of Iraq and Afghanistan, the basic idea of uncoordinated spontaneous volunteers emerging to support Al Qaeda's objective to end military occupation of Muslim countries has been more or less constant. Mohammed Atta, and other members of the Hamburg cell,[23] the 7/7 bombers in London in 2005, and the Christmas bomber in December 2009 are all part of a constant stream of grassroots volunteers, who join Al Qaeda specifically to conduct attacks in response to foreign occupation of Muslims.

Popular Support

Understanding public opinion regarding the vision, strategy, and tactics of Al Qaeda is critical for assessing the prospects for their success. As an aspiring pan-Islamic nationalist movement, they need the Muslim public to get behind their mission in order for them to achieve their ultimate objectives. We find that what support exists for Al Qaeda's objectives is mostly confined to their opposition to U.S. military policy. Conversely, support for reestablishing the Caliphate is, overall, quite low, although it varies from country to country. This suggests that absent U.S. military presence in Muslim countries, public support for Al Qaeda would be insufficient to maintain and expand the movement.

In this section, we review Arab public opinion surveys taken by Shibley Telhami, Anwar Sadat Chair for Peace and Development at the University of Maryland. We look at trends from year to year as well as a more detailed snapshot of the latest survey to disaggregate the data with respect to nation (the countries included in the survey are Jordan, Lebanon, Morocco, Egypt, United Arab Emirates, and Saudi Arabia). We examine the data for five questions that were asked in each survey: 1) favorability toward the United States, 2) whether the clergy have enough influence on government, 3) sources of personal identity (citizen of one's country, Arab ethnicity,

22. Sageman, *Leaderless Jihad*.
23. For a comprehensive exposition of the Hamburg cell and the September 11 hijackers, see Wright, *The Looming Tower*, and McDermott, *Perfect Soldiers*.

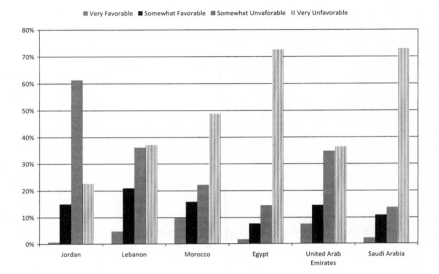

FIGURE 6.2 Views of the United States, 2008

or Muslim religion), 4) the basis for attitudes toward the United States (American values or American Policy), and 5) support for Al Qaeda goals and behavior. Not all questions were asked in all years (and no survey was given in 2007), so there will be some gaps in the data.

Favorability toward the United States

First, we look at whether the surveyed populations view the United States favorably or unfavorably. As a precondition of supporting Al Qaeda's choice of America as the "far-enemy," Arabs must hold the United States in disfavor. Though unfavorable public sentiment is not a sufficient condition for supporting Al Qaeda's far-enemy strategy, it is a necessary one. While there is little evidence of a stable trend in either direction, the surveyed population is fairly uniform in its feelings toward the United States, with majorities in all time periods feeling very unfavorably, followed by somewhat unfavorably, somewhat favorably, and very favorably in descending order. However, when viewing the 2008 data broken down by country, a slightly different picture emerges.

In figure 6.2, the countries are listed from left to right in descending order of political rights and civil liberties as measured by the Freedom

House organization.[24] With the exception of the United Arab Emirates, the countries with better scores on liberties and rights are slightly more moderate. Notably, the home countries of al-Zawahiri and bin Laden are the most extreme in their animus toward the United States.

Basis of Feeling

Next, we look into whether Arab feeling toward the United States is motivated more by American values or American foreign policy. Whatever the reasons behind Al Qaeda's strategic motivation, it is instructive to see how the Arab public feels on the matter. There is almost no variation over time in any of the response categories. Overwhelmingly, the public's feelings toward the United States, shown above to be largely negative, are expressed as a consequence of American foreign policy and not values. Attributions of feeling to values only barely outpace nonresponses ("not sure"). Breaking out the data by country shows that there is some variability across countries, but the "policy" response is the vast majority in each case. Furthermore, there is no discernable pattern with respect to Freedom House rankings.

Sources of Identity

Next, we turn to the question of how the respondents view their own source of group identity. This addresses the question of how the Arab public might view Al Qaeda's goal of creating a unified nation. If they already see themselves as citizens of their current countries, they will be more resistant to the idea of subsuming that identity under another. However, if they see themselves more along ethnic or religious lines, they might be more amenable to Al Qaeda's vision. Again, the responses vary little over time. While one's country is the leading source of identity, it never reaches a majority. Religion is the second leading category, and ethnicity is the last. Overall, this seems to show that Arab popular support cuts against Al Qaeda's vision of creating a unified state, although

---

24. Freedom House scores are determined by the strength of various social and political institutions within a given country, such as freedom of speech, the press, and democratic political representation. For a full description of these rankings, as well as country-by-country scores, see www.freedomhouse.org.

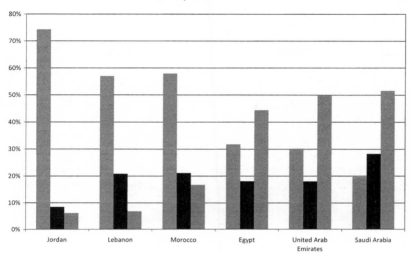

FIGURE 6.3 Sources of identity, 2008

some foundation exists for some form of pan-Arab, pan-Muslim identity formation.

Breaking out the data by country yields a distinct pattern. The lower the Freedom House ranking (on dimensions of both political and rights and civil liberties), the more amenable the population seems to the vision of Al Qaeda with respect to sources of self-identification. Religious identity eclipses nationalism in Egypt, UAE, and Saudi Arabia, and national identity has the lowest response rate in the Saudi Arabia. Thus, in parts of the Arab world, people already see themselves more as members of a religious faith than as citizens of a country.

Role of the Clergy

To continue pursuing the question of the importance of religion in Arab public opinion, we look at the question of whether people feel their clergy are sufficiently active and influential in domestic governance. This goes beyond people's personal feelings about themselves, and asks them to take a position on whether their religious lives and their civic culture

should be more closely coupled. This does not necessarily imply that supporters of religion in government also support Al Qaeda's particular
brand of religion, but it does presume that they are antisecular in their
inclinations.

Over time, Arab populations have seemed to become more satisfied
with the level of clerical-political interaction, with nearly a majority feeling
content with the status quo. A continuation of this trend would not bode
well for Al Qaeda's vision of establishing a Salafist governing regime in the
wider Arab world. In some parts of the Arab world, there would be strong
opposition to increasing the influence of the clergy. However, in others,
there is majority support for increasing religion's role in politics. In short,
this aspect of Al Qaeda's vision has mixed support among different parts
of the Arab world.

Sympathy for Al Qaeda

Thus far, we have approached the question of public support analytically,
breaking out various aspects of Al Qaeda's mission and examining public
support for each piece in turn. Finally, we come to the direct question of
whether and to what degree there is public support for Al Qaeda itself
with respect to those aspects. Very little support exists in any time period
for either Al Qaeda's methods of operation or their efforts to establish an
Islamic state. There is some support, though it may be dwindling, for Al
Qaeda's fighting for Muslim causes ("such as the Palestinian issue"). Most
critically, sympathy with Al Qaeda simply for confronting the United
States has dropped steadily and significantly while the "None" category
(indicating no sympathy for Al Qaeda) has risen substantially and now
represents roughly half the population.

The country-by-country breakdown reveals that some pockets of sympathy with Al Qaeda still exist. Bin Laden's and al-Zawahiri's home countries of Saudi Arabia and Egypt remain largely sympathetic toward Al
Qaeda, as does Morocco. Among the reason for this sympathy, the strategic targeting of the United States is most popular. There is variation with
respect to whether sympathizers favor the methods of operation (tactics)
or Al Qaeda's professed support for Muslim causes. Even in these remaining pockets of sympathy, the Al Qaeda vision of creating an Islamic state
remains relatively unpopular.

Targeting Logic

The vast majority of attacks have employed weapons other than belt bombs. These include car and truck bombs, boat bombs, and (most famously) hijacked commercial airliners. Overall, the lethality of attacks seems to be trending downward, although only slightly. Inherent in these data is the fact that one of Al Qaeda's signatures is the "spectacular" attack, yielding mass casualties and employing an unanticipated tactic (such as the failed "shoe bomber" mission by Richard Reed). One pattern is quite clear: the primary targets of Al Qaeda's campaign have been civilians. Both in number of attacks and number of fatalities, the majority of both measures have fallen on the civilian population.

The logic behind Al Qaeda's targeting of civilians is twofold, and incorporates both strategic and legitimating justification. First, Al Qaeda proposes to break the morale of the U.S. population, thus forcing a change in its foreign policy. This is classic compellence logic, whereby Al Qaeda aims to alter the status quo by inflicting punishment sufficient to alter the U.S. public's position on Middle Eastern political affairs. It is the same logic that both sides applied to strategic bombing in World War II. The Germans waged the battle of Britain, consisting of coercive aerial bombardment, aimed at breaking British resolve to continue its opposition to Hitler's domination of the continent. Similarly, the Allied firebombing of cities in Germany and Japan (most prominently Dresden and Tokyo) was intended to crush the morale of Axis power civilian publics. These punishment policies of both World War II alliances ultimately failed, but not before killing hundreds of thousands of civilians.

Second, Al Qaeda justifies its targeting of civilians as a legitimate warfighting practice. Fully comprehending the moral depravity of civilian punishment strategies, the Allied powers in World War II argued that such missions were aimed at destroying Germany's and Japan's war economies. In a similar vein, bin Laden argues, "[t]he towers were supposed to be filled with supporters of the financial powers of the United States who are abusing the world. Those who talk about civilians should change their stand and reconsider their position."[25] Civilians, in both formulations, are not innocent, but participants in the enemy's war machine. This legitimates their being targeted, even if the strategic intention is to break their morale.

25. David Bamber, "Bin Laden: Yes, I Did It," *Daily Telegraph*, November 11, 2001.

Recruitment

Al Qaeda's recruitment strategy belies the notion that Islamic fundamentalism, per se, sits at the root of its suicide terrorism campaign. Nor does this aspect of its operations emerge directly from its vision of restoring the Caliphate by expanding and consolidating Islamic rule over the former empire. Rather, the Al Qaeda recruitment strategy is a function of what its leaders and target populations view as Western occupation of Muslim nations, or the control via local proxy regimes by the same foreign governments. Religion itself does play a role, but one that differs in important ways from certain common perceptions of inherent Islamic radicalism and proclivity to violence. In all, two interacting factors drive Al Qaeda's recruitment patterns: Western occupation/control and religious difference between Western forces and local populations.

Our data show that Western occupation and/or the perceived control over local governments by Western governments serves as a better predictor of Al Qaeda recruiting success than Sunni Muslim religious affiliation within source country populations. Table 6.1 shows the breakdown of Al Qaeda suicide attackers among Sunni nations with and without an American combat presence.[26] The ratio of attackers per million is nearly ten times higher in Sunni countries with American militaries forces present than Sunni countries without such operations. Table 6.1 also compares countries with significant levels of Salafi influence against other Sunni-majority countries, and the results show similar patterns. These data demonstrate that U.S. military presence contributes substantially more to the recruiting success of Al Qaeda than does religion.

Table 6.2 shows that, by and large, the implementation of U.S. foreign policies aimed at controlling Muslim countries through military occupation or domestic regime support coincides with Al Qaeda recruitment success. On the other hand, the U.S. designation of "terrorist" states fails utterly to account for the recruitment of Al Qaeda suicide attackers. Altogether, these data show that the prime driver of Al Qaeda recruitment is U.S. foreign policy, primarily military occupation as well as regime backing.

26. There have been three suicide attacks in Uzbekistan in this time frame, but there is no hard evidence that Al Qaeda had any role in their execution. Omitting these attacks from our results presents the harder test of our theory, since including them would add increase the ratio of attacks to population among Sunni countries with U.S. military presence. Including the attacks would lend further support to our central proposition.

TABLE 6.1 **U.S. military presence in Sunni and Salafi countries and Al Qaeda, 1995–2009**

Country	Muslims (millions as of 2000)	Al Qaeda suicide attackers
Sunni countries with U.S. combat operations		
Afghanistan	25	3
Saudi Arabia	21	37
Turkey	67	4
Uzbekistan	21	0
UAE	2	2
Oman	2	0
Kuwait	2	0
Yemen	18	5
Jordan	6	1
Total	164	52 (1 per 3.1 million)
Countries with Salafi-influenced populations and U.S. combat operations		
Afghanistan	25	3
Saudi Arabia	21	37
Oman	2	0
Yemen	18	5
Jordan	6	1
Total	72	46 (1 per 1.6 million)
Other Sunni Countries		
Total	912	30 (1 per 30 million)

TABLE 6.2 **U.S. foreign policy and Al Qaeda suicide attackers, 1995–2009**

U.S. combat presence		U.S. backed regimes		U.S. "terrorist" states		Other	
Saudi Arabia	37	Egypt	1	Iraq (pre-2003)	0	United Kingdom	3
Turkey	4	Indonesia (E. Timor)	5	Iran	0	Tunisia	3
Afghanistan (post-2001)	3	Morocco	12	Libya (pre-2004)	0	Lebanon	1
UAE	2			Syria	0	Russia	1
Jordan	1			Sudan	0	Jamaica	1
Yemen	5			Afghanistan (pre-2001)	0		
Pakistan (post-2001)	2						
Total	54		18		0		9

The religious component of Al Qaeda's recruitment success derives not from any intrinsic feature of Sunni Islam, but rather from the difference in religious culture between Islamic populations and Western occupying forces. Viewed from the perspective of recruited populations, the United States has embarked upon an imperialist project to conquer Muslim lands and supplant the native religious culture. Bin Laden himself has repeatedly made reference to the Western "Crusade" in the region, overtly alleging a religious motivation behind U.S. foreign policy, and tying it to the centuries-long religious conflicts between Christendom and Islam. Just as many in the West interpret jihad as a campaign bent on establishing Islamic hegemony, so do Al Qaeda's recruits see the United States and its Western allies as engaged in a struggle to expand Judeo-Christian influence in the region. Thus, they see themselves as engaged in a defensive struggle to beat back the Western "Crusaders."

These two factors are critical in making Al Qaeda's recruitment efforts successful: Western influence (either through military occupation or local regime support) in the region and the religious difference between Western forces and local populations. This has several important implications. First, it challenges the popular notion that Al Qaeda's brand of violence stems from Islamic doctrine or Muslim culture. Second, it points to U.S. foreign policy as a prime motivator of those who offer themselves as martyrs for Al Qaeda's cause. Finally, it bears mentioning that recruits to Al Qaeda's suicide operations need not support the grand vision of restoring the Caliphate. Rather, recruits need simply share the common goal of expelling Western occupiers and severing their support for traitorous local regimes. It is unclear, at this point, whether Al Qaeda would be able to sustain their recent levels of recruiting success were they to call upon these same populations to give their lives for the sake of restoring the Caliphate. In other words, Al Qaeda's recruiting strategy is derived from its strategic, not its visionary, objectives.

Trajectory of Suicide Campaign

Overall, the objective of the campaign is to coerce the United States and its allies to remove their military forces from Muslim territories (especially those on the Arabian Peninsula and Afghanistan) and to cease supporting existing regimes in those countries. This coercion mostly focuses on punishing the countries targeted with suicide terrorism. The broad changes in the trajectory of Al Qaeda suicide attacks reveal a strategic calculus aimed at finding the most efficient way of exerting coercive pressure on the United States. While some commentators have interpreted these changes as evidence of Al Qaeda's defeat, degeneration, or dissolution, this view is mistaken. Instead, the trajectory of the campaign represents an ebb and flow of emphasis between different components of their overall strategy. Over the course of the campaign, Al Qaeda has moved between attacking the United States directly and attacking those of its allies with combat forces fighting side-by-side in Muslim territories, especially Iraq and Afghanistan.

The campaign has unfolded in three main phases. First, between 1995 and 2001, Al Qaeda focused on attacking American-related targets, including U.S. military forces, U.S. embassies, and the U.S. homeland. It is during this time, in 1998, that Osama bin Laden issued a fatwa to kill Americans, with the U.S. military presence in Saudi Arabia as his primary justification.

> The Arabian Peninsula has never—since God made it flat, created its desert, and encircled it with seas—been stormed by any forces like the crusader armies spreading in it like locusts eating its riches and wiping out its plantations. All this is happening at a time in which nations are attacking Muslims like people fighting over a plate of food. In the light of the grave situation and the lack of support, we and you are obliged to discuss current events, and we should all agree on how to settle the matter. . . . The ruling to kill the Americans and their allies—civilians and military—is an individual duty for every Muslim who can do it in any country in which it is possible to do it.[27]

Targets during this time period included the U.S. embassies in Kenya and Tanzania, the U.S.S. Cole in Yemen, and most infamously, the Pentagon in Washington and the World Trade in New York on September 11, 2001.

The second stage runs from 2002 through 2005, during which time Al Qaeda shifted its focus onto U.S. allies participating in the military engagements in Afghanistan and Iraq. Most prominently, the March 11 Madrid[28]

27. Osama bin Laden, "Al Qaeda's Fatwa" (1998), http://www.pbs.org/newshour/terrorism/international/fatwa_1998.html.

28. We consider the Madrid bombing a suicide attack, despite the fact that the bombers did not die in the process of detonating their weapons. They committed suicide in the weeks following the attack rather than allow themselves to be captured or arrange a viable escape.

and July 7 London bombings occur during this period. The immediate goal of this strategic shift was to punish U.S. allies and compel them to withdraw from the battlefield. The indirect goal was to punish the United States by making their attainment riskier and more costly, both materially and diplomatically. The fewer major allies the United States has in its active coalition, the harder it becomes to meet its goals. Moreover, Al Qaeda knows this, and has made this calculus explicit. In a 2004 document titled "Jihadi Iraq, Hopes and Dangers," presumed to have been written by an associate of Yusuf al-Ayira, Al Qaeda's media coordinator until his death in 2003, these strategic aims are laid out clearly. "If the mujahidin can force U.S. allies to withdraw from Iraq then America will be left to cover the expenses on her own, which she cannot sustain for very long."[29]

Furthermore, the document analyzes in some detail the vulnerabilities to coercion of three major U.S. allies in Iraq. Poland, the author claims, is rather invulnerable to coercion, its support for the United States being the deepest of the three. "[W]e are able to say that despite her clear weakness and poverty, [Poland] will be the country most willing to stay in Iraq."[30] Spain, on the other hand, is most vulnerable. "[W]e say that in order to force the Spanish government to withdraw from Iraq the resistance should be dealt painful blows to its forces. This should be accompanied by an information campaign clarifying the truth of the matter inside Iraq. It is necessary to make utmost use of the upcoming general election in Spain in March of next year."[31]

Prior to the bombing, the opposition Socialist Party was behind in the polls, and the governing Popular Party was enjoying the benefits of a strong economy. The attack came just two days before the election, and it seems to have played a critical role in tipping the election to the opposition by provoking a clumsy media response by the government (which tried to blame Basque separatists for the attack) and by raising the issue salience of Spain's military participation in Iraq, which had long been opposed by the Spanish public.[32] The Madrid bombing was a clear success for Al Qaeda with respect to its immediate objective of coercing withdrawal from Iraq

29. Brynjar Lia and Thomas Hegghammer, "FFI Explains Al-Qaida Document" (2004), http://www.mil.no/felles/ffi/start/article.jhtml?articleID=71589.

30. Unknown, "Jihadi Iraq, Hopes and Dangers" (2004), translation by Chicago Project on Security and Terrorism, http://www.mil.no/multimedia/archive/00038/_Jihadi_Iraq_Hopes_38063a.pdf.

31. Ibid.

32. "Spain Grapples with Notion That Terrorism Trumped Democracy," *New York Times*, March 17, 2004.

by the Spanish government. Within 24 hours of his swearing in as Spanish prime minister, Socialist Party leader José Luis Rodríguez Zapatero ordered the withdrawal of his country's troops from Iraq.[33]

The case of Great Britain and the London bombings is less clearly characterized as a success for Al Qaeda, but fits neatly into the strategic logic outlined in the 2004 "Jihadi Iraq" document, which argues that direct coercive pressure on Britain would be most effective if it were to follow the withdrawal of other major U.S. allies, particularly Spain.[34] While the British did not respond to the London bombings with a complete withdrawal, and the incumbent Labor government was not ousted, they did begin to draw down some forces and adjust their military presence to soften its impact on the Iraqi population. In all, the targeting and sequencing of Al Qaeda attacks between 2002 and 2005 (Spain first, then Great Britain, with no attacks against Poland) reflects a strategic calculus aimed at coercing coalition allies to withdraw their troops from Iraq and increasing the costs to the United States of occupying Iraq.

The third phase of the Al Qaeda campaign trajectory runs from 2006 to the present, and it entails a shift back to targeting the United States more directly. This return follows directly in the shadow of bin Laden's January 2006 videotaped message directed at the United States, wherein he claims the bombings in Madrid and London as service to Al Qaeda's cause and promises that attacks on the United States will resume.

> [T]he mujahideen, praise be to God, have managed to breach all the security measures adopted by the unjust nations of the coalition time and again.
>
> The evidence of this is the bombings you have seen in the capitals of the most important European countries of this aggressive coalition.
>
> As for the delay in carrying out similar operations in America, this was not due to failure to breach your security measures.
>
> Operations are under preparation, and you will see them on your own ground once they are finished, God willing.[35]

During this period, police and intelligence agencies in Europe and North America successfully discovered and disrupted a major number of Al

33. "Spanish Premier Orders Soldiers Home From Iraq," *New York Times,* April 19, 2004.

34. Lia and Hegghammer "FFI Explains Al-Qaida Document."

35. Osama Bin Laden, "Text: Bin Laden Tape" (2006), BBC News, http://news.bbc.co.uk/2/hi/4628932.stm.

Qaeda plots that might have killed hundreds or thousands of civilians. In August of 2006, the British police arrested 25 suspects, charged with conspiring to destroy 10 transatlantic airliners en route to the United States and Canada using liquid explosives brought aboard in carry-on luggage.[36] In 2008 six men were convicted of surveilling, purchasing automatic weapons, and training with these weapons for imminent attack on Fort Dix army post in New Jersey; they subsequently claimed bin Laden and Al Qaeda as their inspiration.

In 2008, there appears to be a lull in Al Qaeda operations against the United States, seemingly corresponding to an "Iraq fatigue." In the last year of the Bush administration, it becomes clear to both Western and Muslim publics and elites (including Al Qaeda) that a change in U.S. Iraq policy is coming. With the political ascension of Barack Obama, the presidential candidate most closely associated with opposition to the war, the lull continues. Interestingly, President Obama's actual election seems to end Al Qaeda's fatigue, and in 2009 bin Laden's statements become both more numerous and more pointedly about President Obama. From the time of President Obama's Cairo speech in May 2009, bin Laden's statements consistently paint President Obama's policies as merely a continuation of the most aggressive tendencies of the Bush administration. Bin Laden has gone to particularly great lengths to paint President Obama as pro-Zionist and anti-Palestinian, dovetailing with his overall argument for years that a Christian, Jewish "cabal" is the principal driving force behind American policies to conquer and damage Muslim societies.

President Obama's decision in the fall of 2009 to increase troop presence in Afghanistan has further dovetailed with Al Qaeda's general efforts to support new attacks on the American homeland, including new plots—one of which succeeded and one which came dangerously close to success. The Fort Hood suspect, Nidal Malik Hasan, who allegedly murdered 13 people in a shooting rampage protesting his unit's deployment to Afghanistan, is believed to have been in communication with a purported bin Laden affiliated cleric, Anwar al-Awlaki.[37] This same cleric instructed Umar Farouk Abdulmutallab, the so-called Christmas Bomber who attempted to destroy a Detroit-bound airplane by igniting a bomb sewn into his underwear.[38] Al-

36. In response to the foiled plot, transportation safety procedures were changed to limit the volume of liquids permitted to passengers.

37. "U.S. Knew of Suspect's Tie to Radical Cleric," *New York Times,* November 9, 2009.

38. "Cleric in Yemen Admits Meeting Airliner Plot Suspect, Journalist Says," *New York Times,* January 31, 2010.

Alwaki is also purported to be a member of an Al Qaeda inspired upstart group in Yemen. Altogether, these attacks demonstrate a strategic shift back to targeting the United States directly.

Conclusion

Since September 11, many terrorism experts and policy pundits have claimed repeatedly that Al Qaeda is on its deathbed, thrown off by some combination of its incompetence and our strategic brilliance, or cowering in the face of Western resolve. On the contrary, the facts show that changes in Al Qaeda's behavior are only at most moderately related to internal changes in Al Qaeda as an organization. Instead, the variation in Al Qaeda's attacks reflects an adaptation to changing circumstances and opportunities. When the United States has been, by and large, on its own as a military presence in the region, it has suffered the brunt of Al Qaeda's attacks. Alternatively, when the United States has benefited politically and militarily from the presence of coalition partners, its most valuable and vulnerable allies have become the targets of Al Qaeda's campaign. The pattern of major attacks, with respect to timing and targeting, makes evident a deliberate strategic calculation that follows directly on the threats and promises contained in their public statements. Far from revealing a degeneration of Al Qaeda's capabilities, the ebb and flow of their suicide attacks reflects a purposeful strategic logic: to force the United States to withdraw its military from the region. As long as U.S. combat forces remain stationed on the Arabian Peninsula and other Muslim countries, Americans should expect the threats from Al Qaeda to continue.

CHAPTER SEVEN

Lebanon

S tarting in the early 1980s, Lebanon witnessed the world's first campaign of suicide attacks since the Kamikazes in World War II.[1] Aside
from an isolated attack in 1981, all the suicide attacks in Lebanon were
directly or tacitly coordinated by Hezbollah, a loose federation of Shia
and other terrorist organizations that emerged in the country in 1982 and
remains in existence to this day. As figure 7.1 shows, from 1982 to 1999,
this campaign of suicide terrorism comprised 39 attacks, the vast majority
of which occurred up through 1986, with only a handful after that point.
These attacks were mainly against American, French, and Israeli military
forces as well as Western political targets, and killed a total of some 900
people, including the infamous suicide truck attack upon the U.S. Marine
Barracks in Beirut in October 23, 1983, killing 241 U.S. Marines as they
slept. Although no suicide attacks have occurred in Lebanon since 1999,
this campaign remains important both because the key events served to
inspire a variety of other terrorist groups to conduct suicide attacks, including Hamas, Al Qaeda, and the Tamil Tigers, and because close study
of this case helps to clarify the causal logic of suicide terrorism.[2]

1. Major contributors to this chapter were Sylvia Hammad and Martin Wolberg-Stok. Research assistants for this chapter were Vanessa Bernick and Rana Mikati.

2. Prominent literature on suicide terrorism in Lebanon includes Robin Wright, *Sacred
Rage: The Wrath of Militant Islam* (New York: Simon and Schuster, 1985); Juan R. I. Cole
and Nikki R. Keddie, eds., *Shi'ism and Social Protest* (New Haven, CT: Yale University Press,
1986); Martin Kramer, "The Moral Logic of Hizballah," and Ariel Merari, "The Readiness to
Kill and Die: Suicidal Terrorism in the Middle East," both in *Origins of Terrorism: Psycholo-
gies, Ideologies, Theologies, States of Mind,* ed. Walter Laqueur (Washington, DC: Woodrow
Wilson Center Press, 1990), pp. 131–60 and 192–210, respectively; Hala Jaber, *Hezbollah: Born
with a Vengeance* (New York: Columbia University Press, 1997); Robert Risk, *Pity the Nation:
Lebanon at War* (New York: Oxford University Press, 2001); Reuven Paz, "The Islamic Legacy
of Suicide Terrorism," in *Countering Suicide Terrorism: An International Conference* (Hezliya:

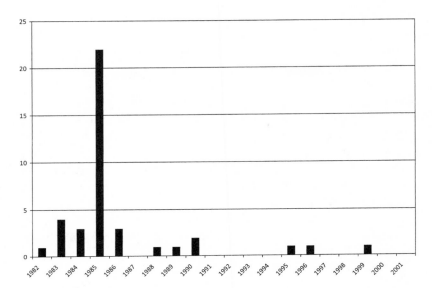

FIGURE 7.1 Suicide attacks in Lebanon, 1982–2001

As the suicide campaign unfolded in the early 1980s, there was relatively little information available about the suicide attackers or the organizations associated with them. Since many of the attackers were Shia Muslims and Hezbollah was known as a Shia Islamic fundamentalist organization, many observers at the time presumed that Islamic fundamentalism was driving the suicide attacks. Indeed, Thomas Friedman, then the New York Times bureau chief in Beirut, wrote numerous articles focusing on the role of religion as central to the suicide bombings.[3] Many other journalists and scholars, such as Robin Wright and Martin Kramer, also produced work similarly claiming that radical Shia Islam was the key motivating factor. It is not too much to say that this early wave of journalism and scholarship on

Gefen Books, 2002); Amal Saad-Ghorayeb, *Hizbu'llah: Politics and Religion* (London: Pluto Press, 2002); Christoph Reuter, *My Life Is a Weapon: A Modern History of Suicide Bombing* (Princeton, NJ: Princeton University Press, 2004), pp. 52–78; and Augustus Richard Norton, *Amal and the Shia: Struggle for the Soul of Lebanon* (Austin: University of Texas Press, 1987), and *Hezbollah: A Short History* (Princeton, NJ: Princeton University Press, 2007).

3. For instance, Thomas L. Friedman, "Suspicion in Beirut Is Now Focused on a Shiite Splinter Group," *New York Times,* October 27, 1983, and "Boy Says Lebanese Recruited Him a Car Bomber," *New York Times,* April 14, 1985.

Hezbollah contributed significantly to current conventional wisdom that suicide terrorists are religiously motivated.

Today, however, we have abundant new information about the cause of the rise and fall of suicide terrorism in Lebanon as well as about the identity of the Lebanese suicide attackers. This data presents a picture far different from the conventional wisdom, fundamentally challenging the idea that Islamic fundamentalism is the root cause of suicide attacks in Lebanon. As we shall see, of the 32 suicide attackers who actually killed themselves from 1982 to 1999 and whose ideology we can identify, 22 were communists and socialists with no commitment to religious extremism, while five were Christians. While religion did play a role as a recruiting tool, it was at most a secondary factor.

The principal cause of suicide terrorism in Lebanon is foreign military occupation. In June 1982, Hezbollah did not exist. On June 6, 1982, Israel invaded southern Lebanon with 78,000 combat soldiers and 3,000 tanks and armored vehicles and one month later Hezbollah was born. Then Hezbollah appears to have experimented with the tactic of suicide attack over the course of the next year and the third attack was on the U.S. Marines in Beirut in October 1983 (French soldiers were also struck by suicide truck bomber that same day). In February 1984, U.S. President Ronald Reagan chose to withdraw all American combat forces from the country rather than face another suicide attack, and the French and other international troops left at the same time. Then, in 1986, Israel reduced its military deployment to a six-mile "buffer zone" in southern Lebanon, and, in May 2000, Israel troops left Lebanon altogether. What is significant about the foreign troop withdrawals is that Lebanese suicide attackers did not follow the Americans to New York, the French to Paris or the Israelis to Tel Aviv—since Israel's military withdrawal in 2000, there has not been a single Lebanese suicide attack, not even during the three-week war between Israel and Hezbollah in the summer of 2006. This pattern—both the origin and end of the suicide attacks—fits tightly with the ebb and flow of foreign occupation and poorly with Islamic fundamentalism, which did not change during the period. Accordingly, the Lebanese suicide terrorist campaign is powerful evidence for foreign occupation as the root cause of the phenomenon.

This chapter explains the suicide terrorism campaign and its relation to Israel's military occupation of Lebanon by examining 1) the origins of the conflict, 2) the motivations and goals of the different organizations in this conflict, 3) the trajectory of suicide attacks themselves, 4) the groups' operational patterns and weapon tactics, 5) the demographic profile of the suicide bombers, 6) levels of state sponsorship for such attacks, and 7) local Lebanese support for martyrdom and the aims of the terrorist groups.

Origins

The phenomenon of suicide terrorism in Lebanon evolved from a long history of political, social, and military developments driving discontent and fear among the Shia. After Lebanon's independence from France in 1943, the political system that emerged recognized 17 sects, with representation according to each sect's community size. Because of the Maronite majority, this Christian group was accorded the presidency. Sunni Muslims, the second largest community, were accorded the office of prime minister. The Shia community was the third largest and was awarded the speakership of parliament, a position far weaker than the first two with little political influence. The official source for the allocation of power was a 1932 census of doubtful reliability, which remains the last official census conducted in Lebanon. Over time, the Shia population grew at a faster rate than the others, creating a demographic shift that was increasingly out of balance with the structure of political power. This encouraged the growing politicization of the Shia, a process also shaped by a mixture of social facts, regional conflicts, and domestic policies, such as the influx of 100,000 Palestinians (Sunnis) who moved to southern Lebanon after the establishment of Israel.[4]

In the 1970s, the most important Shia organization was Harakat Amal, a nationalist movement founded in the Shia heartland of southern Lebanon in 1975. It was created as the military wing of the "movement of the deprived" (Harakat al-Mahrumin) as a response to the armament of other Lebanese militias. Amal leaders advocated the restructuring of the Lebanese political system to prevent the subordination of Shia interests and, after 1975, organized militias to protect the security of villages in southern Lebanon during the civil war. The Amal political platform called for equality for all citizens, social justice, and a nonsectarian commitment to national unity; it did not propose the creation of an Islamic state in Lebanon. By the early 1980s, Amal was the most powerful organization within the Shia

4. Richard A. Gabriel, *Operation Peace for Galilee: The Israeli-PLO War in Lebanon,* (New York: Hill and Wang, 1985), pp. 30–34; Norton, *Hezbollah,* pp. 12–15.

community, numbering in the tens of thousands by 1982. However, the perceived corruption of Amal's leaders and its welcoming stance toward Israel's incursion in 1978 led to disagreements within the group.[5]

Hezbollah came into being one month after Israel's major invasion in June 1982 as a result of a split in the Amal militia. Hussain Mussawi, a second in command of Amal, and his followers rejected Amal's initial collaboration with Israel's military program and established a new group with headquarters in the Bekaa Valley dedicated to active resistance to Israel's military presence. Calling itself "Islamic Amal," the new group was joined in July by a contingent of 800 to 1,000 Iranian fighters and soon became associated with the creation of an Islamic state on the model of Iran. Still, the causal effect of Israel's invasion on the rise of Hezbollah was profound. As then–Defense Minister Ehud Barak noted, "When we entered Lebanon, there was no Hezbollah. We were accepted by perfumed rice and flowers by the Shia in the south. . . . It was our presence there that created Hezbollah."[6]

Initially, Hezbollah had little popular support. After many years of growing tensions between the Shia and the Palestinians, the Shia were willing to allow Israel to push the Palestinians out of Lebanon and generally did not oppose Israeli military forces during the summer of 1982, even though Israeli military forces probably killed 3,000 to 5,000 civilians and rendered as many as 80,000 Shia homeless. However, the longer Israeli troops remained in the country, the more the sense of foreign occupation deepened, a result aggravated by the introduction of American, French, and other Western troops in August 1982 (even though their purpose was to stabilize the country and reduce violence). As more and more Shia came to resent and resist Israeli and Western military forces, Lebanese militants grew from a handful in the summer of 1982 to over 7,000 members by 1986. Accordingly, Hezbollah progressively expanded into an umbrella organization coordinating the resistance operations of a loose collection of preexisting social groups—many with no ties to Iran—such as the Lebanese Da'wa Party, the Association of Muslim Ulama in Lebanon, and the Association

5. Gabriel, *Operation Peace for Galilee,* pp. 60–126. The first Israeli incursion of 1978, dubbed Operation Litani, aimed according to Israeli sources to drive the PLO forces operating in Lebanon north of the Litani River. The second invasion in June of 1982, Operation Peace for Galilee, claimed to be in retaliation for the assassination attempt of the Israeli ambassador Shlomo Argov in London and had the main objectives of competing the task of the 1978 Incursion by crushing the PLO and facilitating the installation of an Israel friendly Lebanese government.

6. "A Brief History Of: Hizballah," *Time,* June 8, 2009.

of Muslim Students. Although these groups differed in many ways, Israel's invasion gave them a new, common purpose—to resist Israel's occupation. Sheik Hassan Nasrallah, the general secretary of Hezbollah, summarizes the origins of the group as "at its inception centered on resisting occupation, nothing else. . . . Naturally, we asked for assistance. From any party . . . then our relations began with Syria and Iran."[7]

Group Goals

What spurred the expansion of Hezbollah was Israel's deepening control and regulation of local villages in southern Lebanon. Starting in the fall of 1982 and formalized in the "Organization for a United South" in January 1983, Israel sought to replace existing local Shia leaders in the 30 largest villages in southern Lebanon with Israeli-backed village committees who would work closely with Israeli military patrols. This policy of control dashed the initial hopes among many Shia that Israel's eviction of the Palestinians would lead to greater self-determination for their community, and fomented powerful resistance to Israeli and Western military forces. As Augustus Norton puts it, "Having begun to throw off the shackles of the PLO presence, the Shia community was not about to wrap itself in the chains of Israel's occupation."[8]

Although conventional wisdom has attributed the use of suicide terrorism to religiously motivated, specifically Islamic fundamentalist groups, more than two-thirds of the suicide bombings in southern Lebanon were carried out by secular organizations. The only clearly religious party carrying out suicide attacks in Lebanon was the "Islamic Amal," linked to at least 9 and possibly as many as 16 suicide bombings, depending on how one counts the 7 unattributed attacks in Lebanon. The groups responsible for the remaining attacks were secular, nationalist, or leftist parties that were in existence years before Israel's invasion in 1982, such as the Syrian Social Nationalist Party (SSNP), the Lebanese Ba'ath, the Lebanese Communist Party (LCP), AMAL, the Popular Front for the Liberation of Palestine (PFLP), and al-Sa'iqa. None of these groups, including AMAL, had a religious agenda.

7. Shimon Shapira, "The Origins of Hizballah," *Jerusalem Quarterly,* vol. 46 (Spring 1988), pp. 115–30; Interview with General Secretary Sheikh Hassan Nasrallah, *Middle East Insight* (May–August 1996), pp. 39.

8. Norton, *Amal and the Shi'a,* p. 114.

What motivated these groups with vastly different ideologies to cooperate in a campaign of suicide terrorism was the belief that suicide attacks were a legitimate means of self-defense against foreign occupation, and not that religious martyrdom was an end in itself. Indeed, arguments for "self-martyr" operations tied the act to the advancement of the local community. An individual, the argument goes, has a purpose on earth and should end that purpose only for another legitimate aim. Ending a foreign occupation that would oppress the local community is viewed as a possible legitimate purpose, but only if the self-sacrifice would in fact contribute toward that end. This core justification was offered in literally hundreds of public speeches and interviews by resistance leaders explaining the need for what they termed self-martyr operations.

Looking closely at Hezbollah's discourse on martyrdom reveals a three-part justification that effectively redefined operations that would normally qualify as suicide and murder as martyrdom and legitimate self-defense. First, the central purpose of martyrdom operations was to end the occupation of Lebanon by American, Israeli, and other Western military forces. In February 1985, Hezbollah's "Open Letter" stated, "America and its allies and the Zionist entity . . . have attacked our country, destroyed our villages, massacred our children, violated our sanctities, and installed over our heads criminal henchmen. . . . We have risen to liberate our country, to drive the imperialists and the invaders out of it, and to determine our fare by our own hands."[9]

Second, suicide operations are a last resort, justified by the Lebanese inferiority in conventional military power compared to Israel and the West. According to the secretary general of Hezbollah, "the outcome [of ordinary attacks] would be 3 or 4 deaths due to the strong fortifications of the enemy. On the other hand, one single martyr without any training or experience, driving a bus without any military backups or supporting groups, was able to kill 8 or 9, wound 21, and scare the entire Israeli entity."[10]

Third, suicide operations have real coercive value in compelling the opponent to withdraw the occupying forces. Again, Hezbollah's "Open Letter" says, "With the blood of its martyrs and the struggle of its heroes, the

9. Ibid., p. 170.
10. Sheikh Hassan Nasrallah, secretary general of Hezbollah, speech "In Memory of His Eminence Martyr Sayyed Abbas al-Musawi" (February 16, 2001).

Islamic resistance has been able to force the enemy for the first time in the history of the conflict against it to make a decision to retreat and withdraw from Lebanon."[11]

This is not to say that religion played no role. The Israeli and Western forces were predominately Jewish and Christian, while the southern Lebanese community was predominately Islamic, encouraging many in the occupied community to believe that foreign military presence threatened their way of life. Indeed, many attackers, even those with secular backgrounds, stressed in their final testimonials that they were motivated by the religious identity of the enemy. Wajdi Sayedh, a 19-year-old member of the Syrian Socialist National Party (SSNP), said "we have no enemy who fights us to take our rights and homeland but the Jews"; Sana Youssef Mhaydali, the 16-year-old member of the Communist Party who was the first female suicide bomber, explained her motive as "to liberate the south from the occupation of the Zionist terrorists . . . who are not like us"; Bilal Fahs, an 18-year-old member of the Communist Party, spoke about "liberation from occupation as Jihad and obligation"; and Khaled al-Azark, a 20-year-old member of the SSNP, said his "main motive" was "to liberate this land from the Jewish enemies."[12]

Trajectory of Suicide Attacks

The initiation and trajectory of the Hezbollah-coordinated suicide terrorism campaign closely paralleled Israel's control of the Shia communities in southern Lebanon. The campaign began in late 1982, reached a peak in 1985–86 when Israel decided to reposition its forces into a security zone in the southernmost region of Lebanon, and stopped completely in December 1999 just before Israel left the country in May 2000.

Before Israel's invasion of Lebanon in June 1982, the country experienced the only suicide attack in its history, an isolated case in 1981 where an unknown individual killed himself in a bombing of the Iraqi embassy in Beirut. Within six months of Israel's invasion, however, Hezbollah began an extended suicide campaign with a series of attacks against Israeli, Ameri-

---

11. Norton, *Amal and the Shia*, p. 179.

12. These statements are collected in Lebanese Resistance Movement, "Martyrdom Operations" (Beirut, n.d.); translation by Chicago Project on Suicide Terrorism.

can, and French targets. Israel's stated goals in invading Lebanon were to destroy the 15,000 troops of the Palestinian Liberation Organization who resided in the south, to force the PLO leadership near Beirut to leave the country, and to compel Syria's military forces, which had been in Lebanon since the 1975 civil war, to leave as well. By September 1982, Israel had accomplished its first two objectives, forcing the PLO leadership and remaining combatant forces to leave Lebanon. However, Syria refused to withdraw from Lebanon, and Israel retained 20,000 forces in southern Lebanon and began to implement a long-term plan to stabilize the central government controlled by the Maronites and to empower Israel-supported village committees throughout southern Lebanon. From the fall of 1982 on, the Shia population in southern Lebanon began to view these Israeli Defense Forces (IDF) preparations as those of a foreign occupier, preparing for a prolonged occupation.[13]

A multinational force (MNF) comprised of American, French, and Italian troops, arrived in Lebanon in August 1982, as neutral observers to oversee the departure of the PLO from Beirut, in a move that would ultimately make matters worse. The PLO left the country by early September, and the MNF began to depart as well, but new events caused the MNF to reverse its decision.

On September 14, the newly elected Maronite president and close Israeli ally, Bachir Gemayel, was assassinated, causing Israel to extend its invasion forces to Beirut in fear of the collapse of the Maronite-controlled government and the loss of an acceptable peace deal with Lebanon. After Israeli forces entered Beirut, three groups of Christian militiamen, known as the Phalange, and the pro-Israel South Lebanon Army (SLA) entered the Sabra and Shatilla Palestinian refugee camps supposedly looking for remaining PLO combatants, and brutally massacred over 800 refugees. In response to the violence against civilians, the MNF was redeployed with the mission to help the new Lebanese government maintain stability.

However, the Shia community did not accept the MNF as "neutral stabilizers," since it was seeking to stabilize a pro-Israel government.[14] This situation eventually led to the beginning of the Lebanon suicide terrorism campaign against Israel and the MNF. The massacres of Sabra and Shatilla along with continued U.S. and French support for the Maronite-dominated government exacerbated Shia hostility. The MNF became increasingly as-

13. Gabriel, *Operation Peace for Galilee: The Israeli-PLO War in Lebanon,* pp. 68–81.
14. Kechichian, "The Origins and the Social Production of Suicide Bombings," p. 25.

sociated with the Maronite regime as they were drawn into the civil war as active participants.[15] As these events progressed, suicide attacks began against Israeli, American, and French targets.

The first suicide bombing of Hezbollah's campaign was on the Israeli headquarters and intelligence center in the southern city of Tyre on November 11, 1982 (this date is celebrated as Martyrs Day by Hezbollah). It was carried out by 17-year-old Ahmad Qasir.[16] The attack killed 74 people including 60 Israeli officers. The events that gave rise and led to this bombing began with demonstrations by women with close male relatives detained by the IDF. In August, two months after Israel invaded, four demonstrations took place and four more in September. The IDF's response to this opposition was more raids and more detentions. The occupation forces built their infrastructure of control on checkpoints, interrogation centers, mass prisoner camps, and village militias. These militias were predominately led by Christians who were viewed as treating the Shia with disdain.[17]

The second suicide bombing occurred on April 18, 1983, and targeted the U.S. embassy in Beirut. The main targets were Philip Habib and Morris Draper, President Reagan's special envoys to the Middle East who were negotiating the peace deal between Lebanon and Israel. They escaped, but the attacks led to the death of about 63 individuals, including 7 CIA agents, and 11 Americans. This bombing followed an attempt by the United States to broker a peace deal between Israel and Lebanon which would have reinforced Maronite dominance. The signing of such a treaty was antithetical to all of Hezbollah's goals. It would have given Israel permanent political influence in Lebanon, allowed its forces to remain in south Lebanon, and given the Maronites international legitimacy as Lebanon's political rulers.[18] Hence, the main political issue for Hezbollah bombers was the Israeli-supported Lebanese regime and U.S. support for Maronite hegemony in Lebanon.[19]

Soon there was a third suicide attack, a simultaneous suicide bombing of

15. Magnus Ranstorp, *Hizb'allah in Lebanon: The Politics of the Western Hostage Crisis* (New York: Palgrave MacMillan, 1997), p. 90.

16. The name of the attacker was only made public in 1985 after the Israeli withdrawal from Tyre.

17. Sevag Kechichian, "The Origins and the Social Production of Suicide Bombings in Lebanon, 1982–2000" (Chicago: CPOST Research Paper, 2007), pp. 26–27.

18. Daniel Helmer, "Hezbollah's Employment of Suicide Bombing During the 1980's," *Military Review*, July–August 2006, p. 78.

19. Kechichian, "The Origins and the Social Production of Suicide Bombings, p. 16.

the U.S. Marine barracks and the French multinational headquarters. The Marine barracks bombing took place on the morning of October 23, 1983, killing 241 marines. It was carried out using a yellow Mercedes Benz truck. Almost simultaneously, another suicide bomber killed 58 paratroopers at the French multinational headquarters. These attacks, among the deadliest single bomb explosions since WWII, were attributed to Hezbollah. Massive U.S. naval support, the presence of the MNF, and Israel in Lebanon led militant Shia organizations to seek to destroy any foreign influence in Lebanon. November 4, 1983, a few days after the October bombings, Hezbollah launched another suicide attack on the Israeli Security Services base in Tyre. Islamic Jihad, another network under the umbrella of Hezbollah, claimed responsibility. The organization announced that its operation had abrogated the Israeli-Lebanese peace treaty and that suicide attacks would continue until the treaty was nullified.[20]

The double bombings of the American and French contingents in Beirut on October 23 resulted in their withdrawal from Lebanon in the first half of 1984.[21] Years later in President Reagan's memoirs, he explains the decision to withdraw: "The price we had to pay in Beirut was so great, the tragedy at the barracks was so enormous . . . We had to pull out . . . We couldn't stay there and run the risk of another suicide attack on the Marines."[22]

The final attack in Beirut took place around noon on September 20, 1984, and was directed again at the U.S. embassy located on the outskirts of Beirut. It killed 24 people. The suicide bombings in Beirut targeted U.S. and French forces after their direct involvement and support of Amin Gemayel's regime. These attacks were successful in inflicting harm and damage on the most powerful of the military actors on the ground. The suicide bombings produced results that would have been unobtainable by any other means. The aim was to get rid of the most powerful and threatening foreign influence in Lebanon.[23] According to Captain Daniel Helmer in his 2006 *Military Review* article, "The attack demonstrated that not even the ambassadors of foreign powers seeking to influence Lebanon could operate with impunity."[24] Suicide bombings shifted to southern Lebanon, and no other suicide bombings have occurred in Beirut since the U.S. embassy bombing in 1984.

20. Helmer, "Hezbollah's Employment of Suicide Bombing," p. 79.
21. Ranstorp, Hizb'allah in Lebanon, p. 90.
22. Ronald Reagan, *An American Life* (New York: Simon & Schuster, 1990), p. 465.
23. Kechichian, "The Origins and the Social Production of Suicide Bombings," p. 22.
24. Helmer, "Hezbollah's Employment of Suicide Bombing," p. 79.

After the first bombing in Tyre in 1982, the repressive practices of the occupying forces alienated the Shia in southern Lebanon and caused anti-Israeli violence. As more and more Shia came to resent and resist Israel's occupation, Hezbollah expanded into an umbrella organization coordinating the resistance operations of a loose collection of groups with a variety of secular and religious aims. The stimulus for Hezbollah's growth was Israel's increasingly strong control and regulation of the Shia community in southern Lebanon from the fall of 1982 onward.[25]

From 1982 to 1984, there were four suicide bombings in southern Lebanon, aimed at IDF security targets, and three bombings in Beirut aimed at MNF political and security targets. After the bombings from 1982 to 1984, the aim of Hezbollah and its organizations was partly achieved. In early 1984 the MNF withdrew from Lebanon, and Hezbollah focused on getting Israel to evacuate from all of Lebanon. Part of their goal, as stated in the open letter of 1985 was to oust any foreign intervention in Lebanon by utilizing any means possible, including suicide attacks. Now they came to understand the capabilities of this weapon—suicide terrorism—and the political goals it might help attain.[26]

After the removal of the MNF, the trajectory of suicide bombings indicates a strategic use of the suicide weapon before, during and after the withdrawal of Israel into a security zone in the southernmost region of Lebanon. The largest concentration of suicide bombings, 22 altogether, took place in 1985, the year of Israeli withdrawal to the security zone. Prior to this, between 1982 and 1984, only seven attacks took place. The remainder of the 39 attacks in the campaign were carried out in the period between 1986 and 1999—a total of 10. Hezbollah has not carried out a suicide bombing since the Israeli forces' complete withdrawal from Lebanon in May 2000.

Targeting and Weapons

Hezbollah's suicide campaign was directed at those it viewed as foreign occupiers or as supporting foreign occupation, and carried out its campaign in the regions where the foreign presence was geographically located—Beirut and southern Lebanon. The first bombing on November 11, 1982, was against the IDF headquarters in the city of Tyre in southern

25. Norton, *Amal and the Shia*, p. 114.
26. Helmer, "Hezbollah's Employment of Suicide Bombing," pp. 77–79.

Lebanon, while the next two moved to Beirut and were aimed at the U.S. embassy, U.S. Marine barracks, and the French barracks. This early series of bombings were considered a great success for Hezbollah and its organizations, as an important portion of their overall goal was relatively quickly achieved with the withdrawal of Israeli forces from Beirut and the MNF from Lebanon by early 1984. With the withdrawal of the Israeli forces from Beirut, the emphasis of the suicide campaign shifted to the remaining military forces of the IDF in southern Lebanon. It is notable that suicide attacks took place only in those two areas of Lebanon, Beirut and southern Lebanon, which came under Israeli control. The suicide bombing campaign largely ended in Beirut with the withdrawal of the MNF in 1984, and totally ended in Lebanon with the withdrawal of Israeli forces in 2000.[27]

Analyzing the operational patterns and weapon tactics of the Lebanese suicide campaign illustrates the coercive logic behind the attacks. Fadlallah, a spiritual leader of Hezbollah, stressed the coercive value of suicide attack, "We believe that suicide operations should only be carried out if they can bring about a political or military change in proportion to the passions than incite a person to make of his body and explosive bomb."[28]

Overall, the campaign shows a strategic targeting effort directed at achieving a political goal—the withdrawal of a foreign occupier and those viewed as supporting that occupier. At the operational level, the campaign focused on security and political targets to punish the military and political representatives of the occupier and its allies with the strategic hope that public support in their respective countries would soon turn against continued involvement in the conflict.

Target Types

Of the 39 suicide attacks in Lebanon, two were deliberate attacks on political targets, with both being directed at the American Embassy in Beirut. These political attacks, along with the one coordinated attack upon American and French MNF barracks, were conducted for the purpose of weakening American and French support for any agreements that would further compromise the political future of the Shia in Lebanon by stabi-

27. Kechichian, "The Origins and the Social Production of Suicide Bombings," p. 11.
28. Interview with Fadlallah, December 16, 1985, quoted in Martin Kramer, "The Moral Logic of Hizballah," in *Origins of Terrorism,* ed. Walter Reich (New York: Cambridge University Press, 1990), p. 148.

lizing a central government that did not reflect the current demographic balance within the country.

The vast majority of the remaining 37 attacks were directed against Israeli occupation forces' military posts or convoys and against military targets associated with Israel's ally, the South Lebanese Army. While these attacks were not expected to render the Israeli military incapable of holding specific territory, they did seek to inflict enough punishment upon the IDF that the Israeli public would begin to question the wisdom of continuing the conflict, and eventually pressure the Israeli government to withdraw the IDF. Unlike subsequent suicide terrorist campaigns around the world, there was no purposeful targeting of civilians in Lebanon.

Weapon Choice

By far, the Lebanese suicide campaign's primary weapon was the car bomb. A car or truck bomb is typically the largest and most destructive bomb that can be successfully maneuvered into position and detonated, and operationally, the Lebanese had already mastered its use in earlier nonsuicide operations.[29] Of the 39 attacks, the car bomb was used 32 times while the belt bomb was used only twice, with various other methods used during the five other attacks, including an animal, a suitcase, and handbag. The car bomb never ceased to be an important weapon and was used throughout the campaign.

Marrying the car bomb with a suicide driver had the additional tactical advantage of maximizing the number of casualties, since the driver stayed with the vehicle and could move it as close to the target as possible before detonating the bomb. Afterward, the driver could not be arrested or interrogated, minimizing the risk to the organization.[30]

The Campaign's Coercive Logic

Since the Shia community could not match the conventional military power of Israel and the West, or hope to overcome it through asymmetric unconventional warfare, suicide operations were justified as a last resort to coerce the occupiers out of Lebanon. Suicide campaigns were not de-

---

29. Kechichian, "Origins and Social Production of Suicide Bombings," p. 12.
30. Helmer, "Hezbollah's Employment of Suicide Bombing," p. 77.

signed or expected to militarily defeat Israel and the West, but, rather, to threaten future and continued punishment. They were designed to punish the political representatives and military forces, not civilians, of the occupier and his allies, with the expectation of changing their respective governments' policies that supported the continued Israeli occupation of Lebanon.

In a July 8, 1985 *Newsweek* article, the Muslim cleric Sheikh Ibrahim Al Amin, at the time the chief spokesman of Hezbollah, stated, "the truck bombers fought these people the only way they could. These people don't have the same strong quality of weapons as the enemy. They only have the willingness to die, to become an example for all freedom seekers in the world. They are not terrorists. We have not gone to America; the Americans came to us."[31] In regards to future punishment, the Hezbollah leader Sheikh Hassan Nasrallah vowed "an era of suicide attacks on targets in Israeli-occupied southern Lebanon." This statement was made after an attack against an Israeli convoy that took place on March 20, 1996. Nasrallah states, "This attack heralds a new era in southern Lebanon. This type of operation is the next stage of the confrontation which aims to overturn the enemy's military domination and free the occupied zone.... Our armed resistance is not subject to negotiations. It will continue as long as the occupation continues . . . this is a war of attrition against Israel."[32] Through such threats of future punishment, Hezbollah sought to influence public opinion in Israel and the West against continued occupation of Lebanon.

Demographic Profile and Recruitment

Many observers have long argued that Hezbollah is the definitive example of how Islamic fundamentalism is the driving force behind suicide terrorism. Based on this conventional wisdom from the 1980s and 1990s, the standard stereotype of a suicide bomber has been a poor, uneducated religious fanatic. At the time the majority of the attacks were occurring, this conventional wisdom was difficult to evaluate given the limited understanding of the complex network that made up Hezbollah.

However, an updated comprehensive survey of native language sources

---

31. "We Expect U.S. Aggression," *Newsweek,* July 8, 1985.
32. Agence France Presse, "Hezbollah Vows Era of Suicide Attacks on Israeli Targets," March 29, 1996.

paints a far different picture of suicide attackers in Lebanon. From 1982 to 1999 there were 39 suicide attacks in Lebanon, involving a total of 46 suicide attackers. For this group, CPOST has identified the names and gender of 41 attackers (7 were women); the age of 29 (21 years on average); the ideological affiliation of 32; the education level of 11; and the income level of 9 attackers.

The most important new information concerns the ideological affiliation of the suicide terrorists. The Hezbollah organization, including its related groups and the individual attackers, were supremely proud of their willingness to launch suicide attacks to compel Israeli and Western forces to leave their country. The attackers made martyr videos and left written statements that were distributed and prominently displayed in their local communities. These native language sources provide extensive demographic information on the attackers. They also contain reliable information on the ideological affiliations of the individuals, since one purpose of these documents was to encourage those with similar ideological affiliations to join the cause.

An analysis of religious affiliation illustrates how religion was, at best, a minor factor the decision to self-martyr. Of the 46 attackers, CPOST can reliably identify the ideology of 32. Of these, 27 do not fit the description of Islamic fundamentalism; 22 were communists or socialists with no commitment to religious extremism, and 5 were Christians. Only 5 of the 32 suicide attackers were affiliated with Islamic fundamentalism. Hence, even if we count all 14 of the unidentified also as Islamic fundamentalists, this would mean at most 19 of the total of 46 suicide attackers in Lebanon (41%) were Islamic fundamentalists.

CPOST has also identified the nationality of 19 suicide attackers, all of whom were native Lebanese. Most came from the "extended Shia family, village and kin networks," and many members of this extended family were leftists and Marxists. Some had worked for the PLO and other secular parties and Shiite movements. In addition, most Hezbollah fighters were integrated into Lebanese society with jobs, families and social networks, "choosing resistance not because [they] had no choice but because it suited their ideals."[33]

The earlier suicide bombings in the 1980s were rarely about acquiring instant fame, and these attacks received minimal publicity in most cases because of the need to protect the identity of the families still living under

33. Augustus Richard Norton, "Hizballah and the Israeli Withdrawal from Southern Lebanon," *Journal of Palestine Studies* 30, no. 1 (Autumn 2000): 26–27.

Israeli occupation. This changed as the suicide attacks became more numerous in 1985. The first martyr videos appeared at this point, giving publicity to the individual suicide attackers as well as encouraging volunteers
for future attacks. Indeed, many Lebanese suicide terrorists were walk-ins,
who had little connection to terrorism before they carried out their suicide
missions. All attackers claimed in their final statements to have been volunteers, and none of the 46 made an effort to surrender to Israeli forces
rather than carry out their mission.

The socioeconomic status of the bombers fails to support much of the
conventional wisdom that bombers are poor and uneducated. Suicide terrorism is commonly ascribed to poverty; the underlying logic is usually
that suicide attackers come from among society's losers, individuals who
are so poor now and so unlikely to prosper in the future that they have
little to live for and so are more likely to sacrifice a pathetic existence for
some illusory blessing. If this explanation were correct, one would expect
suicide terrorists to score low on the main indicators of socioeconomic status, education and income level, both in absolute terms and by comparison
with their society.

However, the socioeconomic facts present a different picture. Of the 11
suicide attackers for whom there is reliable education information, nearly
all (9) had secondary or postsecondary schooling. Of the 9 suicide attackers
for whom there is reliable income information, two-thirds (6) were working
or middle class. Overall they resemble the kind of politically conscious individuals who might join a grassroots movement more than they do wayward
adolescents or religious fanatics.

Finally, the list of suicide attackers in Lebanon shows that seven of the
46 suicide bombers were females, all of whom belonged to secular parties (Syrian Social Nationalist Party, Lebanese Communist Party, and the
Lebanese Baath).

State Sponsorship

Although Iran did provide money and other support to the Lebanese resistance fighters, the rise of Hezbollah and large popular support for the
movement would most probably not have occurred without a clear external event—Israel's massive occupation of southern Lebanon in 1982.
A group of cadres from Amal formed "Islamic Amal," a movement that
professed support for an Islamic state on the model of Iran, and was soon

joined by a contingent of 800 to 1,000 Pasdaran (Revolutionary Guards) that Iran dispatched to Lebanon in July 1982. In addition to the ideological and material Iranian influence, Hezbollah was supported by Syria with whom they coordinated their attacks.[34]

Syrian and Iranian support for Hezbollah's military and political activities is not grounded as much in ideology as it is in common interests, primarily against Israel. Ideologically, Syria and Iran were competitors. At the time, Syria was governed by a secular, Sunni-based regime, while Iran was led by a Shia Islamic fundamentalist movement. Hezbollah's activities furthered Syria's aim of reemergence and dominance in Lebanon, which had significantly decreased following Israel's 1982 invasion and occupation of areas formerly controlled by Syria. For Iran, Hezbollah activity furthered its interest in containing Israeli expansion and American influence in Lebanon and elsewhere in the Middle East.[35]

Further, the relationship between Iranian and Syrian state support for Hezbollah and Lebanese suicide terrorism is weak and at times contradictory. Most importantly since 2000, Iran and Syria have provided significant economic and military support to Hezbollah, but this has not led to suicide terrorism. In 2006 American government officials reported, "Hezbollah leaders deny that they are agents of Iran or Syria. But they publicly acknowledge Tehran's financial support, which some Western intelligence agencies say may amount to more than $200 million a year."[36] Despite this material support, however, Hezbollah did not carry out any suicide bombings in its month-long war against Israel in 2006, most likely because Israeli ground forces were quickly compelled to leave Lebanon, and therefore the suicide attacks would have served no strategic purpose. Overall the pattern shows that although Hezbollah has foreign allies it regularly acts independently according to its own interests. As White House officials concluded in 2006:

Hezbollah can also move on its own initiative, for its own reasons, even as it seeks to avoid any move that would displease its chief patrons. "It sometimes does act on its own," said Wayne White, who was a senior official in the State Department's intelligence arm until last year. White said intelligence agencies have differed on how much Iran might be spending on Hezbollah but that

34. Norton, *Amal and the Shia,* p. 24.
35. Ranstorp, *Hizb'allah in Lebanon,* pp. 53–54.
36. "Despite Hezbollah's Ties to Iran and Syria, It Acts Alone." *Los Angeles Times,* July 14, 2006, http://articles.latimes.com/2006/jul/14/world/fg-hezbollah14.

they agree there are very strong ties between that country and the group. Even so, he said, it would be an overstatement to say that Hezbollah is a "pawn" of Iran.[37]

Local Popular Support

Community support for martyrdom played a key role in encouraging individuals to become suicide terrorists. Although they varied in other ways, the individuals who carried out suicide terrorist attacks in Lebanon attached tremendous importance to how the community would understand and remember their actions. The overwhelming majority of these individuals left detailed statements, either in writing or on video that they expected to be made public after their death.[38] Most of these testaments did become public soon after the individual's mission and circulated widely among the Shia community, either in newspapers or as items available in local markets. Of course, we should assume that the terrorist organization was instrumental in producing them; indeed, many are quite professional.[39] The key fact, however, is that they were created with the local community in mind. Among ordinary suicides, less than 20% leave suicide notes, and virtually none of these are directed at the community at large.[40]

The prevalence of "martyr" testimonials indicates that the suicide terrorists and their organization attach great importance to establishing themselves as martyrs in the eyes of their community. In many of these testimonials, the individuals use the word "martyr," either to describe those who went on similar missions in the past or to name what they hoped to become. They also explain why their actions are directly related to foreign occupation, often explicitly describing Israeli military forces as barbaric invaders who must be ousted from the country at any price. Few, if any, suicide terrorists would bother making such statements if they felt that community support for their actions was unimportant.

37. Ibid.

38. At least 31 of the 41 Lebanese suicide terrorists left public testimonials. See Lebanese Resistance Movement, "Martyrdom Operations" (Beirut, n.d.).

39. Reuter, *My Life Is a Weapon,* p. 74.

40. Ronald W. Maris, Alan L. Berman, and Morton M. Silverman, *Comprehensive Textbook of Suicidology* (New York: Guilford Press, 2000), pp. 284–310; Antoon A. Leenars, *Suicide Notes: Predictive Clues and Patterns* (New York: Human Science Press, 1988).

Hezbollah engaged in extensive social service activities to enhance its legitimacy in the local community. From the beginning of its first resistance operations, Hezbollah has built cultural centers, orphanages, clinics, and welfare centers. It also set up vocational courses like sewing classes for the handicapped, and in 1986 built two major hospitals to care for the local community. Contrary to the belief that Hezbollah primarily recruits using religious appeals, it seems to have established popular support by beneficially embedding itself in its surrounding society, which came to view Hezbollah as more legitimate than the national government.[41]

Furthermore, to implement their suicide terrorism campaign and recruit suicide bombers, Hezbollah leaders addressed the public through hundreds of public speeches and interviews to explain the need for altruistic support for what they call self-martyrdom operations. Rather than a religious justification, the main theme for the speeches is that martyrdom operations are justifiable because they are a response to foreign occupation. Although religion is interspersed in Hezbollah's recruitment, it does not take center stage because Islam prohibits suicide. Instead it is placed in the context that self-martyrdom is acceptable when it is instrumental in protecting the local community from the oppression of foreign occupation. Hezbollah's discussion on martyrdom ties together three themes that jointly work to make this argument: the purpose of martyrdom operations is to end the foreign occupation of the Shia homeland; martyrdom operations are needed for this purpose because of the imbalance of conventional military power between the occupiers and the occupied community; and martyrdom operations are in fact likely to achieve this goal because the target society is susceptible to coercive pressure. Considering Hezbollah's deep commitment to the welfare of its community and strong association of suicide terrorism as instrumental in ousting foreign occupiers, it is not surprising that Hezbollah's suicide campaigns had many volunteers who would contribute to their society and be honored for it in this way.

There is also important evidence of public support for martyrdom. Since no opinion surveys of the Shia community were taken during the period, we cannot provide precise figures. However, there were highly visible signs of pervasive public support for and commemoration of "martyrs" who killed themselves to kill American, French, and Israeli troops. Major city streets

41. Hilal Khashan, "The Developmental Programs of Islamic Fundamentalist Groups in Lebanon as a Source of Popular Legitimation," *Indian Journal of Politics*, vol.27, no. 3 (1993): 1–13.

were named in honor of these fallen heroes; their pictures were widely used as positive symbols in political discourse; and large public rallies were commonly held in their honor on annual public holidays and at other special events. Such public commemoration continues to this day. Among the best sources of information about Hezbollah's leaders' thinking are the speeches given on "Martyrs Day," held annually on November 11 to venerate the first suicide attacker, who killed himself in order to attack an Israeli military post on that date in 1982.

Even in the absence of opinion polls, these facts suggest that Lebanon's suicide terrorists are probably widely respected as "martyrs" by their local community. By contrast, there are no visible signs of public disaffection with Hezbollah's suicide operations. No community leader or movement condemned Lebanon's suicide attackers, either at the time or since.

Conclusion

For decades Hezbollah has been viewed as the paradigm for suicide terrorism, particularly, for the idea that Islamic fundamentalism is its root cause. Powerful new evidence, however, shatters this conventional wisdom. Like suicide campaigns around the world, the strategy behind the suicide campaign in Lebanon was centered around specific territorial and political goals, not the pursuit of an Islamic fundamentalist state or any religious vision. In particular, these goals stressed ending foreign occupation of southern Lebanon, which played a significant role in 1984 when American and French military forces were compelled to leave Lebanon; in 1985 when the IDF withdrew from most of southern Lebanon; and finally in May 2000 when Israel fully retreated. Although Hezbollah continues to fire rockets into Israel, there have been no civilian casualties since the Israel-Hezbollah War in 2006 and no suicide attack has taken place since the complete withdrawal of Israeli forces from Lebanon in 2000. Clearly, the Lebanon suicide campaign was the direct result of the IDF occupation.

One might wonder if the Israeli withdrawal from Lebanon in 2000 was a good idea. After all, Hezbollah has continued ordinary terrorist activities against Israel, including missile and other attacks in the summer of 2006 that killed approximately 43 Israeli civilians. However, a broader look shows that the security of the average Israeli has improved since 2000. From Israel's military withdrawal on May 25, 2000, until January 2010, there have been no suicide attacks by any Lebanese or Hezbollah fighters and a grand total of 165[42] Israelis killed by Hezbollah activities, compared to about 1,787[43] from June 6, 1982, until May 25, 2000. The situation for Israel is better than even these numbers suggest, since nearly all of the Israeli deaths in the past 10 years occurred in the 2006 war, during a few weeks following Israeli air strikes.

42. Israel Ministry of Foreign Affairs Web site, "Behind the Headlines: The Second Lebanon War-Three years Later," "July 12, 2009, http://www.mfa.gov.il/mfa/terrorism-%20obstacle%20 to%20peace/terrorism%20from%20lebanon-%20hizbullah/.

43. Stephanie Fronk, "An Evaluation of Israel's Counterterrorism Strategies," (student paper, University of Chicago, 2010); Global Terrorism Database, START, accessed on February 23, 2010, available at http://www.start.umd.edu/gtd/; Israel Ministry of Foreign Affairs Web site.

CHAPTER EIGHT

Israel and Palestine

The Palestinian-Israeli dispute is one of the most enduring and explosive conflicts, and repeatedly attracts the attention of world leaders
and publics at-large, who are politically, religiously, and historically drawn
to the tensions among Jews, Christians, and Muslims.[1] The conflict has its
roots in the historic claim to the land that lies between the eastern shores
of the Mediterranean Sea and the Jordan River. For the Palestinians the
last 100 years have brought colonization, expulsion, and military occupation, followed by a long and difficult search for self-determination and for
coexistence with the nation they hold responsible for their suffering and
loss. For the Jewish people of Israel, the return to the land of their fore-
fathers after centuries of persecution around the world has not brought
peace or security. They have faced many crises as their neighbors have
sought to wipe their country off the map.[2]

Violent opposition in the form of suicide terrorism did not appear until
the 1990s, spiked from 2000 to 2005, and then declined to almost no suicide
attacks in the past four years. What accounts for this trajectory?

Most explanations of Palestinian suicide terrorism focus on religious,

---

1. Major contributors to this chapter were Sophia Akbar, Martin Wolberg-Stok, and
Sylvia Hammad.

2. For a discussion of Arab-Israeli relations, see Mark Tessler, *A History of the Israeli-
Palestinian Conflict* (Bloomington: Indiana University Press, 2009); Michael Feige, *Settling in
the Hearts: Jewish Fundamentalism in the Occupied Territories* (Detroit: Wayne State University
Press, 2009); Neve Gordon, *Israel's Occupation* (Berkeley: University of California Press, 2008);
Anton La Guardia, *Holy Land, Unholy War: Israelis and Palestinians* (London: Penguin, 2007);
Benny Morris, *One State, Two States: Resolving the Israel/Palestine Conflict* (New Haven, CT:
Yale, 2009); and Kamal Nawash, "Israel/Palestine Conflict May Lead to Regional War," http://
www.arabisto.com/article/Blogs/Kamal_Nawash/IsraelPalestine_Conflict_May_Lead_to_Re-
gional_War/28263; and "A History of the Conflict," BBC, http://news.bbc.co.uk/2/shared/spl/hi/
middle_east/03/v3_ip_timeline/html/default.stm.

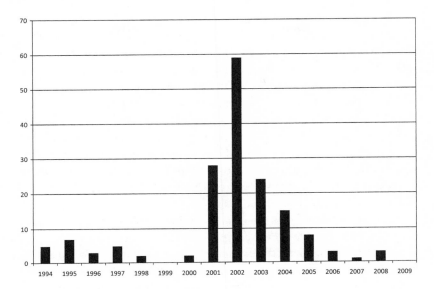

FIGURE 8.1 Suicide attacks in Israel/Palestine

economic, and political causes internal to the Palestinian community.[3] However, these factors change slowly, normally over generations, and so poorly account for the phenomenon. For instance, Islamic fundamentalism in the Palestinian community has existed throughout much of the 20th century, far longer than the existence of the Palestinian campaign of suicide terrorism. With Hamas' recent victory in the 2006 Palestinian Authority elections, many would rate the influence of Islamic fundamentalism higher today than ever—with the result that this religious cause is a poor fit with the rise and decline of suicide terrorism by Palestinians. The economic explanation claims that poverty drives suicide terrorism, though there is

3. For recent work highlighting the Palestinian case as an example of Islamic fundamentalism, see Bruce Hoffman, *Inside Terrorism* (New York: Columbia University Press, 2006); Raphael Israeli, *Islamikaze: Manifestations of Islamic Martyrology* (London: Routledge, 2003); David Frum and Richard Perle, *An End to Evil: How to End the War on Terror* (New York: Random House, 2003). For recent work on the economic argument, see Joyce M. Davis, *Martyrs: Innocence, Vengeance, and Despair in the Middle East* (New York: Palgrave, 2003). For an example of the political explanation, see Mia Bloom, *Dying to Kill* (New York: Columbia University Press, 2005). Among recent scholarship on terrorism, Mohammed M. Hafez's *Why Muslims Rebel: Depression and Resistance in the Islamic World* (London: Lynne Riener Publishers, 2003) comes closest to our position, proposing that Islamist insurgencies occur in environments of political repression (the same type of environment that foreign occupation is likely to create).

little evidence of this being the case in Palestine, where before the First Intifada Palestinians were relatively well off economically and many worked
blue-collar jobs in Israel. It is only after the start of the intifada that Israel
enacted employment and visa restrictions for Palestinians as a response
to the violence, effectively cutting them off economically and driving up
unemployment. On the political front, the claim is that Palestinian terrorist
organizations competing for public support use violence to increase their
reputation, leading in turn to greater extremism as organizations attempt
to outdo each other. However, public opinion polls in Palestine show that
while support for suicide terrorism operations has steadily increased, there
is no evidence that any particular group has made domestic political gains
as a result of suicide operations.

This chapter shows that the primary impetus behind the formation of
the Palestinian suicide attack campaign is Israel's occupation, and particularly Israel's changing cultural, political, and military influence on the
West Bank and Gaza from the mid-1980s onward. This growing Israeli
influence led to increasing resistance to Israeli occupation during the First
Intifada from 1988 to 1992. This ordinary violence ended when Israel and
the Palestinian Liberation Organization adopted the 1993 Oslo Accords
that established a peaceful process whereby Israel would withdraw from
Gaza and the West Bank, eventually creating the conditions for an independent Palestinian self-rule. Breakdowns in the Oslo process, both small
and large, resulted in Palestinian suicide terrorism as a last resort to roll
back Israeli occupation policies.

This campaign of organized suicide attacks launched with the aim of
ending Israeli occupation can be divided into three distinct periods, as illustrated in figure 8.1. The first period is from 1994 to 1999, and is itself
characterized by three distinct subcampaigns: two planned and executed to
coerce Israel into compliance with key provisions of the Oslo agreement,
and the third to stop Israel's targeting of Hamas leadership. The middle period from 2000 to 2005 represents the Second Intifada uprising, or Al-Aqsa
Intifada, which can be distinguished from the previous period both because
of the marked increase of suicide attacks and because negotiations had
ceased during this time. The campaign began shortly after the breakdown
of Camp David, and continued with Israel's expansion of settlements in
Gaza and the West Bank, accompanied by the reintroduction of IDF forces
in Gaza and an expanded IDF presence in the West Bank.

Finally, the period from 2006 to 2009 represents the end and aftermath of the Al-Aqsa Intifada, and shows a marked decrease in suicide attacks during a time of relatively fragile peace.

In examining these three distinct periods, this chapter will provide 1) a brief history of the Israeli-Palestinian conflict from WWI to the 1993 Oslo Accords, 2) a look at the Palestinian suicide terrorist groups and their respective ideology, 3) an assessment of the trajectory of the Palestinian suicide campaign, 4) operational patterns in the suicide attacks, 5) attackers' demographic profile, and 6) an estimation of Palestinian public support for various suicide terrorist groups and their actions. This assessment shows that Palestinian suicide bombing has been driven mainly by strategic, nationalistic aims as opposed to Islamic fundamentalism.

The Israeli-Palestinian Conflict

After WWI, Great Britain was given a mandate by the League of Nations to rule Palestine after the breakup of the Ottoman Empire. Part of the mandate included a commitment to establish a Jewish "national home" in Palestine, as had been expressed in the Balfour Declaration of 1917.[4] However, during WWI, British leaders also committed to establish an Arab state on the same territory as they were eager to incite the 1916 Arab revolt against Ottoman rule.[5] Thus the conflict began between Jews and Palestinians for a homeland in Palestine. In the decades following the Balfour Declaration, Jews began to settle in Palestine. After WWII, Jewish emigration to Palestine increased rapidly in the aftermath of the Holocaust, and riots ensued from both Jewish and Arab sides. The British were faced with a territorial conflict they were ill equipped to deal with, and announced plans to withdraw from Palestine in 1947. The United

---

4. The document ratified by the League of Nations in 1922 for the British mandate over Palestine contained, in its preamble, references to the Balfour Declaration, and called upon Britain to put into effect the promises made in 1917. "League of Nations: The British Mandate (July 24, 1922)," in *The Israel-Arab Reader,* ed., W. Laqueur and B. Rubin (New York: Penguin Books, 2008), pp. 30–36.

5. This commitment found expression in the "Hussein-McMahon Correspondence" of 1915–16. In order to secure Arab land from the breakup of the Ottoman Empire, the sharif of Mecca, Hussein ibn Ali, wrote to the British high commissioner in Egypt, Sir Henry McMahon. In exchange for Arab rebellion against the Ottomans, McMahon promised to assist Arabs in attaining independence in the Levant, Mesopotamia, and the Arab Peninsula. Gudrun Kramer, *A History of Palestine* (Princeton, NJ: Princeton University Press, 2004), p. 144.

Nations stepped in and offered a partition plan, but this was rejected by Arab leaders and the British. Tensions continued to escalate, and Palestine broke into civil war in early 1948. Before the British mandate officially ended in May 14, 1948, Israel announced its independence and was quickly recognized as a state by the United States, France, and the Soviet Union, with Britain abstaining. Invasions by Arab states were countered as Israel successfully regained territory, and after the UN brokered ceasefire ended the war, Israel retained 50% more territory than the original UN partition plan.[6]

After the war, Jordan controlled the West Bank and East Jerusalem and Egypt captured Gaza, but half a million Palestinians were displaced or expelled from their homes in the Israeli territories; this refugee population has continued to grow and in 2009 constitutes over 4.6 million Palestinians living in Jordan, Lebanon, Syria, the West Bank, and Gaza.[7] As Arab states gained independence from Britain and France in the 1950s and 1960s, Egypt called for a unified Arab offensive against Israel. In a preemptive attack, Israel initiated the 1967 Six Day War, which ultimately resulted in the defeat of Arab forces and Israeli control over the West Bank, Gaza, East Jerusalem, the Syrian Golan Heights, and the Egyptian Sinai Peninsula. The way in which the 1967 war altered the map remains the region's most contested issue, as Israeli occupation in these lands continues to adversely affect the Palestinian way of life. UN Resolution 242 responded to the 1967 war and called for withdrawal of Israeli armed forces from the Occupied Territories, encouraging the right of every state in the area to live in peace within secure and recognized boundaries.[8]

Initially, Israel's occupation of the West Bank and Gaza had only modest effects on the Palestinian way of life, and indeed during the 1970s it was common for Palestinians to work in Israel, leaving their homes, traveling to their jobs, and returning on a daily basis, with little incidence of terrorism or violence. Things changed with the increasing encroachment of Jewish settlers on land inhabited by Palestinians. As figure 8.2 shows, during the first 13 years of the occupation (1967–80), only about 12,000 Jewish set-

6. For full texts of the Israeli declaration of independence and the United Nations resolution calling for a cease-fire, see "State of Israel: Proclamation of Independence (May 14,1948)" and "UN General Assembly: Resolution 194 (December 11, 1948)," in *The Israel-Arab Reader,* ed., W. Laqueur and B. Rubin (New York: Penguin Books, 2008), pp. 81–86.

7. "United Nations Relief and Works Agency for Palestine Refugees in the Near East," available at http://www.un.org/unrwa/publications/index.html.

8. UN Security Council, "Resolution 242," available at http://daccessdds.un.org/doc/RESOLUTION/GEN/NR0/240/94/IMG/NR024094.pdf?OpenElement.

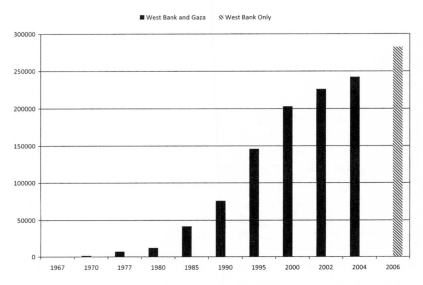

FIGURE 8.2 Jewish settlers in the West Bank and Gaza. Source: Israel's Central Bureau of Statistics, Foundation for Middle Peace Web site (http://www.fmep.org).

tlers resided in the Occupied Territories, a tiny fraction compared to the approximately 2 million Palestinians living there at the time. From 1980 to 1995, this number increased more than tenfold, to 146,000, and a further 60% from 1995 to 2004, to 242,000. The growth of Jewish settlers consumed more and more land, and required progressive expansion of the Israeli military presence to protect Jewish settlements throughout the West Bank and Gaza. In 2005, Israel decided to withdraw its military forces and settlers from Gaza and large parts of the West Bank. From this point on, the number of Jewish settlers continued to grow, but only in the existing Jewish enclaves, immediately on the border of Israel.

Starting in 1987, Palestinian resistance to the growing cultural, political, and military influence of Israel grew progressively—from violent (but unarmed) rebellion in the First Intifada from 1987 to 1992, to protracted guerrilla war and suicide terrorism in the 1990s, to large-scale suicide terrorism in the Second Intifada from September 2000 to the end of 2004. This resistance was not moderated and at times was exacerbated by the Oslo peace process, most likely because it did little to stem the flow of Jewish settlers into the Palestinian territories. Only when Israel unilaterally withdrew from Gaza and large parts of the West Bank in 2005, effectively freezing the encroachment of Jewish settlers on Palestinian land, did suicide terrorism dramatically decline.

Groups and Goals

Hamas, Al-Aqsa Martyr's Brigade, Palestinian Islamic Jihad, and the Popular Front for the Liberation of Palestine (PFLP) are the most important terrorist groups operating in the West Bank and Gaza. Although each group's ideology differs from the others' in significant ways, the common factor uniting all of them is Palestinian nationalism. The shared experience of Israeli occupation has contributed to their uses of nationalistic rhetoric and the common goal of creating an independent Palestinian state.[9] Not only do these groups share the short-term goal of Palestinian nationalism, they also embrace a common method to reach this goal: suicide terrorism. While these groups differ ideologically along two lines, religious versus secular and Sunni versus revolutionary Shiite leanings, they all view suicide terrorism as a viable method in achieving Palestinian nationalism. However, it must be noted that where these groups diverge the most is in their desired ultimate political outcome after this first goal has been achieved. These differences lie, among other factors, in whether to return to 1948 or 1967 borders or whether to rule a newly created Palestine state under an Islamic government or one that is secular. While the groups maintain fairly consistent goals regarding the preferred form of government, some appear to have modified their positions on acceptable borders, since they were originally founded.

Hamas: an Islamic form of government with pre-1967 borders likely acceptable;
PIJ: an Islamic form of government with pre-1948 borders, promoting pan-Islamism across Muslim countries;
PFLP: a nonreligious, socialist form of government brought about through revolution, pre-1967 borders, promoting pan-Arabism across Arab states;
Al-Aqsa: a secular form of government with pre-1967 borders.

One might wonder why, given these incompatible views, Palestinian groups have not carried out attacks against each other. Again, the answer

9. For a comprehensive trajectory of Palestinian national identity, see Rashid Khalidi, *Palestinian Identity: The Construction of Modern National Consciousness* (New York: Columbia University Press, 2010); and Baruch Kimmerling and Joel S. Migdal, *The Palestinian People: A History* (Cambridge, MA: Harvard University Press, 2003).

lies in what they perceive as a shared struggle against Israel and their common goal of Palestinian nationalism—because of these factors, and perhaps
due to current political realities, it seems that these groups are willing to
overlook their differences to achieve this short-term objective.

Hamas—Religious, Sunni

The Harakat al-Muqawama al-Islamiya (Hamas), or Islamic Resistance
Movement, formed in 1987 at the onset of the First Intifada and is the
largest Palestinian militant Islamist organization. With the short-term aim
of driving Israeli forces out of the Occupied Territories, Hamas's long-
term aim is to establish an Islamic state within historic Palestine. Hamas's
militant branch, the Izz al-Din al-Qassam Brigades, was most active before 2005, as the group carried out numerous suicide bombings, rocket
attacks, and shootings against civilians in Israel and security forces and
settlers in the Occupied Territories. It is estimated that this military wing
has several hundred members and coordinates activities with Hamas's
Executive Force, which has reported 6,000 policemen but announced an
expansion to 12,000 in early 2007.[10] Before parliamentary elections in
2006, Hamas also gained popularity among the Palestinian population
through its social programs and building religious institutions, schools,
and hospitals.

As a result of widespread public support, Hamas won the 2006 parliamentary elections by a large margin, 74 out of 132 seats.[11] Fatah, the late
Palestinian leader Yasser Arafat's party and the dominant party in the Palestinian Liberation Organization (PLO), won only 45 seats. After the election, Iran pledged $50 million to the nearly bankrupt Palestinian Authority
(PA) and continues to support Hamas with weapons and training.[12] In light
of the recent 2009 war in Gaza, it is important to note that the resources
Hamas has received from Iran have not resulted in an increase in suicide
attacks. Funding for Hamas also comes from Palestinian expatriates and

10. "Hamas-Led PA expands Executive Force," *Jane's Intelligence and Insight,* January 15,
2007, http://www.janes.com/security/law_enforcement/news/jdw/jdw070115_1_n.shtml.

11. On January 25, 2006, the Palestinian National Authority (PA)—the administrative organization the Oslo Accords created to govern parts of the Gaza Strip and the West Bank—
held elections for the Palestinian Legislative Council, the PA's ruling body. It should be noted
that Hamas is not part of the PLO, the umbrella organization recognized by Arab leaders and
the United Nations in 1974 as the sole legitimate representative of the Palestinian people.

12. Council on Foreign Relations, "State Sponsors: Iran," available at http://www.cfr.org/
publication/9362/state_sponsors.html.

private Arab benefactors, but it is unclear how much of this money goes into militant activities and how much goes into Palestinian Authority ministries and programs.[13]

Classified as a terrorist organization by the United States, EU, and Israel, these major world powers have threatened to limit or end diplomatic or economic relations with Palestine unless Hamas recognizes Israel, renounces terrorism, and accepts all previous Israeli-Palestinian agreements. Supporters of Hamas, on the other hand, maintain that Hamas's activities constitute legitimate resistance against an oppressive foreign occupier.

HAMAS'S IDEOLOGY.   As an offshoot of the Egyptian Muslim Brotherhood, founded in 1928 by Hassan al-Banna, Hamas uses Islamist rhetoric to express nationalistic aims. It is important to note that although Hamas grew out of the Palestinian branch of the Muslim Brotherhood and both groups ascribe to Sunni Muslim ideology, the policies and activities adopted by Hamas from the outset differ markedly from its parent organization, the Muslim Brotherhood. The Muslim Brotherhood's goal has been primarily to establish the Qur'an and the teachings of Prophet Muhammad as the "sole reference point for . . . ordering the life of the Muslim family, individual, community . . . and state."[14] To achieve this aim the group has traditionally focused on religious education and spiritual purification of the community.[15] Hamas, on the other hand, was created with the aim of resisting Israeli foreign occupation and establishing a Palestinian state—a more political, rather than purely religious, goal. This sentiment is reflected in Article 12 of the Hamas charter,

> Nationalism, from the point of view of the Islamic Resistance Movement, is part of the religious creed. Nothing in nationalism is more significant or deeper than in the case when an enemy should tread Muslim land. Resisting and quelling the enemy become the individual duty of every Muslim, male or female.[16]

By couching nationalism in Islamic terms, Hamas makes the Palestinian national struggle a Muslim's duty to overcome. Hamas does intend to

---

13. U.S. Department of State, "Background Information on Foreign Terrorist Organizations," available at http://www.state.gov/s/ct/rls/rpt/fto/2801.htm.

14. "Principles of the Muslim Brotherhood," available at http://www.muslimbrotherhood.co.uk/Home.asp?zPage=Systems&System=PressR&Press=Show&Lang=E&ID=4584.

15. Andrea Nusse, *Muslim Palestine: The Ideology of Hamas* (Abingdon: RoutledgeCurzon, 1998).

16. Hamas, "Charter," available at. http://www.mideastweb.org/hamas.htm.

establish an Islamic form of government, though this is not an immediate aim and Palestinian independence is the primary goal. The form that a Hamas-led Islamic government would take after independence is achieved, however, remains to be seen. The Palestinian population as a whole has historically subscribed to moderate Islam, and religious currents, though increasingly popular, have largely remained peripheral to Palestinian society;[17] consequently, Hamas's election campaign in 2006 minimized its Islamic rhetoric in order to appeal to the entire Palestinian population.[18] In a poll conducted shortly after elections by the Jerusalem Media and Communications Center, 70% of Palestinians said they were "somewhat not worried" or "not worried at all" that a Hamas government would subject Palestinians to social Islamic regulations.[19] This, coupled with Hamas's focus on providing food, education, health care, and social services to Palestinians contributed to its overwhelming popularity. However, Hamas's Muslim Brotherhood roots cannot be discounted either. Religious rhetoric is prevalent in their charter and, according to the same poll, 20% of Palestinians voted for Hamas on the basis of their promises for an Islamic form of government. However, less than 13% believed that Hamas won on religious grounds.[20] Indeed, the way in which Hamas's religious elements might translate into political reality is subject to future consideration.

POSITION ON ISRAEL AND NEGOTIATION.   In an interview with head political bureau chief Khaled Mash'al, Mash'al explains his stance on Israel and the legitimacy of previous negotiations. On an official level, Hamas does not recognize past negotiations or Israel and in fact calls for Israel's destruction in its own charter, a key reason why the international community refuses to recognize the current Hamas-led government as legitimate. Mash'al, however, seems to veer away from this hard-line stance if the concerns of the Palestinian people are advanced by doing so. He states,

> We deal with the signed agreements and the existing ones on the ground in accordance with the interests of the Palestinian people. If they serve my people,

17. Mohammed Dajani, "Hamas and Palestinian Religious Moderation," *Palestine-Israel Journal of Politics, Economics and Culture* 13, no. 3 (2006).

18. Khaled Hroub, "Hamas's Path to Reinvention," available at http://www.opendemocracy.net/conflict-middle_east_politics/hamas_3982.jsp.

19. Matthew Longo, "For the Palestinians, Disco's Last Days?" *International Herald Tribune*, March 22, 2006, available at http://www.iht.com/articles/2006/03/21/opinion/edlongo.php

20. Ibid.

then I'll implement them. . . . It is our right as Palestinians and as a government, irrespective of which one, to tackle these agreements in a way that is realistic, and that takes into consideration the general good and the balance of power.

This statement may serve to explain why Hamas chose to run for PA elections in 2006, a move that was highly contested among Hamas's hardline members, as the PA itself earlier officially recognized the existence of Israel during the Oslo negotiations. Indeed, members participated in elections because they believed Hamas to be the best alternative to Fatah in advancing the Palestinian cause through leadership in the PA.

In this interview, Mash'al also reveals that a cease-fire would be accepted if a Palestinian state within the 1967 borders were to be acknowledged. Rather than viewing this as a "two-state" solution, Mash'al emphasizes that establishing a Palestinian state is the main concern, not recognizing Israel. To clarify, he states,

Why should the establishment of two states become the aim and principle of the Palestinians? Israel does exist in actual fact, and I am asked to give it legitimacy. . . . An entity exists; this is a reality, but as a Palestinian, I am not supposed to recognize the legitimacy of the occupation. There is an entity called Israel. Yes. But recognizing it is not my concern.

Essentially, Mash'al believes that every move, whether it be running for elections, conducting a suicide attack campaign, or calling a cease-fire, should be a strategic step toward advancing the Palestinian cause. A look at the remaining three Palestinian groups will reveal less political participation in pursuit of the goal of Palestinian independence and more focus on violent action.

Palestinian Islamic Jihad—Religious, Shiite Revolutionary Leanings

Palestinian Islamic Jihad (PIJ) violently opposes the existence of Israel and has employed suicide attacks since the mid-1990s with the aim of destroying Israel and establishing a sovereign Palestinian state, within the pre–1948 mandate borders. Similar to Hamas, PIJ has roots in the Muslim Brotherhood in Egypt, but broke away from its parent organization in the 1970s when PIJ members deemed the Brotherhood to be too religiously moderate and insufficiently committed to the Palestinian national cause. Although both Hamas and PIJ aim to establish an Islamic state on historic Palestine, PIJ refuses to participate in the political process and rejects any two-state agreement. Their former leader and founder, Fathi Shiqaqi, was assassinated by Israeli forces in 1995, and was succeeded by Dr. Ramadan Abdallah Shallah.

PIJ is based in Damascus and receives financial support primarily from Iran. It also maintains offices in Beirut, Lebanon; Tehran, Iran; and Khartoum, Sudan. In addition to receiving training from Iran, PIJ members have trained with Hezbollah in Lebanon. Hezbollah supports PIJ's efforts in recruiting Palestinian refugees in Lebanon.[21] The group size is unknown, although it is significantly smaller than Hamas or Al-Aqsa.[22]

PIJ'S IDEOLOGY.[23]   Although PIJ members are Sunni Muslims, the organization ascribes to Shiite revolutionary ideals, most notably those upheld during the 1979 Iranian Revolution that led to the establishment of an Islamic regime in Iran. In addition to its revolutionary leanings, PIJ also adopted the belief of rule by clergy from Shiite ideology. This, however, does not allow the PIJ to be classified as strictly Shiite, since rule by clergy is not specific to Shiism. Rule by descendants from Ali, the Prophet Muhammad's cousin, is specific to Shiism, but the PIJ have not shown evidence of exclusive allegiance to Shiite leaders. Although the Muslim Brotherhood initially accused them of heresy and ascribing to Shiism after the PIJ broke away from their organization, there has since been no evidence of such accusations from the Brotherhood or other major Sunni groups, such as Hamas. In an interview with the PIJ, Shallah lists a number of scholars from which the organization has drawn inspiration, among which are major Sunni and Shiite figures alike, such as Hasan al-Banna (Sunni), Sayyid Abu A'la Mawdudi (Sunni), Ayatollah Khomeini (Shiite), and Hassan al-Turabi (Shiite). A look at the theories of these scholars reveals common threads: a belief in establishing an Islam-based government and belief in the need to overcome Western domination. A few of the Shiite scholars even stress the importance of bridging the Sunni-Shiite divide to overcome Western influence.[24] Thus, it can be concluded that in pursuit of Palestinian liberation,

21. Aaron Mannes, *Profiles in Terror* (New York: Rowman and Littlefield, 2004).

22. U.S. Department of State, "Background Information on Foreign Terrorist Organizations," available at http://www.state.gov/s/ct/rls/rpt/fto/2801.htm.

23. The available literature on the PFLP is limited; in the absence of a publicly accessible charter, this section is based on group and leader statements.

24. "Interview with Hasan al-Turabi," *The Looming Tower: Al-Qaeda and the Road to 9/11* (New York: Knopf, 2006), p. 165.

PIJ members are indiscriminate in their support of Sunni or Shiite Islamist theoretical ideas and successes in practice. In their view, the most successful example of an Islamic revolution to date occurred in Shiite-dominated Iran, but this revolution is not limited to Shiite-dominated countries or groups and can be replicated among Muslim countries worldwide.

Rather than advocating a pan-Arab movement such as the PFLP (discussed in the next section), PIJ considers itself a key player in a pan-*Islamic* movement that began with the Iranian Revolution. In line with this sentiment, Abu-Shahin condemned the international community for exonerating Serbia from the Srebrenica genocide, in which thousands of Bosnian Muslims were massacred in 1995. PIJ sent monetary assistance and arms to the Muslims in the area. To justify involvement in a war outside of Palestine, leader Ali Abu-Shahin stated, "When Islam needs to be defended it does not matter whether this is in Iraq, Palestine, Bosnia, Afghanistan, or any other place."[25] Since Bosnian Muslims are Sunni, this is consistent with their indiscriminate support of the Muslim struggle, Sunni or Shiite.

POSITION ON ISRAEL AND NEGOTIATIONS.   Hamas and PIJ have often been lumped together as organizations with Islamist religious platforms, but it is important to note that PIJ is much more radical in its religious stance and its stance toward Israel. Hamas leaders consider the Palestinian struggle to be essentially political and territorial, summarized by a statement by Mash'al:

> Our message to the Israelis is this: we do not fight you because you belong to a certain faith or culture. Jews have lived in the Muslim world for 13 centuries in peace and harmony; they are in our religion "the people of the book" who have a covenant from God and His Messenger Muhammad (peace be upon him) to be respected and protected. Our conflict with you is not religious but political. We have no problem with Jews who have not attacked us—our problem is with those who came to our land, imposed themselves on us by force, destroyed our society and banished our people.[26]

Speaking for PIJ, Abu-Shahin emphasizes that the struggle is in fact ideological, and not political:

---

25. "We will not sell our people or principles for foreign aid," *The Guardian*, available at http://www.guardian.co.uk/world/2006/jan/31/comment.israelandthepalestinians.
26. Ibid.

You have to understand one thing: we are waging an ideological war, not a political war, against Israel. There are no economic or political issues that we could resolve in a political manner. We will never recognize Israel within its current borders, because we as believers see this as a sin. We will never be at peace as long as our people live like refugees in the world while they bring people from all over the world to live on their hearths. We will fight them to a complete destruction of the Israeli state if necessary, and I guarantee you that we will succeed in this.[27]

Whereas Hamas is willing to participate in the political process if it advances the creation of a Palestinian state, PIJ has never been willing to run for PA elections, citing their illegitimacy under the Oslo Accords. Abu-Shahin expressed this sentiment in an interview:

The moment we become a part of the Palestinian government, it would mean that we recognize Israel and the Oslo agreement signed by Arafat, which has not given the Palestinian people the right to exist. We are a resistance movement and are currently in the phase of liberating our homeland. That is how things will be until the territories where the Palestinian state will be are liberated.[28]

The PIJ also believe that Israeli-Arab coexistence is not possible, citing Zionist expansion as a major threat to Arab peace. Shallah stated, "Peace in this struggle requires the removal of Israel and the return of Palestine, with all its soil, to the map."

Popular Front for the Liberation of Palestine (PFLP)—Secular, Marxist, Sunni

Currently a leading member of the Palestinian Liberation Organization (PLO), the PFLP was founded by George Habash in 1967 as it broke away from the Arab Nationalist Movement. Himself a Palestinian Christian, Habash founded the Arab Nationalist Movement in an effort to unite the Arab world. After the 1967 war and the defeat of Jordan, Syria, Egypt, and Palestine, Habash responded with the creation of the PFLP. Rejecting any two-state solution, the PFLP has historically advocated for one state with an Arab identity in which Jews are allowed to live with minority rights. In

27. "Palestinian Islamic Jihad Member Condemns Acquitting Serbia of Genocide," *Vecernji List (Bosnia-Herzegovina edition)* (Croatian), March 19, 2007.
28. Ibid.

1999, however, the PFLP came to an agreement with PLO leadership regarding negotiations with Israel, but still maintains a hard-line stance. After Habash's resignation in 2000, the PFLP was led by Abu Ali Mustafa. Assassinated by Israeli helicopter rockets in 2001, Mustafa was succeeded by hard-liner Ahmed Sa'adat, who rejects the legitimacy of past negotiations. Sa'adat is currently imprisoned under Israeli custody.

The PFLP receives safe haven from Syria in addition to some logistical assistance from Syria and Libya. Before its collapse, the Soviet Union also provided monetary support to the group. The group's power has been on the decline since leader Sa'adat's arrest, and it is estimated that there are about 800 active members (as of 2004), with a few thousand supporters primarily in the West Bank and Syria. The PFLP and Hamas are the only two groups who have participated in the political scene. However, PFLP's political clout is small in comparison to Hamas; in 2006 elections the group captured only 4.2% of the vote.[29] Currently, the PFLP operates out of the West Bank but has offices in Damascus, Syria, and operates a training camp in Lebanon.[30]

PFLP'S IDEOLOGY.[31]   The PFLP views the Palestinian struggle as a broader revolution against Western imperialism. Their ideology is not only secular but antireligious. Its doctrine is based on three central principles:

- The existence of a rivalry between the Western nations and the Arab world, in which the West seeks to exploit the Arab world's resources either through economic influence or physical occupation of the territory;
- Israel's role as the West's primary regional partner in that process;
- The need for an ideological and organizational framework to guide Palestinians in combating this trend [of exploitation] with revolutionary professionalism, in addition to achieving their national aims—even over a period of generations.[32]

Marxist-Leninist philosophy still guides the PFLP today, believed by the group to offer a well-suited framework for both opposing the West and carrying out a complete revolution over time. The PFLP believes in

29. "PA HAILS Habash as 'Important Symbol of Revolution.' Officials Hope for Moderation in PFLP Following Death of the Organization's Radical Former Leader," *Jerusalem Post,* January 28, 2008.

30. Mannes, *Profiles.*

31. The available literature on the PFLP is limited; in the absence of a publicly accessible charter, this section is based on group and leader statements.

32. Harold M. Cubert, *The PFLP's Changing Role in the Middle East* (London: Routledge, 1997).

the necessity of "a scientific revolutionary ideology, to enable the masses to understand their enemy, its strong and weak points, and the forces which aid it and are allied with it."[33] In line with this view, Habash categorized the 1967 defeat as "the scientific society of Israel against our own backwardness in the Arab world. This calls for the total rebuilding of Arab society into a twentieth-century society."[34] PFLP's ideology goes beyond the call for an independent Palestinian nation, pushing for a revolutionizing of society across all Arab states.

Al-Aqsa Martyrs Brigade—Secular, Sunni

Splitting off from the Fatah political party to pursue militant activities, the Al-Aqsa Martyrs Brigade (Al-Aqsa) formed in 2000 at the outset of the Second Intifada with the aim of driving Israeli forces out of the Occupied Territories and establishing a Palestinian state. Although Al-Aqsa has no central independent leadership, members remain loyal to the Fatah party ideology and were devoted to the Palestinian Authority president Yasser Arafat until his death in 2004. Al-Aqsa was not branded a terrorist organization until 2002, when the group began using suicide bombing against Israeli civilians as a method of attack.

Iran provides funds for Al-Aqsa and reportedly has influence in other aspects of the organization.[35] It is unclear how much of the PLO's finances supported Al-Aqsa during Arafat's leadership before 2004. Lebanon's Hezbollah and Fatah collaborated during the Second Intifada, building cells within the West Bank and Gaza in order to launch sniper and mortar attacks against Israel within the pre-1967 borderlines. The group size is estimated to be around a few thousand.[36]

AL-AQSA'S IDEOLOGY.   Al-Aqsa's ideology is secular nationalist, following its parent organization, Fatah. In the absence of a unique Al-Aqsa charter, we will look to Fatah's ideology for the closest assessment of the militant group's ideology. Unlike Hamas and Palestinian Islamic Jihad, Fatah's charter does not call for an Islamic state based on Islamic jurisprudence,

33. Ibid.
34. "Interview with American Journalist John Cooley, 1973," available at http://www.experiencefestival.com/george_habash.
35. U.S. Department of State, "Background Information on Foreign Terrorist Organizations," available at http://www.state.gov/s/ct/rls/rpt/fto/2801.htm.
36. Ibid.

but rather a Palestinian national state that does not privilege religious interpretations of the law. Rather than being actively antireligious such as the PFLP, Fatah's charter is secular and does not mention the explicit aim of creating an Islamic state, but rather emphasizes national liberation.

POSITIONS ON ISRAEL AND NEGOTIATIONS.   The charter states the following as a goal: "Establishing an independent democratic state with complete sovereignty on all Palestinian lands, and Jerusalem is its capital city, and protecting the citizens' legal and equal rights without any racial or religious discrimination."[37] A statement issued by Al-Aqsa in August 2003 supports resistance in pursuit of this goal, pointing out the failure of negotiations:

> As long as the occupation exists, there will be resistance. We will respond to any aggression, killing and arrest inside the usurper Zionist entity. We also emphasize that these negotiations did not achieve any political goals. The glorious intifada and valiant resistance have shown that placing bets on reaching settlements is an illusion. The Zionist entity, through its military machine and arrogance as well as the continuation of killings, arrests, destruction of houses, and construction of the Nazi segregation wall, has shown that coexistence with it is not possible.[38]

Al-Aqsa has chosen militant activity over political discourse in pursuit of the goals expressed by Fatah: national independence, refugee right of return, Palestinian sovereignty, and the end of Israeli occupation.

Trajectory of Suicide Attacks

Although Israeli occupation of the territories existed since 1967 and Palestinian groups such as Hamas and PIJ had formed in the 1970s and 1980s, we do not see the use of suicide attacks until 1994. Up until that time, Palestinian groups experimented with methods of attack such as guerilla operations and nonsuicide forms of terrorism. The Palestinian suicide campaign is characterized by three periods: 1994 to 1999; 2000 to 2005; and 2006 to the present. The first period is composed of a series of

37. Fatah charter, http://www.mideastweb.org/fateh.htm.
38. "Palestinian Fatah Armed Wing Says Negotiations with Israel 'Useless,'" *BBC Monitoring Middle East,* August 17, 2003.

subcampaigns whose success played an important role in subsequent periods. This section will describe in detail when, how, and why suicide attacks have been employed to achieve the Palestinian groups' stated goals in the three campaigns and the subcampaigns within the first phase.

Period No. 1—1994–1999

The first period, from 1994 to 1999, is important because Israel made significant concessions that increased the confidence of the terrorist groups in the coercive effectiveness of suicide attack, and so encouraged the most intense later campaign, the Second Intifada against Israel.

While the adoption of the Oslo Accords in September 1993 led to the decline of ordinary violence in the First Intifada, breakdowns in the Oslo peace process played a key role in the rise of suicide terrorism. The Oslo Accords marked the first face-to-face agreement between Palestinian and Israeli leaders. It entailed a framework for future relations between Israel and the future Palestinian state, and was signed by Yasser Arafat on behalf of the Palestinian Liberation Organization and Israeli Prime Minister Yitzhak Rabin. The Accords were intended to be a 5-year maximum interim agreement, to allow for resolving major issues such as Palestinian refugees, Jerusalem, security, borders, and Israeli settlements. The most significant features of the Declaration of Principles include

- Creation of the Palestinian Authority (PA) and an elected Council in order to administer Palestinian lands; these lands in the West Bank and Gaza include three types of areas: 1) those allowed full PA control, 2) part PA civilian control and Israeli security control, and 3) Israeli settlements with full Israeli security control and limited PA civilian control. Over the five year-interim period, Israel would grant the PA self-government in phases.
- Withdrawal of the Israeli Defense Forces (IDF) from Gaza and parts of the West Bank
- *Letters of Mutual Recognition:* Israel recognized the PLO as legitimate representation of the Palestinian people while the PLO denounced terrorism and recognized Israel's right to exist.

SUBCAMPAIGN NO. 1—1994 ATTACKS.   Shortly after the signing of the Oslo Accords, the IDF was obligated to withdraw from Gaza and Jericho in the West Bank, called the Gaza-Jericho agreement. The IDF did not withdraw by the March 1994 deadline due to failed negotiations between the two sides; Israel wanted to retain its jurisdiction for criminal prosecution and argued for a smaller Palestinian police force. Hamas then conducted two suicide attacks on April 6 and 13 in Israel, which killed 15 Israeli civilians. Members of the Knesset (Israeli legislature) voted to proceed with the Gaza-Jericho agreement on April 18, forgoing its jurisdiction and security requests, and withdrawal began shortly thereafter on May 4, 1994.

The halting of Hamas's suicide subcampaign at this juncture is significant. In the Hebron massacre of February 1994, an Israeli settler killed 29 Palestinians. Thus, Hamas's suicide campaign was originally intended as retaliation for the massacre, as the group announced a series of five planned attacks. However, after the Knesset voted to withdraw from Gaza and Jericho and concede to Palestinian requests, Hamas did not conduct its final three attacks. A statement by Hamas's then political bureau chief, Musa Abu Marzuq, indicates that this type of change in attack plans is not out of line for Hamas: " the military strategy is a permanent strategy that will not change. The modus operandi, tactics, means, and timing are based on their benefit. They will change from time to time."[39] Hamas, having evaluated its actions as accelerating the withdrawal, changed its operations based on the achieved desired outcome. Notably, former Israeli prime minister Yitzhak Rabin also announced a change of plans in response to the attacks: "We have seen by now at least six acts of this type by Hamas and Islamic Jihad. . . . The only response to them and to the enemies of peace on the part of Israel is to accelerate the negotiations."[40] The outcome of the 1994 attacks could only have bolstered Hamas's belief in the coercive value of suicide terrorism; the deadline of the Oslo Accords did not produce change on the ground, but violent action in fact did.

SUBCAMPAIGN NO. 2 — 1995 ATTACKS.   From October 1994 to August 1995, Hamas and Palestinian Islamic Jihad (PIJ) launched a series of nine attacks combined, but this time with the intended goal of Israeli withdrawal from the West Bank. The sequence of events is illustrated by table 8.1.

As illustrated in the table, Israeli withdrawal seems to have been accelerated by violent action on the parts of Hamas and PIJ, supported by the following interpretations of these events. When questioned about the

39. Shaul Mishal and Avraham Sela, *Palestinian Hamas: Vision, Violence, and Coexistence* (New York: Columbia University Press, 2000).

40. David Makovsky and Alon Pinkas. "Rabin: Killing Civilians Won't Kill the Negotiations," *Jerusalem Post*, April 13, 1994.

TABLE 8.1 **Action-Reaction**

Action	Reaction
Israel did not withdraw from populated areas of the West Bank by the assigned Oslo Accords deadline of July 1994	Hamas launched three suicide attacks resulting in 30 Israeli deaths PIJ launched four attacks resulting in 32 deaths between October 1994 and June 1995
The PA requested a cease fire in March 1995 after Israel agreed to begin withdrawals in July 1995	Hamas and PIJ suspended attacks
Israel withdrawal was delayed due to security road construction setbacks, planned for April 1996 at the earliest	Hamas launched two suicide attacks on July 24 and August 21, 1995, resulting in 11 Israeli deaths
Hamas attacks (aforementioned attacks)	Israel withdrawal was planned and executed on December 1995 without finished construction Hamas and PIJ Suicide attacks halted

decision to withdraw in the face a potential increase in suicide attacks, Prime Minister Rabin responded, "What is the alternative, to have double the amount of terror? . . . All the bombers were Palestinians who came from areas under our control."[41] In an editorial in the *Jerusalem Post,* the writer warns of the danger of appearing to reward terrorism, "They [the attackers] firmly believe that negotiations will achieve little, and that only bloodshed will cause Israel to withdraw quickly and completely. . . . Unfortunately, the messages they receive from Israeli officials do not tend to discourage them."[42] A statement from Hamas leader Mahmud al-Zahhar reflects this encouragement, "Any fair person knows that the military action was useful for the [Palestinian] Authority during negotiations." Adding to this sentiment, PIJ leader Dr. Ramadan Abdallah Shallah stated, "This is the first time in the history of the Zionist entity that martyrdom actions forced the Zionist mind to question the usefulness of establishing a Jewish state on usurped land, on the ruins of a people who will chase them back with resistance and Jihad until the end of time."

SUBCAMPAIGN NO. 3—1996 ATTACKS.   The following two Hamas-led subcampaigns did not result in territorial concessions in the same way as subcampaigns no. 1 and no. 2, nor were such concessions Hamas's stated goal

41. Yitzhaq Rabin, "Interview," *BBC Summary of World Broadcasts,* September 8, 1995.
42. "Suicide Bombers Return," *Jerusalem Post,* November 3, 1995.

in either case. With Palestinian aggression on the rise, Israeli counterterrorism efforts were as well, resulting in targeted assassinations of Palestinian group leaders. On October 26, 1995, PIJ leader Fathi Shiqaqi was assassinated by Israeli forces, in addition to the assassination of Hamas leader Yahya Ayyash on January 5, 1996, through a bomb-laden cell phone.[43] Ayyash was responsible for introducing the suicide bombing tactic to Hamas, and was also the head bomb-maker. Following a six-month lull in suicide attacks, Hamas launched four suicide attacks over two weeks in February and March 1996, reportedly to avenge the assassination of one of their most valuable leaders. Shortly after the assassination, the Izz al-Din al-Qassam Brigades of Hamas issued a statement saying, "The martyrdom of the leader, Engineer Yahya Ayyash will only strengthen the Brigades and emphasize its continuation on his path and proceed on the road of Jihad." Moreover, Hamas leader Imad al-Faluji stated that "Israel will pay a high price for this operation."[44] Indeed, the four suicide attacks resulted in 58 Israeli civilian deaths. After the attacks, Palestinian public support for suicide terrorism was at an all-time low of 5%, compared to nearly 80% who opposed it. The PA's crackdown on militant groups combined with unprecedented Palestinian condemnation of the violence upon Israeli civilians led to a year-long lull in suicide attacks.

SUBCAMPAIGN NO. 4—1997 ATTACKS.   From March 1997 to September 1997, Hamas carried out three suicide attacks in Israel, resulting in 24 Israeli deaths. After the March and July 1997 attacks, Israel attempted to assassinate Hamas's political bureau chief, Khaled Mash'al, in September 1997 in Amman, Jordan.[45] The failed attempt resulted in the capture of the Israeli agents and a third suicide bombing on September 4. After claiming responsibility for the September bombing, Hamas issued a statement promising to continue attacks until release of Hamas members from Israeli prisons:

> We vow to continue our blows as long as our demands are not met and we will not accept any military truce before our prisoners receive their right to freedom. The attack is our explosive message to the government of the enemy which

43. "Gaza: 100,000 Palestinians Protest Assassination," *The Militant*, January 22, 1996.

44. "Israel to Pay 'High Price' for Ayyash Killing," *Radio Monte Carlo*, Paris, France, January 6, 1996.

45. Anne Marie Oliver and Paul Steinberg, *The Road to Martyrs' Square: A Journey to the World of the Suicide Martyr* (New York: Oxford University Press, 2005), p. 45.

blockades our people and which destroys our freedom by destroying houses and waging campaigns of oppression and arrests.[46]

As part of a deal between King Hussein of Jordan and Israel, Israel released Hamas leader Sheikh Ahmed Yassin on October 1 in exchange for the captured Israeli agents, in an effort to "respond to King Hussein's appeal and to take positive steps to help the peace process," stated Israeli Prime Minister Benjamin Netanyahu. Sheikh Yassin's release was demanded by Hamas on several occasions, and there is no evidence that the release was interpreted to be a result of Hamas's 1997 suicide attacks. U.S. and Jordanian pressure, combined with Sheikh Yassin's deteriorating health, has been cited as cause for the release.[47] Despite this fact, Hamas did not continue suicide attacks after the release, virtually halting all suicide attacks until the second uprising, or intifada, of 2000.[48] (There are two suicide attacks in our database in 1998, one by Hamas, the other by Islamic Jihad. There were none in 1999.)

Period No. 2—Al-Aqsa Intifada, 2000–2005

The second period, from 2000 to 2005, involved the most severe suicide campaign against Israel, the Second Palestinian Intifada. This campaign was triggered by the evident failure of the Oslo peace process as a result of the Camp David negotiations in August 2000.

The Second Intifada, also known as Al-Aqsa Intifada, differed markedly from the First Intifada of 1987–92. Palestinian resistance moved from unarmed violent rebellion with no use of suicide attacks in the First Intifada, to large-scale suicide bombing and armed rebellion in the Second Intifada. Hamas leader Mash'al explains the tactical transition:

> Like the intifada in 1987, the current intifada has taught us that we should move forward normally from popular confrontation to the rifle to suicide operations. This is the normal development. . . . We always have the Lebanese experience before our eyes. It was a great model of which we are proud.[49]

46. "HAMAS Claims Responsibility for Jerusalem Blast, Threatens More," *Agence France Presse*, September 4, 1997.

47. Serge Schmemann, "Israel Frees Ailing Hamas Founder to Jordan at Hussein's Request," *New York Times*, October 1, 1997, p. A5.

48. It should be noted that violent attacks in the form of car bombs and planted bombs did occur between 1997 and 2000, but suicide attacks did not.

49. "Hamas Statement," *BBC Summary of World Broadcasts*, November 3, 2001.

The "Lebanese experience" that Mash'al is referring to is the 1982 Israeli invasion into Lebanon. Hezbollah used suicide attacks and violent resistance against U.S. troops after the invasion, and in 1983, U.S. and French troops quit the area. This experience is cited by almost all of the Palestinian groups as proof of the strategic effectiveness of suicide terrorism.

The onset of the Second Intifada came soon after the failure of Camp David negotiations in August 2000 and began a day after Israeli opposition leader Ariel Sharon's controversial visit to the Temple Mount in September 2000, a religious site sacred to both Jews and Muslims. His visit seemed to signal the overall collapse of the Oslo peace process. In the Camp David negotiations U.S. President Bill Clinton invited Palestinian leader and Palestinian Authority Chairman Yasser Arafat and Israeli Prime Minister Ehud Barak to end the overextended five-year interim period of the Oslo Accords and resolve major issues toward a final settlement of the Israeli-Palestinian conflict. Ultimately, no agreement was reached and leaders instead signed a trilateral statement that defined agreed principles to guide future negotiations. The principles simply stated that major issues should be resolved as soon as possible and with good-faith intentions. Both sides blamed the other for the failure of the Summit to reach closure. Loss of confidence in the peace process ultimately led to the Second Intifada, or uprising, of 2000.

All four of the groups—Hamas, PIJ, Al-Aqsa, and PFLP—carried out suicide terrorism during the intifada, with a combined total of 106 suicide attacks. The sudden rise and persistence of suicide attacks on the part of the Palestinian groups can be explained by three key developments: 1) the increasing and punctuated disillusionment with salient negotiation processes, 2) the public shift in acceptance and support of suicide terrorism, and 3) the decreasing legitimacy of the PA and Fatah party under Yasser Arafat. In light of these events, the Palestinian groups increasingly employed suicide attacks, viewing this method as a last resort. Munir al-Makdah, suicide bombing trainer, explains this transition: "Jihad and the resistance begin with the word, then with the sword, then with the stone, then with the gun, then with planting bombs, and then transforming bodies into human bombs." From this quote and Mash'al's quote above, we can see that the Palestinian groups viewed this transition as a strategic choice of attack.

Like Prime Minister Yitzhak Rabin in the mid-1990s, Prime Minister Ariel Sharon's hard-line government, which took office in March 2001, ultimately responded to the suicide attacks with territorial concessions. At first Sharon relied on heavy ground forces. In 2002, Israel launched "Operation Defensive Shield," reoccupying several Palestinian cities and towns,

FIGURE 8.3 Israeli West Bank barrier

constructing a security fence, and pursuing targeted leader assassinations in order to destroy terrorist infrastructure. After these efforts, the number of attacks decreased from 42 in 2002 to 19 in 2003, and fatalities decreased from 250 in 2002 to 126 in 2003. However, the threat of suicide terrorism remained significant.

What brought an end to the Al-Aqsa Intifada was Israel's unilateral disengagement plan, which was announced by Ariel Sharon on December 18, 2003. He stated: "It is not in our interest to govern you. We will not remain in all the places where we are today." He also stated that he would give them back the Gaza Strip by evacuating all Jewish settlements there, withdraw Israeli military forces from a large part of the West Bank, and complete a security barrier between Israel and the abandoned territory on the West Bank, signaling a commitment to keep Israeli forces out of the West Bank as much as a commitment to keep suicide bombers out of Israel.[50] The triple fence security barrier was mostly completed by late 2004 after which Israel's withdrawal from Gaza and part of the West Bank

50. Azzam Tamimi, *HAMAS a History from Within* (Northampton: Olive Branch Press, 2007), p. 205.

began. After the withdrawal process ended in September 2005, suicide terrorism attacks almost completely stopped. Suicide attacks noticeably began to decline just a few months following Sharon's announcement.

Sharon's unilateral withdrawal decision is widely viewed as a response to suicide attacks, a view shared by many Israelis as well as Palestinians. For example, on July 18, 2005, *Haaretz*'s Danny Rubinstein wrote, "Sharon, who never once mentioned or alluded to the need to withdraw from Gaza before, needed suicide bombers, rockets, and mortars to persuade him."[51]

Period No. 3—2006–Present

Despite fears of a resurgence of suicide terrorism following Hamas' electoral victory in January 2006, a third period of very low levels of suicide terrorism continues to this day. The third period, from 2006 to the present, is characterized by a significant drop in suicide attacks and coincides with Israeli disengagement from Gaza and large parts of the West Bank. The vast decline of the Palestinian suicide attacks in response to Israeli withdrawal reinforces the overall patterns that this method of attack is driven mainly by strategic concerns.

Targeting and Weapons

This section will evaluate the operational similarities and differences of the four groups over the entire suicide campaign, examining attack geography, target types (civilian, security, or political), attack lethality, and weapon choice. The only major operational difference between the groups is in attack numbers; the PFLP are responsible for far fewer attacks than the other groups. Hamas has claimed the majority of the attacks in the entire Palestinian campaign (49 out of 136 attacks total); Al-Aqsa has claimed 41 attacks, PIJ conducted 33 attacks, and the PFLP has claimed 8 attacks. Although these groups have different religious and secular ideologies, they behave quite similarly in choosing target types, weapons, and attack regions, as will be discussed.

An important similarity among the groups is the mechanism/target type selection, which is illustrated in figures 8.4 and 8.5. Although the Palestinian resistance groups may proclaim varying ideologies, they share national-

---

51. Danny Rubinstein, "Palestinian Pride, Israeli Capitulation," *Haaretz*, March 21, 2005.

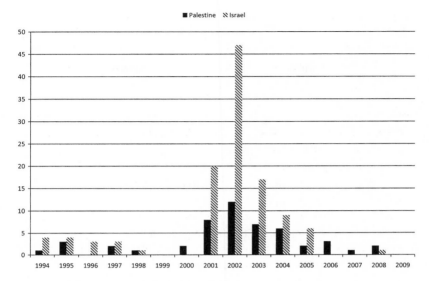

FIGURE 8.4 Attacks by region: Israel versus Occupied Territories

istic rhetoric with the goal of driving Israeli forces out of the Occupied Territories, and creating an independent Palestinian state. These four groups using suicide terrorism share the same political objective, operate within the same geographic setting, and have a common conception of the coercive mechanism best able to achieve their shared political objective—all focusing on Israeli civilian targets more than any other target type.

Attack Geography

As figure 8.4 illustrates, the majority of attacks have occurred in Israel proper. A closer look at the data shows that almost all of the attacks in the Occupied Territories are security targets, whereas most of the attacks in Israel are civilian targets. This finding is in line with figure 8.5, which shows attacks by target type; all other targets are outnumbered by civilian targets. The security target attacks in the Occupied Territories have not been successful in terms of lethality, which is to be expected.

In looking at the each group and their attacks by region, we see that all of them have conducted the majority of their attacks in Israel proper, which is in line with figure 8.4. A look at attacks in the Palestinian territories also yields modest differences:

Hamas: Of 70 total attacks, 13 were in Gaza, 10 in the West Bank, and 47 in Israel;
PIJ: Of 38 total attacks, 6 were in Gaza, 3 in the West Bank and 29 in Israel;
Al-Aqsa: Of 44 total attacks, 7 were in Gaza, 3 in the West Bank, and 34 in Israel;
PFLP: Of 8 total attacks, 1 was in Gaza, 3 in the West Bank, and 4 in Israel.

Considering the groups' relative strongholds within the Occupied Territories, it is to be expected that Hamas conducted all of its non-Israel attacks
in Gaza and none in the West Bank, and Al-Aqsa has had the majority of
its non-Israel activity in the West Bank.

Recently, these group strongholds have been reinforced by political
control. Conflicts between Hamas and rival party Fatah culminated in the
Battle of Gaza in June 2007, which saw a resurge of intra-Palestinian violence. Currently, Hamas is in command of Gaza, and Fatah controls the
West Bank. Approximately 116 Palestinian civilians were killed in the 2007
battle alone, not including fatalities from minor clashes before and after
the battle.[52] Throughout this entire time, however, no suicide attacks were
launched by either side toward the other; the groups instead used gunfire,
shell fire, and rocket-propelled grenades. This strongly suggests that suicide
bombing is reserved for the foreign occupier, Israel.

Target Types

In figure 8.5, we see that civilian targets have consistently outnumbered
all other target types, with a sharp spike in 2002 during the height of the
Second Intifada. A look at each individual group shows a similar trend;
no group has focused exclusively on one target type, and civilian targets
outnumber other targets for each group. This may be because security
targets are difficult to access and the probability of tactical success is low.
Civilian targets, on the other hand, are easily accessible and serve the coercive goals of the Palestinian groups. As an Al-Aqsa leader stated, the
purpose of violent resistance is "to increase losses in Israel to a point at
which the Israeli public would demand a withdrawal from the West Bank
and Gaza Strip."[53] In other words, if occupation continues and Israel does

52. "Gaza-West Bank ICRC Bulletin No. 22 / 2007," *International Committee of the Red
Cross* (June, 15 2007), http://www.alertnet.org/thenews/fromthefield/220224/025f24b73a37ef7
12ad576eb84b22e84.htm.
53. Joel Greenberg, "Suicide Planner Expresses Joy over His Missions," *New York Times,*
May 9, 2002.

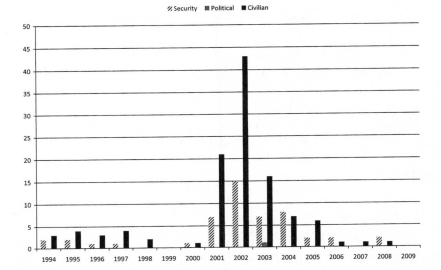

FIGURE 8.5 Attacks by target type

not accept the Palestinians' demands regarding independence, Israel can expect more attacks and escalating civilian costs.

In line with figure 8.5, a summary of each group and their attacks by target type shows that civilian target types outnumber all other targets for all four groups.

Hamas: Of the 70 total attacks, 51 were civilian targets, and 19 security were targets;

PIJ: Of the 38 total attacks, 23 were civilian targets, 13 were security targets, 1 was an unknown target, and 1 was categorized as other;

Al-Aqsa: Of the 44 total attacks, 29 were civilian targets, 14 were security targets, and 1 was a political target;

PFLP: Of the 8 total attacks, 6 were civilian targets, and 2 were security targets.

Attack Lethality

Interestingly, although the number of attacks from 1994 to 1997 was relatively small (see figure 8.2), the lethality of each attack in this time period was greater than the attacks from the Second Intifada. In 1994–97, Hamas and PIJ were the only groups using suicide bombing. As a relatively rare tactic, it is likely that each individual suicide attack was more thoroughly planned at this time than the more numerous and hastily planned later attacks. Indeed, Hamas's target choices in the 1996 attacks ensured devastating outcomes: two of the four attacks were aimed at crowded buses filled with Israeli civilians, killing 44 people total. In the Second Intifada all four of the groups contributed to the 106 attacks resulting in 511 deaths, but fatalities per attack ranged between 6 and 7. Organized planning for each attack was perhaps sacrificed for an overall increase in frequency of attacks, as each group was at the height of militant activity at this time.

Weapon Choice

The weapon choice for this campaign shows a clear preference for belt bombs over car bombs. Group breakdowns reflect a similar pattern; each group has a strong preference for belt bombs and a low preference for car bombs, with PIJ occasionally using motorbike bombs. Even though there are a large number of attacks with unknown weapons, it is safe to assume that the majority of these unknown weapons are not car bombs; in the event of a suicide attack, the use of a car bomb is fairly evident, whereas the use of belt bombs is usually ambiguously referred to as a "suicide bomb."

Hamas: Of 70 total attacks, 39 belt bombs, 10 car/truck bombs, 21 other (most presumed belt bombs);

Al-Aqsa: Of the 44 total attacks, 26 belt bombs, 7 car/truck bombs, 11 unknown/other (presumed belt bombs);

PIJ: Of the 38 total attacks, 19 belt bombs, 8 car/truck bombs, 11 unknown/other (most presumed belt bombs);

PFLP: Out of 8 total attacks, 7 belt bombs, and 1 car bomb.

Interestingly, after 2002 there is a drop and prolonged halt in the use of car bombs. This can be explained by an increase in the monitoring of cars crossing into Israel proper. Prior to and throughout the Second Intifada, car bombs were typically carried out in stolen Israeli-owned cars, ensuring less hassle at border and settlement checkpoints (Palestinian-owned cars are distinguished by white license plates and Israeli-owned cars by yellow license plates).[54] After 2003, however, IDF soldiers began to monitor all cars passing through checkpoints more thoroughly. More recently, the IDF instituted a car ID system to reduce travel time for Israelis; inspection is waived if the Israeli owner enters a secret code when passing through.[55] The 1994–97 attacks had higher fatalities per attack than the Second Intifada. There is no indication that a particular weapon yields higher fatalities; lethality is determined more by target type and the circumstances surrounding the attack, rather than purely by weapon choice. Weapon choice may, however, limit the attacker's ability to attack in an optimally destructive area; belt bombs are more conducive to mobility than car bombs.

In examining this campaign's geography of suicide attacks, target types, attack lethality, and weapon choice, one finds a prominent theme; that is the killing of Israeli civilians in Israel proper. The mobility of the belt bomb, which is the preferred weapon type, has allowed suicide bombers to penetrate the everyday lives of Israeli citizens by conducting suicide operations in markets, discos, cafés, and bus stops. According to a study by Hilal Khashan, these suicide attacks have had devastating effects on Israeli society and have caused economic recession, and delivered a staggering blow to morale.[56] The leaders of the resistance groups have reiterated this, making statements like "the bombings were meant to sow panic among Israelis," which Sheik Ahmed Yassin, the spiritual leader of Hamas, said in 2001.[57] The Palestinian resistance groups, like others around the world, have utilized the killing of civilians to achieve their strategic goal of coercing the occupying government to concede to the groups' nationalistic goals. They have learned this through the concessions that followed each campaign and from statements like the one Yitzhak Rabin made when addressing the Knesset on April 18, 1994, regarding Israel's obligation to withdraw from Gaza and the West Bank. Rabin stated, "We cannot deny that our continuing control over a foreign people who do not want us exacts a painful price. . . . There is no end to the targets Hamas and other terrorist organizations have among us. Each Israeli, in the territories and inside sovereign Israel, including united

54. "Israeli Army to Remain on Seized Palestinian Land in Change of Policy," *Voice of Israel*, June 19, 2002.

55. Yaakov Katz, "IDF launches Car ID System to Speed Up Roadblocks for Settlers," *Jerusalem Post*, September 10, 2008.

56. Hilal Khashan, "Collective Palestinian Frustration and Suicide Bombings," *Third World Quarterly*, 24, no. 6 (December 2003).

57. Karin Laub, "Twin Suicide Attacks as Militants Mark Anniversary of Lebanon Pullout," *Associated Press*, (May 25, 2001).

Jerusalem, each bus, each home, is a target for their murderous plans."[58] If the Palestinian resistance groups assessed the coercive effectiveness of their campaigns, then they have learned that by attacking Israeli civilians, there would be more pressure on Israel to make concessions.

Demographic Profile

Contrary to the belief that suicide bombers are young, unemployed men with little education, our data show that a significant number of identified attackers in fact have postsecondary education levels. Figure 8.6 compares the education level of identified attackers to the Palestinian male population as a whole.

The CPOST database can confidently identify the education level of 55 Palestinian suicide attackers: 65% of them have a postsecondary education, compared to 18% in the entire Palestinian male population. Many held middle-class and working-class jobs, such as teachers, security guards, ambulance drivers, and technicians. Interestingly, Palestinian attackers represent the successful and educated of society, rather than the poor and unsuccessful with nothing to lose (the former is the profile that one might suspect for political activists). Of the 183 attackers identified in our database, only five are not from the Palestinian territory, 173 are male, 10 female, and the vast majority of the attackers are in the age range of 18–24 years.

Popular Support

There is reasonably good information about support for suicide terrorism among the Palestinian public, especially for the period 1995–2007. Public opinion polls taken by the Jerusalem Media Communications Center (JMCC) biannually survey a random pool of an average of 1,500 Palestinian adults (18+) in the West Bank and Gaza.[59] The JMCC is considered a reliable and respected source that repeatedly generates solid data. It has tracked Palestinian views on various issues, especially those concerning support for suicide terrorism, resistance, and Israeli policies, by asking the

58. Yitzhak Rabin, speech to Knesset, *BBC Summary of World Broadcasts,* April 20, 1994.
59. Although many Palestinian public polls exist, the data from the JMCC was the most consistent, making it possible to measure answers to the same question over a long period of time.

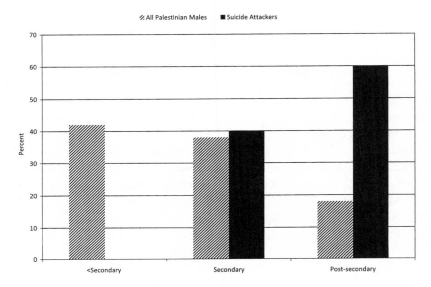

FIGURE 8.6 Education levels: All Palestinian males versus suicide attackers

same basic questions for many years. It is used by American and Israeli media outlets for its consistent Palestinian public opinion polls.

From 1995 to June 2000, just before the Second Intifada, opposition hovered around 60%, with the exception of a spike to 80% in June of 1996. This spike came after the 1996 subcampaign, which was in response to the assassination of PIJ and Hamas leaders. The 1996 campaign did not bring about territorial concessions as did the 1994 and 1995 attacks, and it also resulted in the largest number of Israeli civilian deaths from any campaign up until that time. These two factors combined can explain the sudden spike in Palestinian public opposition to suicide terrorism in June 1996, and the corresponding drop in support to 5%. Overall, the time period before the 2000 intifada shows modest support for suicide terrorism, hovering around 30%.

In the "Trajectory of Suicide Attacks" section, the use of suicide attacks during the Second Intifada is explained to be a result of three key developments: 1) the increasing and punctuated disillusionment with salient negotiation processes, 2) the public shift in acceptance and support of suicide terrorism, and 3) the decreasing legitimacy of the PA and Fatah party under Yasser Arafat. During the time leading up to the intifada and during the uprising itself, we see a steady increase in support for suicide terrorism, peaking at 73.7% in April 2001. Also at this time, the number of suicide attacks were increasing. The use of suicide bombing became a strategic resistance strategy both in terms of attack method and in gaining public support. Developments no. 1 and no. 3 contributed significantly to this rise in public support. As signed agreements between Israel and the PA and negotiations failed to produce results in establishing a Palestinian state, the public increasingly rallied their support behind suicide bombing.

Although developments no. 1 and no. 3 contributed significantly to the rise in support for suicide attacks during the Second Intifada, when looking closely at the JMCC polls from 2000 to 2002, it is evident that development no. 1, disillusionment with negotiations, was the strongest factor. To briefly summarize, in 2000 the poll showed a notable increase in support for military and suicide attacks: 66.2% of the Palestinian people believe that the suicide operations are an appropriate response under the conditions at the time, compared with 26.1% in March 1999. As for the impact of the intifada on the Palestinian public opinion regarding the Oslo Accords, the level of support for the Oslo Accords went down to its lowest mark (39%) compared with 57.9% in June 2000, 64.5% in May 2000, and 74.9% in December 1996, where it was the highest. The level of confidence in Yasser Arafat and his Al-Fatah political party slightly decreased, while support for Hamas and its leader Sheikh Yassin slightly increased; however, when respondents were asked who they would reelect to represent the Palestinians, Yasser Arafat came in first. The polls taken in 2001 and again in 2002 asked the same general questions, yielding the same results. Support for suicide attacks continued to notably increase, while support for any past or future negotiations notably decreased. In 2002, a majority of the respondents (72.1%) said they are either pessimistic or very pessimistic that a peaceful settlement for the Arab-Israeli conflict would be achieved, compared with 67.4 % in December 2001. Yasser Arafat and his mainstream Fatah faction were still the most popular among the Palestinian public with a slight drop in popularity—a slight drop to 25.5 % of Palestinians who said Arafat is the most trusted Palestinian figure compared with 27.6% September 2002 and 24.5% in December 2001. Sheikh Ahmad Yassin and Hamas came in second.[60]

Although Palestinians were well aware of the Islamist ideologies of Hamas and PIJ, suicide terrorism itself garnered more support at this time

60. Jerusalem Media and Communications Center (JMCC), available at http://www.jmcc. org/polls.aspx.

than the Palestinian Islamist groups combined. From the JMCC polls, we see support for suicide operations rising while support for Islamist groups combined rose modestly across the same periods. This evidence strongly suggests that Palestinians, as opposed to turning to Islamic fundamentalism, were in fact supporting resistance in the form of suicide bombing, following the failure of Camp David talks and continued Israeli settlement expansion. The modest rise in support for Islamist groups likely reflects support for their resistance practices and the broader support for suicide bombing among the Palestinian population at this time. Additionally, secular groups such as the PFLP and Al-Aqsa also employed suicide attacks, further distancing the link between support for Palestinian suicide bombing and support for Islamic fundamentalism.

Conclusion

Palestinian suicide terrorism has been mainly driven by the political goal of resistance to Israeli occupation and the encroachment of Israeli cultural, political, and military influence in the West Bank and Gaza. The Palestinians turned to suicide terrorism when negotiations to stem Israeli influence broke down, and turned away from suicide terrorism when Israel complied with previous negotiations or when Israel unilaterally reduced its influence in the Occupied Territories. The most recent and striking drop in suicide attacks coincides with Ariel Sharon's disengagement plan, viewed by the Palestinian groups not only as a huge concession but as a successful result of the suicide attacks.

Has Israel's security improved since 2005? Today, critics of the disengagement plan say no, contending that the withdrawal did not halt terror attacks. The assessment that terrorism continues is correct, but jumping to the conclusion that Israel is now less secure is not.

According to the Israeli Ministry of Foreign Affairs Web site, "Palestinian suicide bombing terrorism, which was the dominant form of attack during the first years of the current confrontation, has continued declining since the peak of 2002. In addition, the decrease in number of Israelis killed in suicide bombing attack also continued."[61] Although other forms of terrorism have not stopped, Israel's Ministry of Foreign Affairs Web site also

61. Israel Ministry of Foreign Affairs Web site: http://www.mfa.gov.il/mfa/terrorism-%20 0bstacle%20to%20peace/palestinian%20terror%20since%202000/.

states that "rocket and mortar shell fire is relatively less lethal than suicide bombing attacks"[62] Given that the number of Israeli deaths to violence related to the West Bank and Gaza declined from an average number of 105 per year in 2000–2005 to 23 in 2006–9, it is more than reasonable to conclude that Israel's security is better now and Sharon's actions saved many lives.

Lastly, it is important to address the consequences of additional Jewish settlers in areas inhabited by Palestinians. While in December 2009 Israeli Prime Minister Benjamin Netanyahu instituted a 10-month lull in building permits for new settlements in West Bank, Israel has continued to approve new construction in East Jerusalem, particularly in neighborhoods with predominantly Palestinian populations. While we cannot say where the threshold for violence lies, historical evidence shows that an expansion of Israeli presence in territory populated by Palestinians is likely to incite resistance. If Israel continues its construction in Palestinian communities, whether in the West Bank or in East Jerusalem, there is good reason to be concerned about a resurgence in suicide violence.

62. Ibid.

CHAPTER NINE

Chechnya

The Chechen separatist suicide terrorist campaign is part of a larger Chechen separatist movement that began with the downfall of the Soviet Union in 1991.[1] The suicide terrorist campaign began on July 7, 2000, approximately six months after the beginning of the Second Russo-Chechen War, in response to Russian occupation and counterterrorism operations. Although the Chechens have a long history of conflict with Russia, the suicide terrorist campaign did not erupt until the brutal Russian occupation of 2000; it then increased in response to counterterrorism operations in 2002 and 2008.

This chapter addresses the historical context of the Chechen separatist suicide terrorist campaign as well as its groups, goals, trajectory, targets, and trends over time. The Russian government and other media sources have often attributed the suicide terrorist campaign to foreign militants imported from countries like Saudi Arabia, Pakistan, and Afghanistan. Our data indicates that these reports are exaggerated, and the more accurate cause is resistance to Russian occupation; suicide terrorism is a weapon of last resort, after ordinary resistance failed to achieve Russian military withdrawal. Furthermore, the ebb-and-flow of the suicide attacks appears to change according to the level of brutality of the Russian occupation forces. The variation in the trajectory of suicide attacks (such as the spikes in 2003 and 2009) corresponds to counterterrorism campaigns that were first initiated by Russian occupational forces and then by the Russian-backed Chechen president Ramzan Kadyrov.

---

1. The major contributor to this chapter was Jenna McDermit.

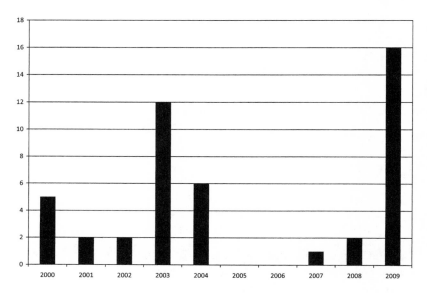

FIGURE 9.1 Suicide attacks in Chechnya, 2000–2009

Chechen Separatists versus Russia

In 1990, Chechnya had approximately 1.2 million people; a large proportion of the 400,000 to 450,000 people in the capital, Grozny, were ethnic Russians and predominantly Christian.[2] Nearly all of the remaining
Chechens were Sunni Muslims. When the Soviet Union collapsed in 1991,
Chechnya declared its independence along with other former Soviet Re-
publics: Ukraine, Uzbekistan, Belarus, and Georgia. Chechnya, however,
was part of the original Russian Federation. Its integration into Russian
territory preceded the era of Soviet expansion that, in the 1920s, absorbed
weak neighbor states like Georgia, Ukraine, and Uzbekistan. The new
Chechen president, Dzhokhar Dudayev, declared Chechnya's independence in 1991, but the Russian government could not accept, first, the collapse of its own federation in addition to the collapse of the U.S.S.R., and,
second, the loss of valuable oil pipelines throughout the Chechen ter-

2. "Chechen Official Puts Death Toll for 2 Wars at Up to 160,000," *New York Times,*
August 16, 2005.

FIGURE 9.2 The Republic of Chechnya

ritory.[3] In 1992, under Dudayev's leadership, Chechnya drafted a completely secular constitution—asserting its right to self-governance by president and parliament. While another president, Aslan Maskhadov, would later bend to local pressures and declare sharia, or Islamic law, it is important to realize that the independence movement had a secular beginning. In 1994, Russia declared the independence movement a rebel uprising; if successful, it could inspire other disenfranchised ethnic groups within Russia's borders. Russia launched the first Russo-Chechen War in December 1994, in order to quell the uprising.

The First Russo-Chechen War

The First Russo-Chechen War began in 1994 after Russian forces invaded Chechnya on three fronts; Grozny was invaded in December of that year.

3. Anne Speckhard and Khapta Akhmedova, "The New Chechen Jihad: Militant Wahhabism as a Radical Movement and a Source of Suicide Terrorism in Post-War Chechen Society," *Democracy and Security* 2 (2006): 1–53, p. 37.

While Russian President Boris Yeltsin anticipated a quick victory,[4] the Russian advance was inhibited by logistical shortcomings from the very beginning: "During the 1994–1996 War, the lack of coordination was one of the major factors responsible for Russia's dismal performance."[5] Russian military performance was also inhibited by a low morale and dissenting soldiers who, like General Eduard Vorobyov, felt it was a crime to "send the army against its own people."[6] Russian troops were poorly trained and disoriented. Many Chechen fighters were tactically advantaged because they had served in the Soviet Army: "Many were familiar with Russian weapons, spoke the language, knew the tactics, and knew many of the Russian commanders."[7] Russia invaded Chechnya with approximately 38,000 troops; as many as 800 of those soldiers dissented.[8]

In February 1995, Chechen separatists retreated from street fighting in Grozny in order to launch attacks from the villages in the Caucasas foothills of the south.[9] Separatist leader Shamil Basayev decided to continue the conflict on Russian soil. In May 1995, Basayev, first, headed 100 miles into Russia and held hostage a hospital in Budyonnovsk. The hostage operation was a great success for the Chechen separatists. Many of the separatists were granted safe passage to Chechnya, and released hostages testified that they had been well cared for and expressed empathy for the rebels' plight.[10] Chechen separatists also targeted pro-Moscow civilians in Dagestan. In 1996, the efficacy of hostage operations was reinforced by Yeltsin's decision to withdraw Russian troops and enter into a cease-fire called the Khasavyurt Accord.[11] The cease-fire included demilitarization

4. Brett Jenkinson, "Tactical Observations from the Grozny Combat Experience," U.S. Military Academy, West Point, NY, 2002, pp. 29–30.

5. Mark Kramer, "Guerilla Warfare, Counterinsurgency and Terrorism in the North Caucasus: The Military Dimension of the Russian-Chechen Conflict," *Europe-Asia Studies* 57, no. 2 (2005): 217.

6. Carlotta Gall and Thomas De Waal, *Chechnya: Calamity in the Caucasus* (New York: New York University Press, 1998), p. 179.

7. Jenkinson, "Tactical Observations from the Grozny Combat Experience, " pp. 29–30.

8. "Grachev: Russia Had No Troop Advantage," *Moscow Times,* March 1, 1995.

9. Brian Glyn Williams, "Commemorating 'The Deportation' in Post-Soviet Chechnya," *History and Memory* 12, no. 1 (2000)" 123.

10. "Chechen Rebels, Volunteer Hostages Leave aboard Buses," *Associated Press,* June 20, 1995.

11. Kramer, "Guerilla Warfare, Counterinsurgency and Terrorism in the North Caucasus: The Military Dimension of the Russian-Chechen Conflict," p. 2.

and withdrawal of forces from Grozny, and was intended as a basis for both parties to negotiate further agreements in 2001.[12] Thoroughly exhausted, Chechen citizens were eager for the cease-fire and anticipated reconstruction.[13] The separatists, however, viewed the cease-fire as borrowed time and as a brief respite to regroup and prepare for the inevitable reinvasion. During this time Basayev traveled with 30 fighters to undergo military training in Khost, Afghanistan: "By that time he envisaged that war with Russia was inevitable. The decision was a reflective and rational one in conditions of relative peace with Russia."[14]

The First Russo-Chechen War resulted in a massive number of civilian casualties (approximately 30,000–40,000), but there was not one suicide attack.[15] The First Russo-Chechen War differed from the Second Russo-Chechen War in three other respects. First and foremost, the Chechen separatists achieved the withdrawal of Russian forces through the utilization of traditional guerilla techniques, such as hostage operations, planned ambushes, and improvised explosive devices. Second, the interim period was marked by the emergence of Wahhabism, which was ultimately only a secondary factor in the suicide terrorist campaign. Lastly (and clearly significant in this case), both the direction and level of military brutality increased between the first and second wars. In the first war, large numbers of ethnic Russians, as well as Chechens, were harmed—primarily during the bombing of Grozny.[16] Afterward, many ethnic Russians evacuated Chechnya. During the Second Russo-Chechen War, nearly all the violence was directed against Chechen civilians. The second war included the previous method of airstrikes but also incorporated new counterterrorism operations: large-scale sweeps, detentions, abductions, communal punishment, "disappearings," and much more. During the Second Russo-Chechen War, there were between 45,000 and 60,000 civilian casualties.

12. "Peace Treaty and Principles of Interrelation between Russian Federation and Chechen Republic of Ichkeria," *Governments of the Russian Federation and the Chechen Republic of Ichkeria,* May 12, 1997.

13. "Lebed Peace Accord Gets Lukewarm Welcome from Yeltsin," *Irish Times,* September 2, 1996.

14. James Hughes, *Chechnya: From Nationalism to Jihad* (Philadelphia: University of Pennsylvania Press, 2007), p. 101.

15. Michael Gordon, "Chechnya Toll Is Far Higher: 80,000 Dead, Lebed Asserts," *New York Times,* September 4, 1996.

16. John Dunlop, "Do Ethnic Russians Support Putin's War in Chechnya?" *North Caucasus Analysis* 6, no. 4 (January 25, 2005).

The Interim Period

Chechnya's infrastructure was demolished after the First Russo-Chechen War: "Huge swaths of Chechnya were destroyed . . . and promises of large-scale reconstruction aid from Moscow never materialised. . . . Public order broke down almost completely."[17] Russia alienated Chechnya and without reconstruction aid, or a means to independently create it, the Chechen economy was strangled. Toward the end of the first war, many Chechen civilians looked to the West for support but were disappointed to find that Western governments considered the war an "internal affair" of Russia.[18]

Recently freed from Soviet-imposed atheism, underground Muslims openly displayed their faith and many younger-generation Chechens reconnected with their spiritual roots as a means of coping with an environment that was "marred by warlordism, rampant criminality, hostage takings, chaotic violence, grisly attacks on foreign aid workers and general lawlessness."[19] In order to cope with the destruction and personal loss caused by the war, Chechens turned to international Islamist organizations. Like Bosnia, the North Caucasus became the target for a number of Middle Eastern 'Islamic charities' in the 1990s, including Benevolence International Foundation, Islamic Relief Organization, al-Haramein and the Joint Committee for the Relief of Kosovo.[20] These organizations offered financial and material support as well as spiritual consolation.[21] Furthermore, given the breakdown of social institutions during the First Russo-Chechen War, the use of sharia courts provided "one of the few useful mechanisms for social regulation."[22] International Islamist organizations were eager to support the resurgence of Islam throughout the entire Caucasus region, and money from wealthier countries supported the rebuilding of mosques,

17. Kramer, "Guerilla Warfare, Counterinsurgency and Terrorism in the North Caucasus: The Military Dimension of the Russian-Chechen Conflict," p. 210.

18. Speckhard and Akhmedova, "The New Chechen Jihad: Militant Wahhabism as a Radical Movement and a Source of Suicide Terrorism in Post-War Chechen Society," pp. 4–5.

19. Kramer, "Guerilla Warfare, Counterinsurgency and Terrorism in the North Caucasus: The Military Dimension of the Russian-Chechen Conflict," p. 210.

20. Monica Duffy Toft, "Religious Violence in the Caucasus: Global Jihad or Local Grievance?" *Program on International Security Policy,* April 13, 2004, p. 12.

21. John Reuter, "Chechnya's Suicide Bombers: Desperate, Devout, or Deceived?" American Committee for Peace in Chechnya, 2004.

22. Hughes, *Chechnya: From Nationalism to Jihad,* p. 99.

schools, and other forms of Islamic expression.[23] Basayev particularly demonstrated an apt interest in Wahhabism—a conservative Sunni Islamic sect from Saudi Arabia—and cultivated an intense bond with a Wahhabi militant known as Khattab.

The religious leanings of Shamil Basayev influenced many young Muslim followers: "It was the success of [Basayev's] units in the battle for Grozny . . . that gave politicized Islam great respect and made it attractive to young fighters."[24] This base of Wahhabi support allowed Basayev to undermine the secular leadership of President Dudayev, as well as the leadership of Aslan Maskhadov later on.[25] Dudayev complained bitterly that Russia "forced us to take the way of Islam even if we were not properly prepared to embrace Islamic values. Now we could succumb to a perverted form of Islam which might be dangerous to the West."[26] In 1997, Aslan Maskhadov was elected the president of Chechnya, but soon found that his government was undermined by radical Islamist elements: "Maskhadov was unable to clamp down on Basayev's forces, and the power of warlords, criminal gangs and Islamic extremist groups increased."[27] Russian-Chechen historians called the rift between secular and religious factions a "meta-cleavage within the Chechen national movement."[28]

The Russian media would eventually blame foreign Wahhabism as the root cause of the suicide terrorist campaign during the Second Russo-Chechen War. Wahhabism, however, is a poor explanation. On a macrolevel, Wahhabism both induced foreign aid to Chechnya and compromised Aslan Maskhadov's secular leadership, but Russia's strangulating behavior created both the financial and political vacuum: "Given the de facto Russian blockade and international isolation, Maskhadov was also dependent on financial support form the Arab world, the bulk of which appears to have been channelled through Wahhabi organizations."[29] On a microlevel, Wahhabism also provides a poor explanation for the suicide terrorist cam-

23. Speckhard and Akhmedova, "The New Chechen Jihad: Militant Wahhabism as a Radical Movement and a Source of Suicide Terrorism in Post-War Chechen Society," p. 3.

24. Hughes, *Chechnya: From Nationalism to Jihad*, p. 100.

25. Yuri Zarakhovich, "Terms of War and Peace: Chechen Leader Jokhar Dudayev," *Time*, March 4, 1996.

26. Ibid.

27. Kramer, "Guerilla Warfare, Counterinsurgency and Terrorism in the North Caucasus: The Military Dimension of the Russian-Chechen Conflict," p. 212.

28. Hughes, *Chechnya: From Nationalism to Jihad*, p. 94.

29. Ibid., p. 102.

paign. Over one-third of the suicide attackers were women; this generally contradicts the ideology of Wahhabism (which discourages female warriors). Furthermore, many of the suicide attackers were Chechens—like Elza Gazuyeva, Shakhida Shabulatova, and Mariam Tashukhadjieva—who were motivated by their harsh experiences under the Russian occupation. Wahhabism may have induced foreign aid to Chechnya, and may have influenced particular leaders and social institutions in Chechnya, but without Russian occupation and oppression, there is little reason to believe that any suicide terrorism would have occurred.

The Second Russo-Chechen War

In September 1999, the Second Russo-Chechen War was declared by Russians in retaliation to two major events. First, in August 1999, Basayev, Khattab, and approximately 200–500 militants invaded Dagestan, Chechnya's southern neighbor, in order to seize several villages and establish control over the area.[30] The militants planned to secure access to the Caspian Sea so that Chechen oil would become sufficiently independent, thereby making it possible to separate Chechnya from the entire Russian economic system.[31] Plans for a Caucasus Common Market drew the eager attention of European financiers as well as the ire of new Russian President Vladimir Putin.[32] "The Russian government hurriedly sent troops . . . to rebuff the incursions. The Russian forces eventually managed to drive Basayev's and [Khattab's] guerillas out of Dagestan, albeit with considerable difficulty. The tension created by these raids and by subsequent clashes was still acute [during] a string of five highly publicised bombings in the late summer of 1999."[33]

A series of bombs destroyed apartment complexes in Moscow, and at the time, these apartment bombings were attributed to the Chechen separatists. Many theories have since linked them to the Russian FSB (Federal Security Service of the Russian Federation).[34] According to popular myth, Vladimir Putin or other members of the Russian security community may

30. Jenkinson, "Tactical Observations from the Grozny Combat Experience," p. 63.

31. Yusup Soslambekov, "Separatism, Islam and Oil, " *Nezavisimaya Gazeta,* March 18, 1998.

32. Igor Rotar, "Islamic Radicals in Dagestan," *Prism* 4, no. 6 (1998).

33. Kramer, "Guerilla Warfare, Counterinsurgency and Terrorism in the North Caucasus: The Military Dimension of the Russian-Chechen Conflict," p. 212.

34. "Bloody September," *Terror-99,* available at http://eng.terror99.ru.

have orchestrated these bombings in order to justify an especially aggressive invasion of Chechnya. "The circumstances of these bombings were never adequately explained," but the Dagestan raid as well as the bombings were cited by Vladimir Putin when he ordered security forces to "reassert control over Chechnya using 'all available means.'"[35] Indeed, the planning for the reinvasion of Chechnya had begun in the March of 1999, when Chechens kidnapped a Russian envoy. Russia amassed 93,000 troops along the Chechen border and began planning a counterterrorist campaign that incorporated three basic phases: "first, block Chechnya's borders and areas containing guerillas; second, destroy Chechen strong points and facilities using air strikes; and third, establish an alternative power structure to challenge the legitimacy of Chechnya's current government."[36]

During the second invasion, the Russian military was unwilling to entertain any risk of defeat and thus adopted a new, tougher strategy for Chechnya: "Russia recognized that it could not win hearts and minds in the sense of ideologically winning over the civilian population of Chechnya from support for national self-determination. Consequently, the logical strategy for Russia to pursue in the second war was one of coercion and control of territory."[37] Defense Minister Marshal Igor Sergeyev vowed that unlike the First War, "Russian troops will never leave Chechnya again."[38] The Second Russo-Chechen War is particularly well known for its scorched-earth campaigns, massive human rights atrocities, and systematic targeting of Chechen civilians through night raids and "zachistkas." (Zachistkas are cleansing operations that typically resulted in the detention, torture, and disappearance of the male populations of entire towns and villages.[39]) As in the First Russo-Chechen War, between 30,000–40,000 civilians were killed. Because many ethnic Russians had evacuated, however, a huge portion of this violence was directed against ethnic Chechens.[40] Russia attacked rural populations by way of zachistkas and attacked urban centers by systematically bombing Grozny, Argun, and Urus-Martan. By February 2000, the Russian military assumed control over Grozny, and by June 2000,

35. Kramer, "Guerilla Warfare, Counterinsurgency and Terrorism in the North Caucasus: The Military Dimension of the Russian-Chechen Conflict," p. 212.

36. Jenkinson, "Tactical Observations from the Grozny Combat Experience," pp. 29–30.

37. Hughes, *Chechnya: From Nationalism to Jihad,* p. 117.

38. Kramer, "Guerilla Warfare, Counterinsurgency and Terrorism in the North Caucasus: The Military Dimension of the Russian-Chechen Conflict," p. 215.

39. "The Critical Human Rights and Humanitarian Situations in Chechnya" (Commission on Security and Cooperation in Europe, April 24, 2003).

40. "Chechen Official Puts Death Toll," *New York Times.*

Russian troops had gained nominal control over all major Chechen towns (with the exception of the south).[41] June 2000 also contained the very first suicide attack of the Chechen separatist suicide terrorism campaign—it began half a year after the beginning of the Second Russo-Chechen War.

In late 2003, command over the Russian operations in Chechnya was transferred from the FSB to the MVD (Ministry of Internal Affairs); it was meant to herald "the gradual end of counterterrorist actions in favour of a more routine maintenance of public order."[42] In 2004, the Second-Russo Chechen War began to taper off with the introduction of Russia's "Chechenization" campaign. As part of Chechenization, Russians transferred power to pro-Russian Chechen officials; first, to Akhmad Kadyrov, then Alu Alkhanov, and most recently, in 2007, to Ramzan Kadyrov. Throughout Chechenization and after, Kadyrov has been widely perceived as a mere extension of Russian power. The pro-Russian government enjoys very little popular support and "relies mainly on violent coercion."[43] In April 2009, Russians declared the end of their military operation in Chechnya, but its proxy, Kadyrov's administration, remains aggressively committed to rooting out the separatist militants.

Groups and Goals

There exists limited information regarding the groups, goals, composition, and cohesion of the Chechen separatist movement due to the lack of Western access to Chechnya. During the interim period, the rampant abductions, murders, and robberies caused many international organizations to withdraw from Chechnya. In 1998, for example, the OSCE (Organization for Security and Co-operation in Europe) Assistance Group moved from Grozny to Moscow.[44] Also, as recently as 2009, the Memorial Human Rights Center temporarily ceased operations in Chechnya after the murder of activist Natalie Estemirova.[45] During the First Russo-Chechen War, Russia estimated there were approximately 15,000

41. Kramer, "Guerilla Warfare, Counterinsurgency and Terrorism in the North Caucasus: The Military Dimension of the Russian-Chechen Conflict," p. 212.

42. Ibid., p. 213.

43. Ibid., p. 214.

44. Hughes, *Chechnya: From Nationalism to Jihad,* p. 97.

45. "Russia-Chechnya-Memorial-Operations" Russia and CIS Military Newswire, December 17, 2009.

Chechen combatants, but "most common sources believe there were 'no more than 3,000 armed fighters in the field at any one time.'"[46] In August 1999, at the time of the second Russian invasion, there were 20,000 armed rebels in Chechnya, 2,000 of them foreign fighters. After the fourth Battle of Grozny, the bulk of the Chechen fighters fled to the south, and the Russian military inventoried over 4,000 dead fighters within the city limits.[47] By 2003, the number of armed separatists appears to have been reduced to as few as 2,000, including 250 foreign fighters.[48] And in 2005, Chechen separatists were thought to number between 1,600 and 1,800.[49] During the first and second wars, Chechen separatists fought effectively within a "loose-knit organization, garrisoning one point then another, without centralized control."[50] Chechen fighters typically self-organized into "cell structures" in which small groups of fighters carried one to two rocket-propelled grenades, a sniper rifle, a machine gun, and one to two assault rifles.[51]

As previously mentioned, there was an enormous secular-religious rift among the Chechen separatist movement. The "meta-cleavage" between the secular and Islamic factions peaked during the interim period. "An intra-elite struggle for power within the Chechen national movement was already apparent by the time Russian forces withdrew from Chechnya at the end of 1996."[52] As foreign funding via Wahhabi groups filled a vacuum of Russian reconstruction aid, the secular faction of separatists were increasingly undermined. Although secular leader Aslan Maskhadov was elected as president in 1997, "he was unable to assert political or military authority over the radicals."[53] As Russia and Chechnya failed to reach the "final status" provisioned by the Khasavyurt Accord, the radical challenge to Maskhadov increased in 1998, and by the summer of 1999, the Islamic faction appeared dominant.[54]

46. Jenkinson, "Tactical Observations from the Grozny Combat Experience," pp. 29–30.

47. Ibid.

48. "Russian General Outlines Numbers and Locations of Chechen Fighters," *BBC Worldwide Monitoring,* June 20, 2000; and Jim Nichol, "Russia's Chechnya Conflict: An Update," *Washington, DC: Congressional Research Service,* April 16, 2003.

49. Kramer, "Guerilla Warfare, Counterinsurgency and Terrorism in the North Caucasus: The Military Dimension of the Russian-Chechen Conflict," p. 213.

50. Jenkinson, "Tactical Observations from the Grozny Combat Experience," p. 80.

51. Ibid., p. 79.

52. Hughes, *Chechnya: From Nationalism to Jihad,* p. 95.

53. Ibid., p. 102.

54. Ibid., p. 94.

The crisis peaked in June–July 1998, when brief armed clashes between Maskhadov's forces and those of [Salman Raduyev] . . . left dozens dead and injured and forced Maskhadov to declare a state of emergency. Basayev resigned from the government, and the radicals increasingly demanded the resignation of Maskhadov on the grounds that he was too conciliatory toward Moscow and had "sold out." Maskhadov, consequently, was squeezed from two sides, internally from the radical opposition, whose ranks were swelling from veterans and new recruits of disgruntled young unemployed Chechens, and externally from Russia, whose blockade stunted economic growth and exacerbated social collapse in Chechnya. Both internal and external enemies of Maskhadov despised his government for being too soft with the other. The choice for Maskhadov was between civil war and concessions. Despite viewing Wahhabism as an "alien" and destructive presence in Chechnya, he chose to make concessions to avert the slide into civil war.[55]

There appear to be three subgroups of the Chechen separatist movement. The distinctions between the three groups appear to be minor, and may have been overdrawn by countries targeted by suicide terrorism, such as the United States and Russia, in order to resemble other suicide terrorist campaigns, like that in Israel and Palestine. There is no discernible difference in territory between groups; instead, all groups retreat to and are based out of Chechnya's southern mountainous region. Although none of the subgroups have formally distinct group goals, we can infer the separatists' overarching goals by examining their demands during the hostage operations between 1995 and 2004.

Groups

Within the Chechen separatist movement, there exist at least three subgroups that the United States added to the U.S. State Department list of foreign terrorist organizations in February 2003.[56] The distinctions between the three groups are minor; all three are linked to Shamil Basayev. The most prominent subgroup is the Special Purpose Islamic Regiment (SPIR), which was led by Movsar Barayev, in order to carry out hostage operations. The remaining two are the Islamic International Peace Brigade (IIPB) and Riyadus-Salikhin Reconnaissance and Sabotage Bat-

55. Ibid., p. 104.
56. Ibid., p. 139.

talion of Chechen Martyrs. These two were founded by Shamil Basayev, and the IIPB was for some time under the control of Basayev's comrade, Khattab.[57] All three groups have personal and organizational linkages; they share fighters, weapons, and materials. Although details exist regarding SPIR, concrete distinctions are lacking between it and the Islamic International Brigade or the Riyadus-Salikhin Reconnaissance and Sabotage Battalion of Chechen Martyrs.

The Special Purpose Islamic Regiment was founded by the separatist Arbi Barayev after the cease-fire with Russia in 1996. SPIR was an extremely small organization with less than 100 members. It was jointly run by Arbi Barayev and his nephew, Movsar Barayev.[58] In 1998, SPIR members had a bitter falling-out with Chechen President Aslan Maskhadov because, as previously mentioned, Islamists felt that Aslan Maskhadov made too many concessions with the Russian government. In an effort to crack down on rampant criminality, Maskhadov attempted to disband SPIR after it had kidnapped and murdered three Britons and a New Zealander.[59] Arbi Barayev was stripped of his formal rank in the Republic's armed forces after this and after attempting to usurp the city of Gudermes against President Maskhadov.[60] Arbi Barayev was killed by Russian forces in 2001 and passed the leadership of SPIR to Movsar Barayev. Movsar Barayev used SPIR to carry out the Moscow Theater hostage operation in 2002 and died in the attack. After Movsar's death, Amir Khamzat became the leader of SPIR. SPIR's activities have since been folded into the mainstream activity of the larger Chechen separatist movement.

SPIR did not seem to possess a unique ideology or goal apart from the wider separatist movement. Many freed hostages and known associates testified that Barayev was neither Wahhabi nor religious. Other sources, however, claim that SPIR wanted to implement a fundamentalist ideology throughout Chechnya and the Caucasus region.[61] SPIR clearly supported suicide bombing as a means to independence. One of the very first suicide bombers, Khava Barayeva, was most likely recruited by one of her infamous relatives, Arbi or Movsar Barayev. All of the subgroups are involved

57. Ibid.

58. Available at www.globalsecurity.org.

59. Robert Parsons, "Chechen President Orders Kidnap Crackdown," *BBC News,* December 13, 1998.

60. "Britons Killed by 'Bin Laden Ally,'" *BBC News,* November 18, 2001.

61. "Terrorist Organization Profile: Special Purpose Islamic Regiment," National Consortium for the Study of Terrorism and Responses to Terrorism, www.start.umd.edu.

in terrorist activities, and are closely enough linked by Shamil Basayev, that there is no reason to conclude that any of them are opposed to the tactic of suicide bombing. The distinction between the three groups would not likely effect any trends in recruitment.

The Wahhabi Influence

Many of the brief references conflate Wahhabism with Arab foreign fighters. However, a closer examination of the geographic distribution of "foreign fighters" in Chechnya shows that the great majority are from border regions, not the Middle East. Although foreign suicide attackers are not unheard of in Chechnya, of the 42 for whom we can determine place of birth, 38 were from the Caucasus. The picture that emerges is mainly of regional resistance to Russia's occupation, not a global jihad to create Islamic fundamentalist states.

Wahhabism emerged in Chechnya after the First Russo-Chechen War via Afghan jihadists. The jihadists intended to aid Chechnya in what they perceived to be the larger jihad against Russia.[62] Sources disagree over the nature and extent of foreign aid to the separatists' cause. Some sources claim that separatists received aid in the form of foreign militants, financial backing, and the use of jihadist training camps. Others, however, believe these claims to be overstated and a result of Russian propaganda.

It appears that the contingent of foreign fighters peaked, around 1999, at approximately 2,000 fighters (between 200 and 700 of which were Arab) out of approximately 20,000 fighters in total. The Russian media attempted to portray the Wahhabis as foreign-born, rabble-rousing Arabs, but most foreign fighters were Dagestanis, Lithuanians, Ukrainians, and Azeris. Even at the peak of Wahhabi influence there were less than 1,000 Arabs. When the Russian military advanced in the December of 1999 many of these Arabs faded away without a fight.[63] Regardless of the number of foreign militants that resided in Chechnya, data suggest that most of the suicide bombers were ethnically Chechen and an overwhelming number were from the Caucasus region.

The response to Russian occupation was *regional* (i.e., Chechens, Dagestanis, Lithuanians, Ukrainians, and Azeris) and not *Arab* in nature. How-

62. Speckhard and Akhmedova, "The New Chechen Jihad: Militant Wahhabism as a Radical Movement and a Source of Suicide Terrorism in Post-War Chechen Society."

63. Michael Wines, "War on Terror Casts Chechen Conflict in a New Light." *New York Times,* December 9, 2001.

ever, after September 11, 2001, it was advantageous for the Russian government to portray the Chechen conflict as *Arab* or *Islamic* in character. "Both
the Russian government and its adversaries have adopted the narrative
of the North Caucasus as a battlefield of global jihad. In both cases, this
rhetorical emphasis has been at least partly tuned to garner international
support and mitigate foreign and domestic criticism."[64] Russians used the
Global War on Terror as a means to justify heavy-handed counterterrorism
policies, portraying its military occupation as a dutiful response to worldwide jihad.

Indeed, Harvard researchers Monica Duffy Toft and Yuri M. Zhukov
found that, overall, less than 15% of all violence in the Caucasus has been
carried out by Islamist fighters. They also found that Islamist violence in
the Caucasus region is exacerbated by Russian repression: "Use of government repression against local Islamic leadership and organizations has an
immediate, direct impact on the probability of experiencing religious violence . . . In other words, repression spreads, rather than contains, Islamist
violence."[65]

In addition to the small contingent of Arab fighters, Chechens may have
received alternative forms of assistance. Some sources have claimed that
the Chechen Wahhabis received approximately $5 million a month in fi-
nancial aid and that foreign militants, like Khattab, opened numerous military training camps. Some sources claim the KavKaz Center was a military
training camp with instructors from Saudi Arabia, Pakistan, Syria, Egypt,
and Algeria.[66] Separatists, however, claim that "financial support from either the West or Arab countries is an absolute lie and a myth. If we received
any support—even meager, not to mention significant—we would be so
much more successful in all respects."[67] Although Chechnya received financial and reconstructive support from Islamist organizations, it is unclear
whether it financed specifically militant activities.

Chechens financed the bulk of their resistance through black market
exchange and financial support from Chechen diaspora.[68] Chechens stole
oil from pipelines that ran from Chechnya to Russia, looted metal from

64. Toft, "Religious Violence in the Caucasus," p. 11.

65. Ibid., p. 4.

66. Speckhard and Akhmedova, "The New Chechen Jihad: Militant Wahhabism as a
Radical Movement and a Source of Suicide Terrorism in Post-War Chechen Society."

67. Emir Sayfullah gave an interview to the Jamestown Foundation. KavKaz.com, March
26, 2009.

68. Toft, "Religious Violence in the Caucasus," p. 12.

bombed factories, and cultivated mountainous poppies for the regional drug trade. Kidnapping pro-Moscow individuals in Chechnya, Dagestan, and other Caucasus states proved one of the most lucrative black market endeavors.[69] Given the frequency of these local black market operations, any financial and military aid from Arab and Islamist organizations would appear to be only a partial contribution to the overall resistance. Furthermore, some academics claim that "External sources of funding have diminished since the implementation of U.S.-led efforts to disrupt terrorist financing following the 11 September 2001 attacks" and that this development may have pushed Chechen separatists to pursue more "cost-efficient" tactics—such as suicide bombs.[70]

Chechen Separatists' Goals: Hostage Operations and Their Overarching Demands

The Chechen suicide terrorist campaign possesses no separately defined goals beyond the overarching goals of the wider separatist movement. These strategic aims can be inferred from the demands made during numerous high-profile hostage-taking operations throughout the First and Second Russo-Chechen Wars, which often lasted for days and allowed the separatists to articulate their demands in full. The suicide attacks that occurred were fully consistent with both the motivation and impetus for a wider group of strategies employed by the resistance.

During the First Russo-Chechen War, the political aims and underlying motivations of the Chechen separatist movement were of a secular and nationalist nature. First, on June 14, 1995, Shamil Basayev and his fellow militants held 1,500–1,800 Russians hostage in the Budyonnovsk Hospital. Despite Basayev's personal religious leanings, the separatists made secular demands. The separatists demanded the cessation of combat operations in Chechnya, the withdrawal of the federal forces, and the holding of free and fair elections in the republic.[71] During the five-day hostage operation, Russian Deputy Prime Minister Nikolay Yegerov offered the separatists "an aircraft to fly to any country of their choice as well as any

69. Valery Tishkov, "The Fund for Humanitarian Assistance to the Chechen Republic: How It Happened and What It Is About," Johnson's Russia List 6191 Research and Analytical Supplement 7, April 2002.

70. Toft, "Religious Violence in the Caucasus," p. 12.

71. *BBC Summary of World Broadcasts,* June 17, 1995.

amount of money for the hostages."[72] Shamil Basayev, however, made one demand: "either begin the immediate withdrawal of troops from Chechnya or face a bloodbath."[73] Although Russia stopped short of promising the immediate withdrawal of Russian troops, President Boris Yeltsin granted a cease-fire, the resumption of peace talks, and safe passage for the rebels to return to Chechnya.[74] Upon his return, Basayev was received as a war hero of folkloric proportions, and Yeltsin was the butt of widespread criticism due to his subservience to separatists' demands.

The effectiveness of the Budyonnovsk operation resonated strongly with the separatists, and they launched a copycat operation in 1996. Separatists held hostage the entire village of Pervomayskoye, Dagestan. This operation was led by Salman Raduyev, who again, demanded the removal of all Russian interior ministry militia from Chechnya as well as safe conduct for a convoy to return home.[75] Two thousand hostages were released and the separatists were once again granted safe passage to return to Chechnya. During the First Russo-Chechen War, separatists demonstrated two central goals: first and foremost, the removal of Russian troops from Chechnya, and, second, safe passage for the hostage takers to return to Chechnya.

Even after the emergence of Wahhabism during the interim period, hostage takers made secular demands during the Second Russo-Chechen War as well. The first hostage operation of the Second Russo-Chechen War took place in October 2002 at the Moscow Theater. Approximately 40 separatists held hostage 800–850 audience members. Throughout the crisis, hostage takers issued several videos that exhibited their belt bombs and made one ultimatum: Russian troops must leave Chechnya in seven days, or the theater would be blown up.[76] One female hostage taker released a tape to Al-Jazeera in which she claimed: "We have chosen this path, the path of struggling for the freedom of [Chechnya].... It makes no difference for us where we will die."[77] Russian Special Forces responded by releasing

72. "Hostage Crisis in Buddennovsk; Buddenovsk Residents Demand Fulfillment of all Hostage-Takers' Demands," *BBC Summary of World Broadcasts,* June 7, 1995.

73. John Kohan, "Assault at High Noon," *Time,* June 26, 1995.

74. Sergei Shargaorodsky, "Chechen Rebels, Volunteer Hostages Leave Aboard Buses," *Associated Press,* June 19, 1995.

75. "Chechen Rebels withdraw Human Shields—Detailed Talks Underway," *Deutsche Presse-Agentur,* January 11, 2006.

76. *ABC News Summary,* October 25, 2002.

77. Michael Wines, "Hostage Drama in Moscow: The Moscow Front; Chechens Kill Hostage in Siege at Russian Hall," *New York Times,* October 25, 2002.

an unknown chemical agent through the theater's ventilation system. This toxic agent killed every hostage taker and 127 hostages.

The year 2004 witnessed the very last hostage operation in Beslan, North Ossetia. The Chechen rebels stormed a middle school and held over 400 people hostage. The separatists demanded, first, the release of jailed insurgents in Ingushetia, and second, the withdrawal of Russian troops from Chechnya. The rebels threatened to blow up the school's gymnasium if their demands were not met. Putin refused to communicate or negotiate with any of the hostage takers.[78] Rebels detonated their explosive vests, and Russian forces stormed the gym (although the order of events is contested by local Ossetians and activist groups). Over 400 hostages were killed, and every single hostage taker was killed or apprehended.

The first two hostage-taking operations, during the First Russo-Chechen War (and preceding Putin's election), demanded the withdrawal of Russian troops as well as safe passage to return home. During the Second Russo-Chechen War, the core demand of Russian withdrawal was reiterated and perhaps even emphasized by separatists' lack of interest in safe passage to return to Chechnya. Hostage operations during the Second Russo-Chechen War were riskier (they took place farther from the Chechen border) and appeared more suicidal in nature—since the hostage takers no longer demanded safe passage home. Bombers aired videos filled with Islamic rhetoric and were undoubtedly influenced by the interim emergence of Wahhabism. Despite the influence of Wahhabism, however, hostage operations clearly retained the original and secular goals of the resistance: political independence and freedom from foreign occupation.

Trajectory of the Suicide Attacks

The separatists' suicide bombing campaign began on June 7, 2000. Two Chechen females, Khava Barayeva and Luiza Magamadova, drove a truck laden with explosives into a Russian Special Forces facility in Alkhan-Yurt, Chechnya. Khava Barayeva was related to two prominent separatist leaders: Arbi and Movsar Barayev. Arbi Barayev was a notorious field commander nicknamed "The Terminator" who was killed in

---

78. "200 Kids Held Hostage; Terror as Armed Gang Storm School on First Day of Term," *Daily Record*, September 2, 2004.

2001. Arbi was well known for the kidnapping and beheading of Russians and orchestrating armed uprisings against President Maskhadov. He also served as the leader of the Special Purpose Islamic Regiment. At the time of his death, Arbi was succeeded by Khava's other infamous relative, Movsar Barayev, who orchestrated the Moscow Theater hostage operation in 2002. In a video before her death, Khava Barayeva announced that men should not "take the women's role by staying home."[79] After her death, a popular singer and songwriter, Timur Mutsurayev, dedicated a song to her operation: "A truck heading toward headquarters, loaded with plastic explosive and destiny. Look at Khava's gentle face behind the wheel; she chose to sacrifice herself."[80]

There were four additional attacks in the year 2000. Two of the attacks were carried out between June 11 and 12. Both suicide bombers targeted checkpoints in and around Grozny. These attacks were carried out by young males: Djabrail Sergeyev and Abdou Rakhmad, both ex-Russian soldiers that converted to Islam. On July 2, 2000, the separatists carried out an operation with four truck bombs and four targets. This attack demonstrated a high level of organization. The attacks were nearly simultaneous and targeted security installations in the Chechen cities of Argun, Naibyora, Gudermes, and Urus-Martan. The last suicide bombing of 2000 was carried out by an unknown male who used a truck bomb to target police headquarters in Gudermes. The suicide bombs in 2000 were predominately carried out by males, and all bombers targeted security installations exclusively.

The year 2001 featured half as many attacks as 2000. The first attack took place on September 18, at a Russian checkpoint in Argun. The second attack occurred on November 29, against a military commander Geidar Gadzhiyev. The bomber, Elza Gazuyeva, carried out this attack against Commander Gadzhiyev because he had killed her husband. Although accounts vary, Gadzhiyev reportedly murdered Elza's husband in the hospital after Mr. Gazuyeva had experienced war-related injuries. According to some, Gadzhiyev brutally forced Elza to witness the murder. When she approached Gadzhiyev with a belt bomb, she asked, "Do you remember me?" and then detonated the explosives.[81] Although suicide bombing is not particularly popular in Chechnya, Elza Gazuyeva is praised by other

79. Adam Dolnik, "Staring Death in the Face," *Straits Times,* October 5, 2005.

80. Ruslan Isayev, "The Chechen Woman and Her Role in the 'New' Society," *Prague Watchdog,* June 21, 2004.

81. Ibid.

Chechen women: "She was, is, and will remain a heroine for us."[82] As in 2000, the suicide bombers in 2001 exclusively attacked security targets.

The year 2002 witnessed two attacks. On May 31, a male bomber detonated a bag bomb at a Russian checkpoint in Minutka Square, Grozny. On December 27, two truck bombs targeted a pro-Moscow governmental complex in Grozny. This attack was carried out by three members of the Tumrievs family. Both truck bombs targeted the same complex; the first was driven by 43-year-old Gelani Tumriyev and his 15-year-old daughter, Alina, and the second was driven by his 17-year-old son. The family members were locals in Grozny and were rumored to have lost their mother at the hands of Russian forces. "Shamil Basayev, the Chechen rebel leader, claimed that the local family—desperate because of the brutality of the Russian forces—had driven the trucks."[83] Additionally, in October 2002, Chechen separatists carried out the Moscow Theater hostage operation. Putin's especially harsh response to the hostage operation fueled the increase in suicide bombings in 2003.

In 2003, Chechen separatists carried out 11 suicide attacks—until recently, the most prolific year of the Chechen suicide campaign. For the first time, suicide bombers attacked targets inside and outside of Chechnya. The attackers bribed their way past military checkpoints and thus showcased weaknesses of the Russian security forces. This generated alarm among Russians and their affiliates in Chechnya, Ingushetia, and North Ossetia. And for the first time, Chechen suicide bombers targeted civilians in addition to military and political installations. Bombers targeted religious festivals, rock concerts, cafés, trains, and hotels. Civilian operations were directed at Russian or pro-Russian civilians in Russia and Chechnya while suicide attacks in Ingushetia and North Ossetia targeted military or political personnel. In 2003, there were seven male suicide bombers and 11 female suicide bombers. Two of the female bombers, Shakhida Shabulatova and Khadijat Mangeriyeva, were recently widowed due to events affiliated with the Russian occupation. Another female bomber, Mariam Tashukhadjiyeva, had also lost her brother to the Russian forces.

In 2004, attacks targeted more civilian populations in Chechnya and Russia. Separatists targeted airplanes, a polling station, a subway station, and a café. There were two noncivilian attacks: one targeted a political

82. Steven Lee Myers, "From Dismal Chechnya, Women Turn to Bombs," *New York Times,* September 10, 2004.

83. Nick Palton Walsh, "At Least 40 Die in Chechnya Blast: Suicide Bombers Drive Explosives-Packed Truck into Security Service Headquarters," *Guardian,* May 13, 2003.

leader in Ingushetia and the other targeted a security building in Chechnya. Chechen separatists also carried out their last hostage operation in Beslan, North Ossetia. Hostage takers targeted children, teachers, and parents in an elementary school. Unlike the Moscow Theater operation, Beslan was met with widespread disdain throughout Russia and the rest of the world for targeting children. The operation was covered extensively by the media, and many expressed outrage that nearly 200 children had been killed. Suicide bombing halted, with the exception of one attack, and did not resume until late 2007.

Although there was one suicide bomb in 2007 and three in 2008, 2009 witnessed a notable increase in the Chechen suicide terrorism campaign. There were 12 new attacks in 2009 that primarily targeted security installations. Refraining from civilian targets may have been a tactical decision to attempt to regain some of the popular support lost when separatists targeted children at Beslan. All of the targets were located inside Chechnya as well as Ingushetia and Dagestan—very much like 2003. Unlike 2003, the majority of the suicide attackers were male.

The Transition from Hard to Soft Targeting

The separatists' transition from hard to soft targeting was caused primarily by Russian brutality and the decision by the Chechen separatists to use more aggressive tactics to compel Russia to withdraw from Chechnya. The transition occurred in 2003 and 2004. In the initial years of the campaign, suicide bombers targeted military or political instillations and their affiliates only. But in 2003, four of the 11 suicide attacks targeted civilians. In 2004, five of the six attacks targeted civilians. After the 2004 lull, the trend toward soft targets began to reverse itself; only one of three 2008 attacks targeted civilians, and in 2009, only one of the 12 attacks targeted civilians. The percentages of civilian targets are as follows: 2000, 0%; 2001, 0%; 2002, 0%; 2003, 36%; 2004, 83%; 2008, 33%; and 2009, 0%. The years 2003 and 2004 demonstrate a transition to and an increase in soft civilian targeting; those two years contain 90% of all civilian-targeted suicide bombs.

In 2002 Russians implemented a new and especially brutal counterterrorism program. In response, separatists increased the number of suicide attacks and began to target civilians in 2003. It seems that separatists transitioned to civilian targets in order to match Russian brutality and influence Russian withdrawal. Shamil Basayev described a similar logic behind the

Beslan hostage operation: "I figured that the more brutal I could make it, the quicker they'd get the message. I thought it would work."[84] Basayev conceptualized a relationship between civilian targets, brutality, and success in achieving Russian withdrawal from Chechnya. The ebb and flow of civilian targeting suggests that this conceptualization extended to the suicide campaign as well. This escalation of attacks directed at civilians may also be explained by an increase in military defenses.

After suffering nine suicide attacks, the Russian military would have been forced to reassess their self-defense. Between 2000 and 2002, Russian security forces had sustained approximately 550 killed or wounded soldiers due to suicide attacks. These casualties, coupled with the loss of military infrastructure, may have prompted the Russian military to strengthen their immediate defenses and better protect soldiers, buildings, convoys, and equipment. If this is the case, a change in Russian behavior likely necessitated a change in separatists' tactics. Suicide bombers, therefore, may have transitioned to soft targets in order to ensure the continued efficacy of their attacks.

The 2003 Spike

The 2003 spike in suicide bombs appears to be a direct response to particularly brutal Russian counterterrorism operations. In June 2000, Russia established nominal control over the Chechen territory. Then, in 2001, Russians announced a transition from conventional warfare to counterterrorism operations because of the success of Chechen guerilla operations. Between November 2000 and April 2001, Chechen separatists clashed with Russian federal forces, causing between 50 and 80 Russian military deaths per month. The Russian position began to weaken as "guerilla hit-and-run attacks on the occupation forces gradually became bolder, more frequent, and better coordinated."[85] Insurgents began to coordinate operations from civilian villages rather than remote camps in the mountains.

Incapable of distinguishing between insurgent fighters and civilians, Russian troops responded with extreme brutality against the noninsurgent population. Exceptionally harsh counterterrorism operations were

84. Jonathan Miller, "Reign of Terror and Another Beslan?" *ABC News,* February 4, 2005.

85. Stephen D. Shenfield, "Checnya at a Turning Point," Johnson's Russia List 6191 Research and Analytical Supplement 7, April 2002.

concentrated between April 2001 and the end of 2002. Russians conducted "sweep operations" in over six villages, where Russian soldiers routinely surrounded an entire village, rounded up the male population, and tortured them in temporary military bases. Some of these villagers were released, but many were kidnapped, maimed, and killed. The most brutal period of the occupation occurred between the end of 2001 and 2002. Although some have argued that these indiscriminate sweeps have not resulted in any increased radicalization or violence against the Russian forces, these studies surveyed the effects on mobilization only over short periods of time (e.g., six months)[86] while it is common for Chechens to take as long as several years to regroup, reorganize, and carry out revenge attacks against the Russian forces. Indeed, Chechens have long had a tradition called *adat,* in which it is acceptable to take years to exact revenge for the death of spouses or family members.

This brutality provoked an especially strong response by Chechen suicide bombers.[87] There were 11 attacks in 2003; this more than doubled the number of attacks from the previous three years. Many of the attackers, in 2003, were individuals that were exacting revenge for the killing of loved ones by the Russian occupation. Both the wife and sister of murdered rebel Ruslan Mangeriyev, for example, carried out separate suicide attacks on July 27 and December 9 of 2003, respectively.[88] There are at least five reported attackers, between May 2003 and August 2008, who lost a family member or spouse in Russian counterterrorism operations. In all likelihood, there are more attackers motivated by similar circumstances that escaped the attention of the news media.

The 2004 Lull

Suicide attacks began in the year 2000 and increased in momentum until the end of 2003. In 2004, the momentum of the suicide terrorist campaign slows; in 2005 and 2006 there are no suicide attacks. They do not resume until the end of 2007. Statistics regarding Russian troop deployment in Chechnya are both sparse and inconsistent, especially since Russia fre-

86. John Lyall, "Does Indiscriminate Violence Incite Insurgent Attacks? Evidence from Chechnya," *Journal of Conflict Resolution* 53 (February 12, 2009).

87. Anne Speckhard and Khapta Akhmedova, "The Making of a Martyr: Chechen Suicide Terrorism," *Studies in Conflict and Terrorism* 29, no. 5 (2006).

88. Sergey Dyupin, "Female Suicide Bomber Attempted to Blow Up Akhmad Kadyrov's Son," *Russian Press Digest,* July 28, 2003.

quently announced and then withdrew plans to decrease troop levels. By most accounts, in the spring of 2004, Russia had nearly 70,000 troops and police in Chechnya.[89] By fall, some sources placed that number at around 55,000.[90] Actual Russian withdrawals were modest—2,400 paratroopers, 150 cars, and 240 armored vehicles in November of 2004[91]—and were often followed by the deployment of new units in the Caucasus.[92] Russia maintained fairly constant troop levels throughout the 2004 lull in order to cope with guerrilla attacks.

The lull is best explained by the consequences of two events: the Beslan hostage crisis, which dramatically eroded separatists' popular support, and the initiation of the "Chechenization" campaign by the Russian government.

The Beslan hostage crisis on September 1, 2004, greatly damaged international public support that Chechen separatists had earned in previous years.[93] The enormity of this crisis, in which nearly 200 schoolchildren were killed, shocked moderate separatists that had previously allowed themselves to be conflated with the Islamists. Exiled Chechen separatist Akhmed Zakayev lamented that those willing to take children hostage gave all separatists a bad name: "A bigger blow could not have been dealt on us.... Now people around the world will think that Chechens are beasts and monsters if they could attack children."[94]

This apparent loss of support coincided with the beginning of "Chechenization," a hearts and minds campaign initiated by the Russian government. Chechenization instituted less brutal policies against Chechen civilians and attempted to sway the local population in support of Russia through policies like amnesty programs for rebel fighters. The amnesty lasted from the summer of 2006 until January 2007; almost 600 Chechen separatists surrendered.[95] Although the Russians half-heartedly pursued Checheniza-

89. Available at http://www.pbs.org/newshour/updates/chechnya_05-11-04.html.

90. Xinhua News Agency, November 20, 2004, available at http://english.people.com.cn/200411/20/eng20041120_164539.html.

91. Xinhua News Agency, available at http://english.people.com.cn/200411/20/eng20041120_164539.html.

92. Available at http://www.jamestown.org/programs/ncw/single/?tx_ttnews[tt_news]=31994&tx_ttnews[backPid]=188&no_cache=1.

93. "International, Russian Human Rights Groups Condemn Beslan Tragedy," *News Bulletin,* September 8, 2004.

94. Valeria Korchagina, "Zakayev Was Asked to Assist in Negotiations at the School," *Moscow Times,* September 6, 2004."

95. Sergei Venyavsky, "Officials: More than 500 Militants Surrendered under Expiring Amnesty in Chechnya, North Caucasus," *Associated Press,* January 15, 2007.

tion since 1991, the assassination of Aslan Maskhadov in March 2005 provided Russia with an opportune moment to construct a "civilized" Chechen leader. "The policy of Chechenization only became viable when Akhmed Kadyrov decided to abandon the insurgency to help Putin. . . . [Kadyrov] was tired of war and pragmatically recognized that Putin's overwhelming use of force made resistance futile."[96]

Rebels acknowledged the success of Chechenization but viewed it with disdain. One separatist complained: "Many of Chechnya's civilians are pleased at what the authorities are doing: the authorities are building homes, they constructed the largest mosque in Europe, they're improving peoples' lives. . . . And all this show is being paid for by our oil. The republic doesn't even get ten percent of the oil revenues. So why do we take their bait? They're grabbing all the oil and throwing us handouts. Telling us meanwhile that 'the Russians feed us.'"[97]

The suicide campaign likely halted in response to the apparent loss of public support following the Beslan crisis and the lessening of brutality associated with Russia's policy of Chechenization. The Chechenization strategy, however, appears unsustainable: "There was an inherent contradiction in the use of the Chechenization policy by Putin, in that its success depended on a level of mutual trust between Russia and the collaborationist administration that could not be realized. Attempts by Russia to build Kadyrov's authority barely moved beyond the rhetorical level, as Chechnya remained under de facto Russian military occupation and emergency rule."[98]

This pattern of, first, separatists responding to the brutality of the occupier and, second, the continuous military occupation by Russia seems to have caused the resurgence of the suicide terrorist campaign in 2008, when pro-Russian Chechen President Kadyrov launched a new brutal offensive to "put an end" to the separatists for good.[99]

The 2008–2009 Resurgence

During Chechenization, Russian troops transferred power to Ramzan Kadyrov, the son of the aforementioned Akmed Kadyrov. "In 2005 and in

---

96. Hughes, *Chechnya: From Nationalism to Jihad,* p. 119.

97. "All That Is Happening Today Is a Mirage," April 21, 2009, available at KavKazCenter. com.

98. Hughes, *Chechnya: From Nationalism to Jihad,* p. 121.

99. Jim Nichol, "Stability in Russia's Chechnya and Other Regions of the North Caucasus: Recent Developments," *CRS Reports for Congress,* August 12, 2008.

early 2006, Ramzan Kadyrov's political power grew substantially. In the spring of 2006, Kadyrov became Prime Minister of Chechnya and following Alkhanov's forced resignation, Kadyrov was sworn in as President of the Chechen Republic in April 2007."[100] Ramzan Kadyrov was the leader of the "Kadyrovtsy, a paramilitary group about three thousand strong . . . after Akhmed Kadyrov's assassination it expanded into a full-fledged paramilitary formation operating under the guidance of the Russian FSB."[101] The Kadyrovtsky, under Ramzan Kadyrov, had been responsible for a great deal of kidnappings and abductions, since 2001, under the guise of death squads: "small clandestine organizations interested in 'deniability' for their 'targeted killings,' which is partly tactical but also reflects the moral shame at the illegal nature of the activity."[102] After the consolidation of his power, Kadyrov—under immense Russian pressure—announced that he would eliminate the separatist movement by the end of that very winter.

The separatists, however, remained active and carried out punitive operations specifically against Chechen civilians that cooperated with the new government. In June 2008, for example, Chechen rebels burned five houses in the village of Benoi-Vedeno. As they left the village, they also left a note saying that anyone who worked for or cooperated with the authorities would be punished in the same way.[103]

Kadyrov had not crushed the resistance by the winter, as promised, and announced a new counterterrorism offensive on June 18, 2008. According to prominent Russian human rights groups, the counterinsurgency operations these forces conducted "frequently involved abduction-style detentions [in which] many of the abductees were placed in illegal prisons and tortured to compel them to sign confessions and testimonies against third parties."[104] This counterterrorism offensive continued the already prevalent kidnappings but also introduced widespread punitive house burnings. "In 2008, high-level officials, including President Kadyrov, made public statements explicitly stating that the insurgents' families should expect to be punished unless they convinced their relatives to surrender"; between

100. "What Your Children Do Will Touch upon You: Punitive House-Burning in Chechnya," Human Rights Watch, July 2009.

101. Hughes, *Chechnya: From Nationalism to Jihad,* p. 124.

102. Ibid.

103. "What Your Children Do Will Touch Upon You: Punitive House-Burning in Chechnya," Human Rights Watch, July 2009.

104. Ibid., p. 14.

the summer of 2008 and the spring of 2009, human rights organizations identified over 25 instances of punitive house burning across seven districts of Chechnya.[105] Soon after the new counterterrorism offensive, the suicide bombing campaign reemerged with three attacks from August to November 2008.

In April 2009, Russians announced the "end of all military operations in Chechnya" and the full transfer of power to Kadyrov who remains committed to harsh measures to root out the rebels. Days after the announcement, the suicide campaign escalated. There were 10 attacks between May 15 and September 15, 2009. Attacks have continued throughout September and October. There exists little evidence to suggest that Russian troops have made significant withdrawal efforts and Chechen rebels continue to enter into skirmishes with both Russian and Pro-Russian Chechen forces. Human Rights Watch expects that new militants are "motivated less by religious militancy and more by revenge for family members killed by security services and personal experiences of abduction and torture"; a resident of Shali district believed his son's motivation for joining the insurgency was due to being severely beaten during an interrogation: "He just could not deal with it any longer. This was no life."[106]

The new wave of separatists perceive Kadyrov as a mere puppet of the Russian government; they have declared a New Caucasus Emirate—much like the Caucasus Common Market of the 1990s. Separatists have begun to articulate economic goals for their overall campaign: "If we had an independent state, our oil would pay for a fine standard of living. That's why we've taken our path of struggle—so we can have our state, so that the Muslims can live in peace."[107] Rebels have even posted, on Web sites, detailed plans for the economic survival and success of the proposed Caucasian Emirate. This new economic cognizance may be an attempt to counter civilians' popular approval of limited Russian reconstruction. This and the resurgence of security-targeted suicide attacks suggests a long-term objective of a separate state; separatists clearly anticipate victory and have developed both economic and political plans to gain popular support for their vision for Chechnya and the Caucasus region. With popular support for this vision, the Chechen separatist suicide terrorist campaign may con-

105. Ibid., p. 20.
106. "What Your Children Do Will Touch Upon You: Punitive House-Burning in Chechnya," Human Rights Watch, July 2009, p. 16.
107. "All That Is Happening Today Is a Mirage (Interview with a Chechen Mujahid)," kavkazcenter.org, April 21, 2009.

tinue for many more years. Indeed, in 2010, Doku Umarov issued video statements warning of attacks yet to come. "The Russians think the war is distant ... Blood will not only spill in our towns and villages but also it will spill in their towns ... Our military operations will encompass the entirety of Russia."[108]

Weapons and Attacker Gender over Time

Weapons usage over the course of the suicide terrorism campaign suggests that belt bombs are affiliated with female suicide bombers. The first reported use of a belt bomb occurred in November 2001 against a military commander. There is a clustering of belt bombs, later, in 2003, which is proportional to the rise in the overall number of suicide attacks. In the 19 instances of confirmed belt bombs, they were utilized in attacks by women in 13 of those instances. This affiliation most likely results from the tactical advantage offered by women's clothing. Very often women can disguise the bombs as a pregnancy, or can disguise them more easily under loose-fitting dresses.

Furthermore, unlike most suicide terrorist campaigns, women were central from the start. The very first Chechen suicide attacker was a woman, and the infamous Black Widows participated consistently over the duration of the campaign. The most recent year of the campaign, 2009, proves a temporary exception. Only one of the 12 confirmed attacks was a female suicide bomber. The year 2003 most closely resembles the size and scope of 2009; of the 18 attackers in 2003, 11 were women. Although this difference cannot be analyzed as a trend over the course of several years, the domination of 2009 by male attackers may be explained by the social network, preference, or religious ideology of two militant brothers, Hussein and Muslim Gakayev.[109] It appears as though Hussein Gakayev may have been involved in the planning of four or more of the 12 suicide attacks in 2009. Then, again, in 2010, two female suicide bombers carried out the Moscow Metro bombings in which 40 people were killed and over 100 injured.

108. "Moscow Metro Blast Kills Dozens," kavkazcenter.com, March 29, 2010.
109. "Kadyrov Urges Law Enforcers to Crack Down on Militants," ITAR-TASS, August 26, 2009.

Recruitment

Most Chechen suicide bombers appear to be self-recruited. It seems as though the trauma associated with Russian occupation caused many secular or modestly religious individuals to orchestrate acts of revenge against the Russian occupational forces. Elza Gazuyeva is a prime example. She attacked Commander Geidar Gadzhiyev to avenge her husband's murder. The Tumriyev family also carried out a suicide attack in retribution for the murder of their mother. Both the sister and the widow of the murdered rebel Ruslan Mangeriyev carried out similar suicide attacks against the Russian forces in 2003. Lastly, the two women that exploded airplanes in 2004, Sazita Jebirhanova and Aminat Nogayeva, had lost brothers to the occupation. We have confirmed at least five instances in which suicide bombers carried out their attacks in retribution for a lost family member, and we expect that there were many more instances in which attackers had similar motivations. Most suicide bombers were Chechens that had lived through the First and Second Russo-Chechen Wars. Approximately 75,000 to 100,000 Chechens died over the course of the two wars, and it is probable that many other bombers had family members among the deceased.[110]

Other academics' work confirms these findings. Anne Speckhard is one of few academics to gain access to suicide bombers' families in Chechnya. In a small statistical sample, she found that 82% of the bombers' families claimed that the bombers were secular prior to an instance of major trauma—like the death of a family member or a near death experience. One family member claimed that a family member "changed immensely after the loss of her brother. She lost a lot of weight, and almost did not go out anywhere after it. She stopped paying attention to her appearance and began to dress as an old woman—putting on the big scarf. She became very religious."[111] Speckhard concludes that many suicide bombers "had no prior relationship to fundamental militant groups but sought out the militant Wahhabi radical groups in direct reaction to the traumas they had endured knowing full well of the groups' beliefs and terrorist practices."[112]

The Russian media has reported many instances of separatists drugging,

110. "Chechnya and the North Caucasus," Thomson Reuters Foundation, http://www.alert-net.org/db/crisisprofiles/RU_WAR.htm
111. Speckhard and Akhmedova, "The Making of a Martyr: Chechen Suicide Terrorism
112. Ibid.

coercing, kidnapping, and blackmailing Chechens—especially the Black Widows—into becoming suicide bombers. Such rumors are largely derivative of the uncharacteristic case of Zarema Murkheyova—a failed bomber who claimed she was given drugs in her orange juice. There is little concrete evidence of recruitment by coercion and also very little evidence of the recruitment of women based on their inability to fulfill societal gender roles. It seems that female suicide bombers self-recruit in much the same way that male suicide bombers do. Throughout the campaign, approximately 21 of the 63 suicide bombers were female, and 67% of all female bombers carried out their operations in 2003 and 2004. They carried out attacks, like their male counterparts, in response to Russian brutality and counterterrorism operations.

The two women that carried out the Moscow Metro bombings, in 2010, for example, carried out their attack in response to the Russian occupation. The seventeen year-old bomber, Abdullayeva, was the widow of a rebel fighter who was killed by Russian forces during the winter of 2009. The second bomber, a university graduate and computer science teacher, was also married to a rebel fighter in the North Caucasus whose whereabouts are unknown. Female Chechen suicide bombers do not demonstrate the widespread allegations of exploitation; instead, female bombers demonstrate clear links to the occupation and a style of self-recruitment that resembles their male counterparts.

Local Popular Support

There is little evidence of local and popular support for the Chechen separatist suicide terrorist campaign. Although there is deep-seated resentment toward Russia, "the desire for revenge has not translated into wider support for continued warfare. The ascendance of Wahhabist leaders among the guerillas, and the damage caused by fighting, have reduced the appeal of the separatist cause."[113] Chechens generally feel that suicide is unnatural, and one man, in response to Satsita Dzhbirkhanova's suicide bombing, questioned, "How can someone do this to themselves? Only God can take a life. She knew very well that to take her life was a sin."[114]

113. Kramer, "Guerilla Warfare, Counterinsurgency and Terrorism in the North Caucasus: The Military Dimension of the Russian-Chechen Conflict."

114. Myers, "From Dismal Chechnya, Women Turn to Bombs."

Anne Speckhard has conducted psychological autopsies of Chechen suicide bombers. She has interviewed family members, friends, teachers, and neighbors of the deceased bombers in order to extrapolate information about the psychological state of the bombers themselves. While doing so, Speckhard has also assessed her interviewees' support for suicide bombing. Speckhard finds that these interviewees (who have intimate relationships to the bombers) generally feel that bombers were manipulated by the terrorist groups and do not express widespread support. Although interviewees may empathize with individual bombers, they seem to demonstrate little support for suicide bombing as a means to independence.

Although there are no public or community-wide celebrations that take place after a suicide attack, it is possible the lack of evidence for public support is due to Russian control. The Russian military and pro-Russian government do not permit independent opinion polls or public displays of support via posters, flyers, or movies. The current lack of popular support may also stem from the harsh counterterrorism initiatives of Russian and pro-Russian security forces. When a suicide bomber elects to carry out a suicide mission, he or she invites a harsh backlash upon his or her family and community members. This phenomenon accounts for Anne Speckhard's small sample sizes, as "many interviewees were at first fearful and reluctant to grant an interview, as nearly all had already been visited and interrogated by Russian special services and continued to fear retaliation."[115]

Russian Democracy

Throughout most of the Chechen conflict, Russia has been viewed as a credible democracy, at least on par with Peru, Thailand, and the Dominican Republic. However, it has also undergone significant political fluctuation, from holding free and fair elections during the 1990s to more questionable elections since 2000. The Russian government has increasingly engaged in undemocratic practices, but has not yet established a clear reputation as a purely authoritarian regime. If both Chechen suicide attacks and Russia's authoritarian trend continue, Russia may well become the first clearly authoritarian state to face suicide terrorism—although the attacks would have begun before it reached that state.

Between 1990 and 1993 Russia was classified by Freedom House as a

115. Speckhard and Akhmedova, "The Making of a Martyr: Chechen Suicide Terrorism."

partly free democracy. There were mostly free and fair elections with the possibility of multiple parties and candidates. The 2000 election in which Putin succeeded President Boris Yeltsin was considered, by outside monitors, also to be free and fair. Prior to election day, Putin's antiterrorism platform boasted a 97% approval rating. He obtained 72% of the popular vote and was reelected in 2004.[116] Between 1997 and 2004, Russian moved from a three to a five on Freedom House's "Political Rights" score. Countries that score between a three and a five are considered to be "Partly Free."

Between 2005 and 2006, Russia's score increased from a five to a six and was therefore classified as "Not Free." After the increase in separatist activity in 2003 and 2004, Putin "consolidated support in the legislature. [He moved] quickly to promote a political agenda dominated by the overarching theme of overcoming internal dissension and increasing internal and external security."[117] At this time the Russian government enacted constitutional changes that allowed Putin control of the governorship of all provinces. It appears as though the spike in separatists' activity legitimized Putin's centralization of power.

In 2006, Freedom House altered its coding categories. There are now nine new categories used to monitor a country's degree of freedom. While these categories have changed from those prior to 2005, they still indicate an increasingly undemocratic trend in Russia. According to Freedom House's new coding rules, from 2006 to 2009, Russia's "Democracy Score" has gone from a 5.75 to 5.96. Russia is presently considered a "Semi-Consolidated Authoritarian Regime." "Countries receiving a Democracy Score of 5.00–5.99 attempt to mask authoritarianism with limited respect for the institutions and practices of democracy. They typically fail to meet even the minimum standards of electoral democracy."[118] If Russia's Democracy Score increases by .04, it will be considered a "Consolidated Authoritarian Regime."

Overall, Russia is a borderline democracy that has been moving increasingly toward authoritarianism in recent years. Russian restrictions upon democracy, in Chechnya, may also exacerbate the local feeling of occupation. After the Beslan hostage operation in 2004, Putin abolished local elections in order to assume greater control over counterterrorism efforts through a proxy force. "[Putin] argued that firm central government control and strong political parties were essential to prevent terrorist attacks such as the Beslan

116. Polity IV Country Report 2007: Russia, http://www.systemicpeace.org/polity/polity4.html.

117. Country Report: Russia (2009), www.freedomhouse.org.

118. "Methodology," 2009 Edition, www.freedomhouse.org.

school siege ... Putin said he wanted the Kremlin to nominate regional leaders, bringing an end to regional elections." The fact that violence resurged
three years later, in 2007, suggests that political restrictions matter most in
combination with corruption, abuse, or oppression. After experiencing several years of Kadyrov's administration, Chechens, in fact, have been frus-
trated by their inability to elect their own leadership. If Chechens continue
to lack legitimate political recourse within the Kadyrov administration, they
will likely continue to pursue violence as a means to nationalist ends.[119]

A Lasting Peace?

With so many Chechen suicide attacks, one could easily be forgiven for
skepticism regarding the prospects of a lasting peace. A close examination of the conflict's history, however, suggests solutions that both sides
may be able to accept. Chechen suicide terrorism is strongly motivated
by both direct military occupation by Russia and by indirect military occupation by pro-Russian Chechen security forces. If Russia were to re-
introduce the moderate policies of 2005 to 2007, it might not end every
attack, but would reduce violence to a level both sides can live with.

The latest generation of Chechen separatists views President Kadyrov
as a puppet of the Kremlin. Any realistic solution must improve the legitimacy of Chechnya's core social institutions. An initial step would be
holding free and fair elections. Others would include adopting internation-
ally accepted standards of humane conduct among the security forces and
equally distributing the region's oil revenues so that Chechnya's Muslims
benefit from their own resources.

No political solution would resolve every issue. But the resurgence of suicide attacks should make clear to Russia that quelling the rebellion with di-
plomacy is in its own security interests. As long as Chechens feel themselves
under occupation—either directly by Russian troops or by their proxies—
the cycle of violence will continue to wreak havoc across Russia.

119. Jeremy Page, "Putin Ready to Seize More Power in Wake of Beslan," *The Times*,
September 14, 2004.

CHAPTER TEN

Sri Lanka

In May 2009, the Sri Lankan president declared victory in the Sri Lankan government's 26-year civil war with the Liberation Tigers of Tamil Eelam (LTTE).[1] The LTTE was an insurgent group committed to creating an independent Tamil state in the Tamil-dominated Northern and Eastern Provinces of Sri Lanka.[2] In its efforts to secure the Tamil homeland, the LTTE sustained the longest running suicide campaign to date. Between 1983 and 2009, LTTE suicide cadres, known as "Black Tigers," were responsible for 116 suicide attacks resulting in 1,643 fatalities. Suicide terrorism was an integral part of the LTTE's overall military and political strategy in prosecuting the war. Nevertheless, there is significant variation in the number and targets of suicide attacks over time. This chapter explains the ebb and flow of the LTTE's use of suicide terrorism over the course of the civil war.

1. Major contributors to this chapter were Jenna Jordon, Keven Ruby, and Sophia Akbar. Research assistants for this chapter were Rajika Jayatilake and Kaan Kadiolu.

2. On the Sri Lankan civil war, see Asoka Bandarage, *The Separatist Conflict in Sri Lanka: Terrorism, Ethnicity, Political Economy* (New York: iUniverse, 2009); K. M. De Silva, *Reaping the Whirlwind: Ethnic Conflict, Ethnic Politics in Sri Lanka* (New Delhi: Penguin Books, 1998); Dagmar Hellmann-Rajanayagam, *The Tamil Tigers: Armed Struggle for Identity* (Stuttgart: F. Steiner, 1994); M. R. Narayan Swamy, *Tigers of Lanka, from Boys to Guerrillas*, 3rd ed. (Delhi: Konark Publishers, 2002); Robert I. Rotberg, ed., *Creating Peace in Sri Lanka: Civil War and Reconciliation* (Cambridge, MA: World Peace Foundation and Belfer Center for Science and International Affairs, 1999); Senaka Silva, *Sri Lanka, Three Decades of Hostilities: The Terror Campaign of the LTTE* (Pannipitiya: Stamford Lake, 2008); Stanley Jeyaraja Tambiah, *Buddhism Betrayed? Religion, Politics, and Violence in Sri Lanka* (Chicago: University of Chicago Press, 1992); Neil DeVotta, "The Liberation Tigers of Tamil Eelam and the Lost Quest for Separatism in Sri Lanka," *Asian Survey* 49, no. 6 (November/December 2009): 1021–51; A. Jeyaratnam Wilson, *The Break-Up of Sri Lanka: The Sinhalese-Tamil Conflict* (Honolulu: University of Hawaii Press, 1989); Mia M. Bloom, "Ethnic Conflict, State Terror and Suicide Bombing in Sri Lanka," *Civil Wars* 6, no. 1 (2003): 54.

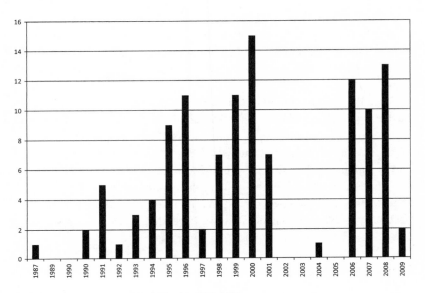

FIGURE 10.1 Suicide attacks in Sri Lanka, 1987–2009

The origins of the LTTE's use of suicide terrorism mirror the causes of the civil war. As the discussion below will show, the LTTE's decision to employ suicide attacks is strategic. Yet the condition of possibility for suicide terrorism to emerge as a strategy was the nature of the conflict between Sri Lanka's ethnic Tamil minority and Sinhalese majority. After independence in 1948, the now Sinhalese-dominated government, in a surge of nationalist fervor, systematically discriminated against Sri Lanka's Tamils. This discrimination generated popular support among ethnic Tamils for increased autonomy in the two Tamil-dominated provinces. Exacerbating the intensity of the nationalist conflict is that the Sinhalese are Buddhist and the Tamils Hindu. This difference in religion casts the conflict in existential terms, a prerequisite for the emergence of a culture of martyrdom that sustains popular support for suicide terrorism necessary to sustain a suicide terrorism campaign.

When the civil war broke out in 1983, the LTTE was poised to capitalize on the Tamil desire for a homeland and support for suicide terrorism to engage the numerically superior military forces of the Sri Lankan government. After 1987, suicide terrorism was integrated into the LTTE's overall military and political strategy for prosecuting the war. Figure 10.1

shows the distribution of LTTE suicide attacks. Accordingly, the pattern of attacks follows the ebb and flow of the major military confrontations between the LTTE and Sri Lankan government forces as they fought for control of the Northern and Eastern Provinces constituting the Tamil heartland.

Since the military defeat of the LTTE in May 2009, there have been no further reported suicide attacks in Sri Lanka. The Sri Lankan policy to end suicide terrorism entailed three components: (1) the military defeat of the LTTE; (2) the internment of Tamils in the conflict zone in order to identify and "rehabilitate" LTTE cadres; and (3) the establishment of High Security Zones around Sri Lankan military installations in the former conflict zone. In the conclusion, we discuss the implications of the three-pronged Sri Lankan strategy as a general model for ending suicide terrorism.

Group and Goals

Group

The Liberation Tigers of Tamil Eelam (LTTE) are a Sri Lankan Tamil separatist group founded by Velupillai Prabhakaran in 1972 as the Tamil New Tigers, becoming the LTTE in 1976. The LTTE claims to represent the interests of the Tamil minority in Sri Lanka, and emerged as the principal Tamil military organization dedicated to the creation of an independent Tamil state, Tamil Eelam, in 1986. Sinhala nationalism, decades of discriminatory policies undermining Tamil cultural, linguistic, and political standing, and outbreaks of anti-Tamil communal violence combined to shape the political will among Tamils to seek an independent homeland. Civil war broke out in 1983, as the LTTE launched its armed struggle against the armed forces of the Sri Lankan government that lasted until the LTTE's defeat in 2009. Suicide bombing is part of the LTTE's larger strategy to shape political and military outcomes in the conflict. LTTE suicide bombers, also called "Black Tigers," carried out their first suicide attack against the Sri Lankan Army (SLA) in July 1987.

The Sinhalese are the largest ethnic group in Sri Lanka. At the time of the 1981 census, they comprised 74% of the population of Sri Lanka. The native language of the Sinhalese is Sinhala, and approximately 93% of Sinhalese are Buddhist. The Tamils are a minority ethnic group in Sri Lanka, who in 1981 made up 18.2% of the population of Sri Lanka (12.7% Sri Lankan

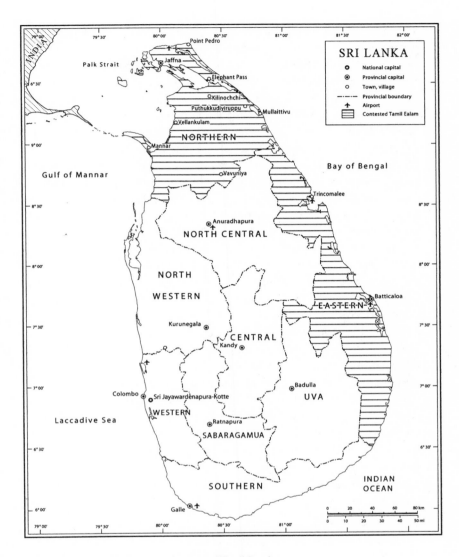

Within the map:

SRI LANKA
- National capital
- Provincial capital
- Town, village
- Provincial boundary
- Airport
- Contested Tamil Ealam

INDIA

Palk Strait

Point Pedro
Jaffna
Elephant Pass
Kilinochchi
Puthukkudiyiruppu
Mullaittivu
Vellankulam

NORTHERN

Mannar

Gulf of Mannar

Vavuniya

Bay of Bengal

Trincomalee

Anuradhapura
NORTH CENTRAL

NORTH
WESTERN

Batticaloa

EASTERN

Kurunegala

CENTRAL
Kandy

Badulla
Colombo
Sri Jayawardenapura-Kotte
UVA

Laccadive Sea

WESTERN
Ratnapura
SABARAGAMUA

INDIAN
OCEAN

SOUTHERN

Galle

0 20 40 60 80 km
0 10 20 30 40 50 mi

FIGURE 10.2 Map of Sri Lanka and contested Tamil Provinces

Tamils and 5.5% Indian Tamils).[3] As figure 10.2 shows, their traditional homelands are in the northern and eastern regions of Sri Lanka, Jaffna, Vavuniya, Batticaloa, and Trincomalee. The Tamils make up the majority in the Northern Province and are a significant percentage of the population in the Eastern Province. Their native language is Tamil, and the majority of ethnic Tamils are Hindu. This religious divide between the Sinhalese Buddhists and the Tamil Hindus is important in understanding the ethnic conflict between the Sinhalese and the Tamils. Jonathan Spencer argues that today, "the formal criterion of membership of the rival Sinhala and Tamil communities is linguistic, but in the colonial period the most salient identities—at least as far as riots and disturbances were concerned—was religious."[4] Thus decades of political conflict can be understood along linguistic and religious divides, even though as we shall see, the LTTE is a secular group.

The conflict between Sri Lanka's Tamils and Sinhalese has its origins in Sri Lanka's colonial past.[5] The ethnic antagonism that originated during the colonial period is a key factor in the development of the civil war and a campaign of suicide terrorism between the Tamil LTTE and the Sinhalese-dominated Sri Lankan government. Sri Lanka started out as a Portuguese colony in 1505, and then came under Dutch control in 1658. Neither Portugal nor the Netherlands controlled much beyond Jaffna and a few additional coastal areas. The Portuguese and the Dutch "encouraged religious intolerance by favoring certain groups and disadvantaging others."[6] This resulted in the "consolidation of a 'Sinhala community' in the central and southwestern parts of the island and of a 'Tamil community' in the north and on the eastern shore."[7] The British wrested control over Sri Lanka from the Dutch in 1796, and it was formally ceded to Britain in 1801. By 1815, Britain had extended its rule over the entire island.

The British governed Sri Lanka using "divide and rule policies" that favored the minority Tamils over the Sinhala majority.[8] The British allocated

---

3. Figures from 1981 Sri Lankan Census, tables 2 and 3 in De Silva, *Reaping the Whirlwind*, 334.

4. Jonathan Spencer, "Introduction: The Power of the Past," in *Sri Lanka: History and the Roots of Conflict*, ed. Jonathan Spencer (London: Routledge, 1990), 8.

5. On Sri Lanka's colonial past and its impact on ethnic division, see especially the essays in part 1 of Jonathan Spencer, ed., *Sri Lanka: History and the Roots of Conflict* (London: Routledge, 1990); Tambiah, *Buddhism Betrayed?*

6. Mia Bloom, *Dying to Kill: The Allure of Suicide Terrorism* (New York: Columbia University Press, 2005), 48.

7. Ibid.

8. DeVotta, "The Liberation Tigers of Tamil Eelam," 1025–26.

Tamils preferential treatment in comparison to their Sinhalese counterparts by providing the Tamils with more access to civil service and high paying jobs.[9] The Sinhalese encountered barriers to economic development during this period, which they saw as being caused by the non-Sinhalese communities. The advantages provided to the Tamils under British rule, and the response of the Sinhalese, are critical in understanding the unfolding of the Sri Lankan civil war and the emergence of suicide terrorism.

Discrimination against the Tamils began after independence in 1948 when democratic elections placed the government into the hands of the majority Sinhalese. Marked by a strong and open Sinhalese nationalism, the new Sri Lankan government sought to redress previous discrimination by passing laws and policies "promoting Sinhalese Buddhist superordination and Tamil subordination."[10] Following the 1956 Sinhala Only Act, speaking Sinhala became essential for promotion in the civil service, even in Tamil-dominated areas, and became the only language allowed in courts. The result was that, while in 1949 41% of civil servants were Tamil, by 1963 the percentage had shrunk to 7%.[11]

In 1972, the Sinhalese government adopted a new constitution in which Buddhism, the primary religion of the Sinhalese, was made the religion favored and protected by the state. This act was seen as a direct threat to the predominantly Hindu Tamil community.[12] According to Spencer, there was "no overarching image of Sri Lankan national identity to hold Tamil sentiment back from the path of separatism; the only images available link the nation to one group, the Sinhala people, and one religion, Buddhism."[13]

Perhaps most threatening to the Tamils, the Sri Lankan government encouraged Sinhalese settlement in Tamil areas to weaken local Tamil majorities. By 1989, 1,673,000 people had been resettled on Tamil lands. These settlers made up about 7% of the size of the Tamil population living in the northern and eastern regions of Sri Lanka.[14] These policies resulted in

---

9. Bloom, *Dying to Kill*, 48.

10. DeVotta, "The Liberation Tigers of Tamil Eelam," 1025.

11. Bloom, "Ethnic Conflict," 61.

12. DeVotta, "The Liberation Tigers of Tamil Eelam," 1025. See also Shawn Teresa Flanigan, "Nonprofit Service Provision by Insurgent Organizations: The Cases of Hizballah and the Tamil Tigers," *Studies in Conflict and Terrorism* 31, no. 6 (2008): 500.; A. J. V. Chandrakanthan, "Eelam Tamil Nationalism," in *Sri Lankan Tamil Nationalism*, ed. Jeraratnam Wilson (Vancouver: UBC Press, 2000).

13. Spencer, "Introduction: The Power of the Past," 9.

14. Sinnappah Arasaratnam, *Sri Lanka after Independence: Nationalism, Communalism, and Nation Building* (Madras: University of Madras, 1986), 74.

an increase in Sinhalese control over Tamil territory.[15] The discriminatory policies designed to reinforce the ethnic balance of power and minimize Tamil political influence contributed to a rise in Tamil militancy.

In this context the LTTE emerged as one of many groups representing the interests of the ethnic Tamils. In 1972 several Tamil political groups came together to form the Tamil United Front (TULF), which sought equal status for the Tamil language.[16] At a conference in 1976, the TULF issued a demand for a separate state to be called Eelam.[17] Tamil political parties, including the nascent LTTE, cited an array of grievances that warrant a separate state: political-economic disenfranchisement, intentional altering of demographics in Tamil-dominated areas, removal from governmental employment, restriction of access to higher education, isolation of support from Tamil brethren in South India, and ethnic cleansing.[18]

The rise in Tamil militancy was widely perceived by the Sinhalese as a threat. When, in 1983, the LTTE carried out an assault on a Sri Lankan Army camp that killed 13 soldiers, anti-Tamil riots broke out.[19] The rioters killed hundreds of Tamils and destroyed Tamil homes and businesses. The Sri Lankan government waited days before calling in its security forces to restore order.[20] These riots are seen as the event that catalyzed large-scale armed conflict between Tamil militants and the Sinhalese Sri Lankan government.[21]

During the 1980s, the LTTE escalated their struggle for a Tamil homeland and solidified their dominance as the primary Tamil militant organization. In the early 1980s, there were several Tamil militant groups such as the Tamil Eelam Liberation Organization (TELO), People's Liberation Organization of Tamil Eelam (PLOTE), Eelam People's Revolutionary Liberation Front (EPRLF), and the Eelam People's Democratic Party (EPDP). At one time, there were as many as 37 militant groups. After 1983, the

15. Amita Shastri, "The Material Basis for Separatism: The Tamil Eelam Movement in Sri Lanka," *Journal of Asian Studies* 49, no. 1 (1990): 63.

16. Bloom, *Dying to Kill,* 51.

17. Robert N. Kearney, "Ethnic Conflict and the Tamil Separatist Movement in Sri Lanka," *Asian Survey* 25, no. 9 (1985): 904.

18. Deirdre McConnell, "The Tamil People's Right to Self-Determination," *Cambridge Review of International Affairs* 21, no. 1 (2008): 59.

19. Suthaharan Nadarajah and Dhananjayan Sriskandarajah, "Liberation Struggle or Terrorism? The Politics of Naming the LTTE," *Third World Quarterly* 26, no. 1 (2005): 87–100.

20. T. D. S. A. Dissanayaka, *The Agony of Sri Lanka: An In-Depth Account of the Racial Riots of 1983* (Colombo, Sri Lanka: Swastika, 1983), 80–90.

21. Wilson, *The Break-Up of Sri Lanka;* Stanley Jeyaraja Tambiah, *Sri Lanka: Ethnic Fratricide and the Dismantling of Democracy* (Chicago: University of Chicago Press, 1986).

LTTE grew from less than 50 militants to over 3,000 active guerillas. While the LTTE initially cooperated with other groups in their attacks against both the SLA and the Sri Lankan government, in February 1986 the LTTE launched a military attack on the TELO, the largest of the armed Tamil groups, killing almost the entire leadership and many of the militants.[22] The LTTE also attacked camps that belonged to another rival organization, the EPRLF, forcing it to withdraw from the Jaffna Peninsula.[23] By 1986, the LTTE emerged as the dominant Tamil separatist organization.[24] It is important to note that contrary to explanations that suicide terrorism is the result of "outbidding" among militant organizations, LTTE suicide terrorism did not begin until after the LTTE established itself as the preeminent Tamil militant group.[25]

In March 2004, one of the key LTTE leaders defected from the LTTE to form a splinter group in the east called Tamil Makkal Viduthalai Pulikal (TMVP).[26] "Colonel Karuna" (Vinayagamoorthy Muralitharan) claimed that the split was the result of marginalization of the Tamils in the east by the dominant northern leadership. In response, the LTTE launched attacks on the Karuna faction. This splintering resulted in a violent struggle for political control of the Eastern Province in which assassinations of many high profile LTTE leaders occurred.[27] The split challenged the LTTE's claim to be the "sole representative of the Tamil people."[28] Hoglund argues that this weakened the bargaining position of the LTTE with the Sri Lankan government. Within four years, the Sri Lankan government will have defeated the LTTE.

Goals

The LTTE is a secular group with no religious agenda. The primary stated goal of the LTTE is to establish an independent Tamil state in the north-

22. Hellmann-Rajanayagam, *The Tamil Tigers,* 164.

23. Edgar O'Ballance, *The Cyanide War: Tamil Insurrection in Sri Lanka, 1973–88,* 1st ed. (London: Brassey's, 1989), 62.

24. On the rise and consolidation of the LTTE, see Hellmann-Rajanayagam, *The Tamil Tigers.*

25. See Bloom, "Ethnic Conflict."

26. Kyle Beardsley and Brian McQuinn, "Rebel Groups as Predatory Organizations: The Political Effects of the 2004 Tsunami in Indonesia and Sri Lanka," *Journal of Conflict Resolution* 53, no. 4 (August 1, 2009): 634.

27. Kristine Höglund, "Violence and the Peace Process in Sri Lanka," *Civil Wars* 7, no. 2 (2005): 163.

28. Ibid.

ern and eastern region of Sri Lanka, Tamil Eelam. In pursuit of Eelam, the LTTE embarked on a military campaign using a combination of guerilla tactics, suicide attacks, and large set-piece battles to challenge the Sri Lankan government's control over Tamil areas. It has been argued, that while the LTTE was inspired by the early suicide attacks carried out by Hezbollah, the LTTE pioneered the use of suicide attacks as a strategic tactic, and carried out more suicide attacks than any other organization.

The LTTE claims to adhere to the "Thimpu Principles," a set of four "cardinal principles" submitted by six Tamil groups to the Sri Lankan government in 1985:

- recognition of the Tamils of Sri Lanka as a distinct nationality;
- recognition of an identified Tamil homeland and the guarantee of its territorial integrity;
- based on the above, recognition of the inalienable right of self-determination of the Tamil people; and
- recognition of the right to full citizenship and other fundamental democratic rights of all Tamils who look upon the island as their country.[29]

The LTTE provided important social services for the community. Like Hezbollah and Hamas, the LTTE used nonprofit service provision as a way to increase communal support for the organization.[30] Through the provision of social services the LTTE increased its support among the Tamil minority in the Northern and Eastern Provinces of Sri Lanka. Flanigan argues that the LTTE used the provision of charitable services within the community as a way to gain acceptance, if not participation, in its violent tactics.[31] While the LTTE relied on coercive tactics of intimidation and violence in ensuring community participation, the provision of social services by the LTTE was an attempt to increase group legitimacy and popular support.[32]

In addition, the LTTE pursued a wide-ranging social agenda to change many traditional Hindu norms. The process of state formation undertaken by the LTTE in the areas that they controlled focused on social welfare,

29. Rohan Edrisinha, "Constitutionalism, Pluralism, and Ethnic Conflict: The Need for a New Initiative," in *Creating Peace in Sri Lanka: Civil War and Reconciliation,* ed. Robert I. Rotberg (Washington, DC: Brookings Institution Press, 1999), 181. Robert N. Kearney, "Sri Lanka in 1985: The Persistence of Conflict," *Asian Survey* 26, no. 2 (February 1986): 219–23.
30. Flanigan, "Nonprofit Service Provision by Insurgent Organizations."
31. See Ibid.
32. Ibid., 516.

economic development, and social equality. In 1994 the LTTE enacted the Tamil Eelam Penal Code and Tamil Eelam Civil Code, which were updated in order to include a focus on social issues such as women's rights and the caste system.[33] According to the LTTE:

> We made special laws for women regarding their property rights, rape, abortion etc. Under our laws women are totally free and on par with men in property transactions. As you know, this is not the case under Jaffna's traditional law, Thesawalamai. Our civil code has done away with the stipulation in Thesawalamai that a woman should obtain her husband's consent to sell her property. We made caste discrimination a crime. These could be considered some of the milestones of the Tamil Eelam judicial system.[34]

The LTTE asserted that the use of female cadres was an important step in emancipating women in what is a traditional patriarchal social structure.[35] Moreover, in constructing a society based on attaining economic and social equality, it has been argued that the LTTE maintained some hope of social revolution.[36] While the LTTE's primary goal was the establishment of an independent Tamil state, the state-building process emphasized the importance of gender equality, economic equality, and the provision of social services.

State Support

During the 1980s, the Indian government provided support to Tamil militant groups, including the LTTE. Under the leadership of Prime Minister Indira Gandhi, the Indian Research and Analysis Wing (RAW), the foreign intelligence agency for India, established training bases for Tamils in India. By 1983, training centers had been established near Dehra Dun. Between 1983 and 1987, the Indian RAW trained an estimated 1,200 Tam-

33. Kristian Stokke, "Building the Tamil Eelam State: Emerging State Institutions and Forms of Governance in LTTE-Controlled Areas in Sri Lanka," *Third World Quarterly* 27 (September 2006): 1067.

34. E. Pararajasingham, Head of the LTTE Judicial Division, TamilNet, October 30, 2003, at http://www.tamilnet.com/art.html?catid1⁄479&artid1⁄410277. Quoted in ibid., 1027.

35. Arjuna Gunawardena, "Female Black Tigers: A Different Breed of Cat?" in *Female Suicide Bombers: Dying for Equality,* ed. Yoram Schweitzer (Tel Aviv University, Jaffee Center for Strategic Studies, Memorandum No. 84, 2006), 85.

36. Jonathan Spencer, "Anthropology and the Politics of Socialism in Rural Sri Lanka," in *Socialism: Ideals, Ideologies and Local Practice,* ed. C. M. Hann (London: Routledge, 1993), 107.

ils in small arms and amphibious sabotage. Militant groups also established camps in the southern Indian region of Tamil Nadu, where those who received formal Indian training would then train new recruits.[37] India's clandestine support of the Tigers and other Tamil groups was later suspended because the Indian government worried that a successful Tamil insurgency would inspire separatism in its own Tamil population in Tamil Nadu. Indeed, the LTTE expanded its ties with Tamil Nadu separatist groups during this time.[38] Ironically, Indian support for the LTTE played a pivotal role in establishing the enemy that it would later fight during India's occupation of northern Sri Lanka from 1987 to 1990.

Indira Gandhi was assassinated by her Sikh bodyguards in October 1984, and in 1985, was succeeded by her son Rajiv Gandhi. The new prime minister tried to settle the conflict in Sri Lanka, even as fighting escalated in 1987. In July 1987, Rajiv Gandhi sought to disarm the LTTE through the Indo-Lanka Peace Accord and through the presence of Indian Peace Keeping Forces (IPKF) in Sri Lanka. The LTTE's suicide assassination of Rajiv Gandhi in 1991 was motivated by fear of another IPKF intervention in Sri Lanka and a renewed crackdown on the Tiger network in Tamil Nadu. Following his death, India hardened its stance toward the LTTE and pressed Sri Lanka for Prabhakaran's extradition to India.

Trajectory of Campaign

The trajectory of the LTTE's suicide terrorism campaign against the Sri Lankan government follows the four major periods of open hostility that mark the Sri Lankan civil war, which lasted from 1983 to the defeat of the LTTE and the death of its leader, Prabhakaran, in May of 2009. These four periods—known as the Eelam Wars I, II, III, and IV—are punctuated by cease-fires, most of them brief, and one lasting several years. The LTTE used suicide attacks throughout the 26-year civil war. Table 10.1 presents an overview of the main phases and LTTE suicide terrorism during the Sri Lankan civil war.

Sri Lankan efforts during the civil war aimed to capture, hold, and clear territory held by the LTTE, especially in the strategically important Jaffna

---

37. Rohan Gunaratna, *International and Regional Security Implications of the Sri Lankan Tamil Insurgency* (St. Albans, Herts: International Foundation of Sri Lankans, 2002), 106–14.

38. Rita Manchanda, "Review: RAW in Sri Lanka," *Economic and Political Weekly* 28, no. 19 (May 8, 1993): 921–23.

TABLE 10.1 **Overview of LTTE suicide attacks in the context of the Sri Lankan civil war**

Period	Key Events	Attacks	Killed
Eelam War I, 1983–87	Sri Lankan offensive to take Jaffna halted by pressure from India, IPKF occupies Northern Province (1987)	1	40
Indian intervention, 1987–90	Civil war suspended, LTTE fight war with IPKF	0	0
Eelam War II, 1990–94	IPKF withdraws (1990), renewed fighting between LTTE and Sri Lanka ends in stalemate	15	402
Eelam War III, 1995–2001	Sri Lanka takes Jaffna (1995), fails to secure overland supply route	62	722
Cease fire agreement, 2002–5	Norway brokers peace deal leading to cease fire agreement (2002), LTTE splits (2004)	1	5
Eelam War IV, 2006–9	Sri Lankan takes Eastern Province (2008), central Northern Province (2008), defeats LTTE (2009)	37	474

Source: CPOST database.

Peninsula, and to secure overland supply routes to government forces stationed in the conflict area. Sri Lanka used military operations—including overland and amphibious assaults, aerial bombardment, and naval interdiction—to weaken the LTTE military capability. It also targeted the Tamil civilian population in hopes of suppressing if not undermining popular support for the LTTE. As demonstrated by the duration of the conflict, the Sri Lankan military was generally ineffective in its counterinsurgency mission until quite recently.

LTTE efforts during the civil war aimed to counter government military gains and raise the cost of resisting LTTE demands for an independent Tamil state controlled by the LTTE. The LTTE's primary mode of conflict was guerilla warfare, though it also engaged in pitched battles against Sri Lankan forces. The LTTE's use of suicide terrorism complemented the LTTE's military and political efforts. Suicide attacks were used to assassinate key political and military leaders, destroy high value but hard-to-reach targets, and raise the cost of war for the Sinhalese civilian population outside the areas of regular combat. The Sri Lankan military was far stronger than the LTTE in manpower and material. Suicide attacks were intended to neutralize this asymmetry.

LTTE suicide attacks are a function of three principal factors: (1) the need to conduct military operations against superior government forces; (2) the desire to influence the course of political negotiations with the government; and (3) third-party military and diplomatic interventions that facilitate cooperation with the government. While it is clear that the

LTTE's use of suicide terrorism is part of its overall strategy for fighting a war against the superior forces of the Sri Lankan government, the Sri Lankan government exacerbated some of the factors fueling LTTE suicide terrorism through its policy choices, i.e., how it conducted the war and negotiations. The remainder of this section explains the ebb and flow of LTTE suicide terrorism throughout the major periods of the Sri Lankan civil war.

1983–1987: Eelam War I

While Eelam War I started in 1983, the LTTE's first suicide attack took place in 1987. The slow adoption of suicide terrorism in the conflict between the LTTE and Sri Lanka is explained by two factors. First, the strategy had only just been demonstrated in Lebanon as an effective weapon against foreign occupying forces. Second, it was not until 1987 that it appeared that the Sri Lankan forces might succeed in dealing the LTTE a major defeat on the LTTE's home turf in Jaffna. The suicide attack came as the Sri Lankan military's Operation Liberation to capture the LTTE stronghold of Jaffna was making significant gains, and it looked as if the LTTE might be defeated. The LTTE targeted Sri Lankan military forces in a truck bombing reminiscent of the Hezbollah suicide attacks five years earlier. Indeed, evidence suggests that the Hezbollah attack and its success in compelling the withdrawal of American forces from Lebanon served as an inspiration. Nevertheless, the effect of the attack was less strategic than organizational: the suicide bomber "Captain Miller" became a central figure in the LTTE's campaign to cement a culture of martyrdom to support the use of suicide attacks in the future. The attack is commemorated yearly on July 5 as "Black Tigers Day," and was the occasion of an annual address by LTTE leader Prabhakaran. After the 1987 attack, there would be no recorded LTTE suicide attacks until 1990.

1987–1990: Indian Occupation

There are no recorded suicide attacks by the LTTE during the period of Indian occupation, from the end of 1987 to early 1990. The prospect of Tamil defeat prompted intervention by India, which pressured the Sri Lankan government to halt its offensive and accept an Indian military force in northern Sri Lanka to monitor a cease-fire between the Sri

Lankan and LTTE forces.[39] While nominally a peacekeeping mission, the the IPKF engaged in a war to disarm the LTTE. The Sri Lankan government took advantage of the cessation in hostilities in the north to quell an insurrection by the ultra-Sinhalese nationalist party, the Janatha Vimukthi Peramuna (JVP), in the southern part of the country. The absence of suicide attacks against the IPKF is explained by the fact that Tamils and Indians are both Hindu. Thus while the IPKF and the LTTE were at war, the conflict was not seen by the LTTE as an existential threat. Under pressure from nationalist elements in the Sinhalese population to remove the Indian military presence from Sri Lankan soil, the Sri Lankan government made common cause with the LTTE in its armed struggle with the IPKF. A new government was elected to power in India in 1989, and, with the cost of occupation mounting, it began to withdraw the IPKF. The last Indian forces left Sri Lanka in March 1990.[40]

1990–1994: Eelam War II

With the common enemy gone, renewed violence between the Sri Lankan forces and the LTTE resumed after only a short period. The renewed fighting, known as Eelam War II, lasted from 1990 until a cease-fire went into effect in January 1995. Militarily, the period is marked by a series of strategic withdrawals by the SLA from vulnerable positions in the Northern Province, including Jaffna and Kilinochchi.

The use of suicide terrorism, especially as a tool for assassinating high profile targets, began in earnest in this period. In the four years from the end of the Indian occupation to the cease-fire of January 1995, the LTTE perpetrated 15 suicide attacks, killing approximately 400 people. Of the 15 suicide attacks, one-third (five) are assassinations. Perhaps the best known such assassination is the May 1991 assassination of former prime minister of India Rajiv Gandhi in Madras, India. The LTTE feared that Gandhi, who stood a good chance of being reelected in the Indian elections later that year, would reinsert the IPKF into northern Sri Lanka.[41] The LTTE also used suicide bombers to assassinate local political and military leaders.

---

39. Chris Smith, "South Asia's Enduring War," in *Creating Peace in Sri Lanka: Civil War and Reconciliation,* ed. Robert I. Rotberg (Washington, DC: Brookings Institution Press, 1999), 19–25.

40. Ibid., 23–25.

41. Ibid., 26.

Political targets included the Sri Lankan minister of defense Ranjan Wijeratne in March 1991 and the Sri Lankan president Ranasinghe Premadasa in May 1993.[42] In November 1992, an LTTE suicide bomber killed Clancy Fernando, the commander leading the Sri Lankan Navy's (SLN's) effort to sever the sea lines of supply between Tamil Nadu and the Jaffna Peninsula. Beyond assassination, the LTTE sporadically used suicide attacks as part of its military campaign against the Sri Lankan armed forces, including attacks on fixed positions and naval vessels at sea.

As 1994 drew to a close, it appeared that the opposing sides had reached a military stalemate. Parliamentary elections in August and a presidential election in November saw Chandrika Kumaratunga of the People's Alliance first assume the prime ministership and then the presidency. A key issue dividing Kumaratunga's platform and that of her United National Party (UNP) challenger was how best to bring the civil war to an end. Kumaratunga favored negotiations; Dissanayake of the UNP assumed a more hard-line position, demanding that the LTTE first disarm.[43] A month before the election that brought Kumaratunga to power, the LTTE sent a suicide bomber to assassinate her UNP rival. Shortly after the election, Kumaratunga and the LTTE agreed to a cease-fire that went into effect in January 1995 and lasted until May. The LTTE acted strategically: it used suicide terrorism to get negotiations, and refrained from further suicide attacks while waiting to see how negotiations with the new government would play out.

1995–2001: Eelam War III

The period from 1995 to 2004, known as Eelam War III, saw a dramatic increase in the number of LTTE suicide attacks over Eelam War II. There were 62 recorded suicide attacks in this period, including 14 assassinations, together accounting for an estimated 722 fatalities.

The dramatic increase in suicide attacks parallels the escalation of the military conflict between the LTTE and the Sri Lankan government. Dur-

42. Associated Press, "Official and 18 Others Die in Sri Lanka Bombing," *New York Times,* March 3, 1991, sec. World, http://www.nytimes.com/1991/03/03/world/official-and-18-others-die-in-sri-lanka-bombing.html; Edward A. Gargan, "Suicide Bomber Kills President of Sri Lanka," *New York Times,* May 2, 1993, sec. World, http://www.nytimes.com/1993/05/02/world/suicide-bomber-kills-president-of-sri-lanka.html.

43. "Sri Lanka Increases Security for Heated Presidential Election," *New York Times,* November 9, 1994, sec. World, http://www.nytimes.com/1994/11/09/world/sri-lanka-increases-security-for-heated-presidential-election.html.

ing the cease-fire, the LTTE was able to resupply Jaffna and regroup. But as it became clear that a workable deal was not forthcoming, the LTTE broke the cease-fire and recommenced suicide attacks against naval targets in late April 1995.[44] The cease-fire was formally abandoned shortly thereafter. In August, the LTTE rejected a new plan for peace proposed by Kumaratunga, a federal solution to the conflict that would grant significant autonomy to Tamil provinces at the expense of LTTE control (the plan was also rejected by Sinhalese nationalists and the Buddhist clergy). With that, the stage was set for the next phase in the Sri Lankan civil war.[45]

Concentrating operations on the northern front, the Sri Lankan government launched two major military offensives to take control of the LTTE stronghold of Jaffna and the strategic overland points of access to the Jaffna Peninsula. In October 1995, the Sri Lankan government launched Operation Riviresa to retake Jaffna.[46] In a series of offensives, the SLA captured Jaffna town in December 1995. In 1995, the LTTE perpetrated 10 suicide attacks, mostly against the SLN but also two oil depots in Colombo on October 20. In January 1996, Sri Lankan forces began an offensive to take control of the entire Jaffna Peninsula. On January 31, 1996, an LTTE suicide bomber attacked the Central Bank building in downtown Colombo, killing 120 civilians. The LTTE was driven out of the Jaffna Peninsula in April 2006, a major setback for the LTTE. The remaining 10 suicide attacks in 1996 targeted military forces as the LTTE took advantage of Sri Lankan military concentration in the Jaffna Peninsula.[47]

In 1997, the Sri Lankan government launched Operation Jayasikurui to secure an overland supply route to Jaffna by attempting to take and hold the highway between Vavuniya and the strategically vital Elephant Pass.[48] Government forces proved unable to secure and hold the road, and the operation was called off after two years in late 1999. During the offensive, LTTE suicide cadres attacked two civilian sites. In October 1997, a suicide truck bomb detonated at the World Trade Center in downtown Colombo.

44. Howard B. Schaffer, "Sri Lanka in 1995: A Difficult and Disappointing Year," *Asian Survey* 36, no. 2 (February 1996): 217–18.

45. Ibid., 219–22.

46. Smith, "South Asia's Enduring War," 27–28.

47. Schaffer, "Sri Lanka in 1995," 143–45.

48. Smith, "South Asia's Enduring War," 28–32.

The bomb and the ensuing firefight with LTTE commandos resulted in 17 deaths.[49] And in mid-February 1998, three Black Tigers detonated a truck bomb at the Buddhist Temple of the Tooth in Kandy, killing 11.[50]

The LTTE had been heavily targeting the Sri Lankan naval forces throughout Eelam War III, for two reasons. First, the LTTE gets much of its supplies from Tamil Nadu, the Tamil-dominated province of India roughly 22 miles off the Sri Lankan coast. But the SLA is also heavily dependent on supply by sea. Having failed to secure land access to the Jaffna Peninsula, and especially after the LTTE captured Elephant Pass in April 2000 (in Operation Unceasing Waves III), Sri Lankan forces were effectively bottled up on the Jaffna Peninsula. The second reason for targeting Sri Lankan naval forces is therefore to weaken the garrison at Jaffna, interdicting and disrupting resupply and reinforcement. Between the fall of Jaffna in 1996 and 2000, there were 10 recorded Sea Tiger suicide attacks on Sri Lankan naval assets, many of these attacks taking place at sea. Between 2000 and 2001, six of the 25 recorded suicide attacks were against naval targets. The most costly LTTE suicide attack in this period, however, fell upon the Sri Lankan Air Force. On the morning of July 24, 2001, 14 Black Tiger suicide commandos attacked the Katunayake Air Base and the terminal area of adjacent Bandaranaike International Airport. Using a mix of rockets and suicide bombs, the Black Tigers destroyed or damaged 26 aircraft, including two Airbus 320s and one Airbus 340. According to Jane's Security News, it was "the most destructive terrorist attack in the history of aviation."[51]

The December 21, 1999 presidential election prompted another round of suicide attacks against Sri Lanka's top leaders. On December 18, LTTE suicide bombers simultaneously attacked President Kumaratunga and a nearby opposition rally. Kumaratunga's position had become increasingly hard line, promising significant Tamil autonomy but no talks before the LTTE disarmed. She survived with injuries, and a total of 33 civilians were

49. "17 Die, 100 Wounded by Huge Bomb and Gunfire in Sri Lanka," *New York Times,* October 15, 1997, sec. World, http://www.nytimes.com/1997/10/15/world/17-die-100-wounded-by-huge-bomb-and-gunfire-in-sri-lanka.html.

50. "11 Killed in Truck Bombing at Sri Lanka Buddhist Site," *New York Times,* January 26, 1998, sec. World, http://www.nytimes.com/1998/01/26/world/11-killed-in-truck-bombing-at-sri-lanka-buddhist-site.html.

51. "Intelligence Failures Exposed by Tamil Tiger Airport Attack," *Jane's Security News,* September 3, 2001, http://www.janes.com/security/international_security/news/jir/jir010903_1_n.shtml.

killed in the attack.[52] Kumaratunga won the election, securing a second term. Less than a month later, on January 5, 2000, an LTTE suicide bomber detonated in front of the offices of Prime Minister Sirima Bandaranaike (January 5, 2000), but she was not there.[53]

At the end of 2001, the strategic situation had not changed significantly since 1996. The SLA occupied the Jaffna Peninsula, but was cut off from the mainland by the LTTE victory at Elephant Pass. At the same time, LTTE efforts to retake Jaffna met with equal failure. As in 1994, the two sides once again were locked in a stalemate. And, as in 1994, elections would hold promise for a diplomatic way out.

2002–2005: The Memorandum of Understanding and Ceasefire Agreement

On February 22, 2002, the Sri Lankan government and the LTTE signed the Ceasefire Agreement and Memorandum of Understanding, halting military activity and beginning a series of talks between the belligerents to find a diplomatic solution to the bitter conflict. From 2002 to 2005, there was only one suicide attack by the LTTE.

Why did the Sri Lankan government and the LTTE sign a Memorandum of Understanding and Ceasefire Agreement in 2002? Several factors played an important role. First, the military side of the conflict had failed on both sides to produce a decisive victory. Second, 9/11 brought significant international pressure to bear on the LTTE to seek a diplomatic way out of the conflict or risk being caught up in the United States' war on terrorism. Third, control over the Sri Lankan parliament changed to the UNP, whose leader, Ratnasiri Wickremanayake, openly supported unconditional dialogue with the LTTE (though the new prime minister was in an awkward political situation as the presidency remained in the hands of Kumaratunga of the rival People's Alliance party). Finally, both sides agreed on Norway as an international mediator. Talks between the Sri Lankan government and the LTTE brokered by Norway began in September 2002 in Thailand. In the course of negotiations, the LTTE moderated its demands, agreeing

---

52. Celia W. Dugger, "Sri Lanka Votes, with War Strategy as the Dominant Issue," *New York Times,* October 11, 2000, sec. World, http://www.nytimes.com/2000/10/11/world/sri-lanka-votes-with-war-strategy-as-the-dominant-issue.html; "Injured Sri Lankan Leader Urges Tamils to Help End Terrorism," *New York Times,* December 20, 1999, sec. World, http://www.nytimes.com/1999/12/20/world/injured-sri-lankan-leader-urges-tamils-to-help-end-terrorism.html.

53. "Bomb Attack Kills 11 in Sri Lanka Capital," *New York Times,* January 5, 2000, sec. World, http://www.nytimes.com/2000/01/05/world/bomb-attack-kills-11-in-sri-lanka-capital.html.

to accept a federal solution. Restrictions for travel by air and land between Colombo and Jaffna were lifted.

But this period of negotiated peace would end in 2005. The Sri Lankan government faced significant domestic (Sinhalese) opposition to any plan that divided the country with the LTTE in control over a Tamil de facto state in the northeast. And the LTTE refused any plan that threatened its political control over a Tamil Eelam.[54] In October 2003, citing the need to formalize the political situation in the Tamil provinces, the LTTE offered its own solution to the conflict: the Interim Self-Governing Authority, which would give the LTTE de facto control over the Northern and Eastern Provinces. President Kumaratunga, under pressure from nationalist elements in her party and political base to halt negotiations with the LTTE, declared a state of emergency and used her executive power to dissolve parliament, effectively ending UNP control. New parliamentary elections were scheduled for April 2004. To strengthen her hand against the UNP, Kumaratunga joined with the Sinhalese nationalist party JVP to form the United People's Freedom Alliance (UPFA), which promised a tough stance on future dealings with the LTTE. The UPFA subsequently won the election and Wickremanayake, "the key architect of the peace process," returned to the opposition.[55] Now the UPFA controlled both the parliament (with Mahinda Rajapaksa taking the position of prime minister) and the presidency (which remained with Kumaratunga). Presidential elections in November 2005 would confirm the UPFA's control of the government, with Mahinda Rajapaksa winning the presidency for the UPFA (Kumaratunga had reached her term limit) in large part because LTTE leader Prabhakaran ordered Tamils to boycott the elections, hurting the more moderate opposition UNP candidate.[56]

Perhaps the most significant event impacting the future of the civil war was the split and subsequent defection in 2004 of Vinayagamoorthy Muralitharan (Karuna), leader of the LTTE's eastern wing. While the LTTE quickly moved to put down Karuna's faction, he, his top advisors, and a significant number of supporters managed to escape. In addition to the loss of military forces, the defection promised the Sri Lankan government

54. Neil DeVotta, "Sri Lanka in 2003: Seeking to Consolidate Peace," *Asian Survey* 44, no. 1 (February 2004): 50–53.

55. Chris Smith, "The Eelam Endgame?" *International Affairs* 83, no. 1 (2007): 70.

56. Somini Sengupta, "Hardliner Is Elected Sri Lankan President," *New York Times,* November 18, 2005, sec. International/Asia Pacific, http://www.nytimes.com/2005/11/18/world/asia/18iht-lanka.html.

detailed intelligence on LTTE operations. As a result, the LTTE's position in the Eastern Province was severely weakened.[57]

The only suicide attack perpetrated by the LTTE in this period appears to have been a response to Karuna's defection. In July 2004, a female suicide bomber was apprehended by the police in Colombo. She detonated her suicide vest after arriving at the police station for questioning. Her target appeared to be a Tamil politician known for openly criticizing the LTTE. Because Karuna had gone into hiding, authorities speculate that the politician, Douglas Devananda, leader of an opposition Tamil party, was targeted instead. The attack was spawned by LTTE internal politics; it was not directed at the Sri Lankan government.[58]

While both the LTTE and the Sri Lankan government maintained a public commitment to the Ceasefire Agreement throughout the period and into 2006, violence between the two sides increased toward the end of 2005. Both sides used the time to begin preparations for renewing open hostilities. The LTTE gradually increased guerilla activity, and expanded its recruitment efforts.[59]

2006–2009: Eelam War IV and the Defeat of the LTTE

Eelam War IV would bring two major offensives by the Sri Lankan government to take the Eastern Province in 2007 and then the Northern Province in 2008–9, resulting in the military defeat of the LTTE. In this period, LTTE suicide cadres perpetrated 37 suicide attacks, killing an estimated 372. Interestingly, a little under half the total deaths caused by LTTE suicide attacks during Eelam IV happened in the first year. One attack alone—the October 16, 2006 suicide truck bombing of a bus carrying SLN sailors[60]—accounts for over 25% of the total fatalities (103) for the three-and-half-year period. The most attacks (13) happened in 2008—the year after the LTTE's defeat in the Eastern Province (there were ten attacks in 2007) and during the Sri Lankan Army's northern campaign

57. Smith, "The Eelam Endgame?," 70–71; Höglund, "Violence and the Peace Process in Sri Lanka."

58. David Rohde, "Tamil Suicide Bomber Kills 4 Policemen in Capital of Sri Lanka," *New York Times,* July 8, 2004, sec. World, http://www.nytimes.com/2004/07/08/world/tamil-suicide-bomber-kills-4-policemen-in-capital-of-sri-lanka.html.

59. Smith, "The Eelam Endgame?," 74.

60. Christine Hauser, "Scores Killed in Attack on Sri Lankan Convoy," *New York Times,* October 16, 2006, sec. International/Asia Pacific, http://www.nytimes.com/2006/10/16/world/asia/17lankacnd.html.

against the last remaining LTTE strongholds. There were only two recorded attacks in the five months before the LTTE defeat in 2009.

While the number of violent incidents between the LTTE and Sri
Lankan forces had already started increasing in 2005, major hostilities did
not begin until 2006. On January 7, a suicide attack by Sea Tigers sank a
SLN patrol boat, killing 13 sailors.[61] Indeed, seven of the 12 attacks recorded for 2006 targeted naval assets, including the October 16 attack on
the convoy transporting SLN sailors. LTTE suicide bombers also made
assassination attempts against two high-ranking military leaders: in the
first, a female suicide bomber posing as a pregnant woman failed to kill
Lieutenant General Fonseka on April 25;[62] in the second, a suicide bomber
on a motorcycle succeeded in killing the third-highest-ranking officer of
the SLA, Major-General Parami Kulatunga on June 26.[63] In August, Sri
Lankan government forces moved into LTTE-controlled Eastern Province
to reopen sluice gates closed by the LTTE and restore water to villagers.
In response, the LTTE declared the Ceasefire Agreement "null and void
at the moment," though there is general agreement among diplomats that
the LTTE had been deliberately provoking escalation.[64]

In 2007, the SLA began the first of two major offensives that ultimately
lead to the LTTE's defeat. The first offensive, which began in July 2007,
targeted the eastern theater. In fierce fighting in the Batticaloa area, the
SLA handed the LTTE a major defeat, going on to take control of the Eastern Province and pushing the LTTE north.[65] The 10 LTTE suicide attacks
in 2007 show no clear pattern, though military targets remain prominent.
All but two attacks were against military targets. The attack with the highest casualties was carried out by Sea Tigers including three suicide boats
against a Jaffna naval base, killing 35.[66] On November 28, a female suicide

61. "'Rebels Sink' Sri Lanka Navy Boat," *BBC,* January 7, 2006, sec. South Asia, http://
news.bbc.co.uk/2/hi/south_asia/4589758.stm.
62. "Bomb Targets Sri Lanka Army Chief," *BBC,* April 25, 2006, sec. South Asia, http://
news.bbc.co.uk/2/hi/south_asia/4941744.stm.
63. "Sri Lanka General Killed in Blast," *BBC,* June 26, 2006, sec. South Asia, http://news.
bbc.co.uk/2/hi/5115968.stm.
64. Justin Huggler, "Sri Lanka's Ceasefire Is Over, Say Tamil Tigers," *Independent,* August
1, 2006, sec. Asia, World, http://www.independent.co.uk/news/world/asia/sri-lankas-ceasefire-is-
over-say-tamil-tigers-410066.html.
65. "'War Victory Party' in Sri Lanka," *BBC,* July 12, 2007, sec. South Asia, http://news.
bbc.co.uk/2/hi/south_asia/6895809.stm.
66. "Tamil Rebels Launch Naval Attack," *BBC,* May 24, 2007, sec. South Asia, http://news.
bbc.co.uk/2/hi/south_asia/6686359.stm.

bomber failed to assassinate Douglas Devananda, the second attempt by the LTTE to kill him.[67]

In 2008 and 2009, the SLA launched its second offensive, targeting the remaining LTTE forces in the northern theater. While the SLA pushed the LTTE into a smaller and smaller area, LTTE suicide attacks in Eelam War IV peaked in 2008 with 13 attacks. Four of the 13 attacks took place in Colombo, well outside the combat zone. The Colombo attacks together account for a total of 24 deaths. This includes the February 3 attack on the main rail terminal that killed 11 on the day before the celebration of Sri Lanka's 60th year of independence.[68] It also includes the April 6 assassination of Highways Minister Jeyaraj Fernandopulle at a New Year's commemoration, killing a total of 14.[69] Other high profile assassinations by suicide attack included the attack on a retired army general and prominent UNP politician on October 6, which killed 22,[70] and a failed attempt by a female suicide bomber to kill Agriculture Minister Maithripala Sirisena on October 10.[71]

In December and January 2009, government forces converged on the last remaining LTTE strongholds. On January 3 they took the LTTE capital Kilinochchi.[72] On January 9, government forces recaptured Elephant Pass.[73] Mullaittivu fell on January 25.[74] In March and April, the Sri Lankan Army continued to whittle away at the remaining LTTE fighters at Puthukkudiyirippu, killing several LTTE leaders and pushing the remaining LTTE fighters into the no-fire zone set aside for civilians fleeing the fighting.[75]

With the LTTE defeat imminent in 2009, there was concern that there

67. "Deadly Bomb Attacks in Sri Lanka," *BBC*, November 28, 2007, sec. South Asia, http://news.bbc.co.uk/2/hi/south_asia/7116335.stm.

68. "Fear in the Capital of Sri Lanka," *BBC*, February 4, 2008, sec. South Asia, http://news.bbc.co.uk/2/hi/south_asia/7226031.stm.

69. "Blast Kills Sri Lankan Minister," *BBC*, April 6, 2008, sec. South Asia, http://news.bbc.co.uk/2/hi/south_asia/7332952.stm.

70. "Suicide Blast Hits Sri Lanka Town," *BBC*, October 6, 2008, sec. South Asia, http://news.bbc.co.uk/2/hi/south_asia/7653945.stm.

71. "Sri Lanka Minister Survives Blast," *BBC*, October 9, 2008, sec. South Asia, http://news.bbc.co.uk/2/hi/south_asia/7660829.stm.

72. Rhys Blakely in Mumbai, "Sri Lankan Army Captures Tamil Tigers' Capital, Kilinochchi," *The Times* (London), January 3, 2008, http://www.timesonline.co.uk/tol/news/world/asia/article5435492.ece.

73. "Army 'Takes Key Sri Lanka Pass,'" *BBC*, January 9, 2009, sec. South Asia, http://news.bbc.co.uk/2/hi/south_asia/7819386.stm.

74. "'Civilians Die' in S Lanka Battle," *BBC*, January 26, 2009, sec. South Asia, http://news.bbc.co.uk/2/hi/south_asia/7850603.stm.

75. "Heavy Fighting in North Sri Lanka," *BBC*, March 11, 2009, sec. South Asia, http://news.bbc.co.uk/2/hi/south_asia/7938113.stm.

would be a sharp increase in suicide attacks. But in the five months of 2009 before the collapse of the LTTE, there were only two recorded suicide attacks. On March 10, an LTTE suicide attacker on a bicycle attacked six Sri Lankan ministers attending a Muslim religious procession in Akuressa, killing 15 (but none of the ministers).[76] There were also reports that 17 civilians were killed in a suicide attack on April 20 as they fled the no-fire zone to escape behind Sri Lankan Army lines.[77] This is the last recorded LTTE suicide attack.

The end of the LTTE came rapidly. On May 16, the Sri Lankan president declared victory over the LTTE, followed by the LTTE's public admission of defeat a day later. On May 18, Velupillai Prabhakaran, leader of the LTTE since its inception in the early 1970s, was killed.[78]

Managing the Postconflict Period

Since May of 2009, there have been no reported suicide attacks in Sri Lanka. The reason for this is the military defeat of the LTTE. While the LTTE has been defeated, the future of Tamil Eelam remains open. The Sri Lankan civil war has resulted in the displacement of hundreds of thousands of ethnic Tamils since fighting began in 1983.[79] In 2008 Sri Lankan forces intensified their fighting in the north, especially in the Vanni region, and from October 2008 to June 2009 more than 280,000 Tamils, approximately half of the Northern Province's population, fled fighting to government-controlled territory.[80] Most of those displaced were placed in camps located in Vavuniya, Mannar, Jaffna, and Trincomalee, with a majority being held in the Vavuniya district.[81] The Sri Lankan government gives two rationales for holding internally displaced

76. "Sri Lanka 'Suicide Bomb Kills 14,'" *BBC,* March 10, 2009, sec. South Asia, http://news.bbc.co.uk/2/hi/south_asia/7934095.stm.

77. "Thousands Flee Sri Lanka Combat," *BBC,* April 20, 2009, sec. South Asia, http://news.bbc.co.uk/2/hi/south_asia/8007465.stm.

78. "Sri Lanka Says Leader of Rebels Has Died," *New York Times,* May 19, 2009, sec. International/Asia Pacific, http://www.nytimes.com/2009/05/19/world/asia/19lanka.html. Mark McDonald, "Tamil Tigers Confirm Death of Their Leader," *New York Times,* May 26, 2009, sec. International/Asia Pacific, http://www.nytimes.com/2009/05/26/world/asia/26lanka.html.

79. "Continuing Humanitarian Concerns and Obstacles to Durable Solutions for Recent and Longer-Term IDPs," *Internal Displacement Monitoring Centre,* November 10, 2009, 105, http://www.internal-displacement.org/8025708F004CE90B/(httpCountries)/0BB9CBD990450F5F802570A7004C148F?opendocument&count=10000.

80. Ibid., 12.

81. Ibid., 35–36.

persons (IDPs) in the detention camps. First, the government has claimed a screening process is necessary to determine which individuals are suspected of being LTTE cadres. Second, the Sri Lankan government has cited safety concerns and is holding IDPs in camps until their places of origins have been determined. However, according to the International Crisis Group, "tens of thousand of IDPs could be released to their place of origin or live with host families in towns and villages which were free of mines."[82] While in December 2009 many Tamils were allowed to leave the detention camps, they were required to register with local authorities so that their movements could be tracked.[83]

In addition, the Sri Lankan government has set up "High Security Zones" (HSZs) around military installations. These zones are intended to prevent attacks against the predominantly Sinhalese Sri Lankan military forces by creating buffer zones. Those living in the HSZs have been displaced, and those in the detention camps are not allowed to return to the HSZs. The majority are near the Jaffna area. It is estimated that between 70,000 and 100,000 people have been displaced because of the HSZs.[84] As of January 2010, there were still nearly 100,000 people in the military-run camps, nearly 20,000 have been released and restrictions on leaving camps have been loosened.[85] Resettlement efforts have begun, but not in the HSZs.[86] The acceleration of resettlement is largely a function of international pressure from Western governments.[87]

In an effort to quell the likelihood of future LTTE attacks, as of February 2010, the Sri Lankan military is holding 11,000–13,000 people suspected of having ties to the LTTE, including former LTTE child soldiers, in extralegal detention centers.[88] These detainees do not have access to lawyers, families, the International Committee of the Red Cross, or other protection agencies. According to Human Rights Watch, "many individuals were taken into custody without regard to the protections provided under

82. ICG, October 1, 2009. Quoted in ibid., 14.

83. Lydia Polgreen, "Sri Lankans in Camps Allowed to Leave," *New York Times,* December 2, 2009, sec. International/Asia Pacific, http://www.nytimes.com/2009/12/02/world/asia/02lanka.html.

84. "Sri Lanka: Continuing Humanitarian Concerns and Obstacles to Durable Solutions for Recent and Longer-Term IDPs," 12–19.

85. "Sri Lanka: A Bitter Peace," *International Crisis Group,* January 11, 2009, http://www.crisisgroup.org/home/index.cfm?action=login&ref_id=6462.

86. Ibid., 16.

87. "Sri Lanka: Continuing Humanitarian Concerns and Obstacles to Durable Solutions for Recent and Longer-Term IDPs," 280.

88. "Sri Lanka: A Bitter Peace," 8.

Sri Lankan law. In many cases, the authorities have not informed family members about the whereabouts of the detained, leaving them in secret, incommunicado detention or possible enforced disappearance, and, as a result, especially vulnerable to abuse."[89] The Sri Lankan government has stated that aside from about 200 people who will be tried, most of the detainees will undergo a process of "rehabilitation" and then be released.[90]

Elections have played a prominent role in the trajectory of the conflict. Future elections are likely to affect the future of currently detained IDPs. Army commander General Sarath Fonseka challenged President Rajapaksa for the presidency in elections held in January 2010. While both Rajapaksa and Fonseka are strong Sinhalese nationalists, Fonseka showed more of a commitment to the protection of minority rights. According to the International Crisis Group, Tamil and Muslim voters were a decisive factor in the election. The effort to appear more moderate to Tamil voters before the election was a primary motive in the Rajapaksa government's decision to further the resettlement of IDPs held in camps.[91] Fonseka had also committed to a 10-point program of relief for war-affected areas to speed up the return of displaced people to their places of origin, rebuild infrastructure damaged in the war, and release detainees held under antiterrorism laws in rehabilitation camps.[92] While Rajapaksa won the election, it is clear that electoral politics will play a part in the future of IDPs in Sri Lanka.

Targeting and Weapons

The LTTE began as a conventional guerilla group, but gradually became one of the deadliest terrorist groups in the world, achieving a sophisticated edge to their strategies and tactics. The planning and use of suicide attackers on land, sea, and air reflects the underlying nature of the LTTE as a guerilla organization engaged in civil war. While the LTTE has carried out both suicide and conventional attacks in its struggle against the Sri Lankan government, the suicide missions carried out by the "Black

89. "Sri Lanka: World Leaders Should Demand End to Detention Camps," *Human Rights Watch,* September 22, 2009, http://www.hrw.org/en/news/2009/09/22/sri-lanka-world-leaders-should-demand-end-detention-camps.

90. "Sri Lanka: A Bitter Peace," 8

91. Ibid., 16.

92. Ibid.

TABLE 10.2 **Number of suicide attacks by target**

Period	Attacks	Civilian	Political	Security	Unknown
Eelam War I, 1983–87	1	0	0	1	0
Indian intervention, 1987–90	0	0	0	0	0
Eelam War II, 1990–94	15	0	4	11	0
Eelam War III, 1995–2001	66	11	8	46	1
Cease fire agreement, 2002–5	1	0	0	1	0
Eelam War IV, 2006–9	37	7	6	24	0

Source: CPOST database.

Tigers" are seen as more accurate and effective than conventional attacks. The LTTE were inspired by the early suicide attacks of Hezbollah, and had in fact been training with Palestinian militants in Lebanon since 1975.[93] Islamic groups, including Al Qaeda, later imitated the LTTE by carrying out similar suicide attacks.

The Black Tigers have used suicide terrorist attacks against civilian, military, and political targets. See table 10.2 for an overview of the number of attacks by target. While they have attacked fewer civilian targets, civilian casualties are often inevitable. For example, the Black Tigers carried out a suicide truck attack against the Sri Lanka Central Bank on January 31, 1996, killing 120 and injuring 1,400.[94] In spite of civilian casualties, the number of civilian targets has been significantly lower than political or military targets.

Assassination has been used as a tool to shape both political and military developments by the LTTE. The Black Tigers have assassinated many Sri Lankan leaders since conducting suicide operations. In other suicide campaigns, such as in Palestine or Pakistan, the number of political target attacks is close to zero. From 1990 through 2009, the LTTE carried out 21 assassinations. From 1990 to 1994 (Eelam War II), the LTTE assassinated five leaders (four political and one military). From 1995 to 2001 (Eelam War III), it carried out 17 assassinations (one civilian, six political, 10 security). Finally, from 2006 to 2009 (Eelam War IV), the LTTE carried out eight assassinations (six political and two security).

In addition to political and security assassinations, the Tamil Tigers have also targeted the country's political, economic, and cultural infrastructure.

93. Swamy, *Tigers of Lanka,* 97.

94. These numbers are the high estimate. There is always variation on the number of individuals reported killed or injured depending on the source reporting the attack.

TABLE 10.3 **Number of Suicide Attacks by Weapon**

Period	Attacks	Vehicle	Boat	Belt	Unknown
Eelam War I, 1983–87	1	1	0	0	0
Indian intervention, 1987–90	0	0	0	0	0
Eelam War II, 1990–94	15	6	4	3	2
Eelam War III, 1995–2001	62	5	11	16	30
Cease fire agreement, 2002–5	1	0	0	1	0
Eelam War IV, 2006–9	37	8	10	4	15

Source: CPOST database.

They destroyed the center of Sri Lanka's security operations, the Joint Operations Command, and targeted individuals who were at the forefront of counterinsurgency operations. They struck at the heart of the country's economy by bombing the Central Bank, the World Trade Center, and the oil storage installations in Kolonnawa. They tried to destroy the Temple of the Tooth Relic, the most hallowed Buddhist shrine.

The Sea Tigers, the naval wing of the LTTE, carried out 25 attacks using explosives-laden suicide boats. In April 2003, the Sea Tigers acquired 34 sets of underwater scooters from Denmark. In planning their attacks against anchored vessels, they knew it was not possible to target Fast Attack Crafts because of their speed.[95] The Sea Tigers increased the number of attacks on Sri Lankan naval vessels in 2006.[96] As noted earlier in the chapter, there were important reasons for targeting the Sri Lankan naval forces. The LTTE needed to maintain access to Tamil Nadu in southern India, and the LTTE used these attacks to weaken the garrison in Jaffna by disrupting the resupply efforts of the SLN.

The Air Tigers, the air-wing of the LTTE, carried out their first attack on March 26, 2007. Two aircraft attacked an engineering facility at Katunayake Air Force Base near Colombo. While the physical damage was insignificant, the psychological damage was substantial. The LTTE had exhibited its night-flying capability with the ability to return to base after flying about 500 to 600 kilometers, mostly over enemy territory.[97] Less than a month

95. Rajat Ganguly, "Sri Lanka's Ethnic Conflict: At a Crossroad between Peace and War," *Third World Quarterly* 25, no. 5 (2004): 903–17.

96. See "Conflict in Sri Lanka: A Change of Gear." *International Institute of Strategic Studies,* March 2007, http://www.iiss.org/search/?q=conflict+in+sri+lanka&x=0&y=0.

97. R. S. Vasan, *LTTE Air Attack: Air Defence and Related Issues* (South Asian Analysis Group, Paper no. 2193, April 3, 2007), http://www.saag.org/common/uploaded_files/paper2193.html.

later, on April 24, 2007, LTTE planes unsuccessfully tried to bomb the Palaly Air Base in Jaffna, instead dropping bombs on a nearby army camp, killing six soldiers. Four days later, on April 28, 2007, Air Tigers bombed key oil storage facilities at Kolonnawa and Muthurajawela in and around Colombo city. None of these attacks involved suicide bombers. The physical damage was minimal, but the attacks generated a significant amount of public fear.[98]

On October 22, 2007, Tamil Tigers carried out their first-ever simultaneous air and ground attack. A single-engine, propeller-driven aircraft bombed the Sri Lankan Air Force Base at Anuradhapura, in the North Central Province, while their ground forces attacked the base at the same time.[99] The Black Tigers occupied the air base from 3 a.m. to 9 a.m., during which time they blew up three helicopters, two fixed-wing aircraft (one of them a trainer), and three unmanned drones.[100] Having lost communication with the air base, the Sri Lanka Air Force Base at Vavuniya dispatched a helicopter to Anuradhapura to find out what had happened. As it neared the air base, Black Tigers, operating the base's antiaircraft gun, shot it down. The Black Tigers also destroyed an ammunition storage depot in the air base and damaged its runway. While the attack caused significant destruction, the Tigers were not able to destroy the Indian-made Indra-2 radars installed at the base. Air force fighter jets intercepted the two Tiger light aircraft fleeing after the failed mission, and shot one down over Mullaitivu.

The LTTE relied heavily upon female suicide bombers in its campaign.[101] See table 10.4 for an overview of attackers by gender. From 1987 to 2009, almost 18% of LTTE suicide bombers were female. Female suicide bombers are used when the target is hard to reach, such as an individual under high security. Examples of prominent female Black Tigers include Thenmuli Rajaratnam who approached her victim, former Indian prime minister Rajiv Gandhi, at an election campaign, greeted him, and bent

98. Jyoti Thottam, "A Surprise Attack by Sri Lanka's Tamil Tigers," *Time*, February 20, 2009, http://www.time.com/time/world/article/0,8599,1881087,00.html.

99. Haroon Siddique, "Tamil Tigers Attack Airforce Base," *Guardian*, October 22, 2007, sec. World, http://www.guardian.co.uk/world/2007/oct/22/srilanka.

100. "There is a significant discrepancy between the Sri Lankan government and LTTE claims regarding the number of aircraft destroyed. The LTTE claims to have destroyed 15 aircraft, while the Prime Minister claimed that the LTTE destroyed only 8 aircraft. See "'Eight Lankan Planes' Destroyed," *BBC*, October 24, 2007, sec. South Asia, http://news.bbc.co.uk/2/hi/south_asia/7059661.stm.

101. Gunawardena, "Female Black Tigers"; Lindsey A. O'Rourke, "What's Special about Female Suicide Terrorism?" *Security Studies* 18, no. 4 (2009): 681; Miranda Alison, "Cogs in the Wheel? Women in the Liberation Tigers of Tamil Eelam," *Civil Wars* 6, no. 4 (2003): 37–54.

TABLE 10.4 **Number of LTTE suicide attackers by gender**

Period	Attacks	Attackers	Female	Male	Unknown
Eelam War I, 1983–87	1	1	0	1	0
Indian intervention, 1987–90	0	0	0	0	0
Eelam War II, 1990–94	15	35	5	29	1
Eelam War III, 1995–2001	62	114	28	61	25
Cease fire agreement, 2002–5	1	1	1	0	0
Eelam War IV, 2006–9	37	85	5	21	59

Source: CPOST database.

down to touch his feet in customary Hindu greeting, then exploded herself. A female suicide bomber in Jaffna detonated a belt bomb targeting housing and construction minister Nimal Siripala de Silva on July 4, 1996. Over the years, Tigers innovated in their use of female suicide bombers. For example, in assassinating army commander Lieutenant General Sarath Fonseka on April 25, 2006, they used a female disguised as a pregnant woman.

Local Community Support

The LTTE called its suicide missions thatkodai, which is Tamil for "giving oneself."[102] The LTTE held public ceremonies to commemorate their martyrs. "Heroes Day" is held every July 5 in Jaffna in memory of the first Black Tiger suicide attack. The LTTE's use of suicide attackers could not have occurred without sustained popular support from the Tamil community. Expectation of community support was a key factor in the decision of many Tamil Tigers to carry out a suicide attack.

The LTTE glorified suicide attackers immediately after their death by displaying their pictures on posters and holding public processions with pomp and pageantry in their honor. After completion of a suicide attack, the identity of the attacker is highly publicized in displays of commemoration, in newspapers, and in commemorative albums. Public monuments are often built on Tamil towns to commemorate Black Tigers. The largest is the life-size statue of Captain Miller that sits near a well-traveled intersection in Jaffna. These displays are conscious efforts to cultivate broad public support for martyrdom. Tigers also carried identity cards on their missions

102. The LTTE thus distinguishes suicide operations from *thatkolai,* "killing oneself." De-Votta, "The Liberation Tigers of Tamil Eelam," 1035.

with their names written in Tamil, English, and Sinhalese in order to ensure that they are recognized and credited with carrying out the attack. The card read, "I am filled with a huge explosive. If my journey is blocked I will explode it. Let me go."[103]

Black Tiger attacks are frequently associated with advancing the welfare of the Tamil community. Prabhakaran, the leader of the group has said, "Tamil Eelam can be achieved in 100 years. But if we conduct Black Tiger operations, we can shorten the suffering of the people and achieve Tamil Eelam in a shorter period of time."[104]

In understanding levels of support for the LTTE, it is important to note that the LTTE itself constituted a significant fraction of the total Tamil population. There were 10,000–15,000 LTTE members during the 1990s. Surveys indicate that the LTTE has significant support from the Tamil community. Popular support for LTTE armed resistance could be interpreted as sympathy, if not support, for suicide operations.

Surveys on Tamil public opinions have shown varied attitudes toward armed resistance. While there are very few surveys on Tamil support of suicide terrorism, there are local surveys documenting support for LTTE armed resistance. According to Mia Bloom, Tamil attitudes toward violence can "constrain what the organization can and cannot do and who they can target."[105] Bloom's survey of Tamil public attitude in 2002 was consistent with existing reports. She found that Tamils were "war weary and anticipated a significant peace dividend in the near future."[106] Her survey also found that Tamils differentiated between support for attacks targeting civilians and those attacking military personnel or politicians. While there was no support for attacking civilians, support for attacking military targets was more varied. Specifically, Bloom found that individuals under the age of 30 were more likely to support violence, while Tamils with a university education were less likely to support armed resistance.[107] Surveys demonstrate that Tamil popular support for the LTTE remained strong long after the Tigers began to use suicide operations. Data show that 72% favored the establishment of an independent Tamil state in 1986, while only 10% op-

103. Bruce Hoffman and Gordon H. McCromick, "Terrorism, Signaling, and Suicide Attack," *Studies in Conflict and Terrorism* 27, no. 4 (2004): 260.

104. Louise Richardson, *What Terrorists Want: Understanding the Enemy, Containing the Threat,* 1st ed. (New York: Random House, 2006), 164.

105. Bloom, *Dying to Kill*, 67.

106. Ibid.

107. Ibid., 68.

posed. Forty-seven percent of Tamils surveyed supported the use of armed force even after more than a decade of protracted suicide operations.[108]

Support for the LTTE can be traced in part to the provision of social and economic resources to the Tamil population. According to a study on social service provision by the LTTE, "the Tamil Tigers have ensured that the communities in LTTE controlled provinces perceive health and social services as coming from the LTTE itself."[109] The LTTE created a "public image of a welfare 'state,'" and doing so is intended to ensure the local Tamil population that they are the "primary provider of relief and rehabilitation."[110] In 1991, the LTTE's Center for Women's Development was opened to deliver humanitarian relief, vocational training, psychological counseling, and childcare to women and children in a series of centers that expanded over time. In 1992, the Tigers established a police and judicial system in the areas under its control. The LTTE recruited female police officers and administrators in order to expand the roles of women in Tamil society. In 1993, the Tamil Eelam Bank was established, providing low-interest loans to stimulate small businesses.[111] The LTTE attempts to break down boundaries between the local Tamil community and the LTTE itself—generating widespread popular support.

> Why does the LTTE have so much support among the population? [It] is the only group that is accepted by the population as "one of our own," "our boys," even "our sons." . . . The LTTE are the one militant group that has managed to build up grassroots support and loyalty among the population for reasons of both ideology and organization and got a grip on the political and social structure of Jaffna.[112]

The success of the SLA's final offensive against the LTTE was facilitated by the defection of Karuna in 2004. The defection reflected a growing dissatisfaction in the Eastern Province with the LTTE leadership. In 2008

108. See Bloom, "Ethnic Conflict"; Bloom, *Dying to Kill,* 3; Ambalavanar Sivarajah, *Politics of Tamil Nationalism in Sri Lanka* (New Delhi: South Asian Publishers, 1996), 158–59; Robert A. Pape, *Dying to Win: The Strategic Logic of Suicide Terrorism* (New York: Random House, 2005).

109. Flanigan, "Nonprofit Service Provision by Insurgent Organizations," 504.

110. Ibid.

111. Sarath Munasinghe, *A Soldier's Version: An Account of the On-Going Conflict and the Origin of Terrorism in Sri Lanka,* 1st ed. (Colombo: Market Information Systems, 2000), 184–87.

112. Hellmann-Rajanayagam, *The Tamil Tigers,* 136 and 44.

Karuna joined the Sri Lankan parliament as a member of the ruling United People's Freedom Alliance, and was appointed Minister of National Integration in 2009.[113] This political move signaled to the Tamils in the Eastern Province that the Sri Lankan government would take their interests into account, resulting in almost half the Tamil population withdrawing their support of the LTTE.[114]

Recruitment

Over three decades, the LTTE grew to approximately 10,000–15,000 fighters. The LTTE was comprised of infantry brigades, women's brigades, commando units, and specialized divisions for laying mines, sniping, firing mortars and artillery, and resisting tanks and armored cars. The LTTE developed specialized wings to carry out suicide attacks, naval attacks, and air attacks.

All LTTE fighters must be willing to die for the group. Since the early 1980s, male and female LTTE fighters have been required to carry a potassium cyanide capsule around their necks. Prabhakaran ordered that all fighters were obligated to bite the cyanide capsule if captured. Over 600 cadres have chosen to die in this manner rather than betray the cause. This extreme devotion is a vital component of the LTTE's success in terrorist attacks. A former military spokesman, Brigadier Sanath Karunaratne, spoke of the suicide bomber: "It is a one-way soldier and there is very little stopping. Once you get someone into that mentality, there can be no limit."[115]

According to India's Research and Analysis Wing, Black Tigers are recruited from among the LTTE's fighters who have already proved extraordinary commitment to the LTTE. The LTTE was extremely selective in recruiting members for suicide operations. These individuals, from tough combat units, volunteer for suicide operations. The success of suicide operations rests on the protection of suicide bombers' identities prior to the attack. Successful Black Tigers received elaborate gravestones that mark

113. "Renegade Sworn in as S Lanka MP," *BBC*, October 7, 2008, sec. South Asia, http://news.bbc.co.uk/2/hi/south_asia/7657668.stm. B. Muralidhar Reddy, "Karuna Joins Cabinet," *The Hindu*, March 10, 2009. Online edition, sec. International, http://www.hindu.com/2009/03/10/stories/200903106261500.htm.

114. Ibid.

115. Amantha Perera, "Suicide Cadres Still Evoke Fear," *Inter Press Service Agency*, July 16, 2003, http://ipsnews.net/srilanka/str1607.shtml.

their achievements, even though there is no body left for burial. The pres-
tige associated with martyrdom motivated young Tamils to become suicide
bombers. The immediate family members of Black Tigers received financial
assistance and employment opportunities within the LTTE.

The LTTE recruited volunteers from local schools, while forcibly taking
children, mainly teenagers, from their families. The Human Rights Watch
report, "Living in Fear," states that, in the Batticaloa district, the LTTE employed a door-to-door, family-by-family recruitment program. The recruit-
ers would contact families either in writing or in person at their homes and
request that they volunteer one of their children. According to the report,
the ages of these child recruits varies, but they were usually at least 15 years
old.[116] The United Nations Children's Fund (UNICEF) documented 3,516
new cases of underage recruitment as of October 31, 2004. Since the signing of the cease-fire agreement in 2002, the average age of a Tamil Tiger
suicide bomber was 21.9 years.

Conclusion

Since the military defeat of the LTTE in May 2009, there have been no
further reported suicide attacks in Sri Lanka. Does the defeat of the
LTTE spell the end of suicide terrorism in Sri Lanka? Can the Sri Lankan
case serve as a model for policies to end suicide terrorism in other
contexts?

Put simply, the prospect of future suicide attacks in Sri Lanka is tied to
the future of the civil war. As we show in the trajectory section, the course
of LTTE suicide terrorism was a function of the course of the civil war.
During the four Eelam wars, the LTTE used suicide terrorism as an integral
part of its military and political strategy to achieve a Tamil homeland. Militarily, it deployed Black Tiger cadres against Sri Lankan ground, naval, and
air forces as well as Sri Lanka's military leadership. Politically, the LTTE
used suicide attacks to influence the course of negotiations by eliminating
politicians that posed a threat to the LTTE's political goal: an independent
Tamil state under LTTE control. The destruction of the LTTE's leadership
and military organization, and the end of the civil war suggest that there
will be no further suicide attacks by the LTTE. However, the underlying

116. "Living in Fear," *Human Rights Watch*, November 10, 2004, http://www.hrw.org/en/
node/11900/section/6.

cause of the civil war—a Sinhala-dominated state that, through its discriminatory practices against the Tamils, has repeatedly reinforced the Tamil minorities' desire for an autonomous homeland—has yet to be resolved. But the prospects for meaningful Tamil autonomy, in the Northern and Eastern Provinces where Tamils are concentrated, are uncertain. The implication is that, while the LTTE may be out and the fighting over, it may be too soon to tell whether the civil war will resume in the future. And if the civil war resumes, we can expect renewed suicide terrorism campaigns, whether by a reconstituted LTTE or its successor.

The Sri Lankan government's postwar security strategy, while contributing to the absence of suicide terrorism in the short term, may ultimately make a return to suicide terrorism more likely in the future. Displacement and internment of a large fraction of the entire Tamil population does separate the terrorist organization from much of its social base of support, and compels individuals to focus on their own immediate welfare in the short term. In the long term, however, the mass displacement and internment of ethnic Tamils is a potent source of resentment. The harsh conditions in these camps have the potential to provide a basis for future resistance by the Sri Lankan Tamils. To minimize this possibility, the Sri Lankan government should consider a large-scale economic and social reconstruction of the Tamil homeland.

The End of Fear, the Beginning of Understanding

In the decade since 9/11, the United States has

- Conquered and occupied two large Muslim countries (Afghanistan and Iraq);
- Compelled a huge Muslim army to root out a terrorist sanctuary (Pakistan);
- Deployed thousands of special forces to numerous Muslim countries (Yemen, Chad, Niger, etc.);
- Imprisoned hundreds of Muslims without recourse;
- Waged a massive war of ideas involving Muslim clerics to denounce violence and creating new institutions to bring Western norms to Muslim countries.

Have these actions—which some have called "World War IV"—made America safe?

In a narrow sense, America is safer. There has not been another attack on the scale of 9/11. Our defenses regarding immigration controls, airport security, and the disruption of potentially devastating domestic plots have all improved. This is the positive side of the ledger.

In a broader sense, however, America is not safer. Anti-American suicide terrorism is rapidly rising around the world. In 2003, then Defense Secretary Donald Rumsfeld famously asked, "Are we capturing, killing or deterring and dissuading more terrorists every day than the madrassas and the radical clerics are recruiting, training and deploying against us?" As even a casual glance at the facts shows, the answer is a disappointing no. The negative side of the balance sheet is daunting.

Each month, there are more suicide terrorists trying to kill Americans and their military allies in Afghanistan, Iraq, and other Muslim countries than in all the years before 2001 combined. Yes, these attacks are mostly (although not exclusively) focused on military and diplomatic targets. However, so too were the anti-American suicide attacks before 2001. It is important to remember that the 1995 and 1996 bombings of U.S. troops in Saudi Arabia, the 1998 bombings of the U.S. embassies in Kenya and Tanzania, and the bombing of the USS Cole in Yemen in 2000 were the crucial dots that showed the threat was rising prior to 9/11. Today, such dots are occurring by the dozens every month.

American military policies have not stopped the rising wave of extremism in the Muslim world. The reason has not been lack of effort. The reason has not been a lack of will among the American people or Western publics. The reason has not been a lack of bipartisan support for aggressive military policies. The reason has not been a lack of funding. The reason has not been a lack of genuine patriotism.

No. American military policies are not failing for the standard excuses. Something else is creating the mismatch between America's effort and the results.

Misunderstanding the Root Cause and Its Consequences

Emergence of "the Narrative"

America has been waging a long war against terrorism, but without much serious public debate about what is truly motivating terrorists to kill us. In the immediate aftermath of the 9/11 attack, this was perfectly understandable and even desirable. Caught by surprise and with no sense of what the coming weeks would bring, virtually any U.S. leader would have sought to retaliate hard and quickly by destroying Al Qaeda's camps in Afghanistan, some of which were as large as Western military bases, with little or no thought given to the root causes of the threat. If toppling the Taliban was necessary to take out Al Qaeda's sanctuary, so be it.

But, in an instant, there was also a great need to know or, perhaps better to say, to "understand" the events of that terrible day. In the years before 9/11, few Americans gave much thought to what drives terrorism—a subject long relegated to the fringes of the media and the periphery of even the government, the military, and universities. This understanding would not wait for new studies, collection of facts, and dispassionate assessment of alternative causes. Terrorism produces fear and anger, and such emotions are not patient.

A simple narrative was readily available, and a powerful conventional wisdom began to exert its grip. Since the 9/11 hijackers were all Muslims, it was easy to presume that Islamic fundamentalism was the central motivating force driving the 19 hijackers to kill themselves in order to kill us. Within weeks after the attack, surveys of American attitudes show that this presumption was fast congealing into a hard reality in the public mind. Americans immediately wondered, "Why do they hate us?" and many quickly came to the conclusion that it was because of who we are, not what we do.

Why was this presumption so readily adopted? Most importantly, because the president of the United States said so. On September 20, 2001, President George W. Bush said in his address to Congress on the September 11 attacks:

> Al Qaeda is to terror what the Mafia is to crime. But its goal is not making money, its goal is remaking the world and imposing its radical beliefs on people everywhere. The terrorists practice a fringe form of Islamic extremism. . . .
>
> "Why do they hate us?" They hate what they see right here in this chamber: a democratically elected government. . . . They hate our freedoms: our freedom of religion, our freedom of speech, our freedom to vote and assemble and disagree with each other.

Then, the media leapt into action. Within weeks—and for years—television, radio, newspapers, college campuses, Internet media, local libraries, and all manner of other public forums were full of wall-to-wall shows, stories, reports, and discussions about "What's Wrong with Islam?" "Why Do Only Muslims Carry Out Suicide Attacks?" "Why Do They Hate Us?" Many carefully avoided broad stereotyping of Islam or Muslims, but nearly all emphasized "Islamic extremism" and the internal roots of Muslim rage.

A prime example is Fareed Zakaria's October 15, 2001 cover story for *Newsweek,* in which one of America's most respected journalists laid out the heart of the emerging conventional wisdom. Zakaria writes:

> The problem is not that Osama bin Laden believes that this is a religious war against America. It's that millions of people across the Islamic world seem to agree. . . .
>
> Only when you get to the Middle East do you see in lurid colors all the dysfunctions that people conjure up when they think of Islam today. In Iran, Egypt, Syria, Iraq, Jordan, the occupied territories and the Persian Gulf, the

resurgence of Islamic fundamentalism is virulent, and a raw anti-Americanism seems to be everywhere. This is the land of suicide bombers. . . .

If there is one great cause of the rise of Islamic fundamentalism, it is the total failure of political institutions in the Arab world. . . .

The United States must help Islam enter the modern world. . . . America—indeed the whole world—faces a dire security threat that will not be resolved unless we can stop the political, economic and cultural collapse that lies at the roots of Arab rage. Obviously we will have to help construct a new political order in Afghanistan after we have deposed the Taliban regime. But beyond that we have to press the nations of the Arab world. . . . We have no option but to get back into the nation-building business.[1]

So, with little public debate—but endless discussion—of the role of Islam promoting hatred of America, it is little wonder that a significant number of Americans surveyed in the months after September 11, 2001, came to believe that the "main reason" that "they hate us" was related to Islamic fundamentalism. For instance, in November 2001, 30% of Americans said that the reason the terrorists attacked the World Trade Center and Pentagon was "mostly their religious beliefs," similar to the fraction in late September reporting that they hate us because of our "values and way of life" (20%).[2]

In fall 2001, the narrative of Islamic fundamentalism was fast gaining traction, but had not yet seized the public mind in a truly large way. Further, during this period, the public was focused on retaliating against Al Qaeda and the Taliban in Afghanistan. For these reasons the idea of waging a broad war on terrorism against many states in the Arab world had little appeal.

Almost immediately after 9/11, senior Bush officials planted the first seeds for what would become a grand plan for the war on terrorism. On September 13, 2001, Deputy Secretary of Defense Paul Wolfowitz said, "It's not just simply a matter of capturing people and holding them accountable, but . . . ending states who sponsor terrorism."[3]

At first, respectable opinion found the idea far-fetched. On September 15, the New York Times wrote in a dismissive editorial: "Paul Wolfowitz . . . spoke of 'ending states who sponsor terrorism.' That may work as a form of

1. Fareed Zakaria, "The Politics of Rage: Why Do They Hate Us?" *Newsweek,* October 15, 2001.

2. Harris Poll (September 24, 2001); and Pew Research Center, "Post September 11 Attitudes (December 6, 2001).

3. Elisabeth Bumiller and Jane Perlez, "After the Attacks: Bush and Top Aides Proclaim Policy of 'Ending' States That Back Terror," *New York Times,* September 14, 2001.

intimidation, but we trust he does not have in mind invading and occupying Iraq, Iran, Syria and Sudan, as well as Afghanistan, nations with a combined population of more than 160 million people."[4] Secretary of State Colin Powell and other Bush officials also took exception to the grand ambition to transform the Arab world.

And then the Taliban fell and . . .

The events in the run up to the Iraq War are well known. President Bush's "axis of evil" speech in January 2002 began a broad campaign to persuade the U.S. Senate and the public at large that American security hinged crucially on the political transformation of Iraq as the only way to prevent the country from gaining nuclear weapons and using them.

In the years since, a small forest has been cut down to print books and articles about the exaggerations (or not) in U.S. intelligence on whether Iraq would gain nuclear weapons.[5] This issue is surely important. However, lost in the massive effort to review and reconstruct what senior leaders knew about Iraq's nuclear and other weapons of mass destruction programs and when they knew it has been this salient fact. At no point did the U.S. Senate demand a detailed review of American intelligence on Iraq's WMD, not even before the crucial vote in October 2002 in which 77 senators—including John Kerry, Hillary Clinton, and 20 other Democrats—supported the Bush administration on the war. Even President Bush did not receive a detailed top secret briefing by the CIA on the subject until mid-December 2002, months after he made the decision to deploy large numbers of American ground forces to the theater in preparation for invading Iraq. Further, President Bush responded to CIA Director George Tenet's briefing with dismay—"This is the best we've got?"—but lost no enthusiasm for the war.[6] Further, two-thirds of the U.S. public supported the conquest of Iraq with even less information than those in Washington.

Why so little real debate on the intelligence on Iraq? Indeed, why did the details of the intelligence seem to hardly matter even to the most senior American decision makers let alone to the public at large?

We offer a simple explanation, one based not on the information that

4. "War without Illusions," *New York Times,* September 15, 2001.

5. Chaim Kaufmann, "Threat Inflation and the Failure of the Marketplace of Ideas: The Selling of the Iraq War," *International Security* 29, no. 1, 5–48; and Robert Jervis, *Why Intelligence Fails: Lessons from the Iranian Revolution and the Iraq War* (Ithaca, NY: Cornell University Press, 2010).

6. Bob Woodward, *Plan of Attack: The Definitive Account of the Decision to Invade Iraq* (New York: Simon & Schuster, 2004), 247.

did not exist (intelligence on Iraq WMD) but on the facts that did—the narrative of Islamic fundamentalism.

How "the Narrative" Shaped Support for the Iraq War

America's decision to invade Iraq unfolded from the winter of 2001, following the collapse of the Taliban in Afghanistan, until March 2003, when the United States officially announced its decision to attack. During this period, American leaders made numerous public statements, which increasingly emphasized that Iraq had weapons of mass destruction and would soon acquire more, was linked to terrorist groups seeking to attack the United States, that regime change was the only viable solution, and that a ground war was the only sure means to execute it. Although we do not know if the Bush administration would have attacked without broad public support, we do know that the administration went to great lengths to influence public opinion and appeared to take the views of America seriously.

Assessing American attitudes toward various issues associated with war against Iraq from early 2002 to March 2003 reveals the important contribution that the narrative of Islamic fundamentalism most likely made to broad public support for the invasion. During this year, a wide variety of polling agencies (Gallup, CNN/USA Today, Harris, Pew, etc.) conducted numerous surveys of American public opinion on Iraq, asking many of the key questions consistently over the period and so allowing for an examination of the U.S. attitudes that were and were not changing during the run up to the Iraq War.

American support for war did in fact rise, from 46% favoring the use of ground forces to invade Iraq in March 2002 to 64% favoring this policy in February 2003—an increase of 18%, far beyond errors in polling and replicated across numerous polling agencies.

Why the rise? Perhaps the biggest surprise in the polling data is that American attitudes on the most discussed topic related to Iraq—its possession of weapons of mass destruction—hardly changed. It started high and remained high. In February 2002, fully 95% of Americans believed that Iraq had or would soon have weapons of mass destruction, virtually the same fraction a year later (91%).[7]

These numbers help to explain why there was discussion but little seri-

---

7. CNN/USA Today/Gallup Polls, February 19, 2002, and December 12, 2003.

TABLE II.I **Using ground troops to invade Iraq?**

	March 2002	February 2003
Favor	46	64
Oppose	50	33
No opinion	4	3

Source: CNN/USA Today/Gallup Polls. March 28. 2002. and February 9. 2003.

ous demand by the public or in congressional committees for detailed review of the intelligence on Iraq's WMD programs. Since the public began with a strong consensus that Iraq had or would soon have these capabilities and since it was easy to assume that Saddam Hussein was capable of deception, knowing more about the precise state of affairs of Iraq's weapons programs was not crucial because it would not affect their decision for war. The American public and the U.S. Congress appear to have reached the same conclusion as then Secretary of Defense Donald Rumsfeld: "absence of evidence is not evidence of absence."[8]

So, if American support for war against Iraq did not grow because more Americans came to accept claims by the Bush administration that Iraq possessed or would soon possess weapons of mass destruction, what did cause the shift? Was it growing fear of ties between Iraq and terrorist groups seeking to attack the United States?

Again, the evidence shows no. And, again, for the same reason. There is little change in U.S. views on Iraq's ties to terrorism during the run up to the Iraq War. It started high and stayed high. Whether one focuses on Saddam Hussein's personal ties to the 9/11 attacks or the broader issue of Iraq's links to terrorist groups bent on harming America, the responses by the U.S. public are nearly identical whenever these questions are asked in the year before the U.S. invasion of Iraq. For instance, when Gallup first asked whether "Saddam Hussein is involved in supporting terrorist groups that have plans to attack the United States" in mid-August 2002, 86% of Americans said "yes, is involved." When the same question was asked again in March 2003, 88% of Americans gave the same answer.[9] In short, American support for war against Iraq did not grow because American beliefs that Iraq was tied to terrorism grew.

8. Secretary Donald Rumsfeld, Press Conference at NATO Headquarters, Brussels, Belgium (June 6, 2002).

9. Gallup News Service Polls, August 21, 2002, and March 15, 2003.

TABLE 11.2 **Is Islam likely to encourage violence?**

	March 2002	July 2003
Yes	25	44
No	51	41
Don't know	24	15

Source: "Religion and Politics: Contention and Consensus" (Washington, DC: Pew Forum on Religion and Public Life. July 24. 2003). section IV. "Changing Perceptions of Islam."

TABLE 11.3 **Perceived number of anti-American Muslims around world?**

	March 2002	June 2003
Half or more	36	49
Some	24	24
A few	21	15
Don't know	19	12

Source: "Religion and Politics: Contention and Consensus" (Washington, DC: Pew Forum on Religion and Public Life, July 24, 2003), section IV, "Changing Perceptions of Islam."

So, if changes in U.S. beliefs on Iraq WMD and ties to terrorism do not explain the shift in American support for invading Iraq, what does? Although we still do not know all the specifics, there is good reason to think that "the narrative"—the story that Islamic fundamentalism is driving the threat—made a significant contribution.

Starting in early 2002, American views on Islam and its role in encouraging violence began to change significantly. According to Pew surveys, in March 2002, 25% of Americans believed that Islam was "likely to encourage violence," and 36% believed that the "number of anti-American Muslims around the world" totaled half or more. In July 2003—the next time the questions were asked—both numbers dramatically rose: 44% believed that Islam encourages violence, and 49% that half or more of all Muslims worldwide hate America.

These are major changes. The shift in attitudes on Islam is roughly the same proportion as the shift in favor of invading Iraq—both nearly 20% over nearly the same period. Further, the extreme depth of the fear of Islam is reflected in the shift from a third to a half of Americans thinking that at least half of all Muslims around the world are a threat to them.

Overall, this assessment of American opinion polls paints a stark picture of the pressures driving American support for the Iraq War. The factors of

Iraq WMD and relationship to terrorist groups did not in themselves create a majority in favor of invading Iraq. Something else had to be added—a catalyst—the growing fear of Islamic fundamentalism. The catalyst mattered because it suggested that America was engaged in a struggle for its civilization and that the enemy, driven as it was by religious fanaticism, could not be deterred by the usual threats of retaliation based on a punishing response to any attack. As Americans came to embrace the narrative that Islam was itself the threat, it seemed all the more plausible that any nuclear weapons Iraq produced would, one way or another, be used against the United States.

Simply put: America could not deter Saddam Hussein from giving nuclear weapons to terrorists. America could not deter the terrorists from using nuclear weapons. America, thus, had no choice but to rely on brute force to stop this process before it truly began. The linchpin of this fear was not Iraq's existing capabilities or links to Al Qaeda. The linchpin was the belief that a huge fraction of Muslims hate us and their religion drove that hate. The growing acceptance of the narrative of Islamic fundamentalism was the catalyst that most likely drove a majority of Americans to support the invasion of Iraq.

How "the Narrative" Shaped the Occupation of Afghanistan and Iraq

The narrative of Islamic fundamentalism did more than explain why America was attacked and encourage war against Iraq. It also pointed toward a simple, grand solution—one whose ambition only made it seem all the more worthy in light of the trauma of that terrible day. As Zakaria's *Newsweek* cover story and many others would suggest, if Islamic fundamentalism was driving the threat and if its roots grew from the culture of the Arab world, then America had a clear mission: to transform Arab societies—with Western political institutions and social norms as the ultimate antidote to the virus of Islamic extremism.

By mid-2003, the United States had toppled the regimes in Afghanistan and Iraq and was, for the first time, in a position to consider the future political order in these countries and the Middle East in general. Up until this point, the idea of producing a broad transformation of Muslim countries had become central to the narrative and commonplace among think tanks and advocacy groups in Washington, but had not yet become officially associated with the Bush administration or other senior leaders. This would now change.

Starting in November 2003, President Bush gave a series of speeches focusing on the need to democratize the Middle East:

> [T]he Middle East . . . must be a focus of American policy for decades to come. . . .
>
> [T]he global wave of democracy has barely reached the Arab states. . . .
>
> [G]roups of men, have gained influence in the Middle East and beyond through an ideology of theocratic terror. Behind their language of religion is the ambition for absolute political power. Ruling cabals like the Taliban show their version of religious piety in public whippings of women, ruthless suppression of any difference or dissent, and support for terrorists who arm and train to murder the innocent. . . .
>
> Successful societies protect freedom . . . allow room for healthy civic institutions . . . guarantee religious liberty . . . privatize their economies, and secure the rights of property . . . recognize the rights of women. . . .
>
> These vital principles are being applied in the nations of Afghanistan and Iraq. . . . Next month, 500 delegates will convene a national assembly in Kabul to approve a new Afghan constitution. . . . The establishment of a free Iraq at the heart of the Middle East will be a watershed event in the global democratic revolution.[10]

The goal of transforming Arab societies into true Western democracies had powerful effects on America's commitments to Afghanistan and Iraq. Constitutions had to be written. Elections had to be held. National armies had to be built. Economies had to be restructured. Traditional barriers against women had to be torn down. Most important, all these changes also required domestic security, which meant maintaining approximately 150,000 U.S. and Coalition ground troops in Iraq for many years and increasing U.S. and Western troops in Afghanistan from 2003 on.

Put differently, adopting the goal of transforming Muslim countries is what created the long-term military occupation of Iraq and Afghanistan. Yes, the United States would almost surely have sought to create a stable order after toppling the regimes in these countries in any case. However, in both, America's plans went far beyond merely changing leaders or ruling parties.

As Zakaria had foretold, America was now in the "nation-building"

10. President George W. Bush, "Remarks by the President at the 20th Anniversary of the National Endowment for Democracy," November 6, 2003.

business. The reason was not that Americans were especially good at it. Indeed, numerous scholars and policy analysts have now evaluated the many failures—from disbanding the army in Iraq without considering how Sunni soldiers might turn to terrorism to eradicating poppy fields in Afghanistan without considering how Afghans might turn to the Taliban.[11]

What pushed ineluctably toward transformation and sustained military occupation was "the narrative." The story that Islamic fundamentalism was driving the threat meant that America could be secure only by transforming Muslim societies. The barrel of a gun may not have been the only way to pursue this strategy, but with the nation's security seemingly at stake, the use of the military appeared a rational course of action.

The problem is that we now have strong evidence that "the narrative" is not true.

The Tide Is Turning

The oxygen for America's strategy is, fundamentally, how we understand the root cause of the terrorist threat we face. Political parties may well articulate a narrative for their own advantage. Bureaucratic politics related to unleashing virtually the entire American national security establishment—all branches of the U.S. military, the 16 principal U.S. intelligence agencies, and large parts of the departments of the state, homeland security, and energy—may also create their own dynamics in favor of resources and power. Narrow special interests may also exist. These factors may support "the narrative" of Islamic fundamentalism or discourage active resistance to it. However, today's mismatch between America's efforts and results against terrorism is due importantly to the intellectual climate of opinion.

In recent years, the intellectual climate has begun to change. Although "the narrative" of Islamic fundamentalism remains the leading view among Americans, the idea that Western military policies are provoking more terrorism than they are stopping is becoming a close second. On January

11. For excellent surveys of America's troubled efforts to democratize Iraq and Afghanistan, see Thomas E. Ricks, *Fiasco: The American Military Adventure in Iraq* (New York: Penguin, 2006); David L. Phillips, *Losing Iraq: Inside the Postwar Reconstruction Fiasco* (New York: Perseus Books, 2005); Larry Diamond, *Squandered Victory: The American Occupation and the Bungled Effort to Bring Democracy to Iraq* (New York: Henry Holt, 2005); and Seth G. Jones, *In the Graveyard of Empires: America's War in Afghanistan* (New York: W. W. Norton, 2009).

26, 2010, a Zogby poll found that 27% of Americans now believe that the "most important factor" motivating terrorists to attack the United States is that they "resent Western power and influence," compared to 33% who still think the main motive is "make Islam the world's dominant religion."

This book provides strong evidence that suicide terrorism is particularly sensitive to foreign military occupation, and not Islamic fundamentalism or any ideology independent of this crucial circumstance. Although this pattern began to emerge in the 1980s and 1990s, new information about suicide terrorism in recent years presents a powerful picture.

Here is a summary of what we know:

- Occupation causes suicide terrorism.
- Over 95% of all suicide attacks are in response to foreign occupation.
- The more occupation, the more suicide terrorism.
- As America has occupied two large Muslim countries, Afghanistan and Iraq, with a total population of about 60 million, total suicide attacks worldwide have risen dramatically—from about 300 from 1980 to 2003 to 1,800 from 2004 to 2009. Further, *over 90% of all suicide attacks are now anti-American.*
- Even transnational terrorists are motivated by foreign occupation.
- The July 2005 suicide bombers in London and other transnational suicide terrorists were not driven by the common explanation of economic and social alienation, but by deep anger at the presence of foreign combat forces occupying kindred communities.
- Indirect occupation is the equivalent of direct occupation.
- The United States compelled Pakistan to deploy 100,000 troops against the Taliban in the Federally Administered Tribal Areas, and Pakistani suicide attacks escalated dramatically.
- Suicide terrorist groups can focus on their main enemy or its military allies.
- Al Qaeda's activity has varied. This is not so much because the overall number of attacks and plots has been rising and falling, but rather because of changing strategy—focused first on the United States, the leader of what Al Qaeda considers a foreign occupation of the Arabian Peninsula, then on key U.S. allies, Spain and Britain, and now again on the United States.
- Ending occupation stops suicide terrorism without transforming Muslim countries.
- Since Israel withdrew its army from Lebanon in May 2000, there has not been a single Lebanese suicide attack. Similarly, since Israel withdrew from Gaza and large parts of the West Bank, Palestinian suicide attacks are down over 90%.
- Civilian casualties during an occupation often increase suicide terrorism.

- In Chechnya, Afghanistan, and elsewhere, there is strong evidence linking harm to civilians and the personal motives of suicide attackers.
- Extreme repression can end suicide terrorism, but with long term risk.
- In Sri Lanka, moving about half of the Tamil population in the north to camps did allow the government to isolate the existing terrorists from the population, but at the risk that refugee camps will become breeding grounds for future terrorists.
- Empowering local groups can reduce suicide terrorism.
- In Iraq, the surge's apparent success was not the result of increased U.S. military control of Anbar Province, but rather the reverse—the empowerment of Sunni tribal leaders for their own security, commonly called the Anbar Awakening.
- Taking power away from local groups can escalate suicide terrorism.
- In Afghanistan the ISAF's expansion strategy, designed to exert more central government control over the Pashtun tribes in the western and southern provinces, caused a resurgence in the Taliban and an increase in suicide attacks.

Cutting the Fuse

Suicide terrorism poses the greatest threat to the United States and its allies today. Without the willingness of individuals to die to carry out catastrophic attacks, mass civilian casualties on the scale of September 11, 2001, or worse would be highly unlikely. While it is true that chemical, biological, and nuclear weapons are more destructive than airplanes hitting buildings, it is the potential marriage of any mass casualty technology with suicide operations that most increases the danger of an attack— since having individual terrorists guide these weapons greatly increases the odds of success.

When pursuing national security interests, leaders must be aware of the "Occupier's Dilemma": conventional military power may achieve immediate security goals, but at the risk of stimulating a suicide terrorist campaign to the homeland. There may be times when the immediate benefits of sustained military occupation overseas are worth the risk of suicide attack at home. There may be some special circumstances in which a military occupation does not encourage suicide attack—particularly when there are no major cultural differences between the occupier and occupied communities (the United States in Germany after World War II) or when both face a more serious common threat from a third party (the United States in

Germany and Japan against USSR during the Cold War). However, these special circumstances do not apply to the United States in the Middle East today, both because of the obvious cultural differences and because the United States is undoubtedly stronger than any state in the region. Hence, it is important to recognize that sustained military occupation there is increasing—and not reducing—the risk of the next 9/11, and so any expected benefit must be worth that possible price.

To stop and reverse the recent explosion of suicide terrorism, it is important to reduce the reliance on foreign occupation as a principal strategy for ensuring national interests. We recognize that the United States as well as most of the world's industrialized countries has legitimate national security interests around the world, and especially in the Middle East. For now the world's economy is dependent on a steady flow of oil from the Persian Gulf and is expected to remain so for decades to come. But, military intervention in and prolonged occupation of Middle Eastern countries to stabilize governments and ensure the world's oil supply does come with the risk of suicide terrorist retaliation against our homeland.

While military intervention should be creatively avoided if at all possible, sometimes military action is the only effective, short-term alternative. Under this circumstance—when intervention is unavoidable—one can and should take care to design a national security strategy that avoids the need for a prolonged presence of combat forces. Since the end of the Cold War, America has stationed tens of thousands of combat forces in the Persian Gulf as a hedge against a wide variety of potential scenarios that could lead to instability in the region. This forward deployment of combat power means that the United States has the capability to influence the direction of domestic political systems, but what appears as "stability" for the United States and the West can easily look like imperial influence to the rest.

On September 11, 2001, the United States had deployed over 12,000 combat forces to countries on the Persian Gulf (5,000 in Saudi Arabia and 7,000 in other countries along the rim). We now know that these troops were the principal rallying cry of Osama bin Laden in his efforts to mobilize volunteers for suicide attacks against the United States and that the martyr videos of the 9/11 hijackers—their last video will testimonials—prominently justify their actions as being in response to Western military control of the governments on the Arabian Peninsula. Further, escalation of American combat forces in the region for the Iraq War directly fueled still more anti-American suicide terrorism.

So what is to be done in the future when the United States and its allies face the Occupier's Dilemma, when a vital national security problem demands military intervention at the risk of creating a threat to their homelands? And in particular, what is to be done in the short and long term in Afghanistan, Iraq, and the Middle East where the United States and its allies are already engaged, and where the suicide terrorism threat against our deployed forces and homeland continues?

Some might argue that the appearance of in-theater ground forces as occupiers during a conflict can be softened by minimizing their "footprint," which means reducing their number to the bare minimum needed for current combat operations, stationing them far from local population centers, greatly limiting their interaction with civilians on a daily basis, and abiding by local cultural norms when they do not conflict with military priorities. These steps might be further augmented by culturally sensitive public relations campaigns to manifest value and concern for local religious and social norms and, most importantly, to issue statements of regret when military operations result in civilian collateral damage. Following this logic, one might conclude that a residual ground combat presence could remain in or near the zone of conflict to serve as a hedge against future instability without increasing the threat to our homeland. In fact, the idea of maintaining in-theater combat forces with a minimum footprint was America's policy in the Persian Gulf throughout the 1990s, and it would not be surprising that cautious decision makers would believe this is the prudent posture for the future.

As before, these tactics alone are unlikely to stop foreign combat forces from being viewed as occupiers. The critical issue is not public visibility or even public displays of respect for other cultures, although both are important. What matters most is whether the foreign combat forces are viewed as supporting a government that lacks domestic legitimacy or as preventing a change of government away from the interests of the foreign power. If either condition occurs, an outside power may well be viewed as "occupying" by local communities, especially if the foreign forces are stronger than those of the local government.

There is good news. Although one might think there is really nothing Western forces could ever do to diminish the appearance of an occupying force, there are important strategies that can be implemented. The United States and its allies must fully understand and use our recent experiences in Afghanistan and Iraq, and draw upon our past experience in the Middle East to shape our current and future national security strategy in the Persian Gulf. These important initiatives can be described as "in-country

balancing" during the conflict and "offshore balancing" to help ensure regional stability for the long haul.

What we have seen in both Iraq and Afghanistan are local communities that did not inherently share the terrorists' political, social, and military agenda, eventually supporting the terrorist organization's campaign
against Western forces. It was only after local communities began to perceive the Western forces as an occupier—as foreign forces propping up and
controlling their national government, changing their local culture, jeopar-
dizing their economic well-being, and conducting combat operations with
high collateral damage to obtain and maintain their control—that these
local populations turned to and supported the terrorists organizations as
an effective means of resisting the perceived occupier. But, we have also
seen in Iraq that this perception of occupation can be changed, and in Afghanistan it might yet be changed.

Just because Al Qaeda and Anbar residents are both Sunnis and just
because the Taliban and Afghanistan eastern and southern province residents are both Pashtuns does not mean these local tribal populations want
to willingly surrender their autonomy and way of life to *either* the terrorist
groups or the Western forces.

In Iraq after the Sunnis were militarily empowered with maintaining
their own security in Anbar Province, we saw the Anbar Awakening militias "in-country balance" the terrorists in the province. As support for the
terrorist campaign declined, we also saw a sharp reduction in suicide attacks throughout Iraq.

In Afghanistan there is little ideological loyalty between the local Pashtuns and the Taliban, but the terrorists have managed to gain local support
by capitalizing on the loss of local political and economic power to a corrupt national government and the Western forces who support it. The perception of occupation is aggravated by certain features of the Afghanistan
constitution, drafted by the West and installed in 2004, under which the
president has the power to appoint provincial governors without regard for
traditional local tribal authority. To reverse the perception of occupation in
the short term, the United States and its allies should promote "in-country
balancing" against the Taliban by creating and establishing political, military, and economic opportunities for the local Pashtun tribes.

Although supporting local groups will often mean they cooperate in
military operations with the foreign forces against terrorists, the guiding
principle of empowerment is not to turn local leaders and militias into paid
mercenaries or pseudo-military allies. Rather, the crucial feature of a local

empowerment strategy is to provide resources to local groups that would enable them to provide for their own security so long as they do not attack the foreign troops providing the assistance. From Western experiences in Iraq and Afghanistan, this usually means local tribal leaders and their militias will also fiercely protect their autonomy from terrorist groups seeking to control their communities or to use their territory.

In-country balancing efforts can help defeat the terrorists, reduce the number of suicide attackers, and cultivate in-country local leaders and militias, who along with the national armies, will be the key to successful offshore balancing efforts to help ensure continued regional stability. But in the long run, "offshore balancing" is the best strategy for Iraq and Afghanistan. Otherwise we will be seen and mistrusted as an occupying power, and the suicide terrorist threat to our forces and homeland will continue.

Fortunately the United States does not need to station large ground forces in either Iraq or Afghanistan to keep them from being a significant safe haven for Al Qaeda or any other anti-American terrorists. Nor is onshore presence necessary to deal with other potential threats in the region. America's interests can be achieved by a strategy that relies on over-the-horizon air and naval forces and rapidly deployable ground forces, combined with training and equipping national armies and local militias to oppose the terrorist groups. This strategy worked splendidly to reverse Saddam Hussein's aggression against Kuwait in 1990. This strategy was also successful in Afghanistan in the fall of 2001, when American airpower and a small number of special forces combined with the Northern Alliance to topple the Taliban and to drive the Taliban and Al Qaeda out of the country.

Transitioning to an "offshore balancing" strategy does not mean that the United States can withdraw all its military power immediately. As we are now seeing in Iraq, changing to an approach that relies less on ground power and more on working with the local leaders and militias takes time. What this transition does require is a greater reliance on local allies, and the steady reduction of in-theater American ground power over a period of several years. No matter what happens in Afghanistan and Iraq, the United States will maintain a significant air and naval presence in the Persian Gulf and Indian Ocean for many years, and those forces are well suited to striking terrorist leaders and camps in conjunction with local militias—just as they did so successfully against the Taliban and Al Qaeda in 2001.

The recent political changes in the Persian Gulf are conducive to an offshore balancing strategy. The emergence of Iraq as an American ally creates an opportunity for the United States to return to its traditional, pre–Desert Storm Persian Gulf security policy. Administrations from President Truman to President Reagan used foreign assistance to build alliances with key local states, while developing the capability to rapidly deploy American combat forces into preestablished bases within the region. America is now poised again to forge an alliance with Iraq and Saudi Arabia, rely on naval and air power on ships in the Persian Gulf and bases in the Indian Ocean, and help maintain bases on the Arabian Peninsula—without Western troops—so that ground forces could be rapidly deployed in any future crisis

Stated simply: offshore balancing is the best long-term strategy for the Persian Gulf. Western combat presence in Middle Eastern countries provides diminishing returns to our security. In-country balancing can be a useful transition, provided it seeks not to manage the internal politics of states, but to empower local groups to provide for their autonomy and security. If democratization is the long-run future of Persian Gulf states, it must ultimately remain their responsibility, not ours. Together in-country and offshore balancing strategies offer the United States its most effective way to stop the anti-Western suicide terrorism threat overseas and at home.

America has been great in large part because it promotes and nurtures understanding and discussion of important ideas and concepts, and because it has remained free to choose its own course. But, intelligent debate and decision making requires putting all the facts before us. For over a decade our enemies have been dying to win. By ending the perception that the United States and its allies are occupiers, we can *cut the fuse* to the suicide terrorism threat.

Index